Abolition Geography
Essays Towards Liberation

Ruth Wilson Gilmore

Edited by
Brenna Bhandar
and
Alberto Toscano

VERSO
London • New York

For all of the teachers

First published by Verso 2022
© Ruth Wilson Gilmore 2022

1 3 5 7 9 10 8 6 4 2

Verso
UK: 6 Meard Street, London W1F 0EG
US: 388 Atlantic Avenue, Brooklyn, NY 11217
versobooks.com

Verso is the imprint of New Left Books

ISBN-13: 978-1-83976-170-6
ISBN-13: 978-1-83976-173-7 (US EBK)
ISBN-13: 978-1-83976-172-0 (UK EBK)

British Library Cataloguing in Publication Data
A catalogue record for this book is available from the British Library

Library of Congress Cataloging-in-Publication Data
A catalog record for this book is available from the Library of Congress

Printed and bound by CPI Group (UK) Ltd, Croydon, CR0 4YY

Contents

PART IV. *Organizing for Abolition*

Original Sources
(in order of publication)

"Decorative Beasts: Dogging the Academy in the Late 20th Century." *California Sociologist* 14 (1–2) (1991): 113–135.

"Public Enemies and Private Intellectuals: Apartheid USA" *Race and Class* 35 (1) (1993): 65–78.

"Terror Austerity Gender Excess Theater." In Robert Gooding-Williams (ed.) *Reading Rodney King/Reading Urban Uprising* New York and London: Routledge, 1993.

"Globalisation and U.S. Prison Growth: From Military Keynesianism to Post-Keynesian Militarism." *Race and Class* 40 (2–3) (1998): 171–87.

"You Have Dislodged a Boulder." Transforming Anthropology 8 (1&2) (1999): 12–38.

"Race and Globalization." In R. J. Johnston, Peter J. Taylor and Michael J. Watts (eds), *Geographies of Global Change: Remapping the World*, 2nd ed., Oxford: Blackwell, 2002, 261–274.

"Fatal Couplings of Power and Difference: Notes on Racism and Geography." *The Professional Geographer* 54 (2002): 15–24.

(with Craig Gilmore) "The Other California," in David Solnit (ed., *Globalize Liberation: How to Uproot the System and Build a Better World*, San Francisco: City Lights, 2003.

"Scholar-Activists in the Mix." *Progress in Human Geography* 29 (2) (2005): 177–82.

"From Military-Industrial Complex to Prison-Industrial Complex: An Interview with Ruth Wilson Gilmore." (Interview with Trevor Paglen), *Recording Carceral Landscapes* (2005).

"In the Shadow of the Shadow State." In *The Revolution Will Not Be Funded*, edited by Incite! Women of Color against Violence, Cambridge, MA: South End Press, 2007.

"Forgotten Places and the Seeds of Grassroots Planning." in *Engaging Contradictions: Theory, Politics, and Methods of Activist Scholarship*, In Charles R. Hale (ed.) University of California Press, 2008, 31–61.

(with Craig Gilmore) "Restating the Obvious," in Michael Sorkin (ed.), *Indefensible Space: The Architecture of the National Insecurity State*, London: Routledge, 2008.

"Race, Prisons and War: Scenes from the History of US Violence," *Socialist Register 2009: Violence Today*, London: Merlin, 2009.

"What is To Be Done?" *American Quarterly* 63.2 (2011): 245–265.

"Race, Capitalist Crisis, and Abolitionist Organizing" (interview with Jenna Loyd), in Jenna M. Loyd, Matt Michelson, and Andrew Burridge (eds), *Beyond Walls and Cages: Prisons, Borders, and Global Crisis*, Athens, GA: The University of Georgia Press, 2012.

"The Worrying State of the Anti-Prison Movement," *Social Justice: A Journal of Crime, Conflict & World Order*. Available at: http://www.socialjusticejournal.org/the-worrying-state-of-the-anti-prison-movement/ (2015).

(with Craig Gilmore) "Beyond Bratton," in Jordan T. Camp and Christina Heatherton (eds), *Policing the Planet*, London: Verso, 2016).

"Abolition Geography and the Problem of Innocence," in Gaye Theresa Johnson and Alex Lubin (eds), *The Futures of Black Radicalism*, London: Verso, 2017.

"Prisons and Class Warfare" (interview with Clément Petitjean/ *Période*), http://www.historicalmaterialism.org/index.php/ interviews/prisons-and-class-warfare (2018).

Editors' Introduction:
Reports from Occupied Territory

Brenna Bhandar and Alberto Toscano

The meek shall inherit the earth, it is said. This presents a very bleak image to those who live in occupied territory.
—James Baldwin, "A Report from Occupied Territory"

As with the twentieth, the problem of the twenty-first century is freedom; and racialized lines continue powerfully, although non-exclusively, to define freedom's contours and limits.
—Ruth Wilson Gilmore, "Race and Globalization"

In his unfinished essay "A Philosophical View of Reform," penned in the wake of the Peterloo Massacre, the poet Percy Bysshe Shelley spoke of the "solemnly recorded" maxims of liberation as "trophies of our difficult and incomplete victory, planted on our enemies' land." This aptly geographical image can certainly be applied to the current fate of abolitionism. The past few years have witnessed an apparent erosion of the ideological defenses that prevented the very idea of abolishing prisons and police from being seen as anything more than a utopian distraction from the urgent demands of political pragmatism. Mass movements catalyzed by intolerable acts of state violence have helped to crack open the space of the sayable and the imaginable, allowing the fruits of decades of grassroots organizing and discursive struggle to gain a certain (at times distorted) visibility. In gathering three decades' worth of Ruth

Wilson Gilmore's essays and interviews, we do not just wish to celebrate her singular contribution to the politics of abolition as theorist, researcher, and organizer ("talk-plus-walk"[1]), making her work available to scholars and activists looking for tools, concepts, methods, formulas, or images that will help them articulate knowledge and action in our turbulent present. We also want to stress the extent to which the writings collected here, and the very imperative of abolition geography that animates them throughout, militate against any one-dimensional conception of what liberation demands, who demands liberation, or what indeed is to be abolished. Or: "Who works and what works, for whom, and to what end?"[2] As we hope briefly to sketch, it is in their powerful and distinctive recasting of the oppositional dialectic between practices of freedom and the ravages of racial capitalism that these texts help to set some of the most vital of contemporary debates on different tracks. If ideology is the falsely transparent domain of the taken-for-granted, then these essays towards liberation also double as incisive interventions in ideology critique, breaking our facile associations between neoliberal globalization and anti-statism, dismantling our identification of abolition with mere decarceration, and showing the poverty of any understanding of racialization and anti-racism that evades their uneven planetary dynamics and plural if interconnected histories.

To theorize is, among other things, to try to see differently, to forge imaginaries and representations that have the potential for collective appropriation and use. A telling index of Gilmore's own way of seeing, of her own style of cognitive mapping, comes in her reflection on the debilitating restriction in the scope of a term that has been closely associated to the politics of abolition, namely the *prison-industrial complex*. As Gilmore observes,

---

1   "Public Enemies and Private Intellectuals: Apartheid USA," in this volume, 80.

2   "Terror Austerity Race Gender Excess Theater," in this volume, 157.

The experimental purpose of the term "prison-industrial complex" was to provoke as wide as possible a range of understandings of the socio-spatial relationships out of which mass incarceration is made by using as a flexible template the military-industrial complex—its whole historical geography, and political economy, and demography, and intellectual and technical practitioners, theorists, policy wonks, boosters, and profiteers, all who participated in, benefited from, or were passed over or disorganized by the Department of War's transformative restructuring into the Pentagon.[3]

This "conceptually expansive" understanding of the PIC, there as a lure for the kind of thinking and practice that follow the circuits and mediations of carceral power into spaces and institutions that might seem to have little to do with the prison, is juxtaposed to a rigid, restrictive use whose consequence is "to shrivel—atrophy, really—rather than to spread out imaginative understanding of the system's apparently boundless boundary-making." The experimental expansion of our political imagination is also evidenced in the way that Gilmore articulates the "centering" of the prison in abolition geography. Elsewhere, she enjoins us temporarily to put aside a conception of contemporary geographic transformations in terms of the globalization of capital flows and its effects and to think instead of the nexus between racialization, criminalization, class, and state-building. This methodological and analytical proposal is advanced as a kind of cartographic gestalt switch, as the call

to map the political geography of the contemporary United States by positing at the center the site where state-building is least contested, yet most class based and racialized: the prison.

---

3 "Abolition Geography and the Problem of Innocence," in this volume, 479–80.

A prison-centered map shows dynamic connections among (1) criminalization; (2) imprisonment; (3) wealth transfer between poor communities; (4) disfranchisement; and (5) migration of state and non-state practices, policies, and capitalist ventures that all depend on carcerality as a basic state-building project. These are all forms of structural adjustment and have inter-regional, national, and international consequences. In other words, if economics lies at the base of the prison system, its growth is a function of politics, not mechanics.[4]

This mapping reveals the multiple and interlocking ways in which "mass incarceration is class war."[5]

We will turn shortly to the state's shifting capacities and composition—a pivotal dimension of Gilmore's research—but it is worth noting the dialectical tenor of Gilmore's geographic imagination. A reversal of margins to center, a making visible of the invisible, is but a moment in a much more painstaking work of always partial and provisional totalization. To define the geography of racial capitalism and of struggles against it *through* the prison is not to reduce it *to* the prison. If we wish for our struggles and our analysis to match the scale, complexity,

---

4 "Race and Globalization," in this volume, 123.

5 "Abolition Geography and the Problem of Innocence," this volume, 479. The essays collected in this volume provide detailed responses to the kind of research problem that Michel Foucault sketched after his visit to the Attica Correctional Facility in April 1972 (mere months after the rebellion), only to leave largely unanswered in his subsequent work (not least due to his unwillingness to trace the carceral dialectics of race and class): "prison is an organization that is too complex to be reduced to purely negative functions of exclusion: its cost, its importance, the care that one takes in administering it, the justifications that one tries to give for it seem to indicate that it possesses positive functions. The problem is, then, to find out what role capitalist society has its penal system play, what is the aim that is sought, and what effects are produced by all these procedures for punishment and exclusion? What is their place in the economic process, what is their importance in the exercise and the maintenance of power? What is their role in the class struggle?" John K. Simon, "Michel Foucault on Attica: An Interview," *Social Justice* 18.3 (1974), 28.

and mobility of the punitive and exploitative social relations we are trying to overcome, then we also need to nuance our understanding of "centrality." For, as Gilmore observes, "the modern prison is a central but by no means singularly defining institution of carceral geographies in the United States and beyond, geographies that signify regional accumulation strategies and upheavals, immensities and fragmentations, that reconstitute in space-time (even if geometrically the coordinates are unchanged) to run another round of accumulation."[6] Critically, this work of mapping carceral and capitalist geographies is not the solitary labor of the theorist and her totalizing oversight. Indeed, this is one of the many instances in which scholarship and activism cannot be cleaved apart—for instance when we attend to how grassroots campaigns "to foster anti-prison awareness and action partially reveal, campaign by campaign, bits of mass incarceration's breath-taking structure."[7]

The relationship between scholarship and activism is triangulated, inter alia, by the university, and Gilmore grapples with the institutionalization of the radical work of militant scholars of earlier epochs in the fields of cultural studies, Black studies, and other "oppositional studies" to interrogate the relationship between literary production and political action and, more generally, what in fact constitutes oppositional work. Exploring the various tendencies within these fields, it becomes clear that the organic praxis occasioned by connection to the world outside the campus is, for Gilmore, a crucial part of (drawing here on a formulation by Mike Davis) the "public production of public use values."[8] In view of making public what is all too often privatized in the guise of individualistic careerism, romantic particularism, or luxury production, Gilmore engages

---

6 "Abolition Geography and the Problem of Innocence," in this volume, 471.

7 Ibid., 477.

8 "Public Enemies and Private Intellectuals: Apartheid USA," in this volume, 85.

a critical political economy reading of Audre Lorde's well-known dictum, reminding us that "if the master loses control of the means of production, he is no longer the master."[9] The revolutionary potential of Lorde's theoretical premise lies in the active struggle to transform the architectures, the relations of ownership, the conditions that enable and disable particular ways of using and producing knowledge. This means, at the very least, understanding how apartheid as a governing logic of late capitalism is privatizing and individualizing what ought to be public and collective and that the education system, like the legal system, is a prime site of this political, economic, and racial operation.

It is in this sense that, while not fitting a narrow abolitionist remit, experiments in anti-colonial collective pedagogy from Guinea-Bissau to Palestine are models for that indispensable work of "stretching awareness from the particular (an inoculation, an irrigation ditch, an electrically powered machine) to the general requirements for the ad hoc abolition geographies of that time-space to become and become again sustained through conscious action."[10] Abolition geography is the dialectical counter to the carceral geographies of racial capitalism to the precise extent that "a geographical imperative lies at the heart of every struggle for social justice; if justice is embodied, it is then therefore always spatial, which is to say, part of a process of making a place."[11] "Freedom is a place," as Gilmore likes to remind us: liberation is both momentous and intensely, intimately, collectively quotidian—not the privileged monopoly of singular events, heroic figures, and spectacular manifestations. Abolition geography is thus nothing other than "how and to what end people make freedom provisionally, imperatively, as they imagine *home* against the disintegrating

9 Ibid., 79.
10 "Abolition Geography and the Problem of Innocence," in this volume, 482.
11 "Fatal Couplings of Power and Difference," in this volume, 137.

grind of partition and repartition through which racial capitalism perpetuates the means of its own valorization."[12] In
this regard it materializes into everyday spatial struggles "the
crucial transformation of the concept of freedom as a static,
given principle into the concept of liberation, the dynamic,
active struggle for freedom."[13]

Place-making, then, a core dimension of abolition, is also a
contested and politically fraught terrain. As we read in "The
Other California," drawing on the work of Laura Pulido on
environmental racism and environmental justice, "place-
based identities ... can be both progressive or reactionary."
The political struggle is in part defined by the task of creating
shared meanings of a particular place that build local democracy and, crucially, make connections to broader struggles for
economic justice. That is why "to achieve that goal, activists
must move beyond place-based identities toward identification
across space, from not-in-my-backyard to not-in-anyone's-
backyard."[14] In a moment of rising neofascist nationalisms, this
forensic examination of what is required for meaningful place-
based political struggles and solidarities that are at the same
time internationalist in their horizons and presuppositions is
both urgent and necessary.

Race and space are mutually constituted across a multiplicity of scales and across distinct if interconnected geographies
shaped by crisis and struggle, "power-difference topographies
(e.g. North, South) unified by the ineluctable fatalities attending asymmetrical wealth transfers"[15]—living, mutable legacies

---

12 "Abolition Geography and the Problem of Innocence," 491.

13 Angela Y. Davis, *Lectures on Liberation*, New York: Committee to
Free Angela Davis, 1971, 4.

14 "The Other California" (with Craig Gilmore), in this volume, 256.
On the articulation of environmental-justice and anti-prison struggles, see
also Rose Braz and Craig Gilmore, "Joining Forces: Prisons and Environmental Justice in Recent California Organizing," *Radical History Review*
96 (Fall 2006): 95–111.

15 "Race and Globalization," in this volume, 113. "North" and
"South" are here also *intra*-national designators, as evidenced in Gilmore's

of colonialism, imperialism, slavery, and genocide but also of the liberatory projects arrayed against strategies of domination. From a variety of angles and cleaving to specific conjunctures, the essays collected in this volume provide an extremely original and fecund spatial translation of an understanding of racism as "always historically specific" and conjunctural,[16] manifesting in practices, subjectivities, and regimes that are always "make-shift patchworks" and "contrivances, designed and delegated by interested cultural and social powers with the wherewithal sufficient to commission their imaginings, manufacture, and maintenance"—that is to say their reproduction and repair.[17] This is a racism that "does not stay still; it changes shape, size, contours, purpose, function—with changes in the economy, the social structure, the system and, above all, the challenges, the resistances to that system."[18] Gilmore's crucial contribution to critical theories of the nexus of race and capital is to make palpable the violent abstraction and the concrete, sited specificity that attaches to race-making as it operates through and by physical and political space.

---

geographical genealogy of US prison growth: "1938–68 World War II and Cold War military buildup produced a territorial redistribution of wealth from the urban industrialized northeast and north central to the agricultural and resource dominated south and coastal west" (117). This is not just an economic but a *political* geography, the geography of counter-revolution: "The *contemporary* US crime problem was born, in the context of solidifying the political incorporation of the militarized south and west into a broadening anti–New Deal conservatism. The disorder that became 'crime' had particular urban and racial qualities, and the collective characteristics of the activists—whose relative visibility as enemies inversely reflected their structural powerlessness—defined the face of the individual criminal" (119).

16   Stuart Hall, "Race and 'Moral Panics' in Postwar Britain," in *Selected Writings on Race and Difference*, ed. Paul Gilroy and Ruth Wilson Gilmore, Durham, NC: Duke University Press, 2021, 59.

17   Cedric J. Robinson, *Forgeries of Memory and Meaning: Blacks and the Regimes of Race in American Theater and Film before World War II*, Chapel Hill: University of North Carolina Press, 2007, xii–xiii.

18   Ambalavaner Sivanandan, *Communities of Resistance: Writings on Black Struggles for Socialism*, London: Verso, 1990, 64.

We cannot rest content with a "sentimental political assertion" about the uninterrupted legacies of slavery (or colonialism), with "the uncritical extension of a partial past to explain a different present." Abolition geography is a dialectical, not a sentimental proposition. In Gilmore's words,

> Instead of imagining the persistent reiteration of static relations, it might be more powerful to analyze relationship dynamics that extend beyond obvious conceptual or spatial boundaries, and then decide what a particular form, old or new, is made of, by trying to make it into something else. This—making something into something else—is what negation is. To do so is to wonder about a form's present, future-shaping design—something we can discern from the evidence of its constitutive patterns, without being beguiled or distracted by social ancestors we perceive, reasonably or emotionally, in the form's features.[19]

Abolition geography, as the determined and determinate negation of specific regimes of racial capitalism, calls for this geographic, historical and materialist sensibility. As Gilmore's granular and systemic analyses of the mutable strategies of mass incarceration and coalitions of resistance against it demonstrate, a static comprehension of the articulations of race, state, and capital is immensely debilitating. Far from defining an untrammeled continuum, birthed by the transatlantic slave trade and fundamentally unchanged today,[20] racial

---

19 "Abolition Geography and the Problem of Innocence," in this volume, 477.

20 Many contemporary uses of the notion of racial capitalism are in stark contravention of the terms of Cedric Robinson's pioneering formulation, which discerned its matrix in Europe's own "internal" dynamics of domination (over people who may later have become "white"). As Gilmore observes, "The racial in racial capitalism isn't secondary, nor did it originate in color or intercontinental conflict, but rather always group-differentiation to premature death" ("Abolition Geography and the Problem of Innocence," 494).

capitalism can be understood and fought only if the historical dialectics of its form are attended to.

Capitalist "uneven development," its churning production of identity (or sameness) and difference (or otherness), its "disintegrating grind of partition or repartition," is racially inscribed at the level of bodies themselves, in an insidious dialectic of the abstract and the concrete: "the process of abstraction that signifies racism produces effects at the most intimately 'sovereign' scale, insofar as particular kinds of bodies, one by one, are materially (if not always visibly) configured by racism into a hierarchy of human and inhuman persons that in sum form the category 'human being.'"[21] The history of the prison is intimately bound up with the violent abstraction of bodies. Traces of Bentham's carceral vision of men "by confinement abstracted from all external impressions [and] from these emotions of friendship which society inspires"[22] can still be detected in the Secure Housing Units (SHUs), "developed [in West Germany] as a death penalty surrogate to destroy the political will and physical bodies of radical activists,"[23] and then amply employed in the US as well as exported to sundry jurisdictions. But the violence of abstraction is not just a matter of traveling paradigms of punishment; it sits at the core of the penal logic of capital, as Evgeny Pashukanis suggested long ago:

> Deprivation of freedom, for a period stipulated in the court sentence, is the specific form in which modern, that is to say bourgeois-capitalist, criminal law embodies the principle of equivalent recompense. This form is unconsciously if deeply

---

21 "Fatal Couplings of Power and Difference," in this volume, 137.

22 Jeremy Bentham, *Principles of Penal Law*, cited in Dario Melossi and Massimo Pavarini, *The Prison and the Factory: Origins of the Penitentiary System*, 40th anniversary ed. London: Palgrave Macmillan, 2019, 223.

23 "Race and Globalization," in this volume, 130. On SHUs, see also "Prisons and Class Warfare" and "Abolition Geography and the Problem of Innocence."

linked with the conception of man in the abstract and abstract human labour measurable in time.[24]

Possibly Gilmore's most cited formula, her definition of racism —as "the state-sanctioned and/or extralegal production and exploitation of group-differentiated vulnerabilities to premature death, in distinct yet densely interconnected political geographies"[25]—is also a lesson in the ambivalence of abstraction, which both defines the violent operations of racial capitalism but also characterizes a very significant moment in a dialectical, geographical method, the moment which captures a general logic or pattern discernable across otherwise heterogeneous sites. This is necessary to do justice not just to the viscous and mutant opportunism of racial regimes but also to what, in an incisive refunctioning of Amiri Baraka / LeRoi Jones's formulation, Gilmore dubs racism's "changing same," which she defines in terms of a tripartite structure:

> [1] Claims of *natural* or *cultural* incommensurabilities [2] secure conditions for reproducing *economic* inequalities, which then [3] validate theories of extra-economic hierarchical difference. In other words, racism functions as a limiting force that pushes disproportionate costs of participating in an increasingly monetized and profit-driven world onto those who, due to the frictions of political distance, cannot reach the variable levers of power that might relieve them of those costs.[26]

Racism's structuring contribution to the uneven and combined articulation of a neoliberal global order thereby entails, in a riff on Stuart Hall's powerful elucidation of the mediations of race and class, that "race is a modality through which

---

24 Evgeny B. Pashukanis, *Law and Marxism: A General Theory*, cited in Melossi and Pavarini, *The Prison and the Factory*, 255.
25 "Race and Globalization," in this volume, 107.
26 Ibid., 114.

political-economic globalization is lived."[27] Where much of the critical literature on neoliberalism has only recently begun to treat race as an integral dimension of the constitution of that ideological project and political practice,[28] Gilmore's has long mapped the multiple ways in which race is not just the prism through which capitalist crises and resolutions have been "*thematized*" but has also functioned to provide both affective opportunities and material infrastructures for the politics of capital. The essays in this volume attending to neoliberalism's racial regimes provide ample elaboration of the thesis that racism enacts a *differential* reinforcement of the state, which in its turn compounds and refunctions those "fatal couplings of power and difference" that, according to Hall, define the making, unmaking, and remaking of race.

While Hall had underscored the "anti-statist" strategy that allowed neoliberal authoritarian populism to capture and ventriloquize social discontent,[29] Gilmore's "prison-centered map" of contemporary crisis and struggle foregrounds—with a wealth of historical, spatial, and budgetary research—how the deployment of carceral geographies must be understood in light of the formation of an "anti-state state" and the practices and strategies of those "people and parties who gain state

---

27 Ibid., 107.

28 See Arun Kundnani, "The Racial Constitution of Neoliberalism," *Race & Class*, Vol. 63(1) (2021): 51–69. See also Quinn Slobodian, "Anti-'68ers and the Racist-Libertarian Alliance: How a Schism among Austrian School Neoliberals Helped Spawn the Alt Right," *Cultural Politics* 15 (3) (2019): 372–86.

29 "An 'anti-statist' strategy ... is not one which refuses to operate through the state; it is one which conceives of a more limited state role, and which advances through the attempt, ideologically, to represent itself as anti-statist, for the purposes of populist mobilisation ... [a] highly contradictory strategy ... simultaneously, dismantling the welfare state, 'anti-statist' in its ideological self-representation and highly state-centralist and dirigiste in many of its strategic operations." Stuart Hall, "Authoritarian Populism: A Reply to Jessop et al.," in *Selected Writings on Marxism*, ed. Gregor McLennan, Durham, NC: Duke University Press, 2021, 284.

power by denouncing state power."[30] As *Golden Gulag* magisterially develops—and as these essays both foreshadow and elaborate—grasping the twinned mutations of politics and punishment requires us not only to attend to the temporalities of crisis but also to unfold the materiality and spatiality of surplus:

> Crisis and surplus are two sides of the same coin. Within any system of production, the idling, or surplusing, of productive capacities means that the society dependent on that production cannot reproduce itself as it had in the past, to use Stuart Hall's neat summary of Marx. Such inability is the hallmark of crisis, since reproduction, broadly conceived, is the human imperative. Objectively, crises are neither bad nor good, but crises do indicate inevitable change, the outcome of which is determined through struggle. Struggle, like crisis, is a politically neutral word: in this scenario, everyone struggles because they have no alternative.[31]

To understand the anti-state state as a crisis state rebuilding itself through a reorganization of surplus (capacity, capital, labor, land, populations), we require an analytical distinction between state and government. A state is here defined as "a territorially bounded set of relatively specialized institutions that develop and change over time in the gaps and fissures of social conflict, compromise, and cooperation," while governments are "the animating forces—policies plus personnel—that put state capacities into motion and orchestrate or coerce people in their jurisdictions to conduct their lives according to centrally made and enforced rules."[32] The state is fundamentally understood

---

30 "In the Shadow of the Shadow State," in this volume, 228. On the anti-state state (as well as her political-intellectual trajectory more widely), see also Gilmore's interview in *Revolutionary Feminisms: Conversations on Collective Action and Radical Thought*, London: Verso, 2020, 172.

31 "Globalization and US Prison Growth," in this volume, 210.

32 "Restating the Obvious" (with Craig Gilmore), in this volume, 262.

in terms of capacities—that is, materially enacted, spatially embodied and enforceable powers—to distribute or hierarchize, develop or abandon, care or criminalize, and so forth. As Toni Negri noted long ago, it is futile to discourse in a Marxian vein about the state without ever reading a state budget.[33] Gilmore has read her share. One of the chief aims of what has come to be known as neoliberalism (especially in its overweening obsession with the constitutionalization of a market order) is to "bake in" its principles into these state capacities themselves so that even a nominally socialist or social-democratic government would still be compelled to carry out neoliberal policies.[34] Without foregrounding the politically charged and geographically embodied transformative conflicts over state capacities,[35] a phenomenon like mass incarceration risks being understood through a one-dimensional lens (as a re-edition of racist segregation) and delinked from broader socioeconomic mutations. As Marx once quipped, the state is indeed "the table of contents of man's [sic] practical conflicts."[36]

In polities structured by the long legacies and mutable modes of racial capitalism, the state is also a "racial state," one that may well operate administratively and juridically through a manifest commitment to "colorblindness." In a passage that compellingly encapsulates the virtues of a historical-materialist

33 Toni Negri, "Stato, spesa pubblica e fatiscenza del compromesso storico" (1975), in *La forma stato. Per la critica dell'economia politica della Costituzione*, Milan: Baldini Castoldi Dalai, 2012, 316.

34 See Pierre Dardot, Haud Guéguen, Christian Laval, and Pierre Sauvêtre, *Le choix de la guerre civile. Une autre histoire du néolibéralisme*, Montréal: Lux, 2021.

35 Especially the one that Gilmore has painstakingly traced in these pages and *Golden Gulag* as the shift from the welfare-warfare state (and military Keynesianism) to the workfare-warfare state (and post-Keynesian militarism).

36 Letter from Marx to Arnold Ruge, September 1843, cited in Stuart Hall, Chas Critcher, Tony Jefferson, John Clarke, and Brian Roberts, *Policing the Crisis: Mugging, the State, and Law and Order*, London: Macmillan, 1978, 202.

geographical sensibility when it comes to the nexus of politics and race, we read:

> The state's management of racial categories is analogous to the management of highways or ports or telecommunication; racist ideological and material practices are infrastructure that needs to be updated, upgraded, and modernized periodically: this is what is meant by racialization. And the state itself, not just interests or forces external to the state, is built and enhanced through these practices. Sometimes these practices result in "protecting" certain racial groups, and other times they result in sacrificing them.[37]

Now, while the state has of course been an integral material and symbolic partner across the history of capitalism, the present has come to be defined by a singular rhetoric—bound to the trajectory of neoliberalism but also exceeding it—namely that of the anti-state state, a state that promises its own demise and employs that promise to increase, intensify, and differentiate its capacities. The combative version (think Reagan's dictum "The nine most terrifying words in the English language are: I'm from the Government, and I'm here to help") is doubled by fatalistic academic apologia (think shopworn mantras of "globalization" as the eclipse of the state). Contrary to a widespread if erroneous vision of mass incarceration as the outcome of a drive to privatize and directly extract value from the carceral, the extraordinary, racialized growth in prisons is internal to and emblematic of transmutations in the state, in the composition of its agents and capacities, which a one-dimensional understanding of neoliberalism often obscures. Among the revelations of that "prison-centered map" is a new understanding of the "tendency to strengthening-weakening of the State, the poles of which develop in an

---

37 "Restating the Obvious," in this volume, 264–5.

uneven manner."[38] Race is a crucial operator in this uneven development:

> Because prisons and prisoners are part of the structure of the state, they enable governments to establish state legitimacy through a claim to provide social "protection" combined with their monopoly on the delegation of violence. The state establishes legitimacy precisely because it violently dominates certain people and thereby defines them (and makes them visible to others) as the sort of people who should be pushed around. In modelling behaviour for the polity, the anti-state state naturalizes violent domination.[39]

It is noteworthy that in articulating the entanglement of the prison-industrial complex with the anti-state state as "a state that grows on the promise of shrinking," the Gilmores link back to Toni Negri's pioneering analyses of the crisis state, and in particular to his lucid contention that "the counter-revolution of the capitalist entrepreneur today can only operate strictly within the context of an increase in the coercive powers of the state. The 'new Right' ideology of laissez-faire implies as its corollary the extension of new techniques of coercive and state intervention in society at large." This is accomplished in part through the incorporation of the economic into the juridical sphere so as to solidify the relationship between "capital's productive and political ruling classes" in the state's very foundation.[40] While the state has long wielded "despotic power over certain segments of society" in order to secure its hegemony, contemporary manifestations of the "racial fix" have seen particular kinds of revision to law and jurisprudence. Whereas

---

38 Nicos Poulantzas, *State, Power, Socialism*, trans. Patrick Camiller, introd. Stuart Hall, London: Verso, 2000, 205.

39 "Restating the Obvious," in this volume, 273–4.

40 Toni Negri, *Revolution Retrieved: Selected Writings on Marx, Keynes, Capitalist Crisis and New Social Subjects 1967–83*, London: Red Notes, 1988, 25.

the "welfare-warfare" state was characterized by an oscillation between remedying racial exclusion through the extension of legal recognition of basic norms of equality during "good times" (for instance, "banning discrimination in public-sector employment") and, during "bad times," by formalizing inequality through legal exclusions, the workfare-warfare state is characterized by an overwhelming shift to a generalized punitive and carceral logic and the subordination of the language of injustice to that of inequality. Race and gender are core components in this "aggressively punitive" form of governance, mediums for the implementation of what Gilmore has termed "organized abandonment"—that late capitalist violence of abstraction, both fast and slow, that manifests as "structural adjustment, environmental degradation, privatization, genetic modification, land expropriation, forced sterilization, human organ theft, neocolonialism, involuntary and super-exploited labor."[41] The anti-statist strategy stands revealed as the unleashing of a mutant statism, shored up by politicians, administrators, and intellectuals committed to "the management of a permanent state of belligerence, a management often reduced to an accounting equation."[42]

What Negri's vantage point—that of the mass mobilizations and creeping civil war of 1970s Italy—may not have fully equipped him to grasp, and what we need to dwell on to discern the authoritarian or fascist potentials in the anti-state state, are the forms of subjective participation in the naturalization of violent domination that go together with a certain promotion of a possessive and racialized conception of freedom. Here we need to not only reflect on the fact that neoliberalism operates

---

41 "Race and Globalization," in this volume, 113–14. See also the reflection in "Public Intellectuals and Public Enemies: Apartheid USA" on how "everywhere racism and machismo and exploitation are determined economically, they are also defined culturally" (87).

42 Massimo Pavarini, "Understanding Punishment Today (2017): The Prison *without* the Factory," in Melossi and Pavarini, *The Prison and the Factory*, 265.

through a racial state—or that, as commentators have begun to recognize and detail, it is shaped by a racist and civilizational imaginary that over determines who is capable of market freedoms—but we also need to attend to the fact that the anti-state state could become an object of popular attachment or, better, populist investment, only through the mediation of race. Gilmore grasps this with prescient lucidity in her reflections on the conjuncture of the 1992 Los Angeles uprising, arguing that reckoning with the terror waged by the US "crisis state" demands thinking its articulation with a geo-economic order in which the United States was losing hegemony and the capacity for a pacifying redistribution of imperial dividends. Continuing in the tradition of W. E. B. Du Bois's historical audit of the "psychological wages of whiteness," Gilmore mediates the revanchist white-supremacist ideologies crystallized around the trial of the LAPD officers who brutalized Rodney King on the one hand and the impasse experienced by US imperialism and capitalist hegemony on the other. This is a powerful lesson in method, enjoining us never to lose sight of the fact that race is a modality through which neoliberal globalization and imperialism are lived, while also asking us to "consider both how racism is produced through, and informs the territorial, legal, social, and philosophical organization of a place, and how racism fatally articulates with other power-difference couplings such that its effects can be amplified beyond a place even if its structures remain particular and local."[43]

White nationalism, with its fascist potentials, appears (in 2022 as in 1992, we might say) as a crisis ideology, which is also to

---

43 "Race and Globalization," in this volume, 116. This also pertains to the traveling carceral theories and practices birthed by the racial anti-state state. As Gilmore observes, "As exercised through criminal laws that target certain kinds of people in places disorganized by globalization's adjustments, racism is structural—not individual or incidental. The sturdy curtain of US racism enables and veils the complex economic, political, and social processes of prison expansion. Through prison expansion and prison export both US and non-US racist practices can become determining forces in places nominally 'free' of white supremacy" (131).

say a revanchist victimology haunted by demotion and loss, by vulnerability to psychic and material dispossession: "The idea and enactment of winning, of explicit domination set against the local reality of decreasing family wealth, fear of unemployment, threat of homelessness, and increased likelihood of early, painful death from capitalism's many toxicities."[44] Racial ideologies do political-economic *work*, as civilizational narratives and geopolitical imaginaries fueled by *ressentiment* find outlets in policy platforms, exploiting "the need for an enemy whose threat obliges endless budgetary consideration"—as writ large in the ensuing trajectory of mass incarceration. Gilmore's words from three decades ago continue to resonate with the present:

> The very crisis which we must exploit—the raw materials of profound social change—is the tending toward fascism through the romance of identity, forged in the always already of the American national project. Our work is to rearticulate our own connections in new (and frightening) forward-looking moves in order to describe, promote, organize, bargain in the political arenas.[45]

It is this work of political rearticulation, buffeted by crisis and confronted with state and para-state violence, that requires the collective forging of "infrastructures of feeling," embodied traditions of the oppressed—as well as new figures of intellectual work and "scholarship-activism." Eschewing a catastrophic conception of liberation or a punctual image of revolution, it requires reinventing, while attending to the "discipline of the conjuncture," abolitionist strategies of *non reformist reform*. Over half a century ago, André Gorz had defined a reformist reform as "one which subordinates its objectives to the criteria

---

44 "Terror Austerity Race Gender Excess Theater," in this volume, 161.

45 Ibid., 166.

of rationality and practicability of a given system," while a "not necessarily reformist reform is one which is conceived not in terms of what is possible within the framework of a given system and administration, but in view of what should be made possible in terms of human needs and demands." Crucially—and this is amply explored in Gilmore's accounts of anti-prison coalitions, Mothers Reclaiming Our Children,[46] or abolitionist projects engaging in "grassroots planning" ("future orientation driven by the present certainty of shortened lives"[47]) across multiple intra- and international sites—Gorz set as a condition of his vision of structural reform that it be "by definition a reform implemented or controlled by those who demand it."[48] In her foreword to Dan Berger's *The Struggle Within*, Gilmore has set out, with combative clarity, how that Gorzian distinction can be repurposed to define the stakes of abolition:

> The purpose of abolition is to expose and defeat all the relationships and policies that make the United States the world's top cop, warmonger, and jailer. Practicalities rather than metaphors determine the focus and drive the analysis, because the scope of prison touches every aspect of ordinary life. Thus, it is possible and necessary to identify all those points of contact and work from the ground up to change them. This ambition makes some people impatient, as well it should. Abolition is a movement to end systemic violence, including the interpersonal vulnerabilities and displacements that keep the system going. In other words, the goal is to change how we interact with each other and the planet by putting people before profits, welfare before warfare, and life over death ... The distinction sketched

---

46 See "You Have Dislodged a Boulder," in this volume, 355–409.

47 "Scholar-Activists in the Mix," in this volume, 94. See also "Forgotten Places and the Seeds of Grassroots Planning," in this volume, 410–48.

48 André Gorz, *Strategy for Labor: A Radical Proposal*, Boston: Beacon Press, 1967, 6–7.

out above is the difference between reformist reform—tweak Armageddon—and non reformist reform—deliberate change that does not create more obstacles in the larger struggle. Some of the timidity in the fight against warehousing humans in cages for part or all of their lives results from the lethal synthesis of abandoned optimism and calculated convenience ... Contemporary oppositional political society seems to be constantly reorganizing itself into fragments. While the assertion of particular needs, struggles, and identities must necessarily be part of the project to free ourselves, the structural effect of everyday political disintegration is fatal.[49]

From the earliest text collected here, with its call for "resisting and denouncing the re-objectification of the subaltern subject" and working out "the semiotics and histrionics of critical performance,"[50] Gilmore's writing is deeply attuned to the vexed question of how to foster a *political culture* "on our enemies' land." Besieged as we are by representations of the intellectual that often serve to debilitate, distract, and disintegrate —rather than to orient or organize—there is much to be gained by rethinking, along with Gilmore, what scholarship/activism as "organic praxis" might mean in the present.[51] This is a present that daily reminds us that only the most capacious and intransigent vision of liberation can stand a chance against the catastrophe in permanence organized under the aegis of the anti-state state and exacerbated by its fascistic progeny. Such

---

49 Ruth Wilson Gilmore, foreword to *The Struggle Within: Prisons, Political Prisoners, and Mass Movements in the United States*, by Dan Berger Oakland: PM Press / Kersplebedeb, 2014, vii–viii. For a recent reflection on how increasing condemnation of mass incarceration in a "reformist reform" vein "does not touch the bedrock legitimacy of the carceral state," see Naomi Murakawa, "Mass Incarceration Is Dead, Long Live the Carceral State!," *Tulsa Law Review* 55, no. 2 (Winter 2020): 251–61.

50 "Decorative Beasts," in this volume, 76.

51 "Public Enemies and Private Intellectuals: Apartheid USA," in this volume, 84.

a vision was sketched out by Gilmore in a 2020 interview, in words that can also serve to frame this collection of interventions, inquiries, and illuminations:

> Abolition has to be "green." It has to take seriously the problem of environmental harm, environmental racism, and environmental degradation. To be "green" it has to be "red." It has to figure out ways to generalize the resources needed for well-being for the most vulnerable people in our community, which then will extend to all people. And to do that, to be "green" and "red," it has to be international. It has to stretch across borders so that we can consolidate our strength, our experience, and our vision for a better world.[52]

---

52 "Ruth Wilson Gilmore Makes the Case for Abolition," *Intercept*, June 10, 2020, available at theintercept.com. For a recent effort to draw on Gilmore's work to map the contours of an abolition ecology, see Nik Heynen and Megan Ybarra, "On Abolition Ecologies and Making 'Freedom as a Place,'" *Antipode* 53, no. 1 (January 2021): 21–35.

PART I

WHAT IS TO BE DONE? SCHOLARSHIP AS ACTIVISM, ACTIVISM AS SCHOLARSHIP

1

What Is to Be Done?[1]

I'm going to need your help tonight, as I always do. At some point I'm going to do this. You'll remember. I move a lot when I talk, but I'll only once do this [raises arms over her head]. And when I do this, you will say, other than your gender or transgender or other identity of choice, woman-man, person, human, lover, masculine-center, whatever you're going to say, make it fit, in two syllables, "Other (fill in your blank) like me will rise." So let's practice. "Other ___ like me will rise." Okay, now everybody say it. "Other ___ like me will rise." One more time. "Other ___ like me will rise." And you've got to say it with a little bit more enthusiasm.

So when we do that, and if you want to rise as Marlon did, feel free to rise.

If I had a title tonight that was more specific than "What Is to Be Done?" it would be something like "Universities and Unions: Institutions with Meaning for the People." I grabbed that phrase from Vijay Prashad's fantastic book, which everyone must read, *The Darker Nations*. But just keep that in mind. Universities and Unions: Institutions with Meanings for the People.

I think all American Studies Association presidents must do the same thing. On receipt of the election results from John Stephens, they immediately put fingers to keyboard and start drafting the talk they're going to give in twenty months. Because area studies, of which American studies is a part, is in some profound sense a presentist enterprise—we study

---

1   2011 Presidential Address for the American Studies Association (ASA).

the past to understand the present, we revise the present on new senses of the past—the speech changes and changes and changes until we arrive at the moment, this moment, and the president starts speaking. Weirdly enough, the practice ghosts, of all people, that nightmare specter Frederick Jackson Turner, who was trying to figure out in 1893 the historical geography, or rather the historical-geographic future, of what we, though not he, would call the American empire. The empire had a long historical-geographical past, and he, in thinking about the frontier and its "closure," wanted to figure out what the future might be. However, in the spirit of the antecedents I *do* wish to body forth—W. E. B. Du Bois, for example, and Ida B. Wells—we also ask, in a constantly reglobalizing context, why this? Why this, here? Why this, here, now?

But since there's something irresistible in talking about the present, the paper I started to write after getting John's email burst forth into the world as "Life in Hell," and many of you heard versions of its forced march toward a book at Santa Barbara, Berkeley, Cornell, New York University, and University College Dublin. That project informs what I have to say here today, but this is going to be more like the discussion we could have after the "Life in Hell" book is done—which it's not.

Twenty-one years ago, I gave my first paper at a scholarly meeting. It was a Modern Language Association convention in DC. The rubric was "The Status of Women in the Profession," organized by the MLA commission devoted to the scrutiny of same. The presentations were arranged into a plenary and a series of sessions, with my panel of the series on the last hour of the last day.

In 1989, we were trying to figure out where women in the profession had gotten to, where we could go, and how we might get there. I use "we" advisedly. I was a drama school doctoral-program dropout who caught a break, thanks to a friend from Yale School of Drama, Michael Cadden, who recommended me to his former colleague at Princeton, Val Smith. There are clear benefits to rolling in and with the elites. As was the case in March 2009 when John Stephens emailed, back in January 1989, when Val Smith telephoned me, I immediately grabbed a new notebook and fresh pen to write a radical revisionist history of the world to be delivered in twenty minutes, eleven months in the future. I devised a time-killing title because I wasn't sure I could actually fill twenty minutes: "Decorative Beasts: Dogging the Academy in the Late Twentieth Century; or, What Are Those Bitches Howling About? Check Out Their Golden Chains."[2]

The principal argument was that in 1989 we were in the midst of a passive revolution. I also said a lot of other things, trying to sort out who and what works in the academy, for whom, and to what end. Public speaking was a novel experience for me. I had one pun halfway through that allowed me to breathe thanks to my unseemly habit of busting up at my own jokes. The solution that I offered back then was, "Organize, organize, organize! Take over what already exists and innovate what's still needed. Unshackle ourselves because nobody will do it for us." This evening I don't want to sound like a Spartacist: "I took a position in 1989 and it's still correct." But I do want to sound like a historical materialist. We make history, but not under conditions of our own choosing.

What was in some ways still incipient then has been consolidated over the past generation. There was no NAFTA. There was no European Union. There were no capitalist Chinese export production platforms. There was industrialization in China, but the export processing zones so prominent in today's economy didn't exist. Nelson Mandela was still in prison, as were a suddenly growing number of people here in the States. Well-waged blue-collar jobs had, for more than ten years, been melting away from longtime industrial landscapes across the United States. At the same time, there was a measurable rise

---

2 See "Decorative Beasts," in this volume, 51–77.

in what one wag called "guard duty"; by that he meant both uniformed security positions *and* jobs like assistant manager at fast-food franchises—jobs whose main duties are to ensure workers don't cheat the time clock, keep their hand out of the till, and don't give out free stuff to their customer-friends. Guard duty.

The Berlin Wall had come down six weeks before. However, with all that, it didn't feel like history was over. In a way, the obsessions that drove me into and then rapidly away from drama were those most beautifully summarized in a few thoughts of Marx: by mixing our labor with the earth, we change the external world and thereby change our own nature.[3] That's what drama is; that's what geography is: making history, making worlds. The fact that I went to Yale is often understood as a tale of generational aspiration, assimilation, and achievement. Yale janitor grandfather, Yale machinist father, Yale graduate daughter—the narrative arc of a shape-shifting myth that, in the words of William Jefferson Clinton, goes something like this: "There's nothing wrong with America that can't be fixed by what's right with America." To believe that is to fall prey to what George Kent, in "Richard Wright: Blackness and the Adventure of Western Culture," called "the imprisoning blandishments of a neurotic culture."[4] But to think that also kills life, past, present, and future.

Here's a different story, a more dramatic narrative arc:[5]

The woman seated in the middle in the front row, J, worked for many years as a housekeeper, as a domestic. She worked as a seamstress. She worked to make people's lives more comfortable

---

3   Karl Marx, *Capital, Volume I*, trans. Ben Fowkes, London: Penguin, 1990 [1867], 283.

4   George Kent, "Richard Wright: Blackness and the Adventure of Western Culture," in *Blackness and the Adventure of Western Culture*, Chicago: Third World Press, 1972, 95.

5   The passage in italics refers to a photograph of the author's family, a reproduction of which can be found in the original publication.

so that she and her husband could make the lives of their children more comfortable. Imagine her one day waiting at the stop for the trolley that will take her and her basket of freshly ironed laundry out to her "white lady's" house. The basket was really heavy, and one of her church friends, S, was already in the trolley. S came to the steps and helped her lift the basket into the trolley.

J always envied S. S worked for a white lady who was all alone, Miss M. J worked for a white lady who was not alone, and she spent a lot of time dodging the white men in the white lady's house. She envied S. She envied S a job that she imagined might be easier to do. But as she thought about it that day in the trolley, she thought, "Well, maybe that job isn't easier to do. Maybe that job is actually a difficult job to do." For example, what if Miss M wasn't somebody who just left S alone? After all, S's daughter, E, who, when she graduated from normal school, could not teach in the public schools because the city would not hire Black teachers, went South to teach in a school for Black girls in Florida, and she, E, discovered in Florida that there were girls who loved girls. And E thought that was a wonderful thing that those girls loved girls, and when she came back, she told her sisters, and her sisters told J's daughter and J's daughter told her mother and said, "Mom, is this something new?"

J told her daughter that that was nothing new. In fact, she had heard the men of her family talking among themselves about P, P the musician, who—the men were worried about P and their sons. They had sons. J and her husband had sons, four sons, and the men wanted to know what P's intentions were toward their boys. J could not understand why these men were so frightened, why these men wouldn't just go ask. So she did. She put on her coat one day and took her handbag and she walked down the street to a place where P was practicing the piano and she said, "P, what is your intention toward my boys," and he said with an arpeggio flourish, "J: I don't like boys. I love men."

E came back from the South, and she worked in New Haven. She worked for her mother to keep her mother in her house,

because her father had died. He had died of a botched opera-
tion. Her father was dead and she was the oldest child, so she
worked, she worked, she worked. She couldn't be a teacher. She
could be a secretary. She was also quite a lively person who
spent a lot of time in Harlem. It was the Renaissance. E met a
man, an immigrant, an immigrant named D, from India. D had
come to the United States to go to school, and he fell in love
with E. Oh, he loved her, he loved her so! He wanted her to go
with him, to go to India, to live with him in a place that was
not yet free of colonial rule, but he swore to her that he would
protect her and love her and cherish her, and her mama would
be OK, even though she was so far from home. She couldn't do
it. She couldn't leave. He went back to India and she stayed in
New Haven.

But other immigrants had come to New Haven. Many immi-
grants had come. They had come from throughout the world,
including all over the British colonies. Many had come from the
Lesser Antilles in the first decade of the twentieth century. The
Negroes of New Haven who were already in New Haven raised
their eyebrows when those women and men came from the West
Indies, and they asked, "What do they want here? What do they
plan to do?"

What the Negroes from the West Indies did was the same
thing that the Negroes of New Haven did: they worked. They
worked and they worked and they worked. H, the man whom
E married, worked at Yale, working for a fraternity, as did J's
husband C, who stands behind her in that picture. C worked
seven days a week. The janitors at Yale in those days worked
seven days a week. They never could have a day off. Indeed, the
comptroller, when asked why they couldn't have a day off, said,
"Why, those boys would just get in trouble if we give them a
day off."

The men conscripted their sons. They could never do all the
work that they had to do at Yale University in those days, so
those who had sons, like C, who had four sons, conscripted

the sons as boys to come and work for them. And it was there that one of the sons, my father, as a young teenager, heard communists debating New Deal Democrats about what was to be done. He stood in the back of the room wearing a white coat, serving food to the debaters, thinking, "This makes sense, what the communists say. This makes sense."

The military conscripted the sons and shipped them off to all the theaters of World War II. While the sons were off at war, they heard what the men back home were doing. They heard that the men, like C and others, were organizing with the CIO, the CIO that had so much leadership from the Communist Party. They organized the union at Yale, Local 35, the blue-collar union, the union for the housekeepers and janitors at Yale.

The women organized, too. His sister-in-law M was working in the wartime industries in Columbus, Ohio. She worked all night in the factories, making machines to kill other people's children, and by day she went to Ohio State University, learning to be a teacher to teach the children who did not get killed. When she got a call from her mother that her elderly father in Virginia was very, very sick she took a bus all the way to Virginia, and when she got to Virginia, when she got to Danville, she took a bus to the edge of town, and then she had to get out and walk to the Colored hospital that was far beyond the end of the bus line.

Having called on her father and seen to his well-being, she walked back to the bus and got in the bus. This was 1942. She got in the bus and she sat in the front and she refused to move to the back. When they arrested her, when they arrested her and so many other people who wouldn't move in those days, long before Rosa Parks finally made her refusal to move symbolize a movement, because people had organized, organized, organized, M went to court, and the judge said, "M, what have they done to you up there in the North? They have driven you out of your mind!" And her family agreed. They drove her to the long-distance bus and said, "Go back to the North and never come back." Editors and pundits discussed this refusal up and down the southeastern seaboard, confused by patience's militant face.

When the men came back, when they came back from the military, they were ready to fight. They knew how to shoot. They knew how to work. They fought into jobs. They fought into jobs they had never had before, but they fought into jobs that were jobs making weapons to kill other people's children. They went to work, for example, for Winchester, one of the major firms of the military-industrial complex. They went to work for Winchester and the military-industrial complex, where the machinists were not organized, although they had, for decades and decades and decades and decades, made weapons to commit the genocide against indigenous people in the United States. They made weapons that were used to grab the Philippines and Hawai'i and Puerto Rico and Cuba. They made these weapons, and in that place where they made the weapons, they made a union.

My father, a machinist, a journeyman machinist, led the organizing. He helped to form the union. But he lost his job because of his union work. He went from job to job, working as a wonderfully skilled tool and die maker, and he eventually wound up working at, of all places, Yale, in the physics department. He worked in the physics department helping the physicists make their machines for observation, their machines for seeing the things that cannot be seen. And while they were doing that, he could see all around him at Yale the things that should not be seen because they should not happen. My father decided that something had to be done. When Lady Bird Johnson came to town in 1967, on her Beautify America campaign, the campaign in which she said, "Plant a shrub or a bush or a tree," my father went and picketed at the president of Yale's house. He wrote a sign that said, "Mrs. LBJ, Prez Kingman Brewster works the Dick Lee's white power to keep the blacks suppressed," and the other side of the placard said, "Yale supports apartheid employment policies."

When I applied to Yale, I came to realize much later, there wasn't any question that I would be accepted. It was a different kind of power grouping that I found myself in, quite different from the one, the kind one, the collegial one, that got me to that first Modern Language Association conference in 1989. My father, indeed, kindly offered to burn the place down if they didn't take his number-one daughter, his only daughter. But not being a fool, not one to waste infrastructure that can be turned to other purposes, his talent was to force Yale to burn money and time rather than the physical plant to achieve what he wanted for the communities where he organized: jobs, housing, daycare, health clinics. In other words, his talent was to organize, promote ideas, and obstruct and obstruct, obstruct in the political and legal arenas. When I asked him to go to the bursar's office with me the first day of school in case there were any remaining charges not covered by the university employees' tuition remission, he said, "Why? They owe us." He wouldn't fill out financial aid forms. He refused to ask. He knew that nobody had invited us here.

"I was sent," Lorna Goodison wrote. "Tell that to history."

And as Stuart Hall taught me, it is history that gives us a sense of ourselves as a single political constituency, which is why we keep rewriting it.

Now I'll turn briefly to the relationships among structural adjustment, security enhancement, and the anti-state state. Let me make some sweeping generalizations and then get down to what is to be done.

The world is, as everybody in this room knows, in political, economic, military, environmental, and ideological crisis. Recent scholarship in American studies strives to decenter the United States while remaining meticulously mindful of its forceful, although by no means decisive, role in globalization—as a source of capital and capital organization, as a market for goods, and as a muscular purveyor of culture. Wealth inequality in the United States is at record levels. The bottom 40 percent of earners have negative net worth while the top 20 percent own 84 percent of everything there is to own. We're not talking about houses: we're talking about *everything* there is to own. The broad measure of US unemployment at this writing [in 2011] hovers at just under one in five workers, and long-term unemployment is off the charts ... There's a blip in the early years of the Reagan introduction of deep structural adjustment programs in the United States, and then we see what has happened since the meltdown in 2008. At the same time, one in a hundred US adults is locked in prison or jail. In addition, about 4 million or so people are under direct control of the system, although not locked up, so that gets us to almost 7 million people in that general category of excluded worker.

Structural adjustment. There have been shifts in the location, form, control, and use of public and private capital, including into warfare, on the one hand, and consumer debt, on the other. The effect of these shifts has been the abandonment of many productive, reproductive, and cultural capacities. This is what Kevin Gaines was talking to us about last year in his eloquent and urgent address about public education. Objectively, structural adjustment policies are designed to put the most possible weight on the backs of the most vulnerable people, who are vulnerable by definition of not having the political clout, expressed through votes, contributions, ownership of the means of production, control of vital territory, or organization to refuse their own vulnerability to premature death. In those places with well-developed apparatuses, infrastructure, and institutions for social welfare and benefits, the weight is differently allocated, and in some cases the rich actually pay because they are not the most powerful in a historical bloc.

Security enhancement. Increasing inequality plus the mobility of raw wealth—the fungibility of money and transferability of many goods—means that stuff not put under lock and key might be available for illegal entitlements. Now most of the grand theft we witness these days is the global looting of public wealth by private forces. That said, inequality sets small numbers—call them plutocrats—against larger ones, with the result that the control of access—between countries, into buildings, into warehouses, neighborhoods, and so forth—has led to many changes in the landscape of accumulation and dispossession. One firm called G4S—it looks like teenager texting—has become the largest private employer on the planet. The guard duty joke from twenty years ago became a capital opportunity, both stacked and automated. G4S operates in 110 countries and has 600,000 employees worldwide.

The movement of capital, in other words, both precedes and confirms structural adjustments, but the latter must be guaranteed, as it were, by some combination of coercion and consent. The rise in security work, therefore, is the natural outcome of the renovation and deepening of uneven development throughout the world.

The anti-state state. This novel form is normative in the United States today and is touted abroad, but with uneven results. The anti-state state is the one that candidates run against in order to get state power. Variations of the anti-state state exist outside the United States, but by no means are all sovereign state forms in this era enlivened as anti-state. At the same time, across the spectrum globally, on average, governmental spending in real dollars has climbed, meaning that even though there's global pressure for structural adjustment to be enacted as shrunken states, what's actually happened is a downward relocation of the social wage across the subpolities of a territorial unit, along with bigger expenditures on the military, in addition to rising fractions of state budgets on prisons, policing, and other guard duty while schools, hospitals, arts, and leisure go begging. To date about $780 billion have been spent on the wars in Iraq and Afghanistan.

These three aspects of a singular, although deeply differentiated political process—structural adjustment, enhanced security, and the anti-state state—do not themselves produce something epiphenomenal that we call culture, but they do draw energy and sustenance from culture, including the kinds of changes fought through and in some spectacularly fragile ways won during the long cultural revolution that produced the most obvious changes in the United States over the past century.

The story from my family's picture is one of political and cultural becoming. We are not afraid, and to tell you the truth, we weren't as afraid as you thought we were. The culture of opposition is a sensibility derived from living in a stretched place—across territories on the one hand and through temporalities on the other.

One of the catastrophes of the last thirty years, which I want to elaborate on this evening, is this: the cultural and political revolution that had concentrated into astonishing eruptive potential between, let's say, World War I and the 1970s, drew dynamic force into a number of interlocking contradictions. I will list them: race, gender, class, sexuality, colonialism, territory, and war, which are all central, all fundamental, yet all ideologically and materially available for cooptation, which is nothing new but worth repeating. The armed wing of the counterrevolution—the police forces, the FBI under the organizing aegis of COINTELPRO in the United States, and many such forces in the United States and abroad—smashed the political, and therefore the social, revolution, annihilating much of the Third World left and its allies wherever they were. That was a catastrophe, as culture became decoupled from the political.

As a result, the culture front became *the* front, where the passive revolution hunkered down for the duration, with more stamina, strength, speed, flexibility, agility, and balance than we, not only because they have more money, but also because they are willing to eat the children. In other words, when Allan Bloom blamed rock and roll, feminists, and the Black students with guns, he was not altogether off the mark in marking the enemy. It's just that he got to define what that meant, what *we—the enemy*—meant, in countless fora, including boards of trustees at colleges and universities around the United States whose bulk purchases of *The Closing of the American Mind* made it the best seller that it was.

And still we fought, but increasingly in terrain already absorbed, annexed, turned to purposes other than abolition. Yet, if we imagine the imagined territory from above, which is to say, in an abstract and generalized view, we see movement, lots of movement, many trenches dug, many positions defended, many previously unimagined integrations achieved. That said, the cultivation of the contradictory landscape of production and reproduction, of violence and love, of culture and power characterized by capital in motion, including in flight, involuntary as well as voluntary migrations, new barriers to entry and exit, Rust Belt, Sun Belt, offshore production platforms, endless war, and an entire new array of organic intellectuals on the right producing the news, producing the stories that explain the new landscape, the new set and scene for our daily and intergenerational dramas and what its real vulnerabilities and fearsomenesses would be, has brought forth most peculiar fruit: one Black man in the White House and a million Black men in the Big House; two people of color serving life terms on the Supreme Court, and 100,000 serving life terms in federal and state prisons. And not only men and not only Black people.

In the 1960s and 1970s, the United Farm Workers (UFW) organized, organized, organized, in places and sectors where it was not legal under the Wagner Act to organize. The political revolution that the UFW was part of, stretching deep roots back through radical Filipino, Black, and white organizing in agriculture, and also the Chicano student movement, was not completely wiped out, but its most radical elements were smashed—not killed but smashed. And what remains in some ways, among the very people whom Chávez, Dolores Huerta, and UFW organizers—among the very people they were trying to summon as subjects in the struggle for their own liberation—has been transformed from a reality of significant struggle into a cultural artifact.

This is a poster that was produced by the California Chicano Correctional Workers Association.[6] They have named their annual award and festival the César Chávez Celebration and Pageant. And they say on their poster, "One thing you must remember is that people, no matter how poor, how disadvantaged, still have the same aspirations as you do for their children, for their future." Here's another story. Ten years ago, a group of us organized the Critical Resistance Research Group at the University of California Humanities Research Institute (UCHRI). Sandy Barringer, Nancy Scheper-Hughes, Avery Gordon, Gina Dent, David Theo Goldberg, and Angela Davis. We visited a few prisons as part of our research. In fact, it was the first time Angela had gotten permission to go inside, although she had had a long-standing relationship with the San Francisco County Jail where she had been teaching for a number of years. But this was the first time she had permission to go inside the adult authority.

At our first site, a level-four prison, a maximum but not supermax prison for men, deep in California's Sonoran desert, not far from the Mexico and Arizona borders, we were mobbed in the ladies' room by a group of Black women prison guards who wished to thank Dr. Davis for the opportunities they had as a result of, as they put it, "what you did." I doubt they understood the deeper truth of their observation, imagining rather that somehow her struggle had been to create equal opportunity in any structure for any kind of security, and they had benefited.

Our second site was the California Institution for Women, an older prison built on the rehabilitation rather than the incapacitation model that feels within the gates like a community

6   Image included in original publication.

college campus gone terribly wrong. There, we were mobbed by youthful prisoners, including a young woman who had enacted Dr. Davis in that year's Black History Month play. When asked what the character did, she replied, "I wore the afro wig. I wore the miniskirt."

Now, believe me, I knocked myself out trying to look exactly like Angela Davis, so I don't mean there's something wrong with the aesthetic. But the person and the politics had become the character in this outfit. This was a very sweet young woman who told us this story. So representation as remnant of the cultural—gender equality, notions of beauty, central embodiment of life as abolition—becomes in this story not only notionally corny, but more to the point, practically split off, though perhaps not severed (the jury's out on that), from the deep radical roots that gave forth Dr. Davis and me and the rest of the Third World left and its allies. What has been disappeared—although more likely waiting than dead—underlies both of the stories these women at the prisons tell, and more to the point, what's absent underlies the fact that we were in prisons to hear the stories.

Just as a number of us combined at UCHRI to investigate the prison-industrial complex, its political ecology no less than political economy, combinations of this kind have come together at universities and colleges around the world across time. Plenty of observers teach us that there are central places stretched across space and generally institutional in structure through which lots of people pass while some stay for a variety of reasons. These include the military, churches, prisons, hospitals, and schools. These are places where people who otherwise might never meet have the opportunity to make something happen through the thinking and working their encounters enable. Universities have been and should be such places. If we think about it, we realize how many key thinkers in the world's liberation movements met at schools and used their time together to sharpen analysis, figure out how to link struggles, scale up research, and revolt—Universidade Eduardo Mondlane, University of Dar es Salaam, Howard University—the list goes on and on. The casualization of academic labor today, the fattening of management, the speed-up of support and custodial staff—these are all part of structural adjustment. The abandonment of public education is a crisis that, behind the sturdy veil of racism, is destroying all capacity to think and be. But people are not accepting this lying down.

Like universities, unions are central places where a certain kind of energizing organizing can and must take place. For example, Justice for Janitors and social-movement unionism was partly based in the Los Angeles terrain where C.L.R. James organized dockworkers, and other Black people waged social-movement war for civil rights and employment rights during World War II. The official story about Justice for Janitors is a story about social-movement unionism drawing its inspiration from Latin American anti-dictatorship, pro-democracy, anti-capitalist movements. And that's true. That source is real, and certainly many of the migration paths of the workers who succeeded Black workers in janitorial positions in California connected the Southland to places that were disrupted by US foreign policy and trade policy in the first place: Guatemala, El Salvador, Nicaragua, Mexico, and so on. But the same was true of what was disrupted in Los Angeles: social movement, long-distance migration, places destroyed. A lot of the outmigration of Black people from the southern United States was caused by the huge demographic, land use, and industrial policy reconfigurations best summed up by the term "military-industrial complex." In both cases, people didn't just move for opportunity; they ran from murder.

The destroyed did not, however, die. A delegation from the Sandinista government in Nicaragua attended a socialist scholars conference in Los Angeles one year and heard the wonderful and very inspiring and somewhat triumphal story of the Justice for Janitors campaign. They asked, "What kind of work is J for J doing with the people who used to have these jobs?" Thoughtful consideration of that question suggests how we might, through research and organizing, develop a better sense of the intellectual and political ground on which we stand, in order to build stronger movements. We might also see in a closer look at that tale how the structural adjustment process has, across the world, tried to achieve scorched earth—through outsourcing, criminalization, and a host of other forms of organized abandonment.

* * *

In the face of all this direness, what kinds of practices—of teaching, research, and analysis—might we develop across disciplines toward the goal of identifying and promoting multiple routes out of crisis? We're living, as my friend David Theo Goldberg likes to say, in "critical condition."

Now I must polemicize a theoretical point, so the title for this section is "Negro Demonstrates." Page one of the *Yale Daily News*, October 9, 1967, covered my father's protest at Kingman Brewster's house. The caption writers at the paper thought they were witty and made my point better than I could. In the middle of the main article they wrote "Negro Demonstrates." And beside a picture that doesn't even include my father—though it represents his placard fairly well—they wrote "Wilson pickets." In that round at least, Wilson had the later laugh.

However embattled the academy is, we must direct our energy and resources as workers toward the goal of freedom, which I'm going to call tonight, for the sake of brevity, radical abolition. The abolition I speak of has roots in all radical movements for liberation and particularly in the Black Radical tradition. The abolition I speak of somehow, perhaps magically (meaning we don't yet know how, which is what magic is, what we don't know how to explain yet)—the abolition I speak of somehow, perhaps magically, resists division from class struggle and also refuses all the other kinds of power difference

41

combinations that, when *fatally* coupled, spark new drives for abolition. Abolition is a totality and it is ontological. It is the context and content of struggle, the site where culture recouples with the political; but it is not struggle's *form*. *To have form,* we have to organize.

Organize. For example, here's a very particular project some people could take up, against the intellectuals who say, "Oops, we messed up putting so many people in prison, but now we have to keep them until we figure out how to let them come home and stay home without getting into more trouble." An article by Joan Petersilia and Robert Weisberg recently appeared in *Daedalus* making such an argument.[7] Think about this policy recommendation. Most people are not serving life sentences. They come out of prison. Most people have no support to come home to because of how their communities have been stripped and repartitioned into no-go sites for the formerly incarcerated and felonized. The round-up of so many people, including undocumented workers, has been key to legitimating the increase in total governmental size, rescaled by anti-state state actors. Plus, the laws and check boxes that determine what people who have been arrested, detained, convicted, imprisoned can and cannot do, as many have theorized over many decades concerning the actual conditions in prison, are designed and calibrated—in the same way conditions inside prisons and detention centers are—to keep such persons always a bit more deprived than the most deprived not-convicted person.

This is the culture we live in because we lost the revolution.

Organize. Somebody needs to write the great book about the second Klan, 1915 to 1944. A number of people have made a fine argument. Chomsky and others have made the excellent point that laughing at the Tea Party—or being snarky about "Kansas"—is a stupid idea, and that if we don't understand it,

---

7   Robert Weisberg and Joan Petersilia, "The dangers of Pyrrhic victories against mass incarceration," *Daedalus* 139.3 (2010): 124–133.

it's going to kill us. I think we can understand the Tea Party if we understand the second Klan, whose principles, according to their website, which is available for all to scrutinize, were Americanism, Protestantism, self-sufficiency, chastity, marriage, and looking out for one's neighbor. Let's all look at that website, and then somebody take up the challenge and do the research.

And then, having gathered all that raw material, all that frightful material, we should use Clyde Woods's blues epistemology to analyze the material.[8] We should use oppositional theorizing and thinking to analyze the material, so that the outcome is not another litany of horror but a regrounding of the terrain of the racial modalities of class struggle.

Organize. We can organize through teaching and curriculum.

I recently saw a copy of a political economy exam that Ruth First gave at the Universidade Eduardo Mondlane in Mozambique. It was an exam for a course in development. She asked the students to think and write about these topics: What is developmentalism? What is meant by "modernization"? The exam highlights a need we all share today: the challenge of disentangling modernization, development, industrialization, capitalism. Take those apart and think about what *we* want to do. How to ask and answer questions and hear the world in our asking and answering is the task before us. In the year 1970 an advisor to then-governor Ronald Reagan told his boss the expansion of public postsecondary education was a problem because "an educated proletariat is dynamite." Is "dynamite." He said this for the record.

These two men, members of the Black Panther Party for Self-Defense, are relatively famous, more of the icons who have become sort of cultural decoration for a lot of people—not as prevalent as Che but of that mold. The one on the left is the

---

8 Clyde Woods, *Development Arrested: The Blues and Plantation Power in the Mississippi Delta*, new ed., introd. Ruth Wilson Gilmore, London: Verso, 2017.

son of the woman who married the West Indian after she didn't marry the East Indian, and the one on the right was the child of long-distance migrants out of the south to the promised land of Los Angeles.⁹ They were students at UCLA, and they were gunned down as a result of a well-waged covert war by COINTELPRO. The immediate cause—what they were fighting about at UCLA—what made them dangerous men was not that they were men with guns—because everybody had guns. The Panther bill restricting arms in California had just barely been passed. Rather, they were men who were fighting for a particular curriculum. It was a curriculum battle that killed them. The Black Panther Party was a party of students.

Organize. I had a student who's now my colleague, Jenna Loyd, who taught for a while in women's studies at California State Fullerton. She became really frustrated after a while because the students in her class, who were all working full-time, going to school full-time, and generally had at least a triple (housework) or a quadruple (caring for elderly parents) day ahead of and behind them, were not doing any reading at all. This is familiar to many people in this room. There are the students who are overprivileged who don't read because they don't care, because the instrument they wish to seize by getting a degree has nothing to do with learning anything, and then there are the people who are actually interested in learning who are scrappy and curious but tired. They're extremely tired. And Jenna was trying to figure out how at least to transform her students' interest into engagement with a course in radical, anti-racist feminism.

The wise young professor concluded that what she should do was turn the question in the room from "Why don't you want to study these things with me?" to "Why doesn't the government of California want people like you to study in institutions designed and built by and for the state of California?" It worked.

---

9   The image included in original publication depicts John Huggins (on the left) and Alprentice "Bunchy" Carter (on the right).

Organize.

Student debt. As many of you know, gross student debt in the United States is greater than consumer debt in the United States, more than all the credit card debts, the debts for short-term consumer durables, cars, refrigerators, deep freezers, everything but houses—student debt is greater than consumer debt. And debt robs. But debt also disciplines. I've been saying this from my bully pulpit for a really long time. But let me take you back in the annals of the Ivy League to talk a minute about debt and how it was used in the early part of the nineteenth century.

In the 1840s, the Ivy League schools, particularly Dartmouth, were worried, because they had been giving scholarships to farmers' sons to go to school. They were giving the farmers' sons scholarships to go to school so they would join the clergy and go west in the westward expansion and take the message of the mainline religions with them, be central to that mission—not as missionaries, but central to the mission of conquering the West.

What the farmers' sons were doing, however, was this: the enterprising young men went to school, got their degrees, and then they went off and had their lives. Some of them went west, and some of them didn't. Most of them did not become clergy; they weren't that interested. They just liked learning. They studied "any old thing," complained some of the people in the archive I read. They were studying philosophy. They were studying political economy. They were studying things that were not going to be immediately central to the purposes of Manifest Destiny, before the phrase was coined, but the westward movement was in full attack. The installation of a certain governmental and social and cultural and ideological form across the vast lands coming under US imperial expansion was not a foregone conclusion, hence the need for emissaries from the mainline as against those from other professions with other structures and goals.

45

The Ivy managers got together and decided that they would use debt to discipline the farmers' sons. They would lend them the money to go to school and forgive the loan if and only if they went off and worked as clergymen. They would discipline them in that way, and if they didn't work as clergy, they would be hounded for repayment of the loans, and it would all be due at once. No monthly payments. It worked pretty well. Today, while the imperial imperatives might be different, the role of debt is the same—to compel consent through the coercion of debt.

Organize.

Develop courses in which undergraduate students work in research teams across majors on term projects. Bite the bullet and give them all the same grade. You will produce scholars and activists from this work. It's a form of conscientization; it's a form of each one teach one. There are people in this room who started their research courses in such a course with me. De-individualizing undergraduate education should complement other innovations such as digital learning and the like. While social media might produce interactions not available in the pen, paper, and print-media milieux, the face time required of group projects can powerfully ground the virtual social. Whatever role social media have played in the current uprisings stretching from the Middle West to the Middle East, it was underlying organization, which is to say *organizations*, that made the spontaneous durable even as new relationships and subjectivities emerge in the crucible of action.

Organize. INMEX, Informed Meetings Exchange, is a not-for-profit organization, a meeting planning service that was founded by Unite Here and about 250 not-for-profit organizations. The American Studies Association is the poster child of INMEX. We have a little blurb on the front page of their website. INMEX is a way for scholarly associations and other not-for-profits to write contracts with hotels and other host sites that require them to have good labor practices from the instant the ink is dry until the meetings end. And if anything goes wrong, the association can get out of the contract at no cost to the group. Time after time, associations cry when they don't move a conference being held at a spot with bad labor or other policies: "It will bankrupt the association." There is truth to that claim. INMEX is the way associations can indemnify themselves against the specter of ruin, hold the hotel industry responsible and accountable to the lowest paid workers, and indeed to all the workers in that industry.

Many associations have not joined INMEX. Many members of the American Studies Association are also members of at least one other group. During my year as president, I and the National Council will produce some talking points and tips to help you put joining INMEX on your organization's agenda to make this happen. There is no neutrality when it comes to worker conditions and protections. If somebody makes your bed, as my grandmothers made many, you have a responsibility to see that s/he does so under the fairest conditions possible.

Organize. Schools are workplaces. Some like to talk about the schooling-industrial complex. Think about this, though. How many people in this room went to Yale? Some of you are sitting on your hands. How many here have colleagues from Yale? A lot of people. By some measure, some would say that Yale's American Studies program is the best, although New York University was saying "We're number one" the other day, so I don't know which one it is. One or the other, I'm sure. But here's what I want to ask you, in talking about Yale. Is it a coincidence, do you think, that several of the most creatively powerful faculty at Yale in American Studies and later in African American Studies came out of the Birmingham cultural studies project? And that that's how some of us got to that PhD program and are now here? They chose us because they took that responsibility that they'd set out for themselves in *The Empire Strikes Back* seriously.

So how can we not be thoughtful about the fact that much of the intellectual leadership in this room is the result of mindful decisions by people who think about these things well? Don't tell me you're post-Marxist. I'm not a Birmingham or Yale PhD, but I am very much a student of Stuart Hall as well as Cedric Robinson as well as Sivanandan and Selma James, to name four intellectual giants who really should talk to each other, of Paul Gilroy and Hazel Carby and Barbara Harlow and Sid Lemelle and Robin Kelley and Angela Davis. Stuart Hall wrote a long time ago that we got here, we got to these places that we're in tonight, we got here to this room in the Hyatt in San Antonio, and we didn't think hard enough about how or why. And if we don't think hard enough about it, we're not going to do the most powerful thinking we can do while here and after we leave.

Organize. Infiltrate what already exists and innovate what doesn't.

Some years ago, Cedric Robinson was teaching at the University of Michigan, where he was told, "Oh, Assistant Professor Robinson, it's really unfortunate that we don't have any Black students here in Political Science. We just can't find any." And Cedric said, "Not a problem, let me have a committee." Where are you, Cedric? How many did you admit that year? Twenty-six! It's not that hard! Don't think about pipelines, think about front lines. Others are fighting mightily now at University of Southern California, at the City University of New York Graduate Center, in departments throughout the land. Make unions, not task forces.

The principal products of the town I grew up in, as I've written elsewhere,[10] were for a long-time graduates and guns. While the military-industrial complex's industrial forces have quit New Haven, taking gun production with them, some intellectual forces of the military-industrial complex remain

---

10 See "Race, Prisons and War," in this volume, 176–195.

at Yale while being, of course, stretched across the academic-industrial complex. Such intellectual work remains central to war making, to money making, to regional trading blocs and global administrative apparatuses and infrastructures such as the IMF, the World Trade Organization, GATT, you name it. Perry Anderson's *The New Old World* closely examines work that professional intellectuals (like most of us) are doing to shape and consolidate the European Union. A key feature of what's happening in that other richest part of the world is the de-democratization of everyday life and the upward movement of the huge decisions that are now made in the European Union by administrative rather than deliberative legislative bodies.

High central administrative command is the normalizing mode in large-scale complex institutional structures, and it raises a question about how organized people, how organized labor and workers organized in multiple ways, including as labor, can and should try to consolidate sufficient power to push back globally against transnational forces. There's a lot of great work happening these days on this subject. For example, there's a young man I just met at the Grad Center at City University of New York named Jamie McCallum whose day job is as a researcher for the Service Employees International Union (SEIU), but he's also written a dissertation about a three-country organizing project the SEIU did with security workers who work for that firm G4S I spoke of earlier.[11] Or Laura Liu, who's been doing work on sweatshop labor and immigrant organizing, who recently completed a project in collaboration with Trebor Scholz trying to figure out, through debate, how we conceptualize the kind of data-exhaust sweeping that happens across the social networks where we all play.[12] Value

---

11 See Jamie K. McCallum, *Global Unions, Local Power: The New Spirit of Transnational Labor Organizing*, Ithaca, NY: Cornell University Press, 2013.

12 Laura Y. Liu and Trebor Scholz, *From Mobile Playgrounds to Sweatshop City. Situated Technologies Pamphlets 7*, New York: The Architectural League of New York, 2010.

is swept off from that play, volunteer labor, and transformed into capital. What is it, and how do we organize against forms of obvious and subtle exploitation?

Organize. In the project I started to write for tonight, "Life in Hell," I conclude that policy is the new theory. Policy is to politics what method is to research. It's a script for enlivening some future possibility—an experiment. No matter what we study, scholars are all about the future, about saying something tomorrow or the day after that. I told you that my teenage father found future sense in what he would not have called, but what he encountered as, historical-materialist theory and dialectical-materialist method.

Lorna Goodison's 1984 poem "Nanny" is a splendid approximation of an antecedent future sense: policy, preparation, script, possibility, and self-determination. Would that I could reproduce the entire poem here. The work is a first-person narrative of a legendary woman who organized the fugitives who formed maroon societies in Jamaica during the long nightmare of slavery. The poem describes how Nanny's birth community transformed her body and consciousness, before selling her into the transatlantic trade as a trained warrior—"all my weapons within me." Now watch for your cue: at the end of the poem, Nanny tells us:

> I was sent, tell that to history.
> When your sorrow obscures the skies
> other women like me will rise.

2

Decorative Beasts: Dogging the Academy in the Late 20th Century

In a wholly unconscious and unthinking way, we occupied our position somewhere at the summit of the higher-education system without ever asking how on earth we had got there and why it was our destiny to produce these new things. The degree to which we were totally unreflective about that really terrifies me in retrospect.

Stuart Hall[1]

The marble fireplace was supported by blackamoors of ebony; the light of the gas fire played over the gilded rose-chains which linked their thick ankles. The fireplace came from an age, it might have been the seventeenth century, it might have been the nineteenth, when blackamoors had briefly replaced Borzois as the decorative beasts of society.

John Le Carré[2]

"Symbolic contingencies," E. San Juan Jr. writes, "can metamorphose into nodes of condensation in programmatic goals and actions."[3] The object status of African American women in the Academy is that of Decorative Beasts. That is, we are fixtures

---

1 Stuart Hall, "Remarks," in *Out of Apathy*, ed. Oxford University Socialist Discussion Group, London: Verso, 1989, 139.

2 John Le Carré, *The Looking Glass War*, New York: Coward-McCann, 1965, 166.

3 E. San Juan Jr., "Problems in the Marxist Project of Theorizing Race," *Rethinking Marxism* 2.2 (1989): 58–80.

embodying Le Carré's seventeenth century image of exclusion/
marginality and his nineteenth century image of imperial-
ism/exoticism *plus* the supporting base for the entire modern
edifice: slavery/commodity itself. Decorative Beasts are alibis
for the Academy, living symbols whose occasional display is
contingent on the Academy's need to illustrate certain ideological triumphs: capitalism, for example, or Christianity,
equality, democracy, multiculturalism. If we keep in mind the
representations of marginality/exoticism/commodity, but shift
our analysis from object to subject, we initiate a political and
cultural metamorphosis enabled by economic conditions. From
this strategy Decorative Beasts, as symbolic contingencies, seize
agency. That is, we become able to negotiate positions from
which to disarticulate the power of the alibi—through our
goals and actions to instigate insurgency and provoke transformation. How is this so?

The Academy is in crisis. The effects of two major upheavals
in the political economy of the Academy during the contemporary moment (World War II to present [1991]) condense
in this historical conjuncture. The first upheaval consisted
of the Academy's reluctant then boosterish growth occasioned by federal fiscal interventions and the baby boom. The
second is the Academy's intensive but decentered efforts to
maintain discursive practices and non-discursive operations
into the debt-ridden and demographically alien near future.
I hope to show (using Cornel West's formulation) that there
are "conjunctural opportunities" in, as it were, the interstices
of "structural constraints."[4] The crisis provides a "window of
opportunity" for Decorative Beasts' access to the money, time,
space, books, and equipment, and people constitutive of and
constituted by the Academy. The window will not stay open

---

4   Cornel West, "Marxist Theory and the Specificity of Afro-American
Oppression," in *Marxism and the Interpretation of Culture*, eds. Cary
Nelson and Lawrence Grossberg, Urbana: University of Illinois Press,
1988, 7–33.

long; the area beyond is not reserved in any particular name. The conjuncture unrolls, and with it a corresponding revolution. Who is in the vanguard?

1.

In January 1969 two Black Panthers, my cousin John Huggins and his comrade Alprentice Carter were murdered—politically assassinated—at UCLA. Their lynching took place in a stairwell outside a meeting about UCLA's incipient Black Studies program. The silenced men had been arguing for a curriculum that centered on race *and* capitalism as inseparable elements of US and global analysis. In other words, their challenge to the Academy asked whether UCLA's Black Studies was in danger of functioning as decorative displacement: whether the project would use ideas "to clarify or mystify understanding of the social world."⁵ The assassins, under cover of Ron Karenga's cultural nationalist organization, United Slaves (US), pulled the trigger for the State after roughing up a Panther sister in order to flush their prey from the thicket of a public meeting.⁶

The lynchings at UCLA were part of an extended struggle for power played out in both "legal" proceedings and extra legal

---

5   James Donald and Stuart Hall, "Introduction," in *Politics and Ideology*, Milton Keynes: Open University Press, 1986, ix.

6   The full story has yet to be reconstructed. However, Frank Donner provides the basic framework for how these murders came about: "[The Los Angeles Police Department] Criminal Conspiracy Section supplied [LAPD tipster Louis Tackwood] with funds to transmit to Ron Karenga, the leader of [United Slaves] a black nationalist organization that was the rival of the Panthers, for use in funding armed attacks on the latter, a program conceived by the FBI and implemented locally. The Karenga assignment was part of a combined LAPD-FBI operation to foment a violent feud between the two groups. The operation was highly successful and resulted in the killings of ... Carter and Huggins—for which several members of Karenga's group were convicted," *Protectors of Privilege: Red Squads and Police Repression in Urban America*, Berkeley: University of California Press, 1990, 265–266.

engagements. Operating on behalf of the State, the Regents of the University of California and the military-industrial complex, J. Edgar Hoover's COINTELPRO operation defined through state terrorism the limits of disruption and intervention a program of study at UCLA might pose to the Academy's constituents. The "symbolic contingencies" demanded and represented by the Black Panthers in the curriculum contestation signified potential ruptures of consequence throughout the discursive spaces both *of* and *fed by* the Academy. State terrorism also destabilized any (however unlikely) potential for transformation that might have resulted from the *public* part of governmental higher education policy—an example of which is federal intervention in Academy cohort formation through student aid programs.

Did I say military-industrial complex? The contemporary US Academy is a historical complex committed to the production of knowledge and, therefore, people-in-the-know. The hierarchies of academic epistemological practice reflect and serve the interests of those who control, economically and culturally, the means of that production. Just after World War II, the Academy began to grow, fed by GIs with federal bucks in hand. At first, colleges resisted the intrusion. Fifteen years earlier, a similar resistance greeted students funded by the New Deal's National Youth Administration. But the colleges wised up and used those students to fill alarmingly empty lecture halls; they also used humanities programs like Great Books, and applied sciences like engineering and medicine, to shape and occupy the interests of non-WASPs (Jews and Italians, for example). College presidents who lobbied against the GI Bill (not so much the fact of reward but rather the particulars of largesse—especially choice) asserted that disaster was the necessary result of their inability to predict how adult men could be accommodated within the "natural" age-differentiated power relations of the Academy.[7] The histori-

---

7 John Monro, "Unlocking Minds," Keynote, Annual Meeting of the College Board, New York, October 1984. While a professor and

cally proven methods of exclusion (money and testing) failed to keep out "war heroes" able to pay their own way with federal dollars. Ultimately, the colleges took the money and used it to produce, among other people-in-the-know, lots of engineers.

A celestial marker, Sputnik, led the way to the birth of the Academy's boom. In 1957 the Rosenbergs were barely cold in their graves; television promoted the ideology of patriotism as anticommunism; Churchill's rhetorical flourish—"iron curtain"—provided US show-me common sense with the material definition of the "free world"; people of color in the "free world," including the United States, were engaged in liberation struggles; television (again) brought the civil rights movement's successes and brutal failures into both white living rooms that might never host living Blacks *and* Black households, raising expectations and consciousness. The defense industry, experiencing its first slump since 1939, got the military and the President to sell an extraordinary bill of goods to a voting public who, on average, enjoying steadily increasing wages, could not imagine not affording those goods.[8] Arm for peace. Get into Space. Produce scientists to accomplish these transparently necessary goals. We can see here the cultural and economic preconditions for Star Wars.

US academies after World War II capitalized on the neatly matched forecasts of more students (GIs segueing into boomers) and more money (federal and industrial/corporate investments in academic production) coupled with a science research and development public policy securely articulated throughout the society: Beat the Russkies with nuclear physics; better living

---

administrator at Harvard in the 1950s, Monro was one of the inventors of the postwar financial aid needs analysis system: the Uniform Methodology. Subsequently he went south to teach in a summer freedom school and stayed—for the balance of his career teaching literature and composition at poor, historically Black colleges such as Miles in Mississippi.

8   The data are available many places, notably in the *Digest of Education Statistics* published by the US Education Department Office of Educational Research and Improvement.

through chemistry at home. In the late 1950s for example, Stanford trustees embarked on a thirty-year campaign to transform their university from a provincial Academy to what it is today: a highly rated undergraduate school, a major research center, and a commanding voice in US discursive practice from the Hoover Institution to the notorious lower-division core humanities course: Culture, Ideas, Values.

With the 1958 National Defense Education Act, the State unambiguously intervened in the kinds of people-in-the-know the Academy would produce by funding near-free loans for science and engineering students. Meanwhile, the modern young Deans of the well-endowed academies (led by the congregationalist cadres from Harvard to Pomona) agreed for the first time in more than a century to end their annual bidding war for undergraduate talent. The peace-keeping force consisted of a "scientific, objective" system to award student aid (principally university/college-funded scholarships). The system, called the "Uniform Methodology," purported to deduce from a formulaic interpretation of income and assets a family's annual *ability to pay* for one or more children to attend college. However disruptive the GIs were at this point, the Deans' eyes were on the "traditional" prize: first-time, full-time freshmen in four-year academies between 17–19 years old (the average age of all US undergraduates currently hovers close to thirty). Thus, the immensely wealthy, not-for-profit College Board— arbiter of *ability to learn* via the SATs—formed a subsidiary membership organization, the College Scholarship Service, to fill the lucrative opening occasioned by the Ivy lever. In the new practice the Deans met annually to compare their "objectively" reproducible *penultimate* results, and to fiddle around with conflicting interpretations of family circumstance until they agreed on a text: a single narrative for each student leading, as if inevitably, in a biblical way, to a uniform bottom line. This meeting to discuss and adjust, called the "Ivy Overlap" (versions of which were practiced by non-Ivies as well) ended in 1991 after the Reagan-Bush Justice Department accused the participating institutions of price-fixing. The Department's rather sudden interest in illegal activities, openly admitted for decades in catalogs, recruitment brochures, and interviews was a curious intervention in the current crisis.[9]

Uniform Methodology, the "objective" formulation regularized by the College Scholarship Service, provided the Secretary of the amazing old triumvirate, Health, Education, and Welfare, both method and model for distributing federal student aid. The 1965 Higher Education Act, the mega-act that launched today's multibillion dollar work-study and guaranteed student loan programs, responded to the overt interests of the rapidly expanding military-industrial complex and the perceived needs of the general electorate as ventriloquized by the growing ranks of professional Academy lobbyists. The Act featured President Lyndon Johnson's Depression-era-developed habit of strategically allocating federal bucks to create Democratic voters. In 1965, Johnson sought to amalgamate the ballot-box potential of working-class urban and rural whites (especially women) with the specifically targeted beneficiaries of the Voting Rights Act: Black women and men who were not voters (or those who, despite FDR and JFK, had not yet left the party of Lincoln). Congressmen, of course, dispensed the promise of education for votes. Black activists, seeking to ensure Black students' share of the take, waged a campaign to restrict the funds to academies that disavowed discrimination—financial incentive for George Wallace to get out of the schoolhouse door. The Academy regularly resisted federal interventions in the *details*

---

9 While a number of the Ivy participants reached a plea-bargain resolution with the Justice Department, the Massachusetts Institute of Technology, which vigorously defends the practice as providing "the freedom of opportunity to get a college education regardless of income," was convicted in September 1992 of violating antitrust law. MIT appealed. See Scott Jaschik, "Judge Rules MIT. Violated Antitrust Law as Member of 23-College 'Overlap Group,'" *The Chronicle of Higher Education*, XXXIX:3 (September 9, 1992), 22.

of cohort formation (the poor; GIs; Black and other of-color folk; white women; Bakke[10]; the differently abled; etc.). Yet the Academy regularly capitulated to such intervention. Any adequate accounting for this cooperation must balance liberal, ethical convictions against both increased dependence on funding, failure to comply with which would not only cause funds to be withdrawn, and fear of *juridical* convictions for violating anti-discrimination statutes.

The exigencies of expansion funding left the "traditional" legatees of the Academy where they have been all along—in the center—surrounded by new cohort-fractions. In 1969, for example, Yale's freshman class was half public-school graduates; it was also bigger than ever, coed, and 10 percent Black.

By the time Lyndon Johnson called it quits, the women and men who lived in proximity to and/or worked (as non-exempt employees) for the urban Academy brought resistance organizing to and inside the gates. They labored to expose and combat what lifelong New Haven activist Courtland Seymour Wilson in 1967 called the Academy's "apartheid" practices: these policies ranged from razing affordable housing, to the rigid chromatic striations in hiring from janitor to president, to the absence of students of color in other than undergraduate programs.[11] White boomer students, inspired by Mario Savio and the Free Speech Movement on the one hand and

10   The 1978 Supreme Court of the United States decision in *Regents of the University of California v. Bakke* upheld affirmative action in college admissions.

11   Working solo, Wilson picketed then-President of Yale Kingman Brewster Jr.'s mansion when Lady Bird Johnson was in residence during her Beautify America Crusade ("Plant a shrub, a bush, or a tree."), carrying a placard outlining the apartheid charge. Ideology is powerful; he got an audience with Brewster and used that encounter in his overall strategy to carry on more than a quarter-century of inside/outsider work to make the university materially accountable to the community. Here in California, Education Professor Reginald Clark successfully sued the Claremont Graduate School for $1,000,000 plus damages plus lawyers' fees: CGS denied him tenure because he is Black. Clark, too, speaks of apartheid policies in the academy.

local Black organizers on the other, protested the Academy's roles in both the Vietnam War and the destruction of stateside urban neighborhoods; in other words, they denounced many of the very practices the Academy had undertaken in order to ensure enrolling those very students. Black and other students of color, whom the Academy recruited voluntarily against the economic and juridical sanctions described above (as well as against the specter of "riots") organized to assert autonomy from the Academy's control of epistemology and its consequent support of repressive practices and processes across the social formation.

The Academy responded strategically and not expensively (in the short run) to those challenges: here a daycare center (in exchange for a linear accelerator on the side where the kids had once lived), there an order for ROTC to leave campus (in exchange for much-needed office and classroom space), and high-profile involvement in the race-relations industry: Black Studies, Chicano Studies, Community Liaisons, Assistant Deans, one or two tenure-track faculty, and lots of honorary degrees (Duke Ellington and I graduated the same June day in 1972).

In the 1970s three changes in the political and cultural economies pitched the Academy to the brink of its current disequilibrium: US dollars declined in value; desegregation declined in fashion; and boomer women declined, or were unable, to have babies.[12]

In that decade of declines, the Academy energetically recruited white women, whose raw numbers in the college-age

---

12   Some intrepid scholar has yet systematically to expose the Academy's complicity in involuntary sterilization, performed through teaching hospitals on women of uncertain habits who sought legal abortions; the procedures to manage race and class reproduction include the straightforward (tubal ligations and hysterectomies) and the reckless—such as insertion of a Dalkon Shield immediately after an abortion and with absolutely no follow up care, even after the Dalkon's destructive properties were exposed in the *New York Times* and other presses.

population shot up, of course, with the boom. Federal anti-discrimination statutes, with their protective language of prevention and remedy, achieved the explicit generality of Title IX of the 1972 Amendments to the 1965 Higher Education Act, and included a rule separating admissions decisions from those concerning financial aid eligibility. The Academy absorbed women (who as a group score lower than men on SATs but earn higher grades) and thus ensured stable growth in tuition revenues. Clearly, coeducation opened a new competitive market and marketing system. Between 1968 and 1980 postsecondary undergraduate enrollments increased 60 percent—an increase of 4.6 million students, 3 million of whom were women; the proportion of coeducational academies went from 75 to 91 percent.[13] Black women fit the project in our double countability, while Black men faded from the halls of the white Academy in the late 1970s. Allan Bloom's hysterical distortion in *The Closing of the American Mind*[14] of the action taken by Black students at Cornell expressed the dominant culture's contemptuous fear of Black men; but Bloom invented neither the fear nor the contempt. For example, on Christmas Eve in 1977, I chanced upon a piece in a daily paper reporting the FBI's Freedom of Information Act—coerced "confession" of its role in the 1969 UCLA lynching and related anti-Panther actions (part of the wide-ranging COINTELPRO totalitarian regime); the editor placed the newswire story not as news or as feature but as holiday filler.

When Nixon occupied the White House, federal student aid funds did new work. Where Johnson planned to create voters, Nixon by contrast used these federal bucks to subsume very poor and other financially alienated young men not drafted

---

13   Center for Education Statistics, *Digest of Education Statistics 1987*, various tables.

14   Allan Bloom, *The Closing of the American Mind: How Higher Education Has Failed Democracy and Impoverished the Souls of Today's Students*, New York: Simon and Schuster, 1987.

for Vietnam—and their sisters—by setting up the next stop on The Way Out railroad whose Great Society stations were Head Start and Upward Bound. Nixon intended for the new programs and dollars to protect urban property and to deflect criticism of the warfare state. 1972's irresistible bid consisted of two parts: (1) free money in the federal student aid kitty (Pell Grants) and (2) a federally mandated ratio of grant to self-help (work-and-loan) of about 3:1 throughout a student's undergraduate career. Congress has never adequately funded the grant portion; Nixon quit.

Academies learned to play the high-stakes sophisticated federal funding game in which the richest schools set standards for the lesser endowed sisters. Institutions such as MIT and Stanford spun off defense-support research institutes. The line between "public" and "private" blurred as major research academies became accustomed to drawing down from 40 to 70 percent of their annual operating budgets from federal sources—particularly basic and classified research and development grants and contracts. Institutions took advantage of escalating inflation and especially the post-1973 surge in energy costs by jacking up their average overhead rates (overhead is the university's surcharge on the "actual" costs to carry out a contracted task), combining graduate student tuitions with toilet paper and heat. More charges on the endless account that had been accumulating for twenty years. Who is minding the rest of the store?

In the second year of his doomed presidency, Jimmy Carter signed into law the Middle Income Student Assistance Act (MISAA) of 1978. The most oddly desperate of the oval office desperadoes, Carter tried to hang on to the voters he'd won in 1976. The tightening economic squeeze of the late 1970s (exacerbated by Carter's economic policy) provoked parents, particularly in the middle income range, to resist paying big bucks tuition, *especially* for their daughters who by then accounted for 50 percent of all enrollment. The Academy lobbyists talked MISAA through Congress, knowing that behind the scenes confidential college budget forecasts projected tuitions rising faster than the rate of inflation measured by the Consumer Price Index (CPI). Part of the marketing strategy in the go-go 1960s consisted of off-price maneuverings (lower than CPI tuition hikes) amid the contradictory scares of Academy closures and competition for all those "new" students. By the late 1970s the price of that management strategy swelled, fed by the maintenance costs of faculty tenured in the 1960s, by the cost of energy, and greed. Where would the money come from?

When money is scarce credit is difficult to access, either because of restrictive rules (the scenario in late 1992) or high cost. In 1981, the prime rate hit 21 percent. A new set of profiteers descended on the Academy: postindustrial, labor-power indifferent investment bankers. From 1980–1990 the Academy has run up billions of dollars in public tax-exempt financing to build or renovate facilities and buy equipment (labs, management schools, computers). Students (and, since 1981, their parents) borrow federally guaranteed education loans at nearly market-rate interest. Imagine: a student can borrow more than $70,000 in 10–25 year debt to complete an advanced degree (and, in certain professions such as health sciences, much, much more). The Reagan and Bush administrations have not cut federal expenditures for student aid. Rather, they have consolidated greater benefits for *their* allies, the plutothugs and econocrats who, regardless of party registration, run the US and by extension a good deal of the world. Further, tax exempt financing for construction and equipment costs federal and state treasuries in foregone revenues. After non-discretionary governmental expenditures (such as interest payments), education and other social programs get a diminishing slice of a mean little pie.[15] The independent colleges of California, for

---

15　The last week of August 1992 the California Legislature and Governor Pete Wilson passed a long-overdue state budget that *cut one billion*

example, today owe nearly three-quarters of a billion dollars in facilities and equipment financing; the University of Southern California, for example, is paying on approximately $200 million, or nearly half the 30 June 1989 net book value of its endowment. These growing billions owed by the Academy have 7–12 year maturities, which means that enormous debt service is due at just the moment when baby boomers' kids (the reproduction of a highly educated class pacified by general consumer—if not strictly educational—debt) should have been going to college.

In the late 1970s both trade and popular journals began to investigate and theorize the effects of fundamental demographic shifts on college enrollments in the 1980s and 1990s. Deans of Admission across the US started to rush upstairs to their bosses' offices brandishing "white papers" that demonstrate a simple fact: People who were not born in 1972–1978 will not attend college in 1990–1996. Assuming high school dropout rates remain at about 30 percent, the projected number of college-bound high school graduates drops 12 percent between the fall of 1989 and 1993 and does not recover until the end of the decade. 200,000 vacancies times average tuition equals a minimum of 600 million 1989 dollars per year in unforgoable revenue.[16]

College presidents agree that enrollment is the number one concern for the next five years.[17] Harold Hodgkinson, Director of the Center for Demographics and Public Policy

---

dollars (2.7 million dollars/day) from state education appropriations for the current fiscal year. Meanwhile the Association of Independent California Colleges and Universities (AICCU) is trying to take a student loan bond deal (the second in a decade) to market. Who profits? Who pays?

16   See, for example, J.A. Centra, "Reading the Enrollment Barometer," *Change* 11 (April 1979): 50–51; C. Francis, "Apocalyptic v. Strategic Planning," and F. E. Crossland, "Learning to Cope with a Downward Slope," *Change* 12 (July/August 1980) 18ff.; "Search for Students: Higher Education in the Next 20 Years," *Futurist* 15 (February 1981): 65–67; also, the *Chronicle of Higher Education* annual "Fact File" and *Almanac*.

17   *Chronicle of Higher Education 1989 Almanac*.

in Washington DC, is the Academy's favorite futurologist. For most of the 1980s he toured the US with his hit road show "Guess Who's Coming to College?" While nobody's come up with an adequate answer, it surely isn't suave, smooth, standard-English-speaking Sidney Poitier.

Finally—and this point is exhaustively reported so I won't elaborate—while pursuit of careers in academe was less than feverish in the "make bank" 1980s, 40,000 professors retire in the next ten years.

Cost, cohorts, colleagues. These three Cs are fundamental constitutive elements of the Academy in crisis. I use crisis in Gramsci's sense, as elucidated by Bill Schwarz and Stuart Hall: The Academy "can no longer [reproduce itself] on the basis of the pre-existing system of social relations."[18]

2.

In the midst of contradictions, in the yawning jaws of crisis, across the disciplines, theory is the thing today. Why? In mathematics and science theories posit general rules for how things work. *The* heuristic research organon, theoretical science is a money magnet, its twin attractive forces prestige and practicality. The post-WWII emphasis on science and mathematics throughout the educational system—new math and so on—occasioned the general contemporary *power* of "theory": faith in its directionality granted *a priori* to summon the force. Scientists discoursing in units of agreement within what Cedric Robinson calls their "formal grammar"[19] advance what they assert are "universal, invariable, inviolate, genderless and

---

18 Stuart Hall and Bill Schwarz, "State and Society, 1880–1930," in Hall, *The Hard Road to Renewal*, London: Verso, 1988, 96.

19 Cedric J. Robinson, *Black Marxism: The Making of the Black Radical Tradition*, London: Zed, 1983, 100.

verifiable"[20] approximations of "natural laws," encouraged by and forming the common-sense idea of knowledge: powerful, rigidly ordered, and as mystifying as the Great Chain of Being.

Producers in the humanities positioned themselves to compete in the Academy economy by making theory: the magical praxis that beat fascism, contained communism, deferred death, and brought us black holes. It is no coincidence that Yale, a major research university, housed the originary and now fabulously tarnished Sterling professors of theory. The funding fathers found the extension of theory to non-scientific discourse "natural," emphasizing all at once "American" intellectual brawn (if not hegemony, then uncontested domination) neatly (t)raced to European roots. But further, the ascendance of theory at Yale and other socially "accountable" (urban or public) academies signed and served another function: to create cloisters separate from Black people and white women who were congregating in the humanities in alarming numbers. (Science could invoke the power of other numbers—SATs and so forth—to exclude the intruders.) Here the control of epistemology entails appropriation of the best—that is, the most fundable, secure, and perhaps obscure—mode of thinking, "theory," and thereby reifies the canon (for example) as the literary equivalent of the mechanical universe.

So while the democracy of the mind ought to mean theoretical investigation is open to any "American" with sufficient ingenuity, stamina, and brain-power, such freedom is elusive, especially to the Decorative Beast. The problem with the equal access formulation lies in the Academy's historical contributions to the construction of race, gender, and class power relations as images of "natural" ahistorical laws. Here, theory—or better,

---

20 Remarks by physicist Sheldon Glashow in "Does Ideology Stop at the Laboratory Door? A Debate on Science and the Real World," with Sandra Harding and Mary Hesse, *New York Times*, 139, 22 October 1989, Sec. 4, E24.

"theory"—has become a means to produce more where there is already most.

The Western Academy produces formal grammars—rules of thought—theological, philosophical, philological, scientific, economic. These grammars, serially although not exclusively through the past 500 years, form the discursive ordering force for the structure in dominance, and ultimately the constituent ideologies of "nation" (culture, race, and so forth) within the borders of state. Benedict Anderson argues persuasively that vernacular print-languages enabled communities to imagine themselves as nations—as naturally differentiated aggregates of humankind.[21]

More specifically, the Academy establishes the rules of the page *qua* object, which predominates in every interpretive instance following its establishment until superseded by a more authoritative page. Martin Bernal's *Black Athena,* a sort of intellectual autobiography, demonstrates the extent to which national race-making in the protestant German Academy became naturalized in academic discourse. In particular, Aryan supremacist myths were systematized in the raw material of discursive production: language itself. The systematic displacement of extra-European linguistic roots into the curious concept "loan words" at once mystifies social relations and prefigures contemporary inter-state debt relations in which somehow the Euros ("real" or honorary) always profit.[22]

---

21 Benedict Anderson, *Imagined Communities*, London: Verso, 1983.

22 Martin Bernal, *Black Athena, vol. 1*, New Brunswick: Rutgers University Press, 1987. Issues of debt, profit, the academy, and nineteenth century production of meaning loop back to the concerns of the first part of this essay. Indeed, one of the slickest apologies for imposing debt on the poor I've ever read is an astonishing piece by the President of Amherst College written in 1830: his central claim is that Jesus will save more the more the farmer's son borrows, since debt peonage will confine him to the evangelical mission. See H. Humphrey, *Quarterly Register and Journal of the American Congregational Education Society*, II: iii (February 1830): 129–134.

Just as words, so too the "Negro." Cedric Robinson describes how Europeans abstracted Africans from both the "dark continent" and from the historical reality of 3000 years of "Ethiop-European" relations. The final construct, the "Negro" stood ugly and empty: one of an identical horde, differentiable only by age and genitals.[23] This construct *needed* content, which Harriet Beecher Stowe to Louis Agassiz to Arthur Jensen worked hard to fill according to the formal grammar of racialist science. These three represent a broad range of knowledge-producers: Stowe, the abolitionist novelist (*Uncle Tom's Cabin*); Agassiz, Harvard's theorist of polygeny; Jensen, the University of California's education professor who cautions against wasting time and money on Negroes who can, thus will, never learn. So it wasn't all that egregious for Kenneth Stampp, trying to fix things, to posit in 1957 *another* content: "Negroes *are*, after all, only white men with black skins, nothing more, nothing less."[24] Five centuries of race-making produced *that* version of anagnorisis—of crisis-necessitated recognition of kin.

Through their predictive capacities, grammars control epistemological possibilities—they police knowledge. They are integral to the functions of the state. Today, not surprisingly, with the collapse of the Keynesian welfare state and the boisterous shifts in capital accumulation, economic grammar has taken on a structural relation to thought both in the Academy and in common-sense consciousness. Investment, cost-benefit analysis, management, productivity, diversity, balance: these concepts order theory and practice from biotechnologies and "informatics" on the one hand[25] to this paper on the other. The US passion for counting, measuring, and ordering its wealth in Christians, slaves, citizens, square miles, literates, or

---

23 Robinson, *Black Marxism*, 105–106.

24 Kenneth M. Stampp, *The Peculiar Institution: Slavery in the Ante-Bellum South*, New York: Knopf, 1956, vii.

25 See Donna Haraway, "A Manifesto for Cyborgs," in *Coming to Terms*, ed. Elizabeth Weed, New York: Routledge, 1989, especially 188ff.

pork bellies now extends to failed S&Ls, the Human Genome Project, the human homeless ... especially at the foot of the US-wide twenty-year decline in real wages and ten-year decline in asset net worth. (How many jobless engineers have become MBAs?) Hence the language: Illiteracy might have economic costs. How many Black women can "we" afford to educate? What is the value of life against the cost to maintain it (quality control)? How does the market correct itself? These questions ask for prediction, for forecast, for theory.

Take what literary critics do: Reading. Theory leads to an understanding of "reading" which leads to who is understood to read, which leads to both who is allowed to read and who succeeds in being understood. Or science: In generation after generation mainstream scientists have provided theoretical pliers and empirical wire for the armature of the structure in dominance in the contemporary social formation. For example, the late William Shockley got enriched and en-Nobeled by the transistor invention. But according to his own testimony, as related in his *New York Times* obituary, Shockley's important lifework was to develop a theory of empirical evidence that people of African descent are intellectually inferior to all other races of the planet.[26]

Shockley lived on the Stanford campus until his death in 1989. His public plot against the purpose of and participants in this special journal issue[27] advanced, even as the debate over Stanford's CIV course captivated the trade and popular presses and fast-forwarded Allan Bloom and William (former

---

26 Wolfgang Saxon, "William B. Shockley, 79, creator of transistor and theory on race," *New York Times*, v. 138, 14 August 1989, B15. Shockley's several careers converge in Spike Lee's creation Radio Raheem (*Do the Right Thing*)—who lived by the transistor and died of the material effects of such theory on race.

27 This article was originally published in a 1991 issue of *California Sociologist: A Journal of Sociology and Social Work* on the theme of "Culture & Conflict in the Academy: Testimonies from a War Zone."

Secretary of Education and Drug Czar) Bennett's founding of the National Association of Scholars. So where's the revolution?

Amid much fanfare Stanford starts Culture, Ideas, Values.

Wesleyan enrolls an astonishingly high number of Black students without any significant increase in Black faculty.

The Jepson Foundation endows the University of Richmond with megabucks for a "Leadership" major in which Mr. and Mrs. Jepson are star faculty.

The University of California at Berkeley completely restructures its undergraduate admissions system both to placate the quota-ed Asian Americans *and*, by increasing set-asides for older and far-rural candidates, to maintain the proportion of whites to total enrollment.[28]

The College Board sells Enrollment Management Packages to academies.

Academies use scholarship funds to "buy teachable students" who can pay their own way, but load needy students with future-determining debt.

E. D. Hirsch's coy paean to pluralism, *Cultural Literacy*, is a bestseller.

Academies desperately search for "talking androids"[29] in the hope they will reproduce themselves at no ideological cost.

The United States Justice Department investigates price-fixing at the wealthiest academies.

The same academies fund one-year Decorative Beast pre- and post-doctoral positions at each other's campuses, which they are under no obligation to renew much less to tenure.

These actions, periodically retailed in trade journals such as

---

28 For this particular bit (information plus analysis), I am indebted to Professor William Allen, former Chair of the United States Civil Rights Commission (appointed by Ronald Reagan) and twice conservative candidate for the Republican Party's nomination to run for a California US Senate seat.

29 The phrase, which describes the Clarence Thomas mode of being in this world, is from Ishmael Reed, *Mumbo Jumbo*, New York: Doubleday, 1972.

The Chronicle of Higher Education, and *Change*, and in more popular documents of everyday life, are indicative of top-down crisis containment, the managerial methodology encoded in "strategic planning." In other words, this tendency indicates what Gramsci calls a "passive revolution." The purpose of a passive revolution is "to restore ... the fundamental social relations of production on a more stable basis for the future."[30] The point is to define the rules then win by them; in a nineteenth century card game spun off Stowe's novel, the winning hand consisted of Tom, Eva, and Justice: a dead Black man, a dead white girl, and a concept imaged as a blindfolded female form of apparent European origin.[31]

The conjunctural opportunity for Decorative Beasts is a function of the structural constraints, which is to say (crudely) numbers: the three Cs—cost, cohorts, colleagues. The foundational elements of epistemology—*Who teaches? What is taught? Who learns?*—will be briefly, specifically, vulnerable during the last decade of the century. Black women academics form a tiny class-fraction, or perhaps better a potential collective social subject, which can reproduce only as a result of serious intervention into the technology of class-fraction formation. Practitioners of certain types of discourse, of certain formal grammars, will play disproportionately powerful roles in determining who has access to the Academy as student, teacher, community organizer in need of resources and support. It is the hip, young, and tenured to watch out for. Across the curricula the "effectively hegemonic"[32] control of epistemology

---

30 Hall and Schwarz, "State and Society," 114. See also Antonio Gramsci, *Selections from the Prison Notebooks*, ed. and trans. Quintin Hoare and Geoffrey Nowell-Smith, New York: International Publishers, 1971, 106–114.

31 Thanks to friend and art critic Howard Singerman for tipping me to the game's existence and the configuration of the winning hand.

32 Wahneema Lubiano, comments from the floor following "Psychoanalysis and Race," Panel, annual meeting of the Modern Language Association, Washington DC, December 28, 1989.

requires specifically racialized knowledge as both object and process if the struggle to end racial domination is not to be erased, in theory. Raced: not essentially but rather historically, according to contingent requirements of the social order. The ideology of objectivity is expressed in common sense as *the* incontrovertible way to see, *really* see, the real world. We see here the epistemological condition, loaded with material supports, that allowed and encouraged Shockley's naturalizing —dehistoricizing—of the economic, political, and cultural components of race hierarchy as fundable science rather than egregious hatemongering.

One empirical basis for Shockley science is learning disabilities (LD): a disease discovered, measured, and managed by "handicapping conditions professions" who work in the $100 million-a-year testing industry. As funding to provide appropriate education for all children regardless of special needs wanes, so does the epidemic of LD—which some critics assert is a disease that never existed.[33] LD serves as a convenient holding pattern, a liberal means to track Black, Latino, and other poor kids to intellectual oblivion under the guise of helping them.

For example, at the California Youth Authority (CYA) in Chino, most of the wards (of whom nearly 50 percent are Black) have been measured and found, learning-wise, underdeveloped. The measurements show appallingly subnormal ability to memorize or to read (read: interpret) units of information such as directions. The intervention of rap in these young men's lives proves the lie of science; many CYA wards compose and their works demonstrate, as successful rap must, rhetorical complexities driven by what we might call memory and interpretation. Allan Bloom's need to valorize inequality, to separate the cultures founded by "Jewish, Christian, Greek, Chinese and Japanese ... men"[34] requires that rhetorical complexity cannot be *rap* if it is truly *Shakespeare*. Why? Because

---

33 See the *Fair Test Examiner*, Spring 1988.
34 Bloom, *Closing*, 201.

the moral lessons are different. Otherwise all those wards would not be in prison. We can look at this question in another way: Who killed Edmund Perry? "The imprisoning blandishments of a neurotic culture"?[35] A white cop? Edmund's Black unconscious which refused to notice a full scholarship to Stanford must lift the veil? But here I am talking about another dead Black man when the subject is supposed to be living Black women. I can't see one without the other.

A few years back Michelle Cliff described an encounter at the University of California at Santa Cruz:

> Two of my African-American women students ... are strolling across the wooded campus ... talking about Bessie Head's novel *A Question of Power*. Suddenly, a 4x4 turns the corner in front of the women, passes by so close they can feel the heat of the engine, and a bunch of white boys yell "How much?! How much?!" ... At that moment, the novel these young women are discussing, and the lives they are living, collide.[36]

Behavioral, psychological and medical science practitioners are at this moment producing the latest definition of Black female alterity, a definition that promises to disambiguate the radical complexion of work on sexuality by Hazel Carby, Barbara Smith, Hortense Spillers, et al.[37] Black women as the

---

35   Edmund Perry was a Harlem youth headed to Stanford from the A Better Chance (ABC) prep school program at Andover. The summer before his first year (1988) he was killed by an undercover cop whom he and his brother allegedly tried to mug. His brother was never convicted of any crime; neither was the cop. If we're all just failures, how come they have to keep killing us? See Robert Sam Anson's thoroughly unsatisfactory account, *Best Intentions: The Education and Killing of Edmund Perry*, New York: Random House, 1988. The quotation is from George E. Kent, "Richard Wright: Blackness and the Adventure of Western Culture," in *Blackness and the Adventure of Western Culture*, Chicago: Third World Press, 1972.

36   Michelle Cliff, *Voice Literary Supplement*, May 1990.

37   See Hazel Carby, "It Jus Be's Dat Way Sometime: The Sexual Politics of Women's Blues," *Radical America* (20) (1987): 9–24; Barbara Smith, "Toward a Black Feminist Criticism," in *The New Feminist Criticism*,

repositories of AIDS (we encounter again content-production for an aggregated identity-construct) establishes in contemporary consciousness a historically specific, "objective" and scientific rationale for the US cultural encoding and recoding of *Black/female/sexual/ evil*. Politically and in common-sense consciousness, US AIDS is two pandemics: one affects white gay men whose economic and cultural experience of everyday life, truly precarious in some respects, enables them to believe and to act on the belief that there are measurable rewards for changing behavior. The second pandemic is in the poorest communities, urban and rural, which are saturated from without by drugs in order to extract wealth and create passivity and chaos. Black sisters tell AIDS workers that they don't have the "mindspace" for AIDS education; that AIDS is a top-down conspiracy transmitted *to* brothers *in* condoms; that when it comes to choosing among life preserving necessities (what defines poor) the new scourge does not yet command the privilege of fear in lives fearfully difficult to live. In 1988, 2 out of 3 first-time, full-time freshpersons in four-year academies (ages 17–19) agreed that mandatory AIDS testing is the best way to control the disease. While the same students *disagreed* that homosexual relations should be prohibited, 7 out of 10 *agreed* that employers should be allowed to require drug tests of employees.[38] As AIDS is recreated in the popular consciousness as a disease of the poor, the non-white, the drug user, the Black woman who trades sex for crack, the Academy, which has already and will continue to enroll such students, is discouraged from risking physical contamination of its population. Who can argue with the economy of health?[39]

---

ed. Elaine Showalter, New York: Pantheon, 1985, 168–185; Hortense Spillers, "Interstices: A Small Drama of Words," in *Pleasure and Danger: Exploring Female Sexuality*, ed. Carole S. Vance, Boston: Routledge & Kegan Paul, 1982, 73–100.

38 Alexander W. Astin, et al, *The American Freshman: National Norms for Fall 1988*, Los Angeles: The Higher Education Research Institute, Graduate School of Education, UCLA, 1988, 93.

39 María de Lourdes Argüelles, Pew Faculty Seminar, Pomona College, 1989; see also Vickie M. Mays and Susan D. Cochran, "Issues in the Perception

Academy presidents and senior faculty and staff determine shifts in admissions criteria; they make decisions to include and exclude (for example, Asian quotas today and Jewish quotas up through the 1950s) in sneaky and sometimes subtle ways. Enrollment forecasts present trustees and other donors with the bright surface of the politics of cohort formation which has, as we have seen, a deep and manipulable cultural and political-economic base.

We are engaged in a war of position. Decorative Beasts must understand that our work is at a critical conjuncture. We face formidable adversaries: the passive-revolutionary vanguards in their duplicities and multiplicities are well-versed in the discursive practices of displacement. Our work is very likely to be displaced to some multicultural space within the dominant discourse (for instance, one of the multitude of depoliticized "cultural studies" programs springing up around the US) closed off from insurgency and power by the mind shield of academic freedom. This mind shield—historical arrogance—permits anyone to mimic what the few in Ethnic Studies have been doing without respect, sufficient colleagues, and generally without tenure, and to lure students away with promises we are not in a position to make.

Black women's critical production remains a hot (marginal/exotic) commodity. Decorative Beasts must protect our proper work by at all times and by all means resisting and denouncing the re-objectification of the subaltern subject. Black women must stake out a series of strategic locations and from there deploy our theory, not only to journals, conventions, summer institutes, but also to the students who can carry on the work *if they* enroll in graduate and undergraduate programs in the 1990s. That means *we* must establish standards and make decisions about who enters the Academy, and promulgate our regulative expectations to the administrations flailing around

of AIDS Risk and Risk Reduction Activities by Black and Hispanic/Latina Women," *American Psychologist* 4:11 (1988): 949–957.

for the "guess who's coming to college" answer. (For example, at the University of California Berkeley in the fall of 1990 only half the new students were admitted according to "objective" criteria: SATs, class rank, etc.; *someone* decides both what those "objective criteria" are and how the other half gets in.)

We need to form a union, a collective, an autonomous entity to move forward on admissions as well as other missions. For example, Joyce A. Joyce and Wahneema Lubiano noted in different fora at the 1989 Modern Language Association (MLA) meetings how thoroughly the Academy disregards Black publishing production, both as weight in the tenure-scale and as sites for research in areas of critique new to non-Black scholars.[40]

Decorative Beasts are fighting for power in the Academy in crisis. The stakes are the control of epistemology: *Who teaches? What is taught? Who learns?* Epistemology as historicized and localized unit of analysis is these three elements, which are always unequal and shifting in dominance. The three questions ask: "How will the US intellectual stratum of the next generation be formed?" That intellectual stratum, organic or traditional, will—as it does now—exert disproportionate control over the congeries of discursive practices in which ideologies are articulated and lives lived. We need theories that work: We need guides to action. We need to take apart—to *dis*articulate—theory from decorative imitation if we are to rearticulate its epistemological power in political praxis.

What, after all, is the difference between imitation and disarticulation? What makes Decorative Beasts as subjects radically different from what we are as objects? One approach to these questions is to consider the practical deployment of Black women's theoretical praxis. Remember, the exchange value of theory is its use value.

---

40   Joyce A. Joyce, "The Shifting Status of Blacks in the Profession," Panel, annual meetings of the Modern Language Association, Washington DC, December 28, 1989; Lubiano, comments cited above.

Los Angeles–based international activist Margaret Prescod coorganized Black Coalition Fighting Back Southside Serial Slayings to publicize and combat the Los Angeles Police Department's complicity in covering up torture/murders of sex industry workers. Our students need to understand that Prescod's work and Hortense Spillers's are part of the same project: the women in Los Angeles are fatally "marked."[41] Wilmette Brown, co-founder (with Prescod) of International Black Women for Wages for Housework, writes: "Fundamentally ... it's that you follow your own activity to its own conclusions and connections."[42] In other words, finding out the difference between imitation and disarticulation starts *by attending "with all the pessimism of the intellect"*—in other words *by dogging*—the conditions, the contradictions, the *"discipline* of the conjuncture."[43] That is, Decorative Beasts must work out both the semiotics and histrionics of critical performance. Semiotics/histrionics. Theory/ practice. Part of the ongoing project is to identify the discursive powers in our diasporic condition, enacting the metamorphosis from symbolic contingencies to a new and unified collective social subject. The rest of the project is to open the praxis, to recruit students by appealing to their interests, by interpellating them in subjectivities other than those ordinarily hailed by the Academy in its invitations to Black women (wannabe a lawyer, a doctor, a capitalist?). Black critical theory, for example, has an ineluctably material basis. Insofar as we try to "explain, figure out, make sense of, or give meaning to the social and political world,"[44]

---

41 Spillers writes "Let's face it. I am a marked woman, but not everybody knows my name." "Mama's Baby, Papa's Maybe: An American Grammar Book," *Diacritics* 17.2 (1987), 65.

42 Wilmette Brown, *Black Women and the Peace Movement*, London: Falling Wall, 1984, 83.

43 Gramsci quoted in Stuart Hall, "Gramsci and Us," *Hard Road*, 162: a demystifying piece of work. See also Gramsci, *Prison Notebooks*, 114.

44 James Donald and Stuart Hall, *Politics and Ideology*, ix.

inclusions of Black women in the texts and contexts of production show we are always already standing in the middle of everyday life. If the political purpose of the theoretical enterprise is to articulate transformative power to reading and to read transformation powerfully, what subjects in the broadest sense—what knowledges and people-in-the-know—do we seek to "Yo" to counter-hegemonic discourses? "Leadership," Ramon Gutierrez clarified, "is a product of followership."[45] In other words, there is no difference between the production and the distribution of knowledge.

---

45 Ramon Gutierrez, Ena Thompson Lecture Series Faculty Seminar, Pomona College, April 1989.

3

Public Enemies and Private Intellectuals: Apartheid USA

But the Harlem intellectuals were so overwhelmed at being "discovered" and courted that they allowed a bona fide cultural movement which issued from the social system as naturally as a gushing spring, to degenerate into a pampered and paternalized vogue.

—Harold Cruse, *The Crisis of the Negro Intellectual*

The master's tools will never dismantle the master's house.

—Audre Lorde, *Sister Outsider*

I'm not of the Frankfurt School. One must live a life of relative privilege these days to be so dour about domination, so suspicious of resistance, so enchained by commodification, so helpless before the ideological state apparatuses to conclude there's no conceivable end to late capitalism's daily sacrifice of human life to the singular freedom of the market. Yet, in the context of an avalanche of words on contemporary "bona fide cultural movement"—especially movement by the young, formerly enslaved, or colonized; urban, everyday, popular—Cruse's assessment of the political failure of the Harlem Renaissance rings true.

We are in an epoch of social revolution—capitalism hasn't won, but not for lack of trying. It is both possible and necessary to pass the word that these times too might pass, but not inevitably toward a more secure fascism. At the same time, (passive) counterrevolutionary forces are pampering into being an intellectual comprador class comprised of some of the very people who have been engaged in the post-1945 freedom work to decolonize our minds.

The late poet-warrior, Audre Lorde, warned that the master's tools will never dismantle the master's house. As with any theoretical premise, Lorde's caveat is useful only if the elements whose paring away enables its elegance and urgency are added back, so that the general truth of the abstraction has concrete meaning for day-to-day life. The issue is not whether the master uses, or endorses the use of, some tool or another. Rather, who controls the conditions and the ends to which any tools are wielded? Control is not easy. In the culture of opposition, control, tentative at best, results from risky forays rather than documentable ownership through capital accumulation. Lorde proposes a decisive seizure whose strategy works toward multiple ends. First, Lorde's focus on tools requires us to concentrate on fundamental orderings in political economy. If the master loses control of the means of production, he is no longer the master. Thus, relations of production are transformed in the process. Second, her focus on the master's house guides our attention toward institutions and luxury. The house must be dismantled so that we can recycle the materials to institutions of our own design, usable by all to produce new and liberating work. Thus, the luxurious is transformed into the productive. Without both parts of the strategy at work, nothing much is different at the end of the day.

In the past decade or so, an astonishing number of people housed in and about the relatively secure luxury of institutions of higher education have picked up the work a few politically committed souls began in the earlier postwar decades. The purpose of the work—called variously cultural studies, Black studies, and so on—had been to try to understand the means through which ordinary people do or might organize, promote ideas, and bargain in the political arena. Such understanding might be achieved through figuring out how people make sense in and of their lives. Activist/scholars pursued their inquiries by studying cultures and "subcultures" as politically vital forces in the anatomy of society. Today's plethora of intellectuals who think about marginal, or oppositional, or simply non-Arnoldian, cultural practice are often in, or influenced by, literary theory. Sensibly enough, the realm of literary criticism "from the margins," as bell hooks might say, has focused on a formidable assemblage of neglected letters—both art and polemic—snatched from the dustbins of history by the diligent graduate-student laborers of such Black studies stars as Henry Louis Gates Jr. These texts occasion many reflections: what was said, in forays into the printed page during the last and current centuries, that will tell us what happened and what might happen? How is literary production a political act? What theoretical work might be hidden in a story, a character type, a way of telling? How can the interpretive skills refined through these processes of thought be turned toward understanding cultural expressions that are not bound to the page, such as the various arenas of popular culture—music, dance, movies, costume, language? What are the processes of creating audiences? And, most of all, why bother? Intellectuals studying these questions lay consistent claim to politics as both cause and effect of their work, harking back to the practitioners (themselves mostly still at work) who shook higher education to free up some intellectual and material resources on behalf of the always already excluded.

The need for oppositional work is unquestioned. But what is oppositional work? As the old folks say, if you're going to talk that talk you've got to walk that walk. Oppositional work is talk-plus-walk: it is organization and promotion of ideas and bargaining in the political arena. Oppositional studies programs originated in and through struggle, and their contemporary quality is various—dependent in large measure on the strict or lax attention paid to the questions of dialectics and contradictions with which Audre Lorde demands that intellectuals engage. Of course, the originary communities that occasioned oppositional studies haven't remained suspended outside of history awaiting the return of the native intellectuals. Quite the contrary. The tumultuous upheavals of systemic crisis throughout the overdeveloped world have reached into every corner of society, transforming both the streets and the campuses. When, as is the case in the United States, the fastest growing group of unemployed consists of white, male, white-collar workers, no institution is unaffected: laws, the church, the military, elected and appointed officials, education—all bow beneath the yoke of austerity, as though such penance, rather than control of profits, will banish generally felt want.

The daily management of capitalism's reorganization demands the doctrine of austerity, which is carried out according to time-honored dogmas of the United States: blame the poor, reward the rich, and talk fast to the middle (the economically broad and racially and culturally confusing category to which most people in the United States assign themselves). On the campuses, the "poor" are not necessarily those completely devoid of resources, but they are the johnnies-come-lately, the Black studies and other oppositional studies units which are, like Rodney King, at risk—as stand-ins for the great masses of superfluous human beings whom the state must control, or discard, to organize reliably new relations of production in the New World Order. In response to this threat, a move toward connection outside the campus makes sense. After all, who but those who, in the first instance, let us scale the walls from their shoulders will stand ready to catch us should we be knocked back out? (But here begin strange meanderings, which more often than not lead to culs-de-sac in the shadow of the master's house, which is still standing!)

There are four broad, overlapping tendencies in contemporary oppositional studies which weave through the literary theory world, but not there alone: individualistic careerism, romantic particularism, luxury production (insider trading), and organic praxis. Briefly, these trends are as follows. The first, individualistic careerism, is the competition to know the most about some aspect of the politically and oppositionally "new"—the new text, performance, tune, theory. This competition, driven as it is by the market anarchy of late capitalism, is characterized by a lack of connections. As Margaret Prescod puts it, careerism promotes one particular aspect of social change without integrating that struggle into the larger struggle for social change. In academic work, "careerism" assigns primary importance to the fact—and survival—of oppositional studies within the intellectual and social structure of the university, the master's house. In this regard, "individualistic" refers both to the practitioners of such cloistered studies and to the studies themselves. Their disarticulation from the larger struggle for social change enables the system to reproduce itself through a multiculturalized professional managerial class. The class is disinclined to or incapable of bringing about realignment of what Stuart Hall has called "the fatal coupling of power and difference."

Romantic particularism purports to reclaim an oppositional epistemology and aesthetic that had been obscured by the historical forces of Europe let loose in the world. In fact, it fails to escape the universalism elaborated by the modern university insofar as it reproduces, in form and function, idealist philosophical assumptions about who and what works, for whom and to what end. Romantic particularism has great appeal outside the university through its identification of an "authenticity" in cultural practice that needs recognition, though hardly revision. Henry Louis Gates Jr.'s 1990 Florida courtroom defense of the ultra-machismo rap group 2 Live Crew as "literary geniuses" was a strategically wily move on his part.[1] After all, he helped save some Black men from punishment for "crimes" few white

---

1   2 Live Crew's album, *As Nasty as They Wanna Be*, was banned by a federal judge, and members of the crew were arrested after a live performance and tried for obscenity.

men are charged with committing. However, the result of his approach is to maintain the struggle against racism at a level of abstraction (that is, unacknowledged maleness) that refuses to engage the complexities of power within the ranks of the disfranchised. He reads nauseating lyrics as unassailably valid African American cultural practice ("It's a Black thing; you wouldn't understand"), in spite of many, many Black women's daily struggles to get out from under the crap of that rap.

The third, and most distressing, category is that of luxury production—what Canadian intellectual Melissa Freedman calls insider trading for the advantaged elites of theory high or low. There is certain usefulness in figuring out just how an expressive cultural form does its work. However, in the rush to understand, a theoretical eclecticism, mingled with an institutionally encouraged tendency to substitute adequate abstraction for adequate theory, produces work which readers become servants of rather than work which serves readers. The point is not that reading must always seem transparent and require neither dictionary nor sustained contemplation. Nor is it that complexity is itself bad, nonproductive, or coopted by definition. Nothing could be further from the truth. But what has happened is that an inward-looking practice is effectively closed off, a dead end of all the labors that produced it —perhaps like a diamond forever, but so what, and at what human costs? In universities over the past generation or so, theory has assumed pride of place in most of the traditional academic disciplines—especially in the humanities—and, by extension, in the oppositional studies corners as well. In fact, it is quite possible that the theoretical urgency running through oppositional studies has been sluiced back to the mainstream, refreshing stagnant waters there. In any event, in the United States, "theory," its own discipline and end, pays. Somewhere along the way, intellectuals are so overwhelmed by discovering the production of knowledge that they have forgotten about "just knowing something," as Barbara Harlow puts it.

And yet, in all this, there is also organic praxis, the recognition that the street has always run into the campus, and the majority of campus employees are not paid to think but rather to clean, to type, to file, to shelve, to guard. What is the relation among us all? In different ways, and concentrating on various kinds of cultural production, writers like bell hooks, Edward Said, Barbara Harlow, Hazel Carby, Rosaura Sánchez, and Richard Yarborough have come up through the discipline of literary study and turned their political and hermeneutic attention to making connections that are profound, not facile, meticulous, not contrived. Houston Baker Jr. makes a passionate but curiously abstract plea for such connection in his new book, *Black Studies, Rap and the Academy*.[2] While he points toward many of the issues addressed in this essay, especially the critique of Gates's Florida testimony and questions of careerism, he does not, alas, couple his rhetorical urgency with equally urgent analysis of the rapidly changing material conditions of everyday life. He shows us the police and the military but not the war, employs the liberally sanctioned metaphor of immigration to describe a historical storming of the university's gates, and invokes some places called "positive sites of rap" as the (again, metaphorical) spaces where something ideal— "redemption"—might take place.

The careerist, particularist, and luxe modes waste precious intellectual resources and displace energy from where it is most needed. As such, they are to the current era what many institutional "reforms" such as assistant deans for race/gender relations, daycare centers, and ethnic and women's studies programs were to colleges and universities in the late 1960s and early 1970s: cheap insurance against more expensively redressed claims that the urban university in the United States has, historically and systematically, underdeveloped the neighborhoods where the working poor live in the shadow of the

---

2 Houston A. Baker Jr., *Black Studies, Rap and the Academy*, Chicago: University of Chicago Press, 1993.

ever-growing master's house. In the exploitation of the culture of opposition, these modes tend to incorporate into the private sphere of intellectual property (books, conferences, centers) what Mike Davis insists should be the public production of public use values. Thus, it follows that these modes suffer, as they must, from theoretical sloppiness and political dishonesty at the heart of the enterprise. Political dishonesty, because to call one's work oppositional is not enough. Theoretical sloppiness, because to speak in certain categories—such as "literary geniuses" (Gates) or "cultural capital" (Baker)—is to couple one's work with that of primary definers such as 1992 Nobel Laureate economist Gary Becker. These definers use such categories to explain away historically specific differentiation (the achievements of racism, machismo, and exploitation) through an appeal to cultural difference alleged to inhere in the oppressed more naturally and less alienably than, say, freedom.

Why all this anger? Well, there is a war on.

It makes sense to pause a moment to consider the conditions under which the culture of opposition both produces and works the local crisis. Los Angeles is a formerly industrial city, exemplary for how the contradictions of the New World Order are so clearly manifest, so unveiled since the Rebellion of 1992. As must be apparent to all who followed the Rodney King case, Los Angeles streets are effectively closed, though they seem open to the inexperienced eye. Any apparent exceptions are bold reinforcements of the rule. For example, every Sunday afternoon the boardwalk at Venice Beach is an intensively policed street scene where crowds of young flaneurs, clad in the latest styles, stroll slowly and boisterously. As often as not they are pushing along snazzy little kids in prams that cost less than the high-top leather sneakers on their stubby little feet. Cheap food. Shiny trinkets. Body builders. Sidewalk artists. Con artists. Escape artists. Singers. A child born nearly armless and legless dances and waves his stumps for dollars while his posse snaps and nods with the beat. The police allow the Sunday Venice Beach exhibitionists to hang out but constantly remind them—through high-profile presence, busts, arrests "under suspicion of," random identification checks, and general harassment—that license to pass can be revoked at any time. The officers, eyeless in mirrored shades, scan waves and waves of black, brown, yellow, red, and white young people. The westerly rays of the sun setting across the vast Pacific burnish the crowd whose skin color spectrum eloquently summarizes 500 years of historical capitalism: the combined effects of predatory territoriality and the international labor market, forever commingled through terror and love.

In some extreme cases, physical barriers control the movement of Angelenos. There are sturdy metal gates sunk in concrete that lock in (and out) the residents of Central American neighborhoods as well as African American and Chicano (Mexican American) public housing projects. The generally high degree of neighborhood segregation furthers easy control of the streets. Capital-intensive police forces (mainly the notorious Los Angeles Police Department, the less well-known but even more murderous Los Angeles County Sheriffs, and, of course, the Immigration and Naturalization Service officers—*La Migra*) can "see" who belongs where and who is out of place. The US internal wars nominally waged against gangs, drugs, crime, and dependency gain general endorsement from the citizenry. Today's supporters of more police or longer prison sentences are tomorrow's targets of state terror, beatings, imprisonment, sterilization, murder.

The fifty-year Reich of California's economic miracle is fast going the way of all of historical capitalism's economic miracles, and the resulting unemployment toward the top has a multiplier effect that pushes people out of all job levels—even minimum-wage positions in the service industry. Blue-collar African Americans, Chicanos, and Anglos have been out of work the longest as the deindustrialization of southern California steamrolls into its second decade, with permanent layoffs of workers by such transnationals as General Motors Corporation (which is about to open a US$700 million plant in Germany), Firestone Rubber and Tire, along with single-mission military-industrialists such as General Dynamics and Hughes Aircraft (both partly or wholly owned divisions of General Motors Corporation). At the same time that the economy is bust, the population is growing younger and poorer; Los Angeles County no longer has a racial/ethnic majority, and the younger the resident, the browner her skin.

The crisis is of enormous proportions, and its outcome is thoroughly unpredictable save for two things. First, the social formation cannot reproduce itself according to existing relations. And second, the state is equipped, with both weaponry and consent, brutally to police the crisis at every step of the way. Herein lies the groundwork for a more secure fascism, through American apartheid's geographical enclavism and separate-but-unequal institutions—most notably education and the legal system. In the 1970s, Stuart Hall and colleagues wrote extensively on the methods and outcomes of this sort of policing in the United Kingdom. Their book, *Policing the Crisis*, is helpful for understanding many of the dimensions of the US crisis-management program, even given the substantial differences and specificities of conditions in the United States.[3] An appeal to an originary nativism (not aboriginal, but rather founding—as in the Founding Fathers) has the warfare state armed and active "against all enemies foreign and domestic" (as the US loyalty oath reads). Such are the master's tools.

On the streets, the crisis has produced a complicated wealth of analysis and resistance, for everywhere racism and machismo and exploitation are determined economically, they are also defined culturally. The work ranges across the endlessly discussed rap music, Mothers ROC (Mothers Reclaiming Our

---

3 Stuart Hall, Chas Critcher, Tony Jefferson, John Clarke, and Brian Roberts, *Policing the Crisis: Mugging, the State, and Law and Order*, London: Red Globe Press, 1978.

Children), to the Coalition Against Police Abuse, to the cherished truce between the two major post-1965 African American "gangs" (the Crips and the Bloods), to Justice for Janitors, and so forth. From the grassroots to the most expensively accessed radio/TV airwaves alike, word is circulating about these bad times and what to do about them. The notorious rap group, Public Enemy, describes common-sense understanding of the situation particularly well in the title to their best-selling 1990 album (bought by white suburban youth no less than Black urban kids), *Fear of a Black Planet.*

Fear of a Black Planet.

When contradictions come to the surface in an eruption of confusing meanings and possibilities, people must struggle to resolve (or to displace) the truths produced by the crisis. Mothers ROC is a grassroots organization engaged in such struggle. The urgency is the unveiling of the actual meanings and dimensions of the New World Order, as understood and lived here in the United States where the working poor (especially the youth) are increasingly the wageless poor. How do fundamental social units (households, families, friends, neighborhoods) reconcile the fear of actual drug dealers encountering the children, on the one hand, with the state's new laws that enable local law enforcement to criminalize those same children, on the other? The process of criminalization, of creating public enemies, is sneaky and, as it seems to the less powerful, inexorable. For example, in some areas of greater Los Angeles, it is now [1993] illegal for young people who fit the "gang profile" (age, gender, race, style of clothing) to walk the streets in possession of a flashlight. As Geri Silva of the Equal Rights Congress said, "If that isn't fascism, then I don't know what is."

Mothers ROC consists of women and men, young and old, fighting for the kids who have been snatched into the system, made public enemies under a series of laws enacted since the late 1970s. Those laws have produced today's chilling statistics: one in four African American men between the ages

88

of fifteen and twenty-nine is in prison, on parole, or under indictment; sixty percent of prisoners are non-white; there are more Native American men on California's Death Row than in California's graduate schools; the United States imprisons a greater percentage of its population than any other industrialized state; most jurisdictions in the United States have doubled their prison capacities since the Reagan regime began in 1981.

For Mothers ROC, knowledge is the path to power. The organization works along the lines of liberation theology's organic praxis: to see, to judge, to act. In the world-system division of labor, women do two-thirds of the work for five percent of the income. Women own one percent of the world's assets; their unpaid-for work becomes someone's private property. Since we know the poorest of the planet's five billion inhabitants are people of color, these data quantify racism, machismo, and exploitation on a global scale. Like the mothers' movements in El Salvador, Argentina, Palestine, and elsewhere, Mothers ROC has virtually no material resources; its principal work is to witness and to tell. In the courtrooms where Mothers ROC recruits members from the visitors' gallery, kids are railroaded into plea bargaining (admitting guilt for a shorter sentence) over crimes they did not commit. The state says: "Plead guilty and we'll give you nineteen years; go to an expensive trial and we'll ask the court to sentence you to ninety-nine years with no possibility for parole." ROC also passes out flyers near jails where mothers, lovers, and friends perform the unpaid ("women's") work of holding the accused's life together from the outside.

The Mothers ROC women are lonely, they are tired, they need help. College students can help, if they have some complex idea of what's up. Insofar as the students who wander into oppositional studies classrooms don't walk out knowing something, the forces of displacement will have won out over the forces of change. Everywhere I turn in Los Angeles today, Salvadorean garment workers, African American and Chicana Mothers

ROC, ex-gangsters trying to maintain the truce against the unwavering interests of the police for it to fail, all turn to students for help. How have we been teaching the people among us entrusted with the responsibility to do "intellectual work"? How can they do what is required of them in the twenty-first century? Are we ready?

The formation of private intellectuals is taking place as apartheid, the political logic of late capitalism, arranges our future through control of our space. Apartheid privatizes and individualizes what should be collective and public, and it explains away collective differences through group individualism (Black people don't work hard; Anglos are thrifty). A major success of the passive revolution to date is its deflection of public work to the private sphere, where it then can be exploited for personal gain. Universities, both those supported by tax monies and those supported by private donations, are all in fact publicly subsidized through the combination of state-funded research and development grants and contracts, student financial assistance, and the tax exemption of charitable gifts. Yet access to the resources within their walls is limited—from jobs to the gym to the library to the thinkers.

Both the political economy and the culture of the campus serve to legitimate the movement of what should be public to exclusive and increasingly private spheres. Such movement runs in direct opposition to oppositional culture, which is, originally and finally, public. The privatization of intellectual work reveals the class interests of the professional intellectual elites, no matter the beleaguered oppositional programs or positions in programs they inhabit. The reduction of public spaces and the disappearance of parks, public housing, public hospitals, public schools, and the right to pass freely all point toward their racially differentiated opposite: the privatization of everything. Even prisons are becoming privately managed.

Through production of public enemies, the state safeguards the unequal distribution of resources and reinforces the logic of scarcity by deflecting attention from the real thieves and criminals—the transnationals that are making off with profits which even the state can no longer lay significant partial claim to through tax tribute. Further, the transnationals' way is made easier through the relentless establishment of regional and global capitalist governments: Maastricht, NAFTA, GATT, the IMF. These governments supersede the state's economic "self-determination" while maintaining its role of domination and regulation with respect to the relations of production. Private intellectuals are both cheap insurance for these arrangements and "pampered and paternalized," a costly drain on the communities of resistance who require their labors. Clearly, the systemic enhancements of late capitalism require revelation, analysis, and enormous public oppositional action. The privatization of intellectual work undermines the project at every tum. "The master's tools will never dismantle the master's house." Who will?

4

Scholar-Activists in the Mix

Scholar-Activists and the Production of Geography

When I set out in 1993 to earn a PhD, a bookseller acquaintance praised my choice of field, saying "Geography is the last materialist discipline." Colleagues across the political spectrum generally bristle at his assertion, while I have cherished it as one of two mantras I use when the going gets tough. The second, dating from the same week in 1993, is an exchange I had with a former student who was completely perplexed by my decision. When she asked why an activist lecturer on race, culture, and power would go study "Where is Nebraska?" I replied that actually I was going to study "*Why* is Nebraska?" This explanation was such a hit among geographers that it turned up, without attribution, in the *Lingua Franca* guide to graduate school.

Motivated to learn how to interpret the world *in order to* change it,[1] I found in Geography ways to contemplate and document the vibrant dialectics of objective and subjective conditions that, if properly paid attention to, help reveal both opportunities for and impediments to human liberation. Space always matters, and what we make of it in thought and practice determines, and is determined by, how we mix our creativity with the external world to change it and ourselves in

---

1 See Karl Marx, "Theses on Feuerbach," in Karl Marx and Friedrich Engels, *Selected Works*, vol. 1, Moscow: Progress Publishers, 1969 [1845], 15.

the process.[2] In other words, one need not be a nationalist, nor imagine self-determination to be fixed in modern definitions of states and sovereignty, to conclude that, at the end of the day, freedom is a place.

How do we find the place of freedom? More precisely, how do we make such a place over and over again? What are its limits, and why do they matter? What, in short, is the mix? In this brief essay I wish to outline how the lively hyphen that articulates "scholar" and "activist" may be understood, and enacted, as a singular identity. These pages are not prescriptive but rather suggestive. If they serve to raise Geography's profile in public debate, that will be great, because my interest is in proliferating, rather than concentrating, ways of thinking. The debates that most concern me center on how organizations and institutions craft policies that result in building social movement (through nonreformist reforms) rather than in areal redistribution of harms and benefits.

The projects from which I have derived these lessons all involve novel practices of place-making that revise understandings and produce new senses of purpose. For example, in the effort to dismantle the prison-industrial complex, one trajectory frames prisons as new forms of environmental racism which are equally, if differently, destructive of the places prisoners come from and the places where prisons are built.[3] Such destruction shortens lives, and *all* people caught in prison's gravitational field are vulnerable to its ambient material and cultural toxicities. Through forging links across enormous social and geometric distances, this activism extends the potential array of campaigns that abandoned rural and urban communities may design in their demand for both living

---

2   See Karl Marx, *Capital*, vol. 1, New York: Penguin, 1976 [1867], 283.

3   "The Other California" (with Craig Gilmore), in this volume, 242–258.

and social wages. What rises to the surface is how people who are skeptical of "the government" begin to engage in what I call "grassroots planning"—a future orientation driven by the present certainty of shortened lives.

Moving to another example, which approaches the problem of "planning" for those specifically excluded by state practices, organizations in urban and rural California are beginning to examine, through community design workshops, forums, and other means, the continuum (rather than the *difference*) between undocumented workers and documented felons. Both groups are equally unauthorized to make a living and participate fully in the institutions of everyday life.[4] All these projects have the potential for fostering previously unimagined or provisionally forgotten alignments,[5] and they are connected by the likelihood that the folks who are becoming activists or reviving activism will die prematurely of preventable causes.[6]

Engaged scholarship and accountable activism share the central goal of constituting audiences both within and as an effect of work based in observation, discovery, analysis, and presentation. Persuasion is crucial at every step. Neither engagement nor accountability has meaning, in the first instance, without potentially expanded acknowledgment that a project has the capacity to flourish in the mix. As a result, and to get results, scholar-activism always begins with the politics of recognition. Whether a project is compensatory, interventionist, or oppositional, the primary organizing necessary to take it from concept to accomplishment (and tool) is constrained by recognition. Recognition, in turn, is the practice of identification,

---

4　See Victor Hugo, *Les Misérables,* New York: New American Library, 1987 [1862].

5　See Peter Linebaugh and Marcus Rediker, *The Many-Headed Hydra.*

6　See Michael Greenberg and Dona Schneider, "Violence in American Cities: Young Black Males Is the Answer, but What Was the Question?" *Social Science and Medicine* 39 (1994) 179–187; "Race and Globalization," in this volume, 107–131.

fluidly laden with the differences and continuities of characteristics, interests, and purpose through which we contingently produce our individual and collective selves.[7] Such cultural (or ideological) work connects with, reflects, and shapes the material (or political-economic) relations enlivening a locality as a place that necessarily links and represents other places at a variety of time-space resolutions.[8]

Consistently, then, the scholar-activist works in the context of ineluctable dynamics that force her—deliberately yet *inconsistently*—at times to confirm and at times to confront barriers, boundaries, and scales.[9] This is treacherous territory for all of us who wish to rewrite the world. There is plenty of bad research produced for all kinds of reasons (engaged or not) and lousy activism undertaken with the best intentions. In the following pages I will highlight what I have found to be key conceptual problems and perils, and end by suggesting some promising pathways that might be introduced into the mix.

Problems

Three kinds of problems dog the diligent scholar-activist in her desire to make the hyphen make a difference. Theoretical, ethical, and methodical challenges grip a project from its earliest moments of conception. Let us take them in turn.

---

7   Stuart Hall, "Cultural Identity and Diaspora," in Patrick Williams and Laura Chrisman, eds., *Colonial Discourse/Post-colonial Theory*, New York: Columbia University Press, 1994, 392–403; "'You Have Dislodged a Boulder,'" in this volume, 355–409.

8   Doreen Massey, *Space, Place and Gender*, Minneapolis: University of Minnesota Press, 1994.

9   Gilmore, "'You Have Dislodged a Boulder'"; Cindi Katz, "On the Grounds of Globalization: A Topography for Feminist Political Engagement," *Signs* 26 (2001): 1213–1234; Cindi Katz, "Vagabond Capitalism and the Necessity of Social Reproduction," *Antipode* 33 (2001) 709–728.

Theoretical

Theory is a guide to action; it explains how things work. What can and should be made of this? The way "good theory in theory"[10] stands up to the test of practice partly depends on how the researcher understands quantum physics' key insight that the observer and the observed are in the same critical field.[11] As may be said of all human activity that produces change, scholar-activism is caught in a social-spatial opening—sometimes a full-blown crisis, sometimes only a conjuncture or brief moment of instability—where historical becoming, or subjectivity,[12] meets up with historical constraint, or objectivity.[13] The external world is real, we are of it no matter what we decide to do, its mutability and our own are not without limit, and yet what we decide to do makes it, and us, different. Here, the theoretical does not collapse into an endless contemplation of the researcher and her feelings or insecurities or the compromises and complications inherent in her "location."[14] All of those things matter but, if the object of study is never a thing but rather relations, then the way theory moves to action always exceeds, while being linked to, the researcher's individual mediation. Theory is, in this sense, a method.

---

10 Toni Negri, "Marx on Cycle and Crisis," *Revolution Retrieved*, London: Red Notes, 1968, 47.

11 Karen Barad, "Getting Real: Technoscientific Practices and the Materialization of Reality," *Differences* 10 (1998): 87–128.

12 See Antonio Gramsci, *Selections from the Prison Notebooks*, New York: International Publishers, 1971.

13 Immanuel Wallerstein, *Unthinking Social Science: The Limits of Nineteenth-Century Paradigms*, Cambridge: Polity, 1991.

14 The superb example of a book that successfully negotiates pitfalls while embracing complexity is Leela Fernandes, *Producing Workers: The Politics of Gender, Class, and Culture in the Calcutta Jute Mills*, Philadelphia: University of Pennsylvania Press, 1997.

Ethical

As a result of heinous practices carried out at the expense of people's lives and well-being, researchers rightly hesitate before connecting "human" and "experiment," and US universities have developed complicated apparatuses to safeguard human subjects from inhumane protocols. In addition to the scandal of harmful inquiry, there is another aspect of ethics for scholar-activists to think through in considering the normative dimensions of projects intended for the mix. What scholar-activism does is forthrightly bring the experimentation of academic research into relation with the experimentation of (any) political action. In both, whether predictions turn out to be strong or weak, effects and outcomes matter and provide the basis for a new plan (or theory) to move forward.

Methodical

Theoretical and ethical considerations embed the third problem. If *methodology* is how research should proceed, the *methodical*, short of "ology's" comprehensive brief, more narrowly focuses on the plodding problem of questions. What kinds of questions should scholar-activists ask? Every question is an abstraction made of concentrated curiosity. Curiosity itself is not free-floating, but rather shaped by the very processes through which we make places, things, and selves. Thus, no matter how concrete, a question's necessary abstraction is also always a distortion—as cartographers, artists, and quantum physicists will readily attest. But all this means opportunity, rather than hopeless gloom, when questions have stretch, resonance, and resilience.

Stretch

Stretch enables a question to reach further than the immediate object, without bypassing its particularity—the difference, for example, between asking a community "Why do you want this development project?" and asking "What do you want?"

Resonance

This enables a question to support and model nonhierarchical collective action through producing a hum that, by inviting strong attention, elicits responses that do not necessarily adhere to already-existing architectures of sense-making. Ornette Coleman's harmolodics exemplify how such a process makes participant and audience a single, but neither static nor closed, category.[15]

Resilience

Resilience enables a question to be flexible rather than brittle, such that changing circumstances and surprising discoveries keep a project connected with its purpose rather than defeated by the unexpected. For example, the alleged relationship between contemporary prison expansion and slavery crumbles when the question poses slavery-as-uncompensated labor, because very few of the USA's 2.2 million prisoners work for anybody while locked in cages. But the relationship remains provocatively stable when the question foregrounds slavery as social death and asks how and to what end a category of dehumanized humans is made from peculiar combinations of dishonor, alienation, and violent domination.[16]

Clearly, all three problems are related, and the mode I have presented them in here is an attempt to make what is strange familiar, and what is familiar strange. We will return to that issue, in a brief discussion of categories, further on. First, let

---

15   Jennifer Rycenga, "The Composer as a Religious Person in the Context of Pluralism," PhD dissertation, Graduate Theological Union, 1992, 261–289.

16   Orlando Patterson, *Slavery and Social Death*, Cambridge, MA: Harvard University Press, 1982; *Golden Gulag*.

us pause and consider the substantial perils invoked by the discussion so far.

Perils

The perils inherent in searching for the liveliness in the scholar-activist's hyphen fall into two general tendencies: technocracy and disabling modesty.

Technocracy

Mixing social-science expertise into experimentation in the nonacademic world can reinforce the bad idea—promoted and affirmed in an innumerate culture where statistics are magic (with the hit-or-miss properties of all magical forces)—that better information from better data is what is needed to make the world better.[17] This way of thinking leads to the supremacy of intrastructural policy tweaking and perpetual displacement machines, and reduces the possibilities of complexly thoughtful action to, for example, expanding reliance on narrowly focused nongovernmental organizations[18] that are locked into endless rehearsals of injury and remedy.[19]

---

17 Robert W. Lake, "Structural Constraints and Pluralist Contradictions in Hazardous Waste Regulation," *Environment and Planning* A 24 (1992): 663–681.

18 Jennifer Wolch, *The Shadow State: Government and the Voluntary Sector in Transition*, New York: The Foundation Center, 1989; Andrea Smith, "Bible, Gender and Nationalism in American Indian and Christian Right Activism," PhD dissertation, University of California, Santa Cruz, 2002 (see also her *Native Americans and the Christian Right: The Gendered Politics of Unlikely Alliances*, Durham, NC: Duke University Press, 2008).

19 "Terror Austerity Race Gender Excess Theater," in this volume, 154–175; Gilmore, "'You Have Dislodged a Boulder,'" in this volume, 355–409; Wendy Brown, *States of Injury*, Princeton, NJ: Princeton University Press, 1994.

Disabling Modesty

If, on the one hand, nonacademic activists expect too little from the social scientist's toolkit, on the other hand, the reluctance of engaged scholars to raise challenges in the mix can make the hyphen inactive insofar as the *scholar* becomes irrelevant. Here of course is where the question of *questions* comes most vividly into view. In the constant rounds of discussion and reflection through which engaged work proceeds, the strictly attentive practice of making the familiar strange is as important in extramural circles where projects come into being as it is in the halls of academia where scholar-activists struggle to legitimate our trade.

Careful focus on the interworkings of the theoretical, ethical, and methodical as outlined above at least partially averts these tendencies. The next section touches on what such focus might consist of.

Promising Pathways

One of the key tensions in any kind of experiment (research, activism) centers on the collision between creativity on the one hand and already-existing frameworks and categories on the other. Categories are not only useful but also seem fundamentally to organize human thinking.[20] There is a difference, however, between the general fact (if we wish to accept its accuracy) that human thought *is* categorical and the practice that plagues much research and activism whereby particular social and spatial categories get reified by studying or acting on them as ahistorical durables.[21] So too with frameworks:

20   George Lakoff, *Moral Politics: How Liberals and Conservatives Think*, Chicago: University of Chicago Press, 1996.

21   For exemplary critiques, see the following: on paradigm shifts, see Thomas Kuhn, *The Structure of Scientific Revolutions*, Chicago: University

the challenge is not to be more logical, or more reasonable, but rather more persuasively based in the real material of the everyday, which means performing with the kind of attention Coleman's harmolodics requires to produce beautifully unexpected sound.

Two of the pathways are rather self-explanatory, and I will only name and briefly describe them, saving my scarce remaining space for the third.

Research Design and Analysis

By now it goes without saying that purpose leads, and the way a project's design and analysis proceed depends a lot on what work the outcome is supposed to do. If it is supposed to bring a different solution to a crisis than the remedies current power-blocs propose, then what will it take to mobilize communities to demand certain kinds of decisions? Where might they go wrong? Who will know, and how?

Scale and Rhetoric

Persuasion requires barriers to fall, at least momentarily. Scale suggests the actual and imaginative boundaries in which political geographies are made and undone.[22] A scholar-activist's project both defines and produces an opening on the ground, through which creative possibility can move.[23]

---

of Chicago Press, 1962; on race and categories, see Denise Ferreira da Silva, *Race and Nation in the Mapping of Modern Global Space*, Durham, NC: Duke University Press, 2005; on radical traditions, see Cedric J. Robinson, *Black Marxism and the Making of the Black Radical Tradition*, London: Zed Books, 1982; on theory, see Barbara Christian, "The Race for Theory," *Cultural Critique* 6 (1987): 51–63; and on topography, see Cindi Katz, "On the Grounds of Globalization: A Topography for Feminist Political Engagement," *Signs* 26 (2001): 1213–1234.

22 Neil Smith, "Contours of Spatialized Politics: Homeless Vehicles and the Production of Geographical Scale," *Social Text* 33 (1993): 55–81.

23 See, for example, Laura Pulido, "Rethinking Environmental

Credibility and Afetishism

In order for the scholar-activist to maintain the vitality of the hyphen, she has to toe a line that keeps moving. Her credibility is a function of many relationships—with other academics, with sources, with organizations. Every graduate student learns, at about the time of oral exams, to say, at long last, "I don't know." The important demystification of scholarship makes its work, in my view, stronger. This strength derives from constantly reflecting on the theoretical, the ethical, and the methodical while always acting. Yet the way through the twinned jaws of technocracy and disabling modesty is also marked, provisionally, by care around three troubling categories that can trip us along the route: object, truth, and authenticity. Objectivity cannot ever be passive,[24] truth cannot ever be comprehensive (which means pessimism of the intellect has to be balanced by optimism of the will),[25] and authenticity is a projection of shadow and light that shifts in time and place. Indeed, object, truth, and authenticity return us to an original argument of these remarks, which is how recognition permeates what we do, and how, and why. Recognition and redistribution are, then, two sides of the same coin.

Conclusion

Geography is an interdisciplinary discipline, and its relative irrelevance and "pariah"[26] status in the twentieth century ironically enhances its current promise because it is so wide open for good use. Certainly, the key words of the contemporary moment —globalization, racism, migration, war, new imperialism,

---

Racism: White Privilege and Urban Development in Southern California," *Annals of the Association of American Geographers* 90 (2000): 12–40.
24 Barad, "Getting Real."
25 Gramsci, *Selections from the Prison Notebooks.*
26 Wallerstein, *Unthinking Social Science.*

environmental degradation, fundamentalism, human rights —bespeak and connect (what, in sum, "articulation" is) all kinds of complexities.

In my view, interdisciplinarity and coalition-building are, like recognition and redistribution, two sides of a singular capacity. What the outcome could be, with scholar-activists in the mix, is the harmolodics of novel scales—which we might call a renovated "third world" or Bandung-consciousness—and subsequent differential alignments for the twenty-first century.

PART II

RACE AND SPACE

5

Race and Globalization

Theorizing Racism

While there is no legitimate biological basis for dividing the world into racial groupings, *race* is so fundamental a sociopolitical category that it is impossible to think about any aspect of globalization without focusing on the "fatal coupling of power and difference" signified by *racism*.[1] Racism is the state-sanctioned and/or extralegal production and exploitation of group-differentiated vulnerabilities to premature death, in distinct yet densely interconnected political geographies. Wherever in the world the reader encounters this essay, she will have some knowledge of racism's everyday and extraordinary violences; she will also be sensible of the widening circulation of cultural, aesthetic, and oppositional practices that subjectively mark the difference race makes. For the purposes of this essay, political economy is primary, because so much of globalization concerns material changes in ordinary people's capacities to make their way in the world. Therefore, by emphasizing racism, the next few pages examine how race is a modality through which political-economic globalization is lived.[2] A case study of the

---

1   Stuart Hall, "Old and New Identities, Old and New Ethnicities," in A. D. King (ed.), *Culture, Globalization and the World-System*, London: Macmillan, 1992. Some theorists prefer the plural—racisms—to underscore how there is not a single universal practice. I use the singular because racism, like other forms of violence, tends to produce the same outcomes regardless of technique: premature death and other life-limiting inequalities.

2   Stuart Hall, "Race, Articulation, and Societies Structured in Dominance," in *Sociological Theories: Race and Colonialism*, Paris: UNESCO, 1980, 305–340.

United States demonstrates how the conjuncture of globalization, legitimate-state limits, and white supremacy reorganizes and contains power through criminalization and imprisonment. These significant political practices, while devised and tested behind the sturdy curtain of racism, have broad national and global articulations—connections not impeded by racialized boundaries.[3] The purpose of focusing on the United States in this essay is not to study an "average" much less "original" racism, but rather to consider how fatal couplings of power and difference in one place develop and change. Then we will consider how they connect with, are amplified by, and materially affect, modalities of globalization elsewhere.

Why should race so vex the planet? Variations in humankind can be regarded in many ways, as contemporary genetics demonstrates.[4] However, the coupling of European colonialism's economic imperatives—expansion, exploitation, inequality—with European modernity's cultural emphasis on the visible[5] produced a powerful political belief that underlies racialization. The belief can be summed up this way: What counts as difference to the eye transparently embodies explanation for other kinds of differences, and exceptions to such embodied explanation reinforce rather than undermine dominant epistemologies of inequality.[6] Geographers from Linnaeus

---

3 Ruth Wilson Gilmore, "Globalization and US Prison Growth: From Military Keynesianism to Post-Keynesian Militarism," in this volume, 199–223; Ruth Wilson Gilmore, "From Military Keynesianism to Post-Keynesian Militarism: Finance Capital, Land, Labor, and Opposition in the Rising U.S. Prison State," PhD diss., Rutgers: The State University of New Jersey, 1998; Avery F. Gordon, "Globalism and the Prison Industrial Complex: An Interview with Angela Y. Davis," *Race and Class* 40.2/3 (1988): 145–157.

4 Richard C. Lewontin, Steven Rose, and Leon J. Kamin, *Not in Our Genes*, New York: Pantheon, 1984.

5 John Berger, *About Looking*, New York: Pantheon, 1980.

6 Paul Gilroy, *Against Race: Imagining Political Culture beyond the Color Line*, Cambridge, MA: Harvard University Press, 2000 (published in the UK as: *Between Camps: Nations, Cultures, and the Allure of Race*, London: Allen Lane, 2000).

forward have figured centrally in the production of race as an object to be known, in part because historically one of the discipline's motive forces has been to describe the visible world.[7]

To describe is also to produce. While any number of "first contact" texts show that in fact "all cultures are contact cultures,"[8] the powerful concept of a hierarchy of fixed differences displaced both elite and common knowledges of an alternatively globalized world.[9] For example, in the mid-fifteenth century, Azurara, court historian to Henry the Navigator (intellectual and financial author of Europe's African slave trade), noted how many in the first group of human cargo corralled at Lisbon strongly resembled then-contemporary Portuguese; indeed, the captives' sole shared feature was their grievously wept desire to go home.[10]

The triumph of hierarchy required coercive and persuasive forces to coalesce in the service of domination.[11] While European militarization constituted the key force that produced and maintained fatally organized couplings of power and difference, Catholic and Protestant missionaries explained and reinforced hierarchical human organization in terms of God-given ineffable processes and eternally guaranteed outcomes.[12] National academies—precursors to today's colleges and universities—

---

7   David N. Livingstone, *The Geographical Tradition*, Oxford: Blackwell, 1992.

8   Brackette F. Williams, "Contact Cultures," Panel, Annual Meeting of the Association of American Anthropologists, San Francisco, February 1992.

9   Jim Blaut, *The Colonizer's Model of the World: Geographical Diffusion and Eurocentric History*, New York: Guilford, 1994; Bernard Lewis, *The Muslim Discovery of Europe*, New York: W. W. Norton, 1982; V.Y. Mudimbe, *The Invention of Africa: Gnosis, Philosophy and the Order of Knowledge*, Bloomington: Indiana University Press, 1988.

10   Ronald Sanders, *Lost Tribes and Promised Lands*, New York: HarperPerrenial, 1978.

11   Edward Said, *Culture and Imperialism*, New York: Knopf, 1993.

12   David Stannard, *American Holocaust*, Oxford: Oxford University Press, 1992.

codified the social world in stringently insulated disciplines which further obscured the world's interconnections.[13]

In the long, murderous twentieth century, geographers used three main frameworks to study race: environmental determinism,[14] areal differentiation,[15] and social construction.[16] The variety of frameworks, and the fact of transition from one to another, demonstrates both how geography has been deeply implicated in the development of inequality and how critical disciplinary reconstruction at times seeks to identify and remedy the social effects of intellectual wrongs. In other words, frameworks—or "paradigms"[17]—are not structures that emerge with spontaneous accuracy in the context of knowledge production. Rather, they are politically and socially as well as empirically contingent and contested explanations for how things work that, once widely adopted, are difficult to disinherit.

Geographers who embraced environmental determinism sought to explain domination and subordination—power and difference in terms of groups' relative life-chances—by reference to the allegedly formative climates and landscapes of

---

13   Immanuel Wallerstein, *Unthinking Social Science*, Cambridge: Polity Press, 1989; Omer Bartov, *Murder in Our Midst: The Holocaust, Industrial Killing, and Representation*, Oxford: Oxford University Press, 1996.

14   See Don Mitchell, *Cultural Geography*, Oxford: Blackwell, 2000.

15   See David Harvey, *Explanation in Geography*, London: Edward Arnold, 1969.

16   For example, Peter Jackson and Jan Penrose (eds.), *Constructions of "Race," Place, and Nation*, Minneapolis: University of Minnesota Press, 1993; Audrey Kobayashi and Linda Peake, "Unnatural Discourse: 'Race' and Gender in Geography," *Gender, Place and Culture* 1.2 (1994): 225–43; Ruth Wilson Gilmore, "'You Have Dislodged a Boulder': Mothers and Prisoners in the Post Keynesian California Landscape," in this volume, 355–409; Ruth Wilson Gilmore, "Fatal Couplings of Power and Difference: Notes on Racism and Geography," in this volume, 132–153; Laura Y. Liu, "The Place of Geography in Studies of Geography and Race," *Social and Cultural Geography* 1.2 (2000): 169–82.

17   Thomas Kuhn, *The Structure of Scientific Revolutions*, Chicago: University of Chicago Press, 1996.

conqueror and conquered. The framework assumed, and therefore persistently demonstrated, that inequality is a product of natural rather than sociopolitical capacities; while culture might revise, it can never fully correct.[18] In this view inequality is irremediable, and thus should be exploited or erased. Examples of exploitation and erasure include US and South African apartheid, the Third Reich's "Final Solution," scorched-earth wars against Central American indigenous groupings, and other cleansing schemes.

As if in recognition of environmental determinism's horrifying consequences, the second framework, areal differentiation, seized the seemingly unbiased tools of the quantitative revolution to map distributions of difference across landscapes. The areal approach featured a mild curiosity toward the political-economic origins of inequalities, by suggesting causes for certain kinds of spatial mismatches or overlays. But in the end, taking race as a given, and development as the proper project for social change, the approach described territorialized objects (people and places as if they were things) rather than socio-spatial processes (how people and places came to be organized as they are).[19]

Inquiry into processes shapes a prevalent critical geographical framework. Neither voluntaristic nor idealistic, social construction refuses to naturalize race, even while recognizing its socio-spatial and ideological materiality. At its relational best, the social construction approach considers how racialization is based in the (until recently) under-analyzed production of both masculinity and whiteness (foundation and byproduct of global European hegemony), and how, therefore, race and space are mutually constituted.[20] How do spatially specific

18 For example, Ellsworth Huntington, *The Character of Races*, New York: Scribner's, 1924.

19 Gilmore, "Fatal Couplings of Power and Difference."

20 Vron Ware, *Beyond the Pale*, London: Verso, 1992; Laura Pulido, "Rethinking Environmental Racism," *Annals of the AAG* 90.1 (2000): 12–40. The articulations of race and space—as and through multiscalar

relations of power and difference—legal, political, cultural—
racialize bodies, groupings, activities, and places? Why are such
relations reproducible? For example, how is it that globally
dynamic interactions, organized according to liberal theories
of individual sovereignty, protection, grievance, and remedy
("human rights"), reconfigure but do not dismantle planetary
white male supremacy—as measured by multinational corporate ownership, effective control over finance capital, and
national military killing capacity?

While the three approaches span a wide political spectrum, from racist eugenics to anti-racist multiculturalism and
beyond, all, at least implicitly, share two assumptions: (1) societies are structured in dominance within and across scales; and
(2) race is in some way determinate of socio-spatial location.[21]
A way to understand the first point is to think about all the
components—or institutions—of a society at any scale, and
then ask about differences of power within and between them.
Are corporations stronger than labor unions? Do poor families rank equally with wealthy ones? Does education receive
the same kind of financial and political support, or command
the same attention to demands, as police or the military? Do
small food producers enjoy the same protections and opportunities as agribusinesses? Are industrial pollutants and other
toxic wastes spread evenly across the landscape? Do those who
produce toxins pay to contain them? Are people tried in courts
by juries of their peers? Having thought about these kinds of
institutional relationships, turn to the second assumption:
According to the society's official or common-sense classifica-
tions, how does race figure in and between the institutions?[22]

hierarchies of colonialism, slavery, and other relations of unfreedom—are
more evident in some contexts than in others. For some examples of how
race becomes both amplified and entrenched, see Center for Contemporary Cultural Studies, *The Empire Strikes Back*, London: Hutchinson,
1982; and Mitchell, *Cultural Geography*.

21   Hall, "Race, Articulation, and Societies Structured in Dominance."
22   Susan Christopherson provides an exemplary chart for doing this

While this thought-experiment is only a crude cross-section, the conclusions strongly suggest that—as all the twentieth-century frameworks agree—race, while slippery, is also structural.

But what structures does race make? Let us turn the question inside out and ask how fatal couplings of power and difference might be globally represented. Any map of modernity's fundamental features—growth, industrialization, articulation, urbanization, and inequality—as measured by wealth, will also map historical-geographical racisms. Such a map is the product of rounds and rounds of globalization, five centuries' movement of people, commodities, and people *as* commodities, along with ideologies and political forms, forever commingled by terror, syncretism, truce, and sometimes love. The cumulative effects of worldwide colonialism, transatlantic slavery, Western hemisphere genocide, and postcolonial imperialism—plus ongoing opposition to these effects—appear today, on any adequate planetary map of the twenty-first century, as power-difference topographies (for example, North, South) unified by the ineluctable fatalities attending asymmetrical wealth transfers.

So far, the discussion is pitched at a general level of abstraction. Our map of contemporary globalization circulation models (GCMs) is built on the historical geographies of past GCMs and signifies underlying struggles that indicate global warming of a peculiar kind. Indubitably anthropogenic, the racialized heat of political-economic antagonisms sheds light on the forms of organized abandonment that constitute the other side of globalism's uneven development coin:[23] structural adjustment, environmental degradation, privatization, genetic modification, land expropriation, forced sterilization, human

---

exercise on a global scale. Susan Christopherson, "Changing Women's Status in a Global Economy," in R. J. Johnston, Peter J. Taylor, and Michael J. Watts, eds., *Geographies of Global Change: Mapping the World*, 2nd ed., Malden, MA: Blackwell, 2002.

23   Neil Smith, *Uneven Development*.

organ theft, neocolonialism, involuntary and superexploited labor.

At the same time, the realities of racism are not the same everywhere and represent different practices at different geographical scales—which are connected (or "articulated") in many ways.[24] Within and across scales—respectively configuring nation-states, production regions, labor markets, communities, households, and bodies[25]—anti-racist activism encounters supple enactments and renewals of racialization through law, policy, and legal and illegal practices performed by state and non-state actors. The key point is this: at any scale, racism is not a lagging indicator, an anachronistic drag on an otherwise achievable social equality guaranteed by the impersonal freedom of expanding markets. History is not a long march from premodern racism to postmodern pluralism.[26] Rather, racism's changing same does triple duty: claims of *natural* or *cultural* incommensurabilities secure conditions for reproducing *economic* inequalities, which then validate theories of extra-economic hierarchical difference. In other words, racism functions as a limiting force that pushes disproportionate costs of participating in an increasingly monetized and profit-driven world onto those who, due to the frictions of *political* distance, cannot reach the variable levers of power that might relieve them of those costs.[27]

---

24   See, for example, Allan Pred, *Even in Sweden: Racisms, Racialized Spaces, and the Popular Geographical Imagination*, Berkeley: University of California Press, 2000.

25   Neil Smith, "Contours of a Spatialized Politics," *Social Text* 33 (1992): 54–81.

26   Peter Linebaugh and Marcus Rediker, *The Many-Headed Hydra: Sailors, Slaves, Commoners, and the Hidden History of the Revolutionary Atlantic*, Boston: Beacon Press, 2000.

27   I use "friction of distance" to theorize the metaphorical and material drag coefficients that differentially impede the movements of people, things, relationships, and ideas across geometric as well as social space. For a thoroughly *unmetaphorical* introduction of the term as the regional science's key revision of neoclassical economics, see Walter Isard, *Location and Space-Economy*, Cambridge, MA: MIT/Wiley, 1956.

What is the character of such friction? Why is the cost of mobility so prohibitive for some, especially in the current period that is colloquially characterized by increased (some say *hyper-*) mobilities? Race and racism are historical and specific, cumulative and territorially distinct—although distinct does not mean either isolated or unique. But while already-existing *material inequality* shapes political landscapes, the contested grounds are also *ideological*, because how we understand and make sense of the world and ourselves in it shapes how we do what we do.[28] In any society, those who dominate produce *normative* primary definitions of human worth through academic study, laws, and the applied activities of medical and other "experts," as well as through schooling, news, entertainment, and other means of mass education.[29] Those who are dominated produce counterdefinitions which, except in extraordinary moments of crisis, are structurally secondary to primary definitions. While such counterdefinitions might constitute "local" common sense, their representation in the wider ideological field is as sporadically amplified *responses* to regional norms—rather than as the fundamental terms of debate.[30] On all fronts, then, racism always means struggle. Whether radically revolutionary or minimally reformist, anti-racism is fought from many different kinds of positions, rather than between two teams faced off on a flat, featureless plain. Indeed, organized and unorganized anti-racist struggle is a feature of everyday life, and the development and reproduction of collective oppositional capacities bear opportunity costs which, in a peculiar limit to that fiscal metaphor, are

28 James Donald and Stuart Hall (eds.), *Politics and Ideology*, Milton Keynes: Open University Press, 1986.

29 Michael Omi and Howard Winant, *Racial Formation in the United States*, New York: Routledge, 1986; Bartov, *Murder in Our Midst*; Sarah E. Chinn, *Technology and the Logic of American Racism*, London: Continuum, 2000.

30 Stuart Hall et al., *Policing the Crisis: Mugging, the State, and Law and Order*.

hard to transfer *collectively* to other purposes within "already partitioned" political geographies.[31] Therefore, if, as many activist-theorists note, coercion is expensive,[32] anti-coercion cannot be cheap.

The deepening divide between the hyper-mobile and the friction-fixed produces something that would not surprise Albert Einstein: depending on their socio-spatial location in the global political economy, certain people are likely to experience "time-space compression"[33] as time-space *expansion*. We shall now turn to a case study of the United States to see how intensified criminalization and imprisonment constitute such an expansion and then conclude by considering some global effects of US anti-Black racism. The reader must bear in mind that US racism is not the model but rather the case and that US racism is not singularly anti-Black; the larger point, then, is to consider both how racism is produced through, and informs the territorial, legal, social, and philosophical organization of a place, and also how racism fatally articulates with other power-difference couplings such that its effects can be amplified beyond a place even if its structures remain particular and local.

Prison and Globalization

Ever since Richard M. Nixon's 1968 campaign for US president on a "law and order" platform, the United States has been home to a pulsing moral panic over crime. Between 1980 and 2000 the "law and order" putsch swelled prisons and jails with 1.68 million people, so that today [2002] 2,000,000

---

31 Smith, "Contours of a Spatialized Politics," 66.

32 For example, Frantz Fanon, *The Wretched of the Earth*, New York: Grove, 1961.

33 David Harvey, *The Condition of Postmodernity: An Enquiry into the Origins of Cultural Change*, Oxford: Blackwell, 1989.

women, men, boys, and girls live in cages.[34] The US rate of imprisonment is the highest in the world.[35] African Americans and Latinos comprise two-thirds of the prison population; 7 percent are women of all races. Almost half the prisoners had steady employment before they were arrested, while upwards of 80 percent were at some time represented by state-appointed lawyers for the indigent: in short, as a class, convicts are the working or workless poor. Why did "the law" enmesh so many people so quickly, but delay casting its dragnet for a decade after Nixon's successful bid for the presidency?

The 1938–68 World War II and Cold War military buildup produced a territorial redistribution of wealth from the urban industrialized northeast and north central to the agricultural and resource dominated south and coastal west.[36] While one urban-rural wealth gap was narrowed by state-funded military development, the equalization of wealth between regions masked deepening inequalities *within* regions as measured in both racial and urban-rural terms.[37]

Military Keynesianism characterized the US version of a *welfare* state: the enormous outlays and consequent multipliers for inventing, producing, and staffing *warfare* capacities underwrote modest social protections against calamity, alongside opportunities for advancement. Prior to the military buildup, the New Deal United States developed social welfare capacities, the design of which were objects of fierce interregional

---

34   The figure 2,000,000 does not include persons detained with or without charge by the US Immigration and Naturalization Service.

35   Jenni Gainsborough and Marc Mauer, *Diminishing Returns: Crime and Incarceration in the 1990s*, Washington, DC: The Sentencing Project, 2000.

36   Gregory Hooks, *Forging the Military-Industrial Complex*, Ithaca, NY: Cornell University Press, 1991; Ann Markusen, Peter Hall, Scott Campbell, and Sabina Deitrick, *The Rise of the Gunbelt*, New York: Oxford University Press, 1991.

37   Bruce J. Schulman, *From Cotton Belt to Sunbelt*, Durham, NC: Duke University Press, 1994; Gilmore, "From Military Keynesianism to Post-Keynesian Militarism."

struggle.[38] In concert with the successful political struggle by the Union's most rigorously codified *and* terrorist white supremacist regimes[39] to make the south and west principal sites for military agglomeration, the federal government also expanded to the national scale—via the structure of welfare programs—particular racial and gender inequalities.[40] As a result, under the New Deal white people fared better than people of color; women had to apply individually for what men received as entitlements; and urban industrial workers secured limited labor rights denied agricultural and household workers.[41]

The welfare-warfare state[42] (another way to think of "military Keynesianism") was first and foremost a safety net for the capital class as a whole[43] in all major areas: collective investment, labor division and control, comparative regional and sectoral advantage, national consumer market integration, and global reach. Up until 1967–68 the capital class paid high taxes for such extensive insurance.[44] But in the mid-1960s the rate of profit, which had climbed for nearly thirty years, began

38   John Egerton, *Speak Now against the Day: The Generation Before the Civil Rights Movement in the South*, New York: Knopf, 1995.

39   Ralph Ginzburg, *100 Years of Lynching*, Baltimore: Black Classic Press, 1988 [1962]; C. McWilliams, *Factories in the Field: The Story of Migratory Farm Labor in California*, Berkeley: University of California Press, 1999 [1939].

40   While there was plenty of racism and sexism outside the South and West, the structure of New Deal social welfare programs equalized across a differentiated landscape a series of perspectives about eligibility, need, and merit that became common sense; see, for example, Gwendolyn Mink, *The Wages of Motherhood: Inequality in the Welfare State, 1917–1942*, Ithaca, NY: Cornell University Press, 1995.

41   Linda Gordon, *Pitied but not Entitled: Single Mothers and the History of Welfare, 1890–1935*, New York: Free Press, 1994; Maralyn Edid, *Farm Labor Organizing: Trends & Prospects*, Ithaca, NY: Cornell/ILR, 1994.

42   James O'Connor, *The Fiscal Crisis of the State*, New York: St. Martin's Press, 1973.

43   Toni Negri, *Revolution Retrieved*, London: Red Notes, 1988.

44   Ruth Wilson Gilmore, *Golden Gulag: Prisons, Surplus, Crisis, and Opposition in Globalizing California*, Berkeley: University of California Press, 2007.

to drop off. Large corporations and banks, anxious about the flattening profit curve, began to agitate forcefully and successfully to reduce their taxes. Capital's tax revolts, fought out in federal and state legislatures and at the Federal Reserve Bank, provoked the decline of military Keynesianism.[45] The primary definers of the system's demise laid responsibility at the door of unruly people of color, rather than in the halls of capital— where overdevelopment of productive capacity weighed against future earnings[46] and therefore demanded a new relation with labor mediated by the state.

The 1968 law-and-order campaign was part of a successful "southern strategy" aimed at bringing white-supremacist Democrats from *anywhere* into the Republican fold.[47] Mid-1960s radical activism—both spontaneous and organized—had successfully produced widespread disorder throughout society. The ascendant right used the fact of disorder to persuade voters that the incumbents failed to govern. The claim accurately described objective conditions. But in order to exploit the evidence for political gain, the right had to interpret the turmoil as something they could contain, if elected, using already-existing, unexceptionable capacities: the power to defend the nation against enemies foreign and domestic. And so the *contemporary* US crime problem was born, in the context of solidifying the political incorporation of the militarized south and west into a broadening anti–New Deal conservatism. The disorder that became "crime" had particular urban and racial qualities, and the collective characteristics of activists—whose relative visibility as enemies inversely reflected their structural powerlessness—defined the face of the individual criminal. To deepen

---

45 Edwin Dickens, "The Federal Reserve's Low Interest-Rate Policy in 1970–1972: Determinants and Constraints," *Review of Radical Political Economics* 28.3 (1996): 115–125.

46 Robert Brenner, *Turbulence in the World Economy*, London and New York: Verso, 2001.

47 See, for example, Lisa McGirr, *Suburban Warriors*, Princeton, NJ: Princeton University Press, 2001.

its claims, the right assigned the welfare-warfare state's *social project* institutional responsibility for the anxiety and upheaval of the period.

The postwar liberation movement focused in part on extending eligibility to those who had been deliberately excluded from New Deal legislation. While some factions of the civil rights movement worked to bring about simple inclusion, radical African, Latino, Asian, and Native American groupings fought the many ways the state at all scales organized poor people's perpetual dispossession.[48] Radical white activists both aligned with people of color and launched autonomous attacks against symbols and strongholds of US capitalism and Euro-American racism and imperialism.

Indeed, growing opposition to the US war in Southeast Asia helped forge an international community of resistance. At the same time, activism against colonialism and apartheid on a world scale found in Black Power a compelling renewal of linkages between "First" and "Third World" Pan-African and other liberation struggles.[49] Meanwhile, students and workers built and defended barricades from Mexico City to Paris: no sooner had smoke cleared in one place than fires of revolt flared up in another. The more that militant anti-capitalism and international solidarity became everyday features of US *anti-racist activism*, the more vehemently the state and its avatars responded by "individualizing disorder"[50] into singular instances of criminality—which could then be solved via arrest or state-sanctioned killings.

Both institutional and individualized condemnation were essential because the deadly anti-racist struggle had been

---

48   Jacqueline Jones, *The Dispossessed: America's Underclass from The Civil War to The Present*, New York: Basic Books, 1992.

49   C. L. R. James, *Fighting Racism in World War II*, New York: Pathfinder, 1980.

50   Allen Feldman, *Formations of Violence: The Narrative of the Body and Political Terror in Northern Ireland*, Chicago: University of Chicago Press, 1991, 109.

nationally televised. Television affected the outlook of ordinary US white people who had to be persuaded that welfare did not help them (it did) and that justice should be measured by punishing individuals rather than via social reconstruction.[51] Thus, the political will for *militarism* remained intact, but the will for *equity* (another way to think about welfare), however weak it had been, yielded to pressure for privatizing or eliminating public—or social—goods and services. In other words, the basic structure of the postwar US racial state[52] has shifted, from welfare-warfare to workfare-warfare, and that shift is the product of, and is producing, a new political as well as economic geography.

The expansion of prison coincides with this fundamental shift and constitutes a geographical solution to socioeconomic problems, politically organized by the state which is, itself, in the process of radical restructuring. This view brings the complexities and contradictions of globalization to the fore, by showing how already-existing social, political, and economic relations constitute the conditions of possibility (but not inevitability) for ways to solve major problems. In the present case, "major problems" appear, materially and ideologically, as surpluses of finance capital, land, labor, and state capacity that have accumulated from a series of overlapping and interlocking crises stretching across three decades.

In the wake of capital's tax revolt, and the state's first movements toward restructuring both capital-labor and international economic relations, the United States slipped into the long mid-1970s recession. Inflation consequent to abandonment of the gold standard[53] and rising energy costs sent prices skyward, while at the same time steep unemployment deepened the effects of high inflation for workers and their families.

---

51 Ruth Wilson Gilmore, "Decorative Beasts," in this volume, 51–77.

52 Omi and Winant, *Racial Formation in the United States*.

53 Anwar M. Shaikh and E. Ahmet Tonak, *Measuring the Wealth of Nations*, New York: Cambridge University Press, 1994.

Big corporations eliminated jobs and factories in high-wage heavy industries (for example, auto, steel, rubber), decimating entire regions of the country and emptying cities of wealth and people. Even higher unemployment plagued farmworkers and timber, fishing, mining, and other rural workers. Landowners' revenues did not keep up with the cost of money because of changing production processes and product markets, as well as seemingly "natural" disasters. Defaults displaced both large and smaller farmers and other kinds of rural producers from their devalued lands, with the effect that land and rural industry ownership sped up the century-long tendency to concentrate.[54]

Urban dwellers left cities, looking for new jobs, cheaper housing,[55] or whiter communities, while new suburban residential and industrial districts developed as center-cities crumbled. Those left behind were stuck in space, their mobility hampered by the frictions of diminished political and economic power. As specific labor markets collapsed, entire cohorts of modestly educated men and women—particularly people of color, but also poor white people—lost employment and saw household income drop.[56] Meanwhile, international migrants arrived in the United States, pushed and pulled across borders by the same forces producing the US cataclysm.

The state's ability to intervene in these displacements was severely constrained by its waning legitimacy to use existing welfare capacities to mitigate crises. However, what withered

---

54 Gilmore, "From Military Keynesianism to Post-Keynesian Militarism."

55 About 65 percent of US households are owner-occupied. When the data are broken down by race, we see a different picture: for example, only about 45 percent of Black households are owner-occupied, because of federally mandated racist lending criteria as well as lower-than-average incomes. See Douglas S. Massey and Nancy A. Denton, *American Apartheid: Segregation and the Making of the Underclass*, Cambridge, MA: Harvard University Press, 1993; Melvin L. Oliver and Thomas M. Shapiro, *Black Wealth/White Wealth: A New Perspective on Racial Inequality*, New York: Routledge, 1995.

56 See, for example, Roger Waldinger and Mehdi Bozorgmehr (eds.), *Ethnic Los Angeles*, New York: Russell Sage Foundation, 1996.

was not the abstract geopolitical institution called "the state," but rather the short-lived *welfare* partner to the ongoing *warfare* state.[57] Unabsorbed accumulations from the 1973–77 recession lay the groundwork for additional surpluses idled in the 1981–84 recession, and again in 1990–94, as the furious integration of some worlds produced the terrifying disintegration of others.

Prison Expansion

Many map the new geography according to the gross capital movements we call "globalization." This chapter proposes a different cartographic effort, which is to map the political geography of the contemporary United States by positing at the center the site where state-building is least contested, yet most class based and racialized: the prison. A prison-centered map shows dynamic connections among (1) criminalization; (2) imprisonment; (3) wealth transfer between poor communities; (4) disfranchisement; and (5) migration of state and non-state practices, policies, and capitalist ventures that all depend on carcerality as a basic state-building project. These are all forms of structural adjustment and have interregional, national, and international consequences. In other words, if economics lies at the base of the prison system, its growth is a function of politics, not mechanics.

The political geography of criminal law in the United States is a mosaic of state statutes overlaid by juridically distinct federal law. Although no single lawmaking body determines crimes and their consequences, there are trends that more than 52 legislative bodies have followed and led each other along over the past two decades. The trends center on (1) making previously noncriminal behavior criminal, (2) increasing sentences for old and new

---

57 Seymour Melman, *The Permanent War Economy: American Capitalism in Decline*, New York: Simon and Schuster, 1974.

crimes, and (3) refiguring minor offenses as major ones. More than 70 percent of new convicts in 1999 were sentenced for nonviolent crimes, with drug convictions in the plurality—30 percent of new state prisoners and 60 percent of all federal prisoners.[58] Even what counts as "violence" has broadened over this period.[59] The summary effect of these trends has been a general convergence toward ineluctable and long prison terms.

The weight of new and harsher laws falls on poor people in general and especially people of color—who are disproportionately poor. Indigenous people, and people of African descent (citizens and immigrants), are the most criminalized groups. Their rate of incarceration climbed steeply over the past twenty years, while economic opportunity for modestly educated people fell drastically and state programs for income guarantees and job creation withered under both Republican and Democratic administrations.[60] Citizen and immigrant Latinos in collapsing primary or insecure secondary labor markets have experienced intensified incarceration; and there has been a steady increase in citizen and immigrant Asian and Pacific Islanders in prison and jail.[61] Finally, at the same time that revisions to federal law have curtailed constitutional protections for noncitizens accused of crimes and for all persons convicted of crimes, immigration law has adopted criminalization as a weapon to control cross-border movement and to disrupt settlement of working people who are non-elite long-distance migrants.[62]

Does the lawmaking and prison building fury mean there's more crime? Although data are difficult to compare because of changes in categories, the best estimate for crime as a driving

---

58   Gainsborough and Mauer, *Diminishing Returns*.

59   The meaning of violence used to define racism in this chapter (see footnote 1 above) is far narrower than the meaning of violence used by current lawmakers to expand punishment.

60   Gilmore, "From Military Keynesianism to Post-Keynesian Militarism."

61   Waldinger and Bozorgmehr (eds.), *Ethnic Los Angeles*.

62   José Palafox, "Opening up Borderland Studies," *Social Justice* 27.3 (2001): 56–72.

force of prison expansion shows it to account for little more than 10 percent of the increase. Rather, it is a greater propensity to lock people up, as opposed to people's greater propensity to do old or new illegal things, that accounts for about 90 percent of US prison and jail growth since 1980. People who are arrested are more likely now than twenty years ago to be detained pending trial; and those convicted are more likely to be sentenced to prison or jail and for longer terms than earlier cohorts.[63]

A counterintuitive proposition might also help further understanding of why there are so many US residents in prison. The lockup punishment imperative must be positively correlated with lockup space. Legislative bodies can make any number of laws requiring prison terms, and they can, in theory, drastically overcrowd prisons and then build new prisons to correct for noncompliance with constitutional, if not international,[64] custody standards. However, if one scrutinizes the temporality of prison growth in California, the largest US state, one sees that lawmaking expanding criminalization followed, rather than led, the historically unprecedented building boom the state embarked on in the early 1980s. And the inception of the building boom followed, rather than led, significant, well-reported, reductions in crime.[65] A similar pattern holds true for the other leading prison state, Texas.[66] The new structures are built on surplused land that is no longer a factor in productive activity. Virtually all new prisons have been sited in rural areas, where dominant monopoly or oligopoly capitals have either

---

63   Alfred Blumstein and Allen J. Beck, "Population Growth in U. S. Prisons, 1980–1996," *Crime and Justice* 26 (1999): 17–61.

64   United Nations International Covenant on Civil and Political Rights, 1976.

65   Gilmore, "From Military Keynesianism to Post-Keynesian Militarism"; Gilmore, *Golden Gulag*.

66   Sheldon Ekland-Olson, "Crime and Incarceration: Some Comparative Findings from the 1980s," *Crime and Delinquency*, 38.3 (1992): 392–416; Dana Kaplan, Vincent Schiraldi and Jason Ziedenberg, *Texas Tough: An Analysis of Incarceration and Crime Trends in the Lone Star State*, Washington, DC: Justice Policy Institute, 2000.

closed down or, through centralization and/or mechanization, reorganized their participation in the economy.

In search of new prison sites, state prison agencies and private prison entrepreneurs (to whom we shall return) present lock-up facilities as local economic development drivers. Recent quantitative and qualitative research in the United States[67] demonstrates that prisons do not produce the promised outcomes for a number of reasons. New prison employees do not live in amenities-starved towns where prisons go, while 60–95 percent of new prison jobs go to outsiders. Prisons have no industrial agglomeration effects. The preponderance of local institutional purchases is for utilities, which are usually extra-locally owned. Locally owned retail and service establishments such as restaurants are displaced by multinational chains, which drain already scant profits from the locality.

When a prison site is authorized, land values increase amid the euphoria of expected growth, but after construction values drop again. Anticipatory development—particularly new and rehabilitated housing—fails, leaving homeowners (especially the elderly) with their sole asset effectively devalued due to increased vacancies. Renters bear higher fixed costs because of hikes during the short-lived construction boom. As a result, prisons can actually intensify local economic bifurcation.

At the same time, prisons produce a local economy dependent on constant statehouse politicking to maintain inflows of cash. In one mayor's words: "Beds. We're always lobbying for more beds." "More beds" means more prisoners.[68] Most prisoners come from urban areas, where the combination of

67 Gregory Hooks, Clayton Mosher, Thomas Rotolo, and Linda Lobao, "The Prison Industry: Carceral Expansion and Employment in U.S. Counties, 1969–1994," *Social Science Quarterly* 85.1 (2004): 37–57; Gilmore, "From Military Keynesianism to Post-Keynesian Militarism"; Gilmore, *Golden Gulag*.
68 Tracy L. Huling, *Yes, in My Backyard*. Documentary. Galloping Girls/WSKG Production, 1999.

aggressive law-enforcement practices[69] and greater structural strains[70] produces higher arrest and conviction rates than in rural areas[71]; suburbia is following urban trends.[72]

The movement of prisoners is, in effect, a wealth transfer between poor communities, and there isn't enough wealth in the sending community to create real economic growth in the receiving community.[73] Taxes and other benefits that are spatially allocated on a per capita basis count prisoners where they are held, not where they are from.[74] When prisoners' families make long trips to visit, they spend scarce but relatively elastic funds in motels and eating establishments. Towns disappointed by the lack of prison-induced real growth console themselves with these meager rewards, although modest tax subventions and families' expenditures hardly constitute an income tide to lift ships. Prisons also provide localities with free prisoner labor for public works and beautification, which can displace local low-wage workers.

Global Implications

Throughout the globalizing world, states at all scales are working to renovate their ability to be powerful actors in rapidly changing landscapes of accumulation. Already-existing

---

69   David H. Bayley, *Patterns in Policing*, New Brunswick, NJ: Rutgers University Press, 1985.

70   John H. Laub, "Patterns of offending in urban and rural areas." *Journal of Criminal Justice*, 11.2 (1983): 129–142.

71   Gilmore, "From Military Keynesianism to Post-Keynesian Militarism."

72   Bureau of Justice Statistics 2000.

73   Tracy L. Huling, *Prisons as a Growth Industry in Rural America: An Exploratory Discussion of the Effects on Young African-American Males in the Inner-Cities*, Washington, DC: US Commission on Civil Rights, 2000; Gilmore, *Golden Gulag*.

74   Tracy L. Huling, "Prisoners of the Census," Mojo Wire, 2000, www.motherjones.com.

capacities, antagonisms, and agreements are the raw materials of political renovation; embedded in renovation work, then, is the possibility (although by no means *certainty*) that already-existing frictions of distance may be intensified. The rise of prisons in the United States is a potentially prime factor in future "globalization circulation models" because prison-building is state-building at its least contested, and the United States is a prime exporter of ideologies and systems. The transfer of social control methods, in times of political-economic crisis, is not new. A century ago, Jim Crow, apartheid, racist science, eugenics, and other precursors to twentieth century hypersegregation, exclusion, and genocide took ideological and material form and globalized in conjunction with technology transfers and dreams of democracy.[75]

In the current period the legitimizing growth of state social control apparatuses productively connects with the needs of those who struggle to gain or keep state power. Such political actors (whether parties, corporations, industrial sectors, or other kinds of interest groups makes no difference) are vulnerable to the arguments of private entrepreneurs and public technocrats about how states *should* function in the evolving global arena, when the norm has become neoliberal minimalism. Increased coercive control within jurisdictions is, as we have seen in the US context, one way to manage the effects of organized abandonment. At the same time, the struggle for *international* sovereignty in the context of "postcolonial" globalization can, and often does, feature a rush to institutional conformity—which today includes expanded criminalization, policing, and prisons. As a result, new or renovated state structures are often grounded in the exact same fatal power-difference couplings (for example, racism, sexism, homophobia) that radical anti-colonial activists fought to expunge from the social order.[76]

---

75 Blaut, *The Colonizer's Model of the World.*
76 Fanon, *The Wretched of the Earth*; M. Jacqui Alexander, "Not Just

In other words, structural adjustment—most ordinarily associated with shifts in how states intervene in the costs of everyday-life basic-goods subsidies, wage rules, and other benefits —flags not only what states stop doing, but also what states do instead.[77] Policing and lawmaking are internationally articulated, via professional and governmental associations,[78] and the pressures of international finance capitalists (whether commercial or not-for-profit) seeking to secure predictable returns on investments. In short, while not all countries in the world rush to emulate the United States, the very kinds of state-based contingencies and opportunities that help explain US prison expansion operate elsewhere.[79]

US prison expansion has other broad effects. While most US prisons and jails are publicly owned and operated, the trend toward public service privatization means firms work hard to turn the deprivation of freedom for 2,000,000 into profit-making opportunities for shareholders. Success rates differ across jurisdictions, but privatized market share, currently about 6 percent, grew 25–35 percent each year during the 1990s.[80] The largest firms doing this work also promote privatization in such disparate places as the United Kingdom, South Africa, and Australia.[81]

Any(Body) Can Be a Citizen: The Politics of Law, Sexuality, and Postcoloniality in Trinidad & Tobago," *Feminist Review* 48 (1994): 5–24.

77　Rarely, if ever, does a delegitimated state, or state-fraction, simply disappear.

78　See, for example, Bayley, *Patterns in Policing*.

79　See, for example, Martha Knisely Huggins, *Political Policing: The United States and Latin America*, Durham, NC: Duke University Press, 1998; Paul Chevigny, *Edge of the Knife: Police Violence in the Americas*, New York: New Press, 1995.

80　Judith Greene, "The Rise and Fall—and Rise Again—of the Private Prison Industry," *American Prospect* 12.16 (2001): 23–27; James Austin and Garry Coventry, *Emerging Issues on Privatized Prisons*, Washington, DC: US Department of Justice, Office of Justice Programs, 2001.

81　Julia Sudbury, "Transatlantic Visions: Resisting the Globalization of Mass Incarceration," *Social Justice* 27.3 (2000): 133–149.

Public and private entities package and market prison design, construction, and fund-development; they also advocate particular kinds of prison-space organization and prisoner management techniques. The "security housing unit" (SHU), a hyper-isolation "control unit" cell condemned by international human rights organizations, is widely used in the United States. The United States imported the SHU from the former West Germany, which developed it as a death penalty surrogate to destroy the political will and physical bodies of radical activists. The United States has both the death penalty and the SHU and promotes control units abroad.[82] At the end of 2000 more than 10,000 prisoners throughout Turkey participated in a hunger strike to protest spatial reconfiguration from dormitories to cell-based "American"-style prison, with a particular focus on the punitive SHU.[83]

Exported structures and relationships can take the form of indirect as well as deliberately patterned effects. In addition to the transfer of wealth between poor places, prison produces the political transfer of electoral power through formal disfranchisement of felons. While elections and politics are not identical, the power to vote has been central to struggles for self-determination for people kept from the polls by the frictions of terror and law throughout the world. In the United States, Black people fought an entire century (1865–1965) for the vote. As of 1998, there were nearly 4 million felony-disfranchised adults in the country, of whom 1.37 million are of African descent.[84] The voter effect of criminalization returns the United States to the era when white supremacist statutes barred millions from decision-making processes; today, lockout is achieved through lockup.

---

82   Angela Y. Davis and Avery F. Gordon, "Globalism and the Prison Industrial Complex."

83   Prison Focus, *Turkey Prisoners Protest SHUs*, CPF 14, 2001.

84   Jamie Fellner and Marc Mauer, *Losing the Vote: The Impact of Felony Disenfranchisement Laws in the United States*, New York: Human Rights Watch/The Sentencing Project, 1998.

The 2000 US presidential election, strangely decided by the Supreme Court rather than voters, was indirectly determined by massive disfranchisement. George W. Bush Jr. won Florida, and therefore the White House and the most powerful job on the planet, by fewer than 500 votes. Yet 204,600 Black Floridians were legally barred from voting; additionally, many others of all races who tried to vote could not because their names appeared on felon lists. Had felons not been disfranchised, candidate Bush would have lost; however, candidate Albert Gore's party shares equal responsibility with Bush's for creating widespread disfranchisement and could not protest on that front. Thus, the structural effects of racism significantly shape the electoral sphere with ineluctably global consequences for financial (G8), industrial (WTO and GATT), environmental (Kyoto), and warfare (NATO; Star Wars) policies.

Conclusion

As exercised through criminal laws that target certain kinds of people in places disorganized by globalization's adjustments, racism is structural—not individual or incidental. The sturdy curtain of US racism enables and veils the complex economic, political, and social processes of prison expansion. Through prison expansion and prison export, both US and non-US racist practices can become determining forces in places nominally "free" of white supremacy. Indeed, as with the twentieth, the problem of the twenty-first century is freedom; and racialized lines continue powerfully, although not exclusively, to define freedom's contours and limits.

6

Fatal Couplings of Power and Difference: Notes on Racism and Geography

Who Am I?

I locate my work within the broad areas of social theory, political economy, and labor and social movements. In my research and writing, I investigate, largely in the US context, overdeterminations of race, gender, class, and power. The geographical impulses shaping my analyses are deliberately counterintuitive. What I wish to do is disarticulate common-sense couplings of sites and struggles and disrupt assumptions such as the idea that politics happens in the milieu of the state or that value comes from wage-controlled workplaces. At the same time, I am not throwing out the historical-materialist baby with the well-used bathwaters of three decades of Marxist geography.

My goal is to emulate the work of engaged scholars who try to find in the organizational foundations of social-movement building something other than perpetual recapitulation of ongoing place-based struggles that are displaced but never resolved.[1] By "place" I mean, following Neil Smith's typology

1 Cedric Robinson, *Black Marxism*, London: Zed Books, 1983; A. Sivanandan, *A Different Hunger*, London: Pluto Press, 1983; Laura Pulido, *Environmentalism and Economic Justice*, Tucson: University of Arizona Press, 1996; Leela Fernandes, *Producing Workers*, Philadelphia: University of Pennsylvania Press, 1997; Clyde Woods, *Development Arrested*, New York: Verso, 1998 [new Verso ed. with an introduction by Ruth Wilson Gilmore, 2017]; Claire Jean Kim, *Bitter Fruit*, New Haven, CT: Yale University Press, 2000; Paul Gilroy, *Between Camps: Nations, Cultures, and the Allure of Race*, London: Penguin Books, 2000.

of scale, the *range of kinds of places*—as intimate as the body and as abstract, yet distinctive, as a productive region or a nation-state.[2]

For the past decade [this essay was originally published in 2002], I have focused my scholarly energy on several projects that developed from ongoing political activism. I am finishing a book called *Golden Gulag,* a study of California's remarkable prison growth, and the opposition to it, during the last two decades of the twentieth century. I embarked on *Golden Gulag* and pursued it relentlessly because women in a grassroots organization whose loved ones are in prison asked me to find out: (1) what work does prison do? (2) for whom? and (3) to what end? Those three initial questions prompted a subsequent pair of interrelated questions, which *Golden Gulag* asks and answers. How does the state-in-crisis discipline surplus workers, and how do workers organize against their abandonment within and across oppositional spaces delimited by race, gender, class, region, and violence?

The second project examines how underdevelopment and environmental racism constitute two sides of a single coin, by looking specifically at how environmental-justice activism can be a sturdy bridge between grassroots activists stuck in urban and rural landscapes of disaccumulation.[3] As in the case of justice work, I find that women take the lead in everyday struggles against toxicities. They join forces not only as petitioners to the state in the name of injuries sustained but also—and more provocatively—as petitioners to communities of similar people in the name of reconstructing place so that concepts of "safety" and "health" cannot be realized by razor-wire fences or magic-bullet cures.

---

2   Neil Smith, "Contours of a Spatialized Politics: Homeless Vehicles and the Production of Geographical Scale," *Social Text* 33 (1992): 54–81. All nation-states are at the same scale, though they are highly varied in geometric size, wealth, demographics, military might, urbanization, integration by global capital, and so on.

3   Pulido, *Environmentalism and Economic Justice.*

Women's restless activism sent me down a third research path. In this new project, tentatively called "Political Geographies of Recognition in the Age of Human Sacrifice," I will attempt to piece together a geographical genealogy of radicalism by tracing the development and movement of several mature women activists across territories shaped by state and state-sanctioned racist terror (Nazi death camp, Mississippi lynch mob, El Salvador death squads). My observation of the ways that the women have become materially and discursively able to recognize each other across many contemporary divides demands reconsideration of the historical geography of the present.[4] All projects investigate the present's lived structural antecedents in the long twentieth century[5] toward the end of detailing how that century, which I call the age of human sacrifice, also produced subjects whose ideological and material agency moved in counterpurpose to "fatal couplings of power and difference."[6]

The urgency of all three projects begins with the crisis of the capitalist racial state.[7] Such investigation neither derives from nor leads to either a monolithic view of the state or an "essentialist" view of race.[8] Rather, my purpose is to use research

4   Allan Pred, *Even in Sweden*, Berkeley and Los Angeles: University of California Press, 2000.

5   Giovanni Arrighi, *The Long Twentieth Century*, London and New York: Verso, 1994.

6   Stuart Hall, "Race, Culture and Communications: Looking Backward and Forward at Cultural Studies," *Rethinking Marxism* 5: 1 (1992), 17.

7   Toni Negri, *Revolution Retrieved*, London: Red Notes, 1988; Michael Omi and Howard Winant, *Racial Formation in the United States*, New York: Routledge, 1986.

8   Geographers, and social scientists in general, tend to overblow the threat of "essentialism." The debates about race that loomed large in the 1980s in cultural theory—especially among Marxists such as Stuart Hall (see "Cultural Identity and Diaspora," in Jonathan Rutherford, ed., *Identity: Community, Culture, Difference*, London: Lawrence and Wishart, 1990, 222–37); Gayatri Spivak, *In Other Worlds*, New York: Routledge & Kegan Paul, 1988; and A. Sivanandan (*A Different Hunger*)—have been taken up and awkwardly inserted into geography without much of the

techniques to piece together a complex (and not necessarily logical) series of abstractions in order at once to analyze and produce a multiscalar geographical object of analysis.[9] States are territorial resolutions of crisis.[10] Capitalist states displace and contain highly differentiated moments of class struggle in many ways. As Marx observed, tax struggle is class struggle. The abstraction of class conflict from the multiple sites of production (including sites of reproduction) to state milieux does more than produce a free-floating—or even an interest-group-defined—squabble over the appropriate disposition of public resources.[11] Indeed, the state's mediation is both constitutive of and constituted by extrastate relations. Changing ideological and material infrastructures—institutions—of actual states

nuance that informed the earlier debates. The primary fear seems to be reification, which then leads to, or deepens, fragmentations along the lines of "identity politics." Analytically, those lines can only lead into a cul-de-sac, since identity politics stands in for a range of subjective and objective categories and concerns. The obsessive dismissal of identity politics misses the principal mark that schooling in historical materialism should make apparent. One works with what is at hand; the problem is not the "master's tools" (Audre Lorde, "The Master's Tools Will Never Dismantle the Master's House," *Sister Outsider*, Freedom, CA: Crossing Press, 1984, 110) as objects, but the effective control of those "tools" (see "Public Enemies and Private Intellectuals," in this volume, 78–91). One can and should be able to analyze "Black" materially—which is to say, with contingent accuracy. Such a claim hardly signifies that "Black" then always refers to the same cultural or biological object. Blackness is a spatially and temporally differentiated, produced, and *real* condition of existence and category of analysis.

9   Academic disciplines crudely summarize these abstractions in one direction, by separating objects of study into disciplines with peculiar methods and boundaries. At the same time, the levels of generality appropriate to different aspects of a single analysis indicate another way in which abstraction crosscuts the questions we ask.

10   See, for example, Charles Tilly, "War Making and State Making as Organized Crime," in Peter B. Evans, Dietrich Rueschemeyer, and Theda Skocpol (eds.), *Bringing the State Back In*, Cambridge, UK: Cambridge University Press, 1985, 169–91; Michael Mann, *State, War, and Capitalism*, Oxford: Blackwell, 1988.

11   See "Globalization and US Prison Growth: From Military Keynesianism to Post-Keynesian Militarism," in this volume, 199–223.

widen (or narrow, and sometimes both at once) the distance between categories of social actors and their capacity to realize their own freedom.[12]

If race has no essence, racism does. Racism is singular because, whatever its place-based particularities, its practitioners exploit and renew *fatal* power-difference couplings. Fatalities—premature deaths—are not simply an objective function of any kind of power differential.[13] There is no difference without power, and neither power nor difference has an essential moral value.[14] Rather, the application of *violence*— the cause of premature deaths—produces political power in a vicious cycle.[15] What, then, are nonfatal power-difference couplings? Mutuality for one. For another, my undergraduate students always say "the family"; and while we debate how and why different kinds of contemporary families are structured as they are, to what extent patriarchy is still a family rather than state affair,[16] and how the concept of family defines normative sexuality, there's something in the answer to work with.[17]

Racism is a practice of abstraction, a death-dealing displacement of difference into hierarchies that organize relations within and between the planet's sovereign political territories. Racism functions as a limiting force that pushes disproportionate costs of participating in an increasingly monetized and profit-driven world onto those who, due to the frictions of *political* distance,

---

12 "Freedom" is shorthand for the object of history.

13 Michael Greenberg and Dona Schneider, "Violence in American Cities," *Social Science and Medicine* 39.2 (1994): 179–87.

14 Michael Foucault, *Discipline and Punish*, New York: Pantheon, 1977.

15 Allen Feldman, *Formations of Violence*, Chicago: University of Chicago Press, 1991.

16 See Wendy Brown, *States of Injury*, Princeton, NJ: Princeton University Press, 1995.

17 See, for example, Patricia Hill Collins, *Black Feminist Thought*, Boston: Unwin Hyman, 1990; Leopoldina Fortunati, *The Arcane of Reproduction*, New York: Autonomedia, 1995; Ruth Wilson Gilmore, "You Have Dislodged a Boulder," in this volume, 355–409.

cannot reach the variable levers of power that might relieve them of those costs. Indeed, the process of abstraction that signifies racism produces effects at the most intimately "sovereign" scale, insofar as particular kinds of bodies, one by one, are materially (if not always visibly) configured by racism into a hierarchy of human and inhuman persons that in sum form the category "human being."[18]

The violence of abstraction produces all kinds of fetishes: states, races, normative views of how people fit into and make places in the world. A geographical imperative lies at the heart of every struggle for social justice; if justice is embodied, it is then therefore always spatial, which is to say, part of a process of making a place. For researchers, purpose and method determine whether one reifies race and state—chasing down fetishes—or, rather, discovers dynamic processes that renovate race and state.[19] When I started to work on *Golden Gulag*, I realized that prisons were a consequence of state failure; I had yet to learn that they are a project of state-building. Prisons are geographical solutions to social and economic crises, politically organized by a racial state that is itself in crisis. The complex dynamics of politically organized institutional shifts that reconfigure the economic, cultural, and reproductive landscapes of everyday life are necessarily contradictory. In placing prisons at the center of a multiscalar analysis of contemporary crisis, I found it necessary (1) to chart dynamics of change that articulate landscapes of accumulation and disaccumulation and (2) to document how racism works even when it is officially "over."[20] These twinned goals then set into stark relief

---

18   Giorgio Agamben, *The Remnants of Auschwitz: The Witness and the Archive*, New York: Zone, 1999.

19   Antonio Gramsci, *Selections from the Prison Notebooks*, ed. and trans. Quintin Hoare and Geoffrey Nowell Smith, New York: International Publishers, 1971.

20   Gilmore, "Globalization and US Prison Growth," in this volume, 199–223; compare with Etienne Balibar and Immanuel Wallerstein, *Race, Nation, Class: Ambiguous Identities*, London and New York: Verso, 1992.

the ways that relatively powerless social actors—for example, prisoners' mothers and families—renovate and make critical already-existing activities, categories, and concepts to produce freedom from surplused capacities. As a result, starting from race and state yields, necessarily rather than additively, an analysis that cannot be complete at any level of abstraction without attending to gender, class, and culture in the simultaneous processes of abstracting and reconstructing geographies of liberation.

Where Have We Been?

In the long, murderous twentieth century, geographers used three main frameworks to study race: environmental determinism,[21] areal differentiation,[22] and social construction.[23] While these three approaches span an astonishing political spectrum, from racist eugenics to antiracist multiculturalism, all (at least implicitly) share two assumptions: (1) social formations are structured in dominance within and across scales; and (2) race is in some way determinate of socio-spatial location. In other words, having marched a long way, geographical inquirers into race perhaps have not gotten as far as we might wish. Contradiction was as fundamental to the early as the late twentieth-century work.

---

21 See Don Mitchell, *Cultural Geography*, Oxford: Blackwell, 2000.

22 See David Harvey, *Explanation in Geography*, London: Edward Arnold, 1969.

23 See, for example, Peter Jackson and Jan Penrose, eds., *Constructions of "Race," Place, and Nation*, Minneapolis: University of Minnesota Press, 1993; Ruth Wilson Gilmore, "Behind the Power of 41 Bullets: Interview by Bob Wing," *Colorlines*, (Winter 1999–2000): 16–20; *Golden Gulag*; Laura Y. Liu, "The Place of Geography in Studies of Geography and Race," *Social and Cultural Geography* 1.2 (2000): 169–82.

Where Should We Go?

As I have suggested, race is not only contradictory but also—necessarily—overdetermined as well. That is, the recognition that power and structure are mutually dependent requires that we understand dynamic distributions of power throughout a structure. The object is to figure out what (including "who"—that is, deal with agency in a nonvoluntaristic sense) makes oppressive and liberatory structures work and what makes them fall apart. At the most general level of abstraction, we know that structures change under conditions of power redistribution—that is, during times of crisis. In times of crisis, dynamics are peculiarly apparent, and insofar as we can catch historical or contemporary shifts on the fly, we might recognize something powerful about race and freedom.

For Example?

In my newest project, I am trying to sort out the ways in which organizing is always constrained by recognition.[24] Women who lived through political terror as youth have, in their mature years, become political activists seeking to formulate "public policies" for social movements. They work in the context of the short-lived and weak US welfare state's dismantling and the rise of a punitive postwelfare state that, like its predecessor, ideologically and materially depends on the legitimacy of militarism or warfare.[25] In this political, economic, and cultural geography, premature death is an unfortunate given rather than an intolerable failure. What is the historical geography of the present in which these women's work proceeds? What institutional shapes of twentieth-century human sacrifice produced

---

24 See also "You Have Dislodged a Boulder," in this volume, 355–409.
25 Gilmore, "Globalization and US Prison Growth," in this volume, 199–223.

power through killing and terror sufficient to keep women, for many years, from living whole ways of oppositional life? And why fight now?

The capacities for particular historical blocs to secure local, regional, national, or imperial domination depend in part on the skill and extent to which the blocs socialize the costs of such domination (especially since, as every smart anti-colonialist has pointed out, coercion is expensive).[26] They reduce their own financial and ideological exposure by externalizing such costs to collective structures—that is, to the state. The benefit to such externality lies not only in tapping the public purse but also in expanding lower-cost consent by developing the ideological state apparatuses.[27]

In Franklin Delano Roosevelt's New Deal regime, social welfare apparatuses took shape as Progressive-era-bred reformists used the state's power to resolve the Great Depression's antagonisms. They did so in order both to restore general health to the economy and to disarm radical alternatives such as communism.[28] The programs spread guaranteed effective demand by redistributing wealth, but did so unevenly, to the point that, while labor achieved a modicum of security against economic disasters, lawmakers and agencies of the nascent Keynesian state reworked and made critical the very

26   See Frantz Fanon, *The Wretched of the Earth*, New York: Grove Press, 1961.

27   Louis Althusser, *For Marx*, trans. Ben Brewster, London and New York: Verso, 1996 [1971].

28   Carey McWilliams, *Factories in the Field: The Story of Migratory Farm Labor in California*, Hamden, CT: Archon Books, 1969 [1939]; Elizabeth Faue, *Community of Suffering and Struggle: Women, Men, and the Labor Movement in Minneapolis, 1915–1945*, Chapel Hill: University of North Carolina Press, 1990; Robin D. G. Kelley, *Hammer and Hoe: Alabama Communists During the Great Depression*, Chapel Hill: University of North Carolina Press, 1990; Don Mitchell, *The Lie of the Land: Migrant Workers and the California Landscape*, Minneapolis: University of Minnesota Press, 1996; Doug Dowd, *Blues for America: A Critique, A Lament, and Some Memories*, New York: Monthly Review Press, 1997; Woods, *Development Arrested*.

US hierarchies that activists were fighting to deconstruct in radical organizing. Thus, under the New Deal, white people fared well compared with people of color, most of whom were deliberately excluded from opportunities and protections,[29] men received automatically what women had to apply for individually,[30] and normatively urban, industrial workers secured rights denied agricultural field workers even to this day.[31]

The uneven development of the New Deal's "creative government"[32] resulted not only from the uneven capitulations of capital to a massive social wage, but also—and perhaps more—from the desperately dense relationships between Southern and Northern Democrats. The Southerners' congressional seniority gave them secure legislative foundations from which to engineer limits to any centralized power that would disrupt the region's peculiarly fatal couplings of power and difference.

Both resident and absent planters,[33] who derived enormous fortunes from sharecroppers and tenant farmers, and regional and carpetbagger capitalists, who funded the South's competitive mine- and mill-based (steel, cotton, lumber) industrialization, depended on the expansion, consolidation, and enforcement of Jim Crow rule to keep labor cheap and disciplined.[34] Indeed, securing the capacity to produce power

---

29   Kelley, *Hammer and Hoe*; Gwendolyn Mink, *The Wages of Motherhood: Inequality in the Welfare State, 1917–1942*, Ithaca, NY: Cornell University Press, 1995.

30   Faue, *Community of Suffering and Struggle*; Teresa Amott and Julie Matthaei, *Race, Gender, and Work*, Boston: South End Press, 1991; Linda Gordon, *Pitied but not Entitled: Single Mothers and the History of Welfare*, New York: The Free Press, 1994.

31   Maralyn Edid, *Farm Labor Organizing: Trends & Prospects*, Ithaca, NY: Cornell/ILR Press, 1994; Woods, *Development Arrested*.

32   Sidney Baldwin, *Poverty and Politics: The Rise and Decline of the Farm Security Administration*, Chapel Hill: University of North Carolina Press, 1968.

33   John Egerton, *Speak Now against the Day: The Generation Before the Civil Rights Movement in the South*, New York: Knopf, 1994; Woods, *Development Arrested*.

34   W. David Lewis, *Sloss Furnaces and the Rise of the Birmingham*

through racist terror—lynching—symbolized the metaphorical and material line that separated the South from, and thus connected it to, the rest of the United States. Here, then, we must understand that the anomaly that emerged in the 1930s was not federal reticence to condemn lynching in contrast with the building of institutions of social welfare, but rather the extension to the federal scale—through differentiations of protections from calamity and opportunities for advancement —of the South's apartheid practices.

Although authorized, the New Deal social welfare institutional forms were never fully operationalized. However, in order to execute the World War II buildup, the Department of War appropriated from the political and institutional milieu of social welfare powerful bureaucracies, central planning, and control over large sums of finance capital.[35] Starting in 1938, these formerly underutilized capacities were transformed into the structures of the national security state,[36] and the postwar Department of Defense became a fortress agency, shielded from public scrutiny.[37] The wealth produced in large part by federal expenditures for the maintenance and expansion of Pentagon research and development, equipment, installations, and personnel—accounting for 5–15 percent of the annual Gross Domestic Product (GDP)—effectively underwrote the postwar welfare state; redistribution of wealth in the golden age was made palatable by general prosperity. Meanwhile,

---

District, Tuscaloosa: University of Alabama Press, 1994; Woods, *Development Arrested.*

35 Edward K. Hunt and Howard Sherman, *Economics: An Introduction to Traditional and Radical Views,* New York: Harper and Row, 1972; Gregory Hooks, *Forging the Military-Industrial Complex,* Ithaca, NY: Cornell University Press, 1991; Ann Markusen and Joel Yudken, *Dismantling the Cold War Economy,* New York: Basic Books, 1993.

36 Hooks, *Forging the Military-Industrial Complex.*

37 Fred J. Cook, *The Warfare State,* New York: MacMillan, 1962; Seymour Melman, *The Permanent War Economy,* New York: Simon and Schuster, 1974; Frances Fox Piven, "Reforming the Welfare State," *Socialist Review* 22.3 (1992): 69–81.

in the context of the Cold War—in other words, as an arm of "defense"—the codification of business unionism in the 1947 Taft-Hartley Act narrowed labor's realm of activism.[38] Thus, "military Keynesianism" designates the socioeconomic "welfare-warfare" system practiced in the United States.[39]

At the same time, the war against racism was also a racist war, in that it renovated the US racial state on several fronts. The US state deliberately, self-consciously, and repeatedly declined to intervene in the extermination of Jews by Nazis; it willfully ignored dispatches detailing what the Nazis were doing to Jews (and, I can only presume, to non-Jews who were communists and homosexuals, to Romani, to Africans stuck in Europe, and to the other five million or so industrially killed in the camps[40]). The racist exclusion of European Jews from US shores, effected by obstacles one State Department official named "paper walls,"[41] particularized the racial front to the East, even as, in the West, the coast-long "security zone" provided the pretext for expropriating Japanese and Japanese Americans and deporting them to concentration camps.[42]

The evidence shows how the War Department and members of FDR's administration worked diligently to define the security zone so that it would maximize capture of the "enemy race" (as Japanese/Japanese Americans were named in one of many memos) and minimize capture of others (Germans, Italians) with whom the US was at war. Death stalked the West

---

38 C. L. R. James, *Fighting Racism in World War II*, New York: Pathfinder Press, 1980; Nelson Lichtenstein, *Labor's War at Home: The CIO in World War II*, Cambridge, UK: Cambridge University Press, 1982; Mike Davis, *Prisoners of the American Dream*, London: Verso, 1986.

39 James O'Connor, *The Fiscal Crisis of the State*, New York: St. Martin's, 1973.

40 David S. Wyman, *The Abandonment of the Jews*, New York: Pantheon, 1984.

41 David Wyman, *Paper Walls: America and the Refugee Crisis, 1938–1941*, Amherst: University of Massachusetts Press, 1968.

42 Michi Weglyn, *Years of Infamy: The Untold Story of America's Concentration Camps*, New York: Morrow Quill, 1976.

as much as the East and the South. As this project progresses, I will argue, rather than merely assert, that the security zone provided the pretext for FDR's successor to drop the bomb on Hiroshima and Nagasaki. The internment camps discursively signified and materially produced civil and quasi-social death, which then enabled (or perhaps even required) state terror to obliterate the enemy "over there" whose racial difference (whether understood biologically or understood culturally) could only be dissolved by physical death.[43]

In sum, then, by trying to reconstruct the United States that the activist women moved into and across, I found that my project became thematically and empirically concerned with how the US racial state renovates and makes critical already-existing activities in times of crisis. Through forcefully twinned processes of articulation and abstraction, lived narratives of difference become singularly dramatized as modalities of antagonism, whose form of embodied appearance is the over-determined (racialized, gendered, nationalized, criminal) enemy. Indeed, the central point here is best summarized by Orlando Patterson's elegant statement summarizing slavery's common-sense justifications, which attribute the logic of social death to a mutable object of adversity: "One fell because he was the enemy; the other became the enemy because he had fallen."[44]

The US urban welfare state institutionalized particular gendered dramas of race and class. The most radical tendencies of the African American civil rights movement's "second reconstruction"[45] coalesced during the World War II fight against racism and fascism.[46] We have already seen that Black veterans

---

43   James N. Yamazaki, *Children of the Atomic Bomb*, Durham, NC: Duke University Press, 1995.

44   Orlando Patterson, *Slavery and Social Death*, Cambridge, MA: Harvard University Press, 1982, 44.

45   Manning Marable, *Race, Reform, and Rebellion*, 2nd ed., Jackson: University of Mississippi Press, 1991; compare to W. E. B. Du Bois, *Black Reconstruction in America*, New York: Atheneum, 1992 [1935].

46   James, *Fighting Racism in World War II*.

returning from the front, and their families, were determined not to relive the intensified lynching that punctuated the end of World War I.[47] Nevertheless, it was a bloody time. However, while radical tendencies persisted until they were crushed by the state during the next quarter century,[48] they were also displaced by success in the struggle for access to social welfare programs and equal educational opportunity. This was especially the case in cities outside the South to which Black people had migrated during the century to work in Fordist war and peacetime industries, if almost always at their margins.[49] The "urban pact" was an outcome of reformist struggles characterized by the formation of political coalitions through which Black people achieved access to public resources and employments and wielded relative electoral power.[50]

The welfare state came under sustained attack when military —or "bastard"[51]—Keynesianism failed to prevent the mid-1970s economic crisis that featured both high inflation and high unemployment.[52] Why the failure? In economic terms, Keynes's short-run remedy was not up to the challenge of a

---

47 Ralph Ginzburg, *100 Years of Lynching*, Baltimore: Black Classic Press, 1988 [1962].

48 George Jackson, *Soledad Brother*, New York: Bantam Books, 1970; Angela Y. Davis, *Women, Race, and Class*, New York: Vintage, 1981; Frank Donner, *Protectors of Privilege: Red Squads and Police Repression in Urban America*, Berkeley: University of California Press, 1990; Huey P. Newton, *The War against the Panthers*, New York: Harlem River Press, 1996.

49 Carol Marks, *"Farewell—We're Good and Gone": The Great Black Migration*, Bloomington: Indiana University Press, 1989; Marable, *Race, Reform, and Rebellion*; Ralph Sonenshein, *Politics in Black and White: Race and Power in Los Angeles*, Princeton, NJ: Princeton University Press, 1993; compare to Carol Stack, *Call to Home*, New York: Basic Books, 1996.

50 Marable, *Race, Reform, and Rebellion*; Sonenshein, *Politics in Black and White*.

51 Lynn Turgeon, *Bastard Keynesianism*, Westport, CT: Greenwood Press, 1996.

52 Anwar M. Shaikh and E. Ahmet Tonak, *Measuring the Wealth of Nations: The Political Economy of National Accounts*, New York: Cambridge University Press, 1994.

long-run crisis. Countercyclical investment and guaranteed effective demand were powerless against the key crisis: an apparently secular, rather than cyclical, post-1967 decline in the rate of profit created by excessive capitalist investments in productive capacity.[53] While military buildup in Vietnam temporarily cured the 1970 recession, extreme measures taken by Washington's rising monetarist elite at the Federal Reserve Bank—manipulation of interest rates, abandonment of the gold standard, and devaluation of the dollar—worsened conditions for ordinary people in the United States.[54] However, it was the welfare state, military Keynesianism's *social* face, rather than capitalism's surplus-generated crisis, that bore popular political blame for economic turmoil. In particular, urban dwellers of color who had seized a portion of public resources began to weather the long attack on their right to share in the social wage. At about the same time, decent individual-wage jobs, especially in labor market segments disproportionately filled by modestly educated Black and brown men, began the late twentieth-century urban outmigration, producing the deindustrialized city cores that in turn yield most prisoners today.[55]

Has the delegitimization of Keynesianism produced a post-Keynesian tendency to domestic militarism? Why not simply post-Keynesian monetarism or neoliberalism? Is the domestic state really more coercive, or merely more neglectful? Let us approach the tendency toward militarism through my attempt to theorize the normative aggression of US responses to crisis in

---

53   Robert Brenner, *Turbulence in the World Economy*, New York: Verso, 2001.

54   Edwin Dickens, "The Federal Reserve's Low Interest-Rate Policy in 1970–1972: Determinants and Constraints," *Review of Radical Political Economics* 28.3 (1996): 115–25.

55   David Grant, Melvin L. Oliver, and Angela D. James, "African Americans: Social and Economic Bifurcation," in Roger Waldinger and Mehdi Bozorgmehr, eds., *Ethnic Los Angeles*, New York: Russell Sage Foundation, 1996, 379–413; Gilmore, "Globalization and US Prison Growth"; Gilmore, "Behind the Power of 41 Bullets"; Gilmore, *Golden Gulag.*

terms of the nation's violent history and habits.[56] The domestic turn of the national security state derives from a standard of aggression specific, if not peculiar, to the United States. Thus, while the postwar national security state emerged from crisis conditions and absorbed means and methods designed for peaceful purposes in order to build up the most extensive warfare apparatus in the history of the world,[57] the ideological preconditions for the behemoth post-1945 Pentagon lie in the centrality of state and state-sanctioned violence to the American national project.

In my view, the founding moments of US nationalism, well-rehearsed in mainstream histories, are foundational to both state and culture. First, the United States was "conceived in slavery"[58] and christened by genocide.[59] These early practices established high expectations of state aggression against enemies of the national purpose—such as revolutionary slaves and indigenous peoples—and served as the crucible for development of a military culture that valorized armed men in uniform as the nation's true sacrificial subjects.[60] Large-scale, coercive institutions—prisons and reservations—were established to control freedmen in the postbellum South and dispossessed Native Americans throughout the country. Second, the high incidence of war waged by the United States correlates with high levels of violence, particularly homicide, experienced in the social formation of the United States as compared with 114 other nation-states. Every time the United States goes to war and wins—as happened in 1991—the homicide rate goes up,

---

56   Gilmore, "You Have Dislodged a Boulder."

57   Hooks, *Forging the Military-Industrial Complex*; Markusen and Yudken, *Dismantling the Cold War Economy*.

58   Jacqueline Jones, *The Dispossessed: America's Underclass from the Civil War to the Present*, New York: Basic Books, 1992, 292.

59   David Stannard, *American Holocaust: The Conquest of the New World*, Oxford: Oxford University Press, 1992.

60   Du Bois, *Black Reconstruction*; Stannard, *American Holocaust*; Tom Engelhardt, *The End of Victory Culture: Cold War America and the Disillusioning of a Generation*, New York: Basic Books, 1995.

indicating that the state, in particular the warfare state, models behavior for the polity.[61] Third, the national exculpatory standard for murder committed in "self-defense" is remarkably aggressive. Indeed, in the culmination of nearly fifty years of case law involving white men killing white men, the Supreme Court overturned the murder conviction of a man who pursued a retreating combatant, with Chief Justice Oliver Wendell Holmes explaining that "[a] man is not born to run away."[62]

It is plausible to argue that these three points have sedimented weight, not as remnant ideology, but rather as ballast for common-sense notions of everyday dangers and alternatives to them. In particular, I believe they help to explain the promotion and acceptance of expanded punishment and the attendant apparatuses of criminal justice in the contemporary period, according to the following scheme. First, the legitimate domestic US state is the national security, or defense, or warfare state. Second, the local world is, and has always been, a very dangerous place: indeed, at the very moment when the nation is basking in foreign victory, the domestic turns hostile. Finally, the key to safety is aggression.[63]

But it is more complicated than this. If the legitimate state is the defense or warfare state, and domestic militarism is properly deployed to intervene between—and thereby define—wrongdoers and law-abiding citizens, how else can we characterize these antagonists? I have already noted the importance of chattel slavery and the premeditated murder of indigenous peoples as foundational to US economic and territorial growth. These

---

61 Dane Archer and Rosemary Gartner, *Violence and Crime in Cross-National Perspective*, New Haven, CT: Yale University Press, 1984.

62 Mark De Wolfe Howe, ed., *Holmes–Laski Letters, Volume 1*, Cambridge, MA: Harvard University Press, 1953, 335–36; Richard Maxwell Brown, *No Duty to Retreat: Violence and Values in American History and Society*, Norman: University of Oklahoma Press, 1991.

63 Compare with Foucault, *Discipline and Punish*; Feldman, *Formations of Violence*; Omer Bartov, *Murder in Our Midst: The Holocaust, Industrial Killing, and Representation*, Oxford: Oxford University Press, 1996.

twinned legacies, plus the colonization of Mexico and Puerto Rico[64] and the differentiation of both immigrants and nationals according to hierarchies of origin and religious belief,[65] are central to the production of the US master-race.[66] Justice Holmes's "man" was actually and normatively white. And, insofar as Holmes's "man" individualized the nation-state at the scale of his body, he was also the figure of the citizen. Thus, while the power of the state could be, and was, used against white men as workers,[67] the relatively early universal extension of suffrage to Euro-American males established government as their milieu and state power as their instrument.[68] The development of the US "herrenvolk democracy"[69] or "dictatorship of white men"[70] both depended on and fostered a connection between and among masculinity, state power, and national belongingness, with everyone else thus characterized as to some degree alien.

In other words, the warfare state is also the gendered racial state.[71] Intranational conflicts around inclusion and exclusion require this state to "fix" difference in order to maintain

---

64 Mario Barrera, *Race and Class in the Southwest: A Theory of Racial Inequality*, South Bend, IN: University of Notre Dame Press, 1979.

65 Du Bois, *Black Reconstruction*; Stannard, *American Holocaust*; Alexander Saxton, *The Indispensable Enemy: Labor and the Anti-Chinese Movement in California*, Berkeley: University of California Press, 1995 [1971]; Tomás Almaguer, *Racial Fault Lines: The Historical Origins of White Supremacy in California*, Berkeley: University of California Press, 1994.

66 David Roediger, *The Wages of Whiteness*, New York: Verso, 1990; Theodore Allen, *The Invention of the White Race*, New York: Verso, 1994.

67 Roediger, *The Wages of Whiteness*.

68 Ira Katznelson, "Working-Class Formation and the State: Nineteenth-Century England in American Perspective," in Peter B. Evans, Dietrich Rueschemeyer, and Theda Skocpol, eds., *Bringing the State Back In*, Cambridge, UK: Cambridge University Press, 1985.

69 Roediger, *The Wages of Whiteness*; compare to Saxton, *The Indispensable Enemy*.

70 Howard Winant, *Racial Conditions: Politics, Theory, Comparisons*, Minneapolis: University of Minnesota Press, 1994.

71 Omi and Winant, *Racial Formation in the United States*.

internal pacification.[72] The "fix" follows two general trajectories. In good times, the state remedies exclusion by recognizing the structural nature of racism and institutionalizing means for combating its effects—by, for example, extending the vote, banning discrimination in public-sector employment, or constructing the legal apparatuses through which injured persons may seek courtroom remedies.[73] Such racial state remedies were the order of the day for African Americans starting roughly in 1948, when President Harry S. Truman desegregated the military, and diminished from the late 1960s onward.[74] In bad times, when deepened differentiation pacifies widespread insecurity among the herrenvolk, the "fix" formalizes inequality. Examples of the latter include the 1882 Chinese Exclusion Act; Jim Crow (US apartheid) laws throughout the early twentieth century; the Roosevelt White House refusal to attack lynching, even rhetorically, in the 1930s and 1940s; the use of deportation, asset theft, and concentration camps to alienate and control Japanese Americans during World War II; and the extensive criminalization and imprisonment of people of color today.[75]

The oscillation between reformist and repressive "fixes" is not a simple binary movement but rather overdetermined at the source. A key aspect of the US state's "infrastructural coordination"[76]—its relational power throughout society, manifested in such social goods as laws, currency, education, roads, and so on—is its reliance on racial hierarchy.[77] That is, toward the end of securing or maintaining hegemony,[78] the state reproduces racial hierarchy through its capacity to wield despotic power over certain segments of society—whether the

---

72   Mann, *State, War, and Capitalism.*
73   Omi and Winant, *Racial Formation in the United States.*
74   Marable, *Race, Reform, and Rebellion.*
75   "Globalization and US Prison Growth," in this volume.
76   Mann, *State, War, and Capitalism.*
77   Omi and Winant, *Racial Formation in the United States.*
78   Gramsci, *Selections from the Prison Notebooks.*

decree is to promote a Black woman, put her on workfare, or send her to prison for being a bad, drug-addicted mother.

The contemporary racial state's aggressively punitive stance is made clear in recent revisions to law and jurisprudence, which occurred despite a preponderance of evidence that once produced different results. Take the death penalty. During the height of the civil rights movement in the 1960s, when petitioners persuaded the US Supreme Court to review the racist excesses of the various states' death-dealing zeal, probability mattered. "Scientific" approaches could prove (rather than justify) racism, and policy analysts from the social sciences made a veritable industry of producing the most highly mathematized representations showing whom the state kills, when, and why. Signs mattered. Thus, the evenhanded "objectivity" numbers presented to the policymaker consolidated and made actionable anti–state-racism struggles waged in other arenas. Thirty years later, trial, appellate, and supreme courts are generally unmoved by the arguments that were so persuasive not very long ago.[79] Probability does not matter anymore, in legal terms. As the punishment system is currently constituted, the fact that a Black person is more likely to be arrested, tried, convicted, sentenced, imprisoned, and executed than are others is, in the words of a prominent criminologist emeritus, "inequality, but not injustice."[80]

---

79 Franklin E. Zimring, "Research on the Death Penalty: On the Liberating Virtues of Irrelevance," *Law & Society Review* 27.1 (1993): 9–17. Such change should not be ascribed to rotation of personnel. Judges can be the very same people who wrote completely different opinions years earlier. Supreme Court Justice Roger Taney powerfully exemplifies such a shift. In 1841, he wrote the decision delivering from bondage the captured Africans of the Amistad slave ship, who had killed the crew that was taking them to be sold. The decision concurred with their position that they had been wrongfully enslaved and therefore did not constitute property under US law. In 1857, as the Court's Chief Justice, Taney wrote the landmark Dred Scott decision that included the immortal words: "A [Black] man has no rights that a white man is bound to respect"; *Scott v. Sandford*, 60 U.S. 393 [1856].

80 Ernest van den Haag, "Crime/Criminal Justice," paper delivered at

The context of fatalities for the women whom I am studying was a capitalist racial state-in-crisis that invested in and rewarded diligently revised norms of the applied (legal, medical) disciplines.[81] Such work had the *policy* effect of producing the "inhuman" side of the contradictory unity "human being"[82] through processes of gendered criminalization and racialization that accompany, and indeed ease, the ordinary destructive violences that "appear" to be not structural—all the sites of premature death in the US urban and rural regions that have been abandoned by capital and state in the seismic upheavals we call "globalization," even when the dough and the power are only relocated down the road. Teetering on the verge of the new millennium, we are ready to fall back into the end of the *nineteenth century*—the era of Jim Crow, of *Plessy v. Ferguson*. Or else, we leap into the future.

What Is the Conclusion?

Geographers should develop a research agenda that centers on race as a condition of existence and as a category of analysis, because the territoriality of power is a key to understanding racism. The political geography of race entails investigating space, place, and location as simultaneously shaped by gender, class, and scale. By centering attention on those most vulnerable to the fatal couplings of power and difference signified by *racism*, we will develop richer analyses of how it is that radical activism might most productively exploit crisis for liberatory ends. The usefulness of such an approach enables reconsideration of historical geographies, radical examination of transitional geographies, and the difference between

the "Racism and Public Policy" Conference, Bloustein School of Planning and Public Policy, Rutgers University, April 19, 1996, New Brunswick, NJ.

81   Bartov, *Murder in Our Midst.*
82   Agamben, *The Remnants of Auschwitz.*

the neutral fact of unequal power and its fatal exploitation. Thus, in this view, the focus on race neither fixes its nature nor asserts its primacy. Rather, the focus demands examination of the subjective and objective nature of power and difference as articulated and naturalized through racism; one can follow the reasoning, and adjust the methods, for studying interrelated fatalities. In other words, we must change aspects of both the forces and the relations of knowledge production in order to produce new and useful knowledges.

7

Terror Austerity Race
Gender Excess Theater[1]

[A] civilization maddened by its own perverse assumptions and
contradictions is loose in the world.

—Cedric Robinson, *Black Marxism*

Civilization is nothing but the glory of incessant struggle.

—Gabriele D'Annunzio, quoted in
Colin Mercer, "Fascist Ideology"

The day before I performed this paper at Berkeley, I was driving
the sixty-mile breadth of LA County—my regular commute to
UCLA. When I hit the radio button to get a traffic report I
found instead, at the middle of the AM band, gavel-to-gavel,
opening-day coverage of the trial to determine whether four
Los Angeles Police Department (LAPD) cops used excessive

---

1   This paper was originally presented on March 6, 1992, in slightly
different form at a daylong conference at the University of California at
Berkeley arranged by James Turner, Judith Butler, *and others*, entitled "Performing: Deforming: Inversions: Subversions" (or something like that). I
have not rewritten it in light of the April 29, 1992, verdict and ensuing
rebellion—in part because I was not the least surprised by either event. I
am trying to figure out *how* what is happening works in the minds of mine
enemies and by extension, quite literally, on me. That is, I am treading the
precipice of my fear while also trying to avoid the trap that held Harriet
Jacobs in check for so long 150 years ago. "Both pride and fear" she
wrote, "kept me silent." We have not, as she discovered she had not, time
for the luxuries of pride and fear. Thanks to friends in the struggle: Saidiya
Hartman whose intervention inspired and occasioned the paper; Gilbert
McCauley for listening; *always* C. G. for patient reading and passionate
talk at any hour (especially the eleventh).

force against Rodney King. The prosecutor devoted nearly a third of his 35-minute opening argument to establishing that King had indeed committed several crimes—speeding, driving while intoxicated, failing to yield. As I traveled west on the Foothill Freeway, passing Altadena Avenue at about fifty-five miles per hour in my Subaru, the prosecutor described how King entered the Foothill Freeway at Altadena Avenue and traveled west, achieving more than twice my rate of speed in his Hyundai (yes, Hyundai). Listening to the people's attorney describe the long, high-speed chase, in which the California Highway Patrol (CHP) unit at maximum speed could not catch up, I looked around, expecting to see that the CHP had traded in the force's low-performance Chevrolet V6 and Straight-8 megacube cruisers for speedier, energy-efficient, four-banger imports: a publicly funded endorsement of the Korean manufacturing miracle and American assembly-line decline.

While I do listen to the radio a lot, I don't watch much TV. This austerity in my habits has relatively little to do with moral indignation at stupidifying stuff and perhaps even less to do with an addiction, as long as memory, to print. Rather, my TV-free living results from the material conditions of my house (its situation in a narrow mountain canyon precludes regular broadcast reception) and my income (I can't afford a satellite dish) and, I confess, the cultural politics of front-yard decor (a dish in the front yard would signify an excess of meaning I am not prepared literally to live behind). When the cable crew came to wire Palmer Canyon, they pretended there was not one last house way up the ridge beyond the rickety, twelve-inch, single-plank "footbridge," and we never called to complain that our municipally guaranteed right to consume through the tube had been violated. It is astonishing to think there hasn't been a project of cablizing scale in my corner of LA County since the 1930s when the Rural Electrification Act compelled SoCal Edison to install three poles to run two wires up to one glorified cabin in the live oaks.

As a result of a lengthy separation from television in the living room, effected when I went off to college in 1968, I am still surprised to see what has happened in that medium which, among other events, brought the brutality of the anti–Civil Rights movement, Lee Harvey Oswald's murder, and the horrors of Vietnam into the everyday experience of people who, a half generation earlier, had to go to the movies and catch the newsreels to see this stuff in motion—from life but not, as we say, "live." Nowadays, new brutalities, murders, horrors defy surprise, normalize excess, present terror as entertainment; there are not any limits when it comes to picturing death in motion and its melodramatically visible consequences.

My students insist that I cannot teach them adequately if I do not understand how television affects their consciousnesses—their timing and codes canonized, I can only surmise, in MTV. I recognize their appeal in my own intergenerational battles with professors: the men who told us in 1969 that we did not know real danger as they had in the 1930s and 1940s doing real oppositional work which we students in our acting out only insubstantially performed. I knew I was right (as my students know they are) because around me my family and friends went to jail, were assassinated by agents of the FBI, came home from Vietnam as strangers; those unfettered by prison or trauma spent all their nonwaged time in meeting after meeting after meeting. But then, in 1969, I was not, in the raced (white), gendered (male) institutions I attended, simply, transparently a "student." When Jerry Farber published *The Student as Nigger*, I was taken aback for the first of many times, as a substantive category of my political identity became overtly and publicly metaphorical, symbolic, comparative, abstract.

Toward the end of my sophomoric encounter with God and Man at Yale, I had this exchange with my father (organic intellectual/labor and community organizer/Ivy League drag) after he sat through what was doubtless a dreadful production of Sophocles's *Antigone* (starring you know who/hair bushed halfway to Manhattan/maroon lightweight wool sleeveless bellbottomed jumpsuit/4-inch platform sandals):

> RJW: Daddy! Did you like the show?
> CSW: Are you going to act or are you going to work?

I've never figured out the answer to his retort. Indeed, he knew his question was unanswerable. The substance of the distinction—between drama and realness, between repetition and invention, between spectator and actor, between invention and work, between Fordism and Americanism, between economy and culture—the substance is dialectical, and the tendencies along which the tension both pushes and pulls me are what inform the semiotics and histrionics of my critical performance. So far, I've learned to describe the tension according to this scheme, loading the action (provisionally) into the work: Who works and what works, for whom, and to what end?

Terror Austerity Race Gender Excess Theater

Who works and what works, for whom, and to what end? For the project at hand the question turns toward this particularity: What work do certain kinds of acting—of performance—do, especially when the venue straddles the chasm of a crisis of the crisis state? The crisis state is the warfare state. Toni Negri wrote in 1980 from Trani Special Prison (Italy):

> By transition from "welfare" to "warfare" state I am referring to the internal effects of the restructuration of the state machine—its effect on class relations ... Development is now planned in terms of ideologies of scarcity and austerity. The transition involves not just state policies, but most particularly the *structure* of the state, both political and administrative. The needs of the proletariat and of the poor are now rigidly subordinated to

the necessities of the capitalist reproduction ... The state has an array of military and repressive means available (army, police, legal, etc.) to exclude from [the arena of bargaining or negotiating] all forces that do not offer unconditional obedience to its austerity-based material constitution and to the static reproduction of class relations that goes with it.[2]

The "static reproduction of class relations" is a complicated enterprise. It is hardly accomplished simply from the top down, even with the might of the state's coercive apparatus. A significant proportion of the people whose relations are reproduced must concretely consent to the arrangement, however displaced their understanding. In the US, where real and imagined social relations are expressed most rigidly in race/gender hierarchies, the "reproduction" is in fact a *production* and its by-products, fear and fury, are in service of a "changing same"[3]: the apartheid local of American nationalism.[4]

---

2 Toni Negri, "Crisis of the Crisis-State," in *Revolution Retrieved: Selected Writings on Marx, Keynes, Capitalist Crisis and New Social Subjects, 1967–83,* London: Red Notes, 1988, 181–82. Also particularly helpful to the formulation of this paper's tendency are Marie-Hélène Huet, *Rehearsing the Revolution: The Staging of Marat's Death, 1793–1797,* Berkeley: University of California Press, 1982; Selma James, *Sex, Race and Class,* London: Falling Wall, 1986; A. Sivanandan, *Communities of Resistance,* London: Verso, 1990.

3 The phrase is Amiri Baraka's, but Paul Gilroy put it in my vocabulary. See LeRoi Jones, "The Changing Same," *Black Music,* New York: Apollo Editions, 1970; see also Paul Gilroy, "Sounds Authentic: The Challenge of a 'Changing Same,'" paper delivered at "The Politics of Identities" conference, April 4, 1991, Claremont, CA.

4 Any who doubt my claim need only study the 1992 Democratic Party platform and the party's many pundits whose subtexts resound with the unvoiced but clear desire for Black people to disappear so that liberalism can be reborn as a white, working thang. If the Democrats are committed to "distancing" themselves from Black people, then the distance will require a material force to maintain it. Doubling the prison populations in the past decade, the reinstitution of the death penalty in many states, combined with recriminalization of practices which had become misdemeanors in the 1970s (for example, possession of marijuana for personal use) set in motion both the concrete and the ideological forces

Terror Austerity Race Gender Excess Theater. What kinds of terror are enacted by and on behalf of the US Crisis State, both as response to *and* mystification of power shifts occasioned by the new international economic order during the past decade? How do local—that is, *intra*national—forms of state terrorism work to create and maintain alienated publics in the current crisis, publics who are *contingently* united, if at all, in culs-de-sac of identity politics, most frighteningly realized locally as resurgent American nationalism? By American nationalism I mean an allegedly restorative tendency (back to family values and all that), normatively white, in patriotic revolution against the "stark utopia"[5] of both late capitalism's exportation and the state's domestic squandering of the possibilities of household-based economic security. What's at issue is not simply that things are getting worse (and they are) but that they are getting worse in stark contradiction to still-rising expectations—the ideology of progress embedded in American common-sense consciousness. In no way an anti-capitalist movement per se, this revolution seeks to explain contemporary disorders and structural adjustments in US political, cultural, and libidinal economies in natural terms, as though a transcendent discourse would guarantee the transcendent innocence of the richest, most powerful, most technologically advanced nation-state in the history of the world. The contradictions of fascism deny the social but not the constructed character of US hierarchies. For the new American nationalist, hierarchy is naturally a result of specific "work," the glory of constructing world power (identical with household-based progress toward the good life) in the empty yet threatening wilderness of continental North America. In this formulation,

---

necessary to dispose of a subset of an entire racially marked group of the population without once using the word "fascism" as a rallying cry in mainstream circles. See Dan Baum, "Just Say Nolo Contendere: The Drug War on Civil Liberties," *The Nation* 25: June 29 (1992), 886–8.

5 Karl Polanyi, *The Great Transformation,* New York: Farrar and Rinehart, 1944, 3.

the US is a muscular achievement of ideological simplicity: "White men *built this nation!! White men are* this nation!!!"[6] Antonio Gramsci reminds us that work mediates society and nature. The hierarchical divides of who performs what work define cultural tendencies of gender, race, sexuality, authority; the divides also enforce multiple and, in this moment of danger, *competing* economies of being. When all this identity chat is en route somewhere beyond "self" toward subjectivity, in motion from object to agency, its politics are about these competitions and their possible outcomes.

Terror Austerity Race Gender Excess Theater. First a definition of terrorism from the official US Code:

> "[A]ct of terrorism" means an activity that (A) involves a violent act or an act dangerous to human life that is a violation of the criminal laws of the United States or any State, or that would be a criminal violation if committed within the jurisdiction of the United States or of any State; and (B) appears to be intended (i) *to intimidate or coerce a civilian population*; (ii) to influence the policy of a government by intimidation or coercion; or (iii) to affect the conduct of a government by assassination or kidnapping [emphasis added].[7]

"To intimidate or coerce a civilian population"; which civilians? War, the State of World War, the World Warrior State, is the theater of operations for the production of new

---

6 White Aryan Resistance (WAR) flyer, distributed to windshields throughout the western US. WAR'S headquarters is about twenty-five miles from where I live (same area code). Tom Metzger, founder of WAR, and his son John were convicted of inciting Portland, Oregon, skinheads to commit racist acts of terror, which culminated in the murder of the Ethiopian student Mulugeta Seraw. Morris Dees and the Southern Poverty Law Center successfully prosecuted the case. Dees is now on Metzger's hit list.

7 Cited by Noam Chomsky, "International Terrorism: Image and Reality," in Alexander George, ed., *Western State Terrorism*, New York: Routledge, 1991, 13.

American nationalism, the post-Vietnam syndrome, the idea and enactment of winning, of explicit domination set against the local reality of decreasing family wealth, fear of unemployment, threat of homelessness, and increased likelihood of early, painful death from capitalism's many toxicities. Arthur MacEwan writes:

> U.S. business and the U.S. government are still an extremely powerful set of actors, but the era of U.S. hegemony is past. U.S. corporations have felt the impact in numerous ways, losing their dominant role in many world markets and experiencing substantially lower profit rates in the 1970s and 1980s than in the preceding decades. Capital, however, is highly mobile, and in many instances U.S. firms have been able to detach themselves from the fate of the U.S. economy and, indeed, have been able to use the structures of the international system to shift the burdens of adjustment onto the backs of labor. Working people in the United States have borne a considerable burden from the emergence of a "new international economy" in the post-hegemony era.[8]

One of many debtor nation-states in the world economy, the posthegemony United States is in the process of structural adjustment—the sine qua non of all debt service. In everyday

---

8 Arthur MacEwan, "What's 'New' about the 'New International Economy'?" *Socialist Review* 21: 3 and 4 (July–December 1991), 112. An example of a US corporation successfully detaching "from the fate of the US economy" (or more, *defining* that fate through its detachment!) is General Motors, which idled tens of thousands of workers and closed twelve plants between 1969 and 1989, one of which was South Gate in South Los Angeles. GM plans to close twenty-one more plants and lay off an additional 74,000 by 1995; one permanently idled autoworker means two to three layoffs in businesses where the worker spends her pay. But take note: in 1985 the same transnational ranked thirteenth (right behind Ford and Hughes Medical Institute) among contractors in *arms* exports. See Raul Madrid et al., *U.S. Arms Exports: Policies and Contractors*, Washington, DC: Investor Responsibility Research Center, 1987.

life, enforcement of structural adjustment increasingly takes the form of local and international war. How come that Hyundai beat out the Chevy? Maybe because American workers are on drugs. The War on Drugs will take care of that, doubling the prison population every few years, unless adoption of Charles Murray's starkly utopian recommendations for market regulation (through voucher power) results in more barricaded, death-soaked ghettos à la Warsaw (1940) or Pico Union and Westside and North Las Vegas (1992).[9] Warfare: "Civilization is nothing but the glory of incessant struggle." War is accepted, in common sense, as the principal medium of power, prestige, and means to explain all structural adjustments, including the "fatalities" Benedict Anderson isolates as crucially accounted for in *pre*-national ideological systems: "death, loss and servitude."[10] What this all means for us at this historical moment can be summarized as follows: The ideology of nation demands sacrifice; the enactment of the warfare state demands human sacrifice. And further, both the forces and the relations of ideological production in the warfare state—in other words the crisis state—require an excess of accused, of enemies, especially if the state is successfully to exact austerity from an economy whose polity expects, as a right, indulgence (transcendent, TV-reified innocence), prosperity, excess. Such was the case fifty years ago, with the internment of the Japanese, and the centrally coordinated attacks on US blacks who began many franchisement actions during the war against racism.[11] Such is the case today.

---

9   Charles Murray, "Drug Free-Zones," *Current* 326 (October 1990): 19–24. Thanks to Mike Davis for telling me about this article, originally published in the *New Republic*. *Current* is a reader's digest for the radical right. Also see Mike Davis, "Blacks Are Dealt Out," *Nation* 255: 1 (July 6, 1992) 7–10.

10   Benedict Anderson, *Imagined Communities*, rev. ed., London: Verso, 1991, 36.

11   See C. L. R. James et al., *Fighting Racism in World War II*, New York: Pathfinder, 1980. A debate raged in middlebrow and learned journals on this very topic, with not only activists but also "friends of the Negro" and what Ishmael Reed calls "talking androids" all contributing

Play according to the drama of the moment.

The long-dong batons of the LAPD gangstas who beat Rodney King as he writhed on the ground are too obviously priapic to withstand much discussion. What interests me here are the theatrical venues for the repetition of that act of state terror and the subsequent configuring of the enemy, the accused—the dramaturgical roles of both George Holliday, the "neighbor" cameraman who brought the secret act to light, *and* of television, which brought the secret to "the world," and finally of the courts, which decide how secret the secret must be. Through what work does the "mass mediated society"[12] intertwine local terror with beliefs contrary to what the society is able to know about the system which produces and directs the terror? How, for example, could/have any number of people, including perhaps the jury sitting in judgment of the performance, determine that King deserved, earned, needed what he got? Central to the mission, a massive willing suspension of disbelief, is a dramatic clue: "Arrest is the political art of individualizing disorder."[13] I'd thought to show the video, Holliday's representation of political artists at work—have it loop silently in the background as I describe the meanings of King's torture. But, frankly, I can't display the act as artifact: whether or not it might *be* otherwise, it *was* not. Instead, let's try to summon within the confines of orality a picture of the terror, an image of the enemy, the accused, to "see it and say it ... in theory."

We can propose as explanatory hypothesis Ketu Katrak's description from her study of Wole Soyinka's drama: "The

---

to the argument. See Virginius Dabney, "The Negro and His Schooling," *The Atlantic Monthly* 169: (April 4, 1942): 459–68; Warren H. Brown, "A Negro Looks at the Negro Press," *Saturday Review* 25: 51 (December 19, 1942) 5–6; John Temple Graves, "The Southern Negro and the War Crisis," *Virginia Quarterly* 18 (1942) 500–18; and so on.

12 Robin Erica Wagner-Pacifici, *The Moro Morality Play*, Chicago: University of Chicago Press, 1986, 1–21.

13 Allen Feldman, *Formations of Violence: The Narrative of the Body and Political Terror in Northern Ireland*, Chicago: University of Chicago Press, 1991, 109.

protagonist's personal history is intertwined inextricably with his people's history, which, at any given time embodies the totality of his community's present-past-future. The personal and the historical come together in the actions of the protagonist."[14] Katrak's excursus through Soyinka requires many mappings, not the least of which are routings of her own and Soyinka's active consciousness as "post-independence"[15] historical subjects. The confusion of *American* protagonists in the King/LAPD video is multiple. Who *is* the accuser, who the accused? King? The cops? The busybody Holliday? Dangerously available technology? We who watched the tape on television (I was called from the mountain to witness) over and over and over and over? And what do I mean by "we"? The tangle of violence we encounter in sorting out the "accused" emphasizes layers and layers of effective Americanness as white maleness. The violently abstract work of Blackness in the United States, the growing proportion of guard-duty (cop, etc.) work in the sum of all US employment, the violence of being a stoolie, all propel the question at the heart of the post-Grenada, "when-hegemony-fails-give-'em-a-dose-o'-dominance" ideological enterprise, democratically domesticated as state terror: Is or ain't an "American" a contender? Doesn't a contender have to protect as well as beat up? Two bits of evidence: First, Holliday's videocassette, which the prosecutor showed to the jury during his opening argument, has a length of "extraneous footage" at the beginning: Holliday's "wife" and her "girlfriend" hanging out in the living room, American girls having American fun. Segue to the beating. Second bit of evidence: California Highway Patrolwoman Melanie Singer, on patrol with her husband (!) Tim, was the in-charge officer at the scene

---

14   Ketu Katrak, *Wole Soyinka and Modern Tragedy*, New York: Greenwood, 1986, 129.

15   Ella Shohat, "War, Sexuality, and the Imperial Narrative," paper presented at the annual convention of the Modern Language Association, San Francisco, December 30, 1991.

until LAPD Sergeant Koon told her to back off. Taking the stand against the LAPD officers, she tells us that King was acting silly, that he did a little dance. Stacey Koon's defense attorney tells it differently, citing Koon's deposition: King was "on something"; "I saw him look through me," and, when Singer told King to take his hands away from his butt, "he shook it at her [dramatic pause]. He shook it at her." The women, of course, are what makes the nation possible (and Melanie should give up that job to a man), the "class," as Brackette Williams says, that produces for and serves a "race of men."[16] Here, the protection of womanhood is actually the reassertion of race/gender in the national hierarchy: to keep Singer from being accused (in austere times of having a man's job; of trying to do a man's work without succeeding), King must stand in for both Willie Horton *and* for Melanie Singer. He must become the accused, in service of the rehabilitation of the nation.[17]

Frantz Fanon writes that violence "binds [the oppressed] together as a whole, since each individual forms a violent link in the great chain, a part of the great organism of violence which has surged upward in reaction to the settler's violence in the beginning. The groups recognize each other and the future nation is already indivisible."[18] Manthia Diawara comments:

> There we have it: violence is a system or a machine, or, yet, a narrative, of which the individual desires to be a part in order

---

16 Personal conversation; see also Brackette Williams, *Stains on My Name, War in My Veins*, Durham, NC: Duke University Press, 1991. See also Anne McClintock, "'No Longer in a Future Heaven': Women and Nationalism in South Africa," *Transition* 51 (1991): 105–24.

17 All references to the trial are from notes taken on the road listening to the opening remarks by the district attorney and by Koon's defense attorney. KFWB, Los Angeles, March 5, 1992; the information was substantiated in reports in the daily press.

18 Frantz Fanon, *The Wretched of the Earth*, cited by Manthia Diawara, "Black British Cinema: Spectatorship and Identity Formation in *Territories*," *Public Culture* 3: 1 (Fall 1990), 41.

to participate in the (re)construction of the nation. Furthermore, in order to be actualized, violence "introduces into each man's consciousness the ideas of common cause, of a national destiny, and of a collective history." Violence—"this cement which has been mixed with blood and anger"—in this sense becomes the founding basis of the nation, the process through which the individual articulates his/her relation with the nation.[19]

For good reason we tend to think of this "cement mixed with blood and anger" in terms of the not-white, not dominant, and in fact the topic of Diawara's essay is Black British cinema. But what Stuart Hall calls "new ethnicities," cementing into solidarity in fear of power shifts, include, of course, "Americans." Hall's proposal of such groupings centers on Black diaspora formations.[20] The conceptual extension of new ethnicities to the United States, and to the normatively white United States at that, signifies this: the very crisis which we must exploit—the raw materials of profound social change—is tending toward fascism through the brutal romance of identity, forged in the always already of the American national project. Our work is to rearticulate our own connections in new (and frightening) forward-looking moves in order to describe, promote, organize, bargain in the political arenas.

In a sense, 1992 is the year of the rehabilitation of white, male heterosexuality: its return to sites of centeredness, beauty, prosperity, power. Such a rehabilitation is central both to the European community and to the Columbian quincentenary. The rehabilitation extends to resurrections of some of those legendary dead white men—JFK, Columbus—as well as those who are trying to stay undead: from WAR's Tom Metzger on the ultra "right" to name your pundit on the other side. Metzger's

---

19   Diawara, "Black British Cinema," 41–2. Internal citations are from Fanon.

20   Stuart Hall, "New Ethnicities," in *Black Film, British Cinema*, London: ICA Documents, 1988, 27–31.

laissez-faire terrorism, stage-managed for spontaneous, natural effect, is of a piece with the nationalist power theater which the United States tuned in to with the invasion of Grenada in 1983. The shifts in the production of profit in the United States during the several years immediately preceding that invasion reflect how the circulation of value was less and less a function of productive labor and more and more the direct transfer of capital among competing traders—investment bankers, corporate raiders—and the exportation of labor relations. The major warfare matériel and engineering transnationals are located in the United States—the principal but by no means only state to which the transnationals pay tribute in exchange for defense, both for protection and for patronage. By 1983 they needed the kind of ideological zap (and subsequent funding spurt) which Sputnik provided the military-industrial complex in 1958. (The historical connection between the military-industrial complex and contemporary US white-racist nationalism is explicit, and current; for example, Richard Butler, founder of the Aryan Nation, is an engineer and retired military man who worked in aerospace before he recolonized northern Idaho to maintain and produce the pure.)[21] These ideological zaps are certainly a function of the "I'm proud to be an American" rah-rah, but *more,* they work—they dramatically arouse the sorts of sensations that, if cemented by blood and anger, last even unto the voting box and other fora where Americans are emptying their pockets into the valises of the rich. Thus the need for an enemy whose threat obligates endless budgetary consideration ("I could see him look through me"; "He was on something") and who can perhaps be found and fought as well by the brave American nationals who are sacrificing all for the sake of the nation-state: the dead and undead white men and their cadres who, Tom Metzger's windshield flyers assure us, built and (therefore) *are* this nation. Contenders.

---

21   James A. Aho, *The Politics of Righteousness,* Seattle: University of Washington Press, 1990, especially chapter 2.

A final accusation, expanding the ranks of the potentially accused, is that of being a spectator: only a watcher, a critic, a conscientious objector, gay, lesbian, unwaged, a blackteen-agewelfaremother, a supernumerary who fails to exit on cue. These performances of inadequacy are incompatible with the demands of the crisis state—or so terror teaches. Spectators in judgment, the judge and jury of the LAPD trial are already notorious as the result of an alleged jury-tampering attempt by a member of the Ventura County NAACP. One prospective juror told the press: "*I kind of got the feeling that they wanted me to vote a particular way—because I'm Black,*" lines repeated over the television, simulcast in idiot-card and voice-over. "See it and say it in American." By the way, the jury has no Black members or alternates.

The US Supreme Court, effectively, has no Blacks either. To a degree, whether or not one is white and male (in an old-fashioned sense) does not necessarily determine one's ability to perform "American," in the restricted nation, when power relations allow and indeed require the (formal) subsumption of the Other to the ... Other. Clarence Thomas composed his first dissenting opinion for the case concerning whether prison personnel may beat up a prisoner; he averred they may as long as they don't have so much fun that the stand-in has to go to the hospital. State terrorism, locally defined, is not terrorism at all. State terrorism is the price of misbehavin', of acting out, including acting out in the world in particular mortal casing.

My friend F— tells it this way: she was a teenager in Little Rock, in 1924. The second Klan had reached its apogee: a million white Protestant men and women, organized against the Bolsheviks, the Catholics, the Blacks who did not know their place; Kathleen Blee tells us they even tried to enlist "their" Blacks to help control the in-migration of Black disruptives and other foreigners in an effort to maintain the social order characterized by three generations of Redemption and Jim Crow.[22]

This is the end of the life of a Black man F— never knew. The lynchers tied him to the back of their Ford car and dragged him throughout the city streets, through white and Black neighborhoods alike. All of his skin scraped off. F— noticed the Black man had turned white and she wondered whether that's what they had in mind when they preached in church about how we're all the same underneath. Then the lynchers, some of whom she recognized as prominent members of the Little Rock elite and civil-service cadres, built a bonfire at the intersection where the Black part of town abutted the white, out where the pavement ends. They threw the man in the fire. As the acrid smoke of human sacrifice filled the neighborhood, some of the lynchers, especially the men in training showing off for their girls, pulled pieces of burning flesh and smoldering bone from his body, and walked the streets with their trophies. A high-tech lynching, thanks to that Ford car. State-sanctioned terror. Human sacrifice.

My friend F— lived at that intersection. She watched from the porch for a while, and then horror pulled her down the steps to see more closely what was happening to this man so that she would always know it in its particular and repeated terror across the years.[23] *Until 1960, race riots in the United States were these sorts of enactments, staged by a civilization loose upon the world.*

I went down from the mountains, again, to catch part of the Hill/Thomas story, tuning in at the exact moment when "high-tech lynching" entered the popular imaginary. With that plot twist, Thomas regendered himself, transforming Hill's

---

22   Kathleen Blee, *Women of the Klan,* Berkeley and Los Angeles: University of California Press, 1991.
23   Thanks to my friend, Mrs. FVH, an octogenarian who keeps the rest of us in line.

sexist thug into Ida B. Wells's bourgeois truth teller. If the polls are to be believed, the work of anagnorisis is powerful in its capacity to delimit vision. Thomas had already performed class suicide by marrying up. Now he abstracted himself to an important role in the crisis state—that is, he became a stand-in for "progress," just as junk-bond trading becomes a stand-in for production. In both instances, the aftermath of excess— of excessive abstraction of "race" *and* of "value"—produces a remaining austerity, a scarceness of every sort of resource, a disappearance of types of workers, with the notable inclusion of Thurgood Marshall as a worker type.

Anita Hill is mystified as "Black woman" such that all-we-all, including Thomas's "arrogant, entitled, dependent" sister, and their mother for whom the sister is the unpaid caregiver, fade into an infinitely regressing chorus line, abstracted to a single gynomorphic silhouette. Hill's "personal" history becomes entwined with that of her "people"—and, her people's with her. Educated in an elite university, Hill worked in DC for the better part of the 1980s dismantling regulations the enabling legislation of which two generations fought to enact. In recent, informal conversation, a noted Black feminist journalist asserted that nobody really *knows* what Hill's politics are. In response to my rehearsal of the DC years, my interlocutor curled her lip and said, "But that was her job." This common-sense differentiation of "job" and "politics" reinscribes the fatal space between "work" and "act," or "political" and "economy." The space itself is a result of the disciplinary configurations within and around knowledge-production centers (for example, the university, *itself* in crisis) that make possible the masking of how we act our politics; of how how we act *is* our politics; that politics is not ultimately derived from nor reducible to our gestures at the ballot box. And further, the willful ignorance demonstrated in the assertion of that distinction by a "feminist" argues exculpation on the basis of equal opportunity—for a woman to undo women: logically extended, we ought to celebrate Lynne Cheney Day. The issue returns us to an aspect of the problematic which my unwieldly title foregrounds: austerity, or scarcity—here, both in availability of types of waged work which an overeducated sister may perform (the government, including the armed services, is our principal employer) *and* in the portion of any person's actions one may politically scrutinize even though these actions in aggregate constitute, in the last analysis, material political performance.

The mystification of Hill, her abstraction to general meaning adequate to critique the performance of "Black woman" as a class, entails a general desire by audiences, some Black, some female, for Black women, in general, to disappear: that is, for us to cease our public performing, to carry on with our mediations as though we are not really here in the *flesh*, as Hortense Spillers would have it, especially when the work is flesh work. How can it be otherwise when in *every* case woman, recast through the anti-abortion crusade as national mother, vessel, "fetal container," *is* the performance of (hetero)sex (at whom *should* he have shaken it?) and its consequences: children; and also, when Black, addiction ("he was on something") and AIDS. Los Angeles is the site of at least twenty-nine torture murders of poor women, mainly Black, many of whom earned their livelihoods (and supported their children) working in the sex industry. The police are prominent in this drama as well. A grass-roots organization trying to bring an end to these deaths and take care of the survivors, Black Coalition Fighting Back Serial Murders testified at the Christopher Commission Hearings. "By labelling all the women prostitutes, the police attempted to segregate them from other women, and at the same time gave other women a false sense of security."[24] The

---

24 US Prostitutes Collective Statement, reported in *Update from the Wages for Housework Campaign/LA* (Fall/Winter 1991) 3. In fact, the only time there was any major, sustained coverage of these murders as *news* was on the occasion when a white woman who had been organizing

only arrest made in connection with these murders was that of a cop; the forensic evidence that led to his arrest was "reevaluated" by the same lab that found empirical support for his complicity, and he was released shortly thereafter.

Terror Austerity Race Gender Excess Theater

Here, finally, the title fully represents its dramatic possibility, every element functioning to coerce into silence and invisibility poor Black women who perform, if at all, as the expendable class but who, at the same time, embody, to the terror of the American nation "the [imagined] totality of our community's past-present-future." *Terror:* murder; torture; what to do with the children? The *austerity* of poverty, of turning finally to the body as the means for daily reproduction. The poverty that attaches to *race*—as Immanuel Wallerstein exposes in "The Myrdal Legacy," racism is a necessary component, rather than a passing phase, of capitalism.[25] The poverty that attaches to *gender*: According to the United Nations International Labour Organization, women do two-thirds of the world's work for five percent of the income and one percent of the assets; since we know the poorest among us are people of color, these data quantify racism and sexism on a global scale.[26] The *race/*

against the slayings was found dead in San Diego, gravel stuffed in her mouth. Otherwise, the biggest coverage was in the form of a *Los Angeles Times* feature in 1986 which coordinator Margaret Prescod and others fought for to announce formation of the Coalition. Source: Black Coalition Fighting Back Serial Murders.

25 Immanuel Wallerstein, "The Myrdal Legacy," *Unthinking Social Sciences*, Oxford: Polity, 1991, 80–103.

26 These figures are from the United Nations International Labour Organization; they are also ten years old. What with all the restructuring in the First through Third Worlds as a result of the debt crisis, these income and asset figures have undoubtedly shrunken, while the proportion of work has certainly risen. Thanks to Krishna Ahooja-Patel, an economist with the United Nations International Labour Organization, who worked to produce these data, and the International Wages for Housework

gender excess of these dead women is expendable enough for the LAPD to refuse to state categorically whether or not the murders have ceased. The work of the murdered and their survivors turns on the performance of *excess*, a quick ride on a paying penis—is this the fatal one?—the *theater* of orgasm become Grand Guignol become terror itself become snuff. War is the enemy of the poor.

The attempts to get major, in particular *televised*, coverage of this series of murders, and of deaths in similar circumstances as far away as Kansas City and Florida, encounter no drama-turgical zeal. After all, what work would this revelation do to extend coercion of the least powerful segment of the social for-mation? And, further, the coverage would result in an excess of something else, of attention paid to Black women who are not individually upwardly mobile objects of rape and other male abuses (Hill, [Robin] Givens, [Desiree] Washington, [Oprah] Winfrey). The coercion is already effectively in place, carried by fear and the anti-gospel gossip circuit; women get on the phone and talk, like the women who tried to turn in [Jeffrey] Dahmer before he'd eaten his fill. We talk until we're sure someone is listening—when we know we are performing for the technological apparatuses that turn on a suspect word—and say we'll talk some more when (when?) we meet again. We are the accused (like Anita Hill, who also accuses us), we who conspire to prevent the American nation from regaining its ancient heritage, its accessible white-male identity, clothed in whatever melanogender fits the needs of the political economy of the crisis-capitalist state. Spectators at our own undoing, we are filthy vessels of unwanted offspring, body parts that just won't work in the bodies of those who can afford to buy a spleen, a kidney, a heart—not even Fordism can save us now—separated by the excess of genetics, the fact of race in this era

---

Campaign, for both the data and the contemporary critique of the data. See also Maria Mies, *Patriarchy and Accumulation on a World Scale*, London: Zed, 1986, especially chapter 4.

of neobiologism, from any work/act/performance that does not run up in the face of state terror over and over and over again. I can stay in the mountains for this show; it won't be televised.

Stand-ins. What is so perfect, so perfectly austere in this theater is how nobody is a star—American equality in action. We're stand-ins, as Gloria Anzaldúa says,[27] and so are all the objects of state torture, of state terrorism, targets cast for the fit, the lighting, the camera, the angle, the story, in place of anyone who dares perform a comparable excess of being. But even stand-ins, in times of austerity, might unionize, might move from being objects of organized abandonment, redlined along with the buildings and neighborhoods, to *subjects* who refuse—who refuse to bear the weight of late capitalism's stark utopia, the abstraction of abandonment, the violence of abstraction.[28] We are poised in a performance I've yet to plot, or map, or systematically to theorize the semiotics and histrionics of, beyond these preliminary remarks. I believe it is too late to fight nationalism with nationalism; that bloodily disintegrating process must result in planetary death. I also believe it is not too late to act, to make work *work,* through rearticulation of the "complex skein of relatedness"[29]: organic integrations of the earth, technology, desire.

The Great Leveller Thomas Rainsborough said it in 1637: "Either poverty must use democracy to destroy the power of property, or property, in fear of poverty, will destroy democracy."[30] If we start from where we're at, and organize in and

---

27 Gloria Anzaldúa, "Theorizing, Mestiza Style," lecture delivered in Claremont, CA, February 1991.

28 See David Harvey, "Crises in the Space Economy of Capitalism," in *The Limits to Capital*, Chicago: University of Chicago Press, 1982, 413–45, and David Harvey, *The Condition of Postmodernity*, Oxford: Blackwell, 1989; see also Derek Sayer, *The Violence of Abstraction*, Oxford: Blackwell, 1989.

29 Charles Johnson, "The Education of Mingo," in *The Sorcerer's Apprentice*, New York: Macmillan, 1986, 19.

30 Quoted by Raphael Samuel, "British Marxist Historians, 1880–1980: Part One" *New Left Review* I/124 (March/April 1980), 28.

for work, conceived in the fullness of our imaginative powers, we might push and pull the current tendency of crisis away from a national resolution in fascism: terrorism, imprisonment, deportation, sterilization, state-supervised death. All of these features are everyday elements of life in California, in Arkansas, in Texas, New York, you name it. This is where we're at; where are we headed?

8

Race, Prisons, and War: Scenes from the History of US Violence

> Moreover, the important question for the future in this case is not "can it happen again?" Rather, it is "can it be stopped"?
> —David Stannard, *American Holocaust: The Conquest of the New World*

What can be said about a political culture in search of "infinite prosperity" that is dependent on a perpetual enemy who must always be fought but can never be vanquished? The United States ranks first in military power, wealth, war-making, murder rates, and incarceration rates. At the time of this writing in the summer of 2008, one in 100 US adults was locked in a cage, and an additional 2 percent were under the direct supervision of the criminal justice system. While the vast majority of people in custody did not kill or violently harm anybody, the centrality of violence to all aspects of US life helps explain the continuum from policing and prisons to war. Rather than rehearse well-known critical histories of stolen land, stolen labor, gender domination, and iron-fisted capital expansion, this essay uses them to historicize current events. It constructs a series of scenes from various periods that, in sum, are designed to demonstrate the persistence and convergence of patterns and systems. The resulting narrative arc is more cumulative than teleological, even though I believe with all my heart there's an end to violence in both senses of "end": violence produces power, which under the grow-or-die culture of capitalism seems like a slightly erratic expression of self-interest;

but violence does not produce *all* power, which means perhaps that its effectiveness might come to a finish.

Southern Louisiana: Armed White Men

The violence wrought by Hurricane Katrina in September 2005 focused singularly shocked global attention on the naked, official, and organized depth of US racism. A global chorus—including many residents of the United States—insisted they had not really known how bad it still is to be poor and of color in the richest and most militarily powerful nation-state in the history of the world. The views of dead Black people floating in the floodwater and living Black people huddled on roofs or in rowboats, or crammed into the hold of a troop transport ship in dry-dock, or into the vastness of the Sugar Bowl football stadium, either taught or reminded the world what it used to know about the United States: it is difficult and dangerous to be Black in this country. One particularly outstanding image, shot on both still and motion film from hovering helicopters, demonstrated in stark terms how the disaster was—and remains—a political rather than natural phenomenon. Picture: a line of armed white men pointing their Winchester rifles at a group of mostly Black people to keep them from walking across an interstate highway bridge from New Orleans onto the dryer ground of neighboring Gretna. Professional and amateur pundits marveled at this scene's explicitness. OK, they reasoned, perhaps unorganized neglect had allowed the levees to crumble, and perhaps the cumulative effects of flooding Black neighborhoods to save white ones during previous hurricanes and floods stretching back across the century had increased the vulnerability of those locations. But how could anybody explain officers of the law stopping, rather than helping, people in obvious danger of dying? What is the continuity that produces and exploits group-differentiated vulnerability to premature death so casually, without fear of political consequence or moral shame?

Armed white men of Gretna figured in the media a century earlier, when a ready-to-lynch mob hit the streets one afternoon in the year 1900. A New Orleans newspaper account of the hunt concluded: "The shots brought out almost everybody —white—in town, and though there was nothing to show for the exciting work, except the arrest of the Negro, who doesn't answer the description of the man wanted, Gretna's male population had its little fun and felt amply repaid for all the trouble it was put to, and all the ammunition it wasted."[1] This was a story of a nonlynching (although the "man wanted" and others were slain that day) during the long period of Jim Crow rule committed to destroying Black self-determination. Had the 1900 Gretna gang caught its quarry everybody would still have had "fun"—and used even more ammunition, since one favorite pastime of lynchers was to empty their Winchesters into the victim's *dead* body, to watch the bullets destroy whatever human form remained after burning, cutting, tying, dragging, flaying, disemboweling, dismembering had, in Ida B. Wells's words, "hurled men [and women] into eternity on supposition."[2]

Wells, whose *On Lynchings* was first published in 1892, used the pulpits of international organizations and the press to argue precisely how lynching combined the forces of both violence and ideology—or coercion and consent—to produce and consolidate power. She showed that this combination particularly provided the capacity to stifle association and competition, minimize ownership and independence of thought and action, and therefore guarantee the extraction from Black communities of cheap labor (including sex) and profits from the sale of consumer goods. Her aim was not only to bear witness to the fact

---

1 Ida B. Wells-Barnett, *On Lynchings*, Amherst: Humanity Books, 2002.

2 Wells-Barnett, *On Lynchings*, 48, 53.

of each event—that someone died or nearly died—but also to testify to its context, to trace out the event's underlying or true cause. To achieve her end, she examined not only what people did, but also how the stories of their actions were narrated and used. Her exposition and analysis demonstrated the role of lynching in renovating racist hierarchy, gender subordination, and regional accumulation strategies. To do all this hard work every lynching was exemplary, which means it wasn't quick. Lynch mobs did not just take off after somebody with the intent of killing them extralegally—albeit in most cases with the sanction of sworn state agents from sheriffs to governors to juries. Lynching was public torture, and both press and posse elites encouraged "everybody—white" to get in on the fun. Mobs thrilled to participate in the victim's slow death, to hear agonized cries for pity and smell roasting human flesh, to shoot dead bodies to smithereens, to keep body parts—ears, penises, breasts, testicles, charred bones—as souvenirs, and to read detailed descriptions of torture in the newspapers. Mobs South, North, and West could usually count on the press to explain away the kidnapping, torture, and murder by invoking the naturalness of human sacrifice—particularly through the repetitive ascription of subhumanity to the victim—and thereby to vindicate the torturers ("everybody—white") via the contradictory claim of supremacy.

If "everybody—white" in Gretna were also the "males" of Gretna, their violence ("fun"—in other words, its distance from "criminality") cannot be legitimated in the same way for all males. But that's not an end but a beginning, because a dynamic society in which the victors present themselves as the pattern of human nature (in which *homo economicus* strips off his bourgeois haberdashery and becomes imperially naked human nature in action), invites mighty struggles to establish who counts as masculine. Moreover, Ida Wells spelled out clearly that the "usual crime" of rape pinned on lynch victims was a fiction, a lie known by everybody in the South.

By publishing the open secret that white women had consensual, intimate, illegal sex with Black men, Wells dared name, in black-and-white, a persistent weakness in the hierarchy of entitlements and exclusions organizing white supremacy. People then and now think race is natural because of the biology of reproduction, even though the biology of reproduction proves race is made of the social and political meanings assigned to it. And to complicate the issue, sex is not reproduction, while reproduction is always differentiation.

That's a lot to keep under control, and torture helped to perpetuate the normative view that there *should be* control. Thus, it made no difference that most of the people tortured did not have illegal sex, consensually or not, with anybody. The convolution here is indicative of the paroxysms of thought and argument that stunningly establish a threshold of sanctioned torture (should nonconsensual sex be so punished?) and thereby evade the question of how "criminality" is naturalized by presenting it as the origin of the explosive horror of violence (the illegal sex) that then must be fought with the explosive horror of violence (the torture and lynching). Enshrouding this necessary convolution are the constantly renovated gender relations that give coherence to the rhetoric of vulnerability and perpetration. The rape of women of color, and the pervasiveness of domestic violence in all kinds of households, speak both to the gendered hierarchy of racism and to the notion that masculinity is constituted through differentially legitimated force. Thus, the spasmodically systematic application of violence to secure material and ideological domination over "infinite prosperity" is a consistent practice of, rather than a rude eruption in, everyday life.

Representatives of and advocates for Black and poor people doomed, displaced, or disappeared in the 2005 events in Gretna and New Orleans followed in Wells's footsteps and carried grievances and demands for remedy before international bodies. When the United States showed up for its regularly scheduled interview at the United Nations Human Rights Commission in Geneva in 2006, commissioners asked questions about the usually suspect aspects of US life: Why are there so many poor people? Why are there so many prisoners? Why does racism persist in what Wells termed "the organized life of the country"?[3] And in particular, why hasn't the devastation that slammed Black and poor communities where the Mississippi flows into the Gulf of Mexico been redressed?

Members of the Human Rights Commission struggled to understand how the United States could be lax in living up to the terms of treaties that it had helped to write,[4] but even though Article VI of the US Constitution specifies that Treaties are part of "the supreme Law of the Land," Native Americans do not puzzle over the question that (perhaps just for show) seemed to mystify the Geneva commissioners. The United States has in fact consistently broken every treaty ever written with indigenous peoples, a habit of disregard unmodulated by a single wrinkle of official remorse, much less by redress for the slash-and-burn movement of white people across North America, from Virginia and New England in the seventeenth century, through coast-to-coast horrors of extermination committed in the name of God, lawgiving, freedom, and accumulation. Puritans described the screams of Indians being burned alive in torched villages as "God laughing at his enemies."[5] Indian-killers wore the body parts of those they had killed as jewelry and made other useful and decorative objects from human remains. Through the violent dialectics of murder, dislocation, and disease, more than 95 percent of indigenous Americans were hurled into eternity within the first few generations after contact with European

---

3 Wells-Barnett, *On Lynchings*, 48.
4 Reverend Daniel Buford, Untitled report, CITY: People's Institute for Survival and Beyond, 2006.
5 Michael Mann, *The Dark Side of Democracy: Explaining Ethnic Cleansing*, Cambridge: Cambridge University Press, 2005, 84.

colonizers.[6] The rest were removed, relocated, or "terminated"—an astonishing word, meant to describe dispersal of people from reservations to cities. Weapons of various types, constantly improved to become like the rifles wielded in Gretna in 1900 and again in 2005, enforced indigenous agreement to treaties that consigned first-nation peoples to places and lifeways not their own, the alternative being straightforward extermination.

Southern New England: The Military-Industrial Complex

I was born and raised in New Haven, Connecticut, a small city dominated at first by tightfisted Puritans but then, over the centuries, shaped by Native Americans (many of whom passed as, or into, white or Black), free Black people, southern and eastern Europeans, and Puerto Ricans, Dominicans, and most lately Chicana/os and Mexicans. It became a Catholic city with a significant Jewish population sometime in the early twentieth century, during the height of the biggest immigration boom, in absolute numbers, in the history of the United States. New Haven was ruled, first overtly and then behind-the-scenes, by WASPs, until they didn't care about it anymore, when it ceased being a prosperous polity around 1980. The principle of "dispersed inequality" that Robert Dahl famously and erroneously concluded in 1957 would be the future of the US multiethnic republic appeared to work well enough to warrant his book on New Haven politics during the post–World War II period, when the Elm City's two principal products of economic activity, guns and students, were being turned out in high quality and at high cost. But when things started to get bad, in New Haven and throughout the United States, Dahl wisely repudiated his signature concept (even though US-trained political

6 David Stannard, *American Holocaust: The Conquest of the New World*, Oxford: Oxford University Press, 1992, ix–x.

science doctoral candidates must, to this day, commit its error to heart).

Every New Haven schoolchild of the long twentieth century learned about the political and material marvels achieved by the white men whose names mark many of the city's major streets: Judges Goffe, Dixwell, and Whalley, who signed the death warrant for Charles I and fled to New Haven when Charles II took the throne; Eli Whitney, interchangeable parts innovator, wartime profiteer, and cotton gin engineer; and Oliver Fisher Winchester, developer and manufacturer of the repeating rifle—the gun that "won" the west. Youngsters toured their monuments, reported to each other on their accomplishments, and sang and danced their praise in dead-serious amateur musicals performed for elected and other elites.

Killing kings, mass-producing weapons, and framing accumulation as an inalienable right coalesced into white supremacy —the modern theory and practice that explains how, over the past few centuries, authority devolved from the person of the monarch to one, and only one, sovereign race. That race's divinely conferred and energetically exercised freedom to have, to take, to kill, to rule, and to judge when any of these actions is right or wrong—individually and in the aggregate—kept institutions like Winchester's arms factory and Yale University humming day and night.

Killing *somebody* has always been on the American agenda, and avoiding being caught in American crosshairs an ontological priority. For example, the lessons white supremacists violently offered to Black GIs after World War I can be summed up in a couple of imperatives: expect nothing, and don't wear your uniform. Lynching, which had minimally abated during the United States's brief engagement in the war, heated up in the aftermath. There is always an increase in murder in the United States after the country goes off to war and wins—just as there is always a sudden spike after executions—which together form strong evidence that the "state models behavior for the polity."[7] The bloody "red summer" of 1919, best known for the Palmer raids against Leftist political and labor organizers, was simultaneously a time of intense racist lynching in the name of white supremacy. The class and race wars were related rather than coincidental. Not surprisingly, J. Edgar Hoover began his rise to power as the chief engineer of capitalist white suprem-acist policing by serving as technocratic overseer for many of the 1919 actions. He was still around as head of the FBI when, over an eighteen-month period in 1969–71, federal and local police destroyed the Black Panther Party. In 1969, no less than in 1919, rhetoric about violence and violent action brought into view a perpetual enemy who must always be fought but can never be vanquished, presented as simultaneously criminal (acting outside the law) and alien (not belonging to the polity).

But when Black GIs came back after World War II, they were not about to "expect nothing" or hide their uniforms in the bottom of a trunk. Having heard from wives and fathers, sisters and friends, about the work radicals were doing stateside to advance the double-victory cause—the fight against US racism as part of the fight against fascism—many decided to fight to get well-paying blue-collar jobs in factories. In New Haven, it was making guns. Winchester's was the biggest factory in the New England Gunbelt, and the rifles used to kill indigenous people were still being produced long after the theft of the continent had been completed. Winchester's became the place where Black men went to work after doing their two or three or four years in the armed service—"protecting" Berlin, South Korea, Okinawa, Thailand, Laos, South Vietnam. They knew how to shoot. They worked overtime on the assembly line. The wives worked at Yale in low-paying jobs. Their children sang and danced: when they were not rehearsing "Jump Jim Crow" they warbled about superior inventions and modern points of view.

---

7   D. Archer and R. Gartner, *Violence and Crime in Cross-National Perspective*, New Haven, CT: Yale University Press, 1984.

The modern point of view that sustained the social order was the relentless industrialization of killing, requiring fewer exertions of human physical and mental strength per person hurled into eternity. This was the military-industrial complex: the set of workers, intellectuals, bosses, boosters, places, materials, relationships, ideas, and political-economic capacity to organize these factors of production into the machinery of death. Eventually, President General Dwight David Eisenhower got nervous enough about the military-industrial complex to give it its name. He revered war; he loved capitalism. But he did not like how war-making and profit-making had become so thoroughly intermeshed during the Cold War that, he argued, both entrepreneurial innovation and industrial policy would be shaped (and perhaps squeezed) by their might. His anxiety was about 185 years too late, though perhaps it is never too late to say you're sorry. The United States has never had an industrial policy other than the one cohering around warfare, although it became most fully operationalized with the establishment of the Pentagon and consolidated power of the Department of Defense's many constituents in the post-1945 era.

Winchester's New Haven arms factory was taken over by the Olin-Mathieson Corporation in 1963. After an employee buyout to forestall the factory's closure in 1981 failed, the factory was first acquired by a French holding company, then sold to a Belgian arms-making cartel. By the time the factory was completely shut down in 2006, prosperity had long since exited the city—along with nearly 25 percent of its population. What was left in its wake were poor Black and brown people, a spatially segregated arc of extremely well-to-do white households, and a shrunken middle-income stratum struggling to make public schools and services respond as they had in the earlier period. As has been the case across the United States, especially in places where wide gaps between rich and poor coincided with declining local economies, criminalization became the preferred public response to the problems created by poverty. Young people from households which had been supported by guns produced and exported to kill other people's children now got their hands on imported guns to kill neighbors, family, and friends. Mostly, however, they were busy being poor.

The expansion of criminalization is always explained away by reference to a secular rise in violent activity—rape, murder, child molestation are the unholy trinity. Highly rationalized, interpersonal violence did not account for the kinds of laws and techniques used to lock people up. But it served as an excuse, throughout the United States, to shift infrastructural investment from schools and hospitals to jails and prisons. The same family that bought and later dumped Winchester funds the Olin Foundation, which is among the principal sponsors of intellectual hacks who churn out racist reports and soundbites proving that prison expansion is good for society. The war against the poor has thus oscillated between modes of incorporation (a job in a gun factory or a cot in a cage) that maintain the central force of racial capitalism.

From the Greyhound Station to Abu Ghraib: Prisons as Manifest Destiny

"Criminal" has long been on the rise in the lexicon of putatively transparent or self-explanatory terms—like race or gender —used to designate fundamental (whether fixed or mutable) differences between kinds of people. Ida B. Wells saw the active connection between race-making and outlaw-making when she wrote: "To lynch for a certain crime not only concedes the right to lynch any person for any crime but it is in a fair way to stamp us a race of rapists and desperadoes."[8] The first public infrastructural accomplishment in post-Katrina New

---

8 Wells-Barnett, *On Lynching*, 41.

Orleans was to convert the city's Greyhound station into a jail; Burl Cain, the warden of the notorious Angola State prison —a post–Civil War plantation where 85 percent of prisoners are Black and an equal percentage serve sentences for the rest of their natural lives—was put in charge. In other words, the elites didn't start by burying the dead or feeding the living, but they did close a port—the bus station—in order to lock up as many as possible whose exit from the city had not yet been accomplished through dispersal or death. Of all sites, the bus station! In the United States buses are symbolic of working-class mobility, and also—especially in the South—of the struggle, organized during the height of the long twentieth-century civil rights movement, to desegregate transportation no less than schools.

The conversion of the bus station into a jail occurred not long after Gretna's police blocked the public bridge, whose very existence symbolized the disinvestment in city centers in favor of the suburbanization of the 1950s and 1960s. The failed levees of New Orleans themselves were, in their disintegration, symbolic not simply of urban abandonment but rather of a recalibration of (as opposed to a wholesale withdrawal from) the wealth-producing urban landscapes of the Big Easy, as New Orleans is familiarly called.

In the twenty-five or so years leading up to Katrina, a massive expansion of prisons and criminalization spread across the United States, driven by different, but connected, processes of displacement, abandonment, and control. As was the case with kidnapped African labor and stolen indigenous land, a completely involuntary migration—this time around, via conviction and incarceration—has once again resulted in the mysterious disappearance of millions of people. This ongoing disappearance is apparently not fully grasped, even in its accomplishment, to judge from the calmness with which most people in the United States of all races receive the news that one out of every 100 of the country's adults is locked up in a prison or jail.

The rise of the cage as a large-scale, all-purpose solution to problems is a relatively recent phenomenon in world history. Modern prisons were born and grew up with the United States, as impersonal but individualized sites of large-scale social control, in the long historical turn marked by the consolidation of the bourgeois nation-state as the world's fundamental political-economic unit, the normalization of capitalism, and the development of racist science and philosophy to explain it all. Although the reformist purpose of prisons was to end bodily torture, in the United States prison did not replace torture but rather complemented its role in securing social order. In the case of slavery, prison was beside the point: there was no purpose in locking up a tool with life in it, while there was plenty of purposefulness in demonstrating to that and other living tools the imminence of premature death as the likeliest respite from endless suffering.[9] And in the case of land theft, there was no point in locking people up at public expense when those indigenous people who had not been slaughtered could be deported to reservations to fend for themselves. But what of others?

By the late 1840s, when various US political factions were debating the merits of permanently grabbing part or all of Mexico, the most clear-eyed proponents of "Manifest Destiny" hesitated at the prospect of bringing into the union millions of Mexicans who, whatever they were, were not white. Supremacists claimed they had coaxed from (rather than forced into) the landscape a set of nearly identical, locally controlled governmental institutions run by enfranchised white men. They were determined to maintain the absolute dominion of the sovereign race. Thus, the anxiety was not just about having more not-white folks on US territory but about dealing with the problem of the vote—itself symbolic of their material delusion concerning local governance. If the Mexican-become-American

---

9   Saidiya V. Hartman, *Scenes of Subjection: Terror, Slavery, and Self-Making in Nineteenth-Century America*, Oxford: Oxford University Press, 1997.

men voted, then what of the union of free white men? The master-race republic sought to expand its wealth without diluting its distribution scheme. As we have seen, in the post–Civil War period, public torture was pervasively used, even as the modern prison increasingly became part of rural no less than urban landscapes. Jim Crow, then, did not only work to suppress Black people; it was both template and caution for all who were not members of the sovereign race. That century's globalizing contradictions, characterized by indigenous extermination, wars of territorial expansion, socio-spatial segregation, racist science and eugenics, the redrawing of the world's imperial contours, and the spread of democratized blood-and-soil nationalism, coalesced at the time of the 1898 Spanish-American war, and these forces in sum gave both political and theoretical shape to the twentieth century's continuing human-sacrifice rampage.

The end of the nineteenth century was also defined by the development of the modern business corporation and the rise of engineering and a technocratic view of how to manage systems and structures—whether the DuPont Corporation, the city of Los Angeles, or the State of Mississippi. This combination of "what" and "how" formed the basis of "Progressivism"—a movement misunderstood as an opening through which common people might democratically overcome racial capitalism and white-supremacist imperialism. Rather, Progressives developed large-scale complex public and private institutions in order to guarantee the privatized extraction of value from land and other factors of production. As a result, it should not be surprising that Progressivism developed in the South and that Jim Crow was part of its original structure. Under the aegis of Progressivism, prisons became regulated by specialists and segregated by age and gender. This might not sound so bad—except for the fact that before the Progressive period few youngsters and few women were in any prisons anywhere.

Reform, then as now, opened the door to expanding prison under the guise of social improvement. At the same time, in the South the official end to the convict lease system took uncompensated labor (prisoners) out of competition with unemployed free labor; the struggle to end that system was resolved, in racist terms, by the formation of prison plantations for men (mostly Black) so that free workers (profiled white) could be assured of an exclusive right to jobs, whether or not the work actually existed. In the late twentieth and early twenty-first century, prison expansion has proceeded along these two fronts—as the necessary response to "criminality" and as a reform of that response. The disfranchisement of prisoners gave George W. Bush the 2000 election.

The rationality underlying prison growth uses both rhetoric and practices of violence to make mass incarceration seem other than what it is—a machine for producing and exploiting group-differentiated vulnerability to premature death. The intellectuals who have figured out how to exercise racism without naming race have to work extremely hard to realize their goals, and they draw on a template and legacy of thought developed from and for the kinds of wars they imagine the United States is fighting when it sends troops and matériel abroad. War and incarceration are supposed to bring good things to the places destroyed in the name of being saved; the devastation wrought overseas in Iraq and Afghanistan is both prefigured and shadowed by the history and current experience of life in the United States itself. The convergence of theory and technique comes into view in the construction of the perpetual enemy who must always be fought but can never be vanquished.

For the past twenty-five years the militarization of everyday domestic life in the United States is acted out, in full dress, through—for instance—the intensified criminalization of kids, who in California in 1988 were officially named "street terrorists." Another example is the way that people in the United

States have gotten into the habit of wearing photo identification as though it were jewelry. Everyone expects to be stopped, but the expectation of what happens afterward diverges wildly. In such a milieu of battle-readiness and checkpoint-cheeriness it was remarkably easy for the lawyers defending the Los Angeles policemen who beat up Rodney King to argue, in spite of the visual evidence, that King was "in control" of the situation. A millisecond of the globally circulated film of his beating shows King trying to get up as he is kicked and pummeled. This effort made King a violent desperado; and the jury that acquitted the four cops probably would have let them go anyway, because the jurors came from a community of retired police and military and had a narrative of events on which to hang the cops' plea. "Criminality" worked too well to fail in the courtroom.

The 1992 multicultural uprising against the verdict brought forth both spontaneous and systematic radical understandings of the internal racist logic of US institutions. It also gave a boost to the top-down development of legal and other machinery designed to suppress such opposition to racist policing. Although the Los Angeles police chief at the time was run out of his job, he has been replaced by a series of men for whom policing people of color is the number-one priority. (Gretna in 1900 had a "Black detective" to help in that work, just as apartheid South Africa had Black police.) Each has demanded a larger police force, arguing that every time something happens like Rodney King being beaten up, or thirteen-year-old Devin Brown being shot dead because a policeman said he thought the kid, driving a stolen car, was "a drunk" (which King was), the city will go up in flames if there isn't enough police power to keep it under control. They shop their techniques and demands around the world (getting rich as consultants along the way). Like the military, they want to surge. And as with contemporary warfare, they claim that what they do benefits the assaulted as well as the assaulter. The triggerman is safer and the target is precise. However, just as the outcome of what is called "surgical strikes" in the era of increasingly capitalized warfare has meant that more civilians than ever die in each conflict, so it is the case with policing "the war on the streets" at home.

The police and the military also act to guarantee their institutional role in the apparatus and activities of the state. On the one hand, for a nation conceived in the violence of indigenous extermination and chattel slavery, one might think that the governmental agents charged with "defense" and "internal pacification" would have nothing to worry about. But they do have things to worry about—ranging from the technical capacity to capitalize a lot of their individual human labor, to the fact that their opponents work around the clock to abolish policing, prisons, the military, and capitalism. The constant agitation produces constant effort to shape both thought and action, and those in uniform use bodily violence both as rhetorical pretext and as disciplining practice in order to reproduce power.

The torture of prisoners by US military jailers at Abu Ghraib in Iraq in 2004 focused singularly shocked global attention on the naked and official depth of US racism. The revelation of the hidden spectacle that soldiers staged for themselves and the various audiences they sent pictures to occurred a year before Katrina, and in retrospect the similarity of press and pundit reactions to the two outrages is rather compelling evidence of how successfully the production of power through violence works. Once the pictures came to light, one phrase, invoking a physical action, came up several times in English, French, and Spanish language newspapers of varying political persuasions in both the "First" and "Third" worlds: "when Americans look away." I can't tell you whether the phrase emerged in one place and then traveled, or whether it is a phrase commonly used to describe Americans' ADHD,[10] or something else. What does

---

10 Attention deficit hyperactivity disorder—the condition so commonly attributed to children "acting up."

the phrase assume about "Americans" and where they look? Were these newspapers right in assuming the real audience for the hidden spectacle, who happened to stumble onto it, could, as has happened historically, look and then look away—not out of denial, much less pity or shame, but rather with a deep and perhaps empathetic shrug for the *torturer*? The fact of torture consigns the tortured to a category of undifferentiated difference, an alien-ness underscored by religious or citizenship distinctions, but not reducible to them since both religion and citizenship can be changed. This suggests that the torture of prisoners today is about constructing racial categories no less than when white supremacy was being secured a hundred years ago.

Once the evidence of the outrage at Abu Ghraib was paraded before congressional committees (and in art shows inviting "public" comment in elegant books), the perpetrators were plucked out of the "chain of command" and sent to prison. A lot was made of the fact that two or three of them had been stateside prison guards, and so what could one expect? Analytically, one could expect at least some critics to understand that what the guards did in both the United States and Iraq was to help consolidate policing and prisons' institutional dominance. These institutions aspire to the same degree of security for their existence at the state and local level that the Pentagon enjoys at the federal level. This reduces questions of institutional reform to marginal squabbles over cost-benefits and better practices.

Such a devolution of criticism makes reformist reform very powerful in the way that neoliberalism operates.[11] But it is not only the current set of institutions structured in dominance that matter—though they do. The culture of capitalism—not the culture of *consumption* but of *capitalism*—informs all the tendencies laid out in the scenes depicted in this essay. "Grow or die" works hand-in-hand with structural inequality to keep

---

11   *Golden Gulag.*

producing an outcome that people keep being shocked by. And yet, while being shocked, many are also persuaded of the naturalness of the system and are therefore vulnerable to accepting the proposition advanced by the man who coined "manifest destiny" to describe Anglo Saxons' right to control the planet. As Charles Kingsley, the author of *Westward Ho!*, wrote in a letter to a friend in 1849: "It *is* expedient that one man die for the people. One tribe exterminated if need be to save a whole continent. 'Sacrifice of human life?' Prove that it is *human* life."[12]

Abolition Now

In the dream of advocates for people locked up in Guantánamo and other known and unknown US military-controlled prisons around the planet, the prisoners should be brought into the US criminal justice system where they can be charged, face their accusers, and be judged by their peers. This seems unlikely as a remedy for the real problem, which is violence, prisons, and warfare. It also proposes that things will cure things—better buildings (Bush's promise to remedy Abu Ghraib), training sessions (what US professional has not taken a harassment training session in the past two years?), handbooks, and new laws. Yet in regular US prisons and jails, where one out of every 100 US adults lives, torture and terror happen every day. In California every week a prisoner dies from medical neglect of easily treatable maladies. Throughout the United States the households of prison guards, along with police and military, are more likely to experience domestic violence than households whose income is not organized around the willingness to use bodily violence.

---

12 Quoted in Reginald Horsman, *Race and Manifest Destiny: The Origins of American Racial Anglo-Saxonism*, Cambridge, MA: Harvard University Press, 2002, 77.

The proliferation of new prisons in the United States was followed by the proliferation of laws to guarantee their present size. And contemporaneously with domestic prison growth, there has occurred a US-led global production of a criminal class without rights, designed to evade rather than fulfill the terms of treaties—including the global prohibition against torture. The concept of a rightless person is an indirect legacy of the 1857 Dred Scott Supreme Court decision that used race to define who counts as human and therefore who bears human rights. Today the world is full of activists who try to practice human rights as a science, bringing before courts and the "organized life" of the planet claims of injury and demands for redress. Given the power that violence produces, it is perhaps time to pause and consider how the unfinished work of radical abolition might help us in practical as well as theoretical ways to get out of the trap of reformist reform. The violence of torture and official murder, toward the end of stealing labor, land, and reproductive capacity, has driven the history of the United States. If reform within that history is the pattern for change, it can only result in a "changing same." [13]

---

13   LeRoi Jones (Amiri Baraka), "The Changing Same (R&B and New Black Music)," *Black Music*, New York: William Morrow, 1967, 180–211.

PART III

PRISONS, MILITARISM, AND THE ANTI-STATE STATE

9

Globalization and US Prison Growth: From Military Keynesianism to Post-Keynesian Militarism

Ever since Richard M. Nixon's 1968 campaign for president on a "law and order" platform, the United States has been home to a pulsing moral panic over crime and criminality. The "law and order" putsch has produced an increase of 1.4 million people in the prison and jail population since 1982: by the time this essay goes to press [in 1998], there will be nearly 2,000,000 women and men living in cages. But are the key issues underlying carceral expansion "moral" ones—or are they racial, economic, political? And if some combination of the latter, why did "the law" enmesh so many people so quickly, but delay casting its dragnet until almost fifteen years after Nixon's successful bid for the presidency?

California is a case in point. In mid-1996 the State's attorney general, who is responsible for prosecuting all serious and violent crimes, circulated a report showing that the crime rate peaked in 1980 and declined, unevenly but decisively, thereafter. However, since 1982 when the State[1] embarked on the biggest prison construction program in the history of the world, the number in the California Department of Corrections (CDC) prisons rose 400 percent—to 156,000. African Americans and Latinos (primarily Mexican Americans) comprise

---

1 "State" with an uppercase "S" designates a specific political geography or government (such as the State of California); "state" with a lowercase "s" designates the general political-territorial form (the rising prison state) that ranges, in scale, from municipality to nation-state.

two-thirds of the prison population; 7 percent are women of all races. Almost half the prisoners had steady employment, that is, they were working for the same employer for at least one year before arrest, while upwards of 80 percent were, at some time in their case, represented by state-appointed lawyers for the indigent: in short, as a class, convicts are the working or workless poor. At a cost of $280–350 million *each*, California has completed twenty-two new prisons since 1984. The new prisons, plus the state's twelve previously existing facilities, plus four new prisons being planned, plus internal expansions, plus space contracted with public or private providers, will give the system a lockdown capacity of more than 200,000 by 2001, according to data from the California Legislative Analyst's Office and the CDC.

But California's prison expansion must be situated in the political-economic geography of globalization if its full significance is to be understood. A new kind of state is being built on prison foundations in the world's seventh or eighth largest economy. The importance of California is not that it represents the average case of current conditions throughout the United States but, rather, that the State stands in as a plausible future for polities within and outside national borders: California has long served as an activist exemplar that others keenly emulate.

Why Prisons? Dominant and Counter Explanations

The media, government officials, and policy advisers endlessly refer to the moral panic over crime and connect prison growth to public desire for social order. In this explanation, what is pivotal is not the state's definition of crime *per se*, but rather society's condemnation of rampant deviant behavior—thus a moral, not (necessarily) legal, panic. The catapulting of crime to US public anxiety number one, even when unemployment and inflation might have garnered greater worry in the recessions of the early 1980s and the early 1990s, suggests that concerns about social deviance overshadowed other, possibly more immediate issues.

However, by the time the great prison roundups began, crime had started to go down. Mainstream media reported the results of statistics annually gathered and published by the Federal Bureau of Investigation (FBI) and the Bureau of Justice Statistics (BJS). In other words, if the public had indeed demanded crime reduction, the public was already getting what it wanted. State officials could have taken credit for decreasing crime rates without producing more than a million new prison beds. But the beds are there.

Another explanation for the burgeoning prison population is the drug epidemic and the threat to public safety posed by the unrestrained use and trade of illegal substances. Information about the controlling (or most serious) offense[2] of prisoners supports the drug explanation: drug commitments to federal and state prison systems surged 975 percent between 1982 and 1996. Therefore, it is reasonable to conclude that widening use of drugs in the United States in the late 1970s and early 1980s provoked prison expansion. According to this scenario—as news stories, sensational television programs, popular music and movies, and politicians' anecdotes made abundantly clear—communities, especially poor communities of color, would be more deeply decimated by addiction, drug dealing, and gang violence were it not for the restraining force of prisons. The explanation rests on two assumptions: first, that drug use exploded in the 1980s and, second, that the sometimes violent organization of city neighborhoods into gang enclaves was accomplished in order to secure drug markets.

---

2 Prisoners are classified according to their "controlling" or most serious conviction. Thus, the more than 6,500 people in CDC custody for "petty theft with prior" did not commit other, more serious crimes, such as robbery.

In fact, according to the BJS, illegal drug use among all kinds of people throughout the United States declined precipitously, starting in the mid-1970s. Second, although large-scale traffic in legal or illegal goods requires highly organized distribution systems—be they corporations or gangs—not all gangs are in drug trafficking; for example, according to Mike Davis, in Los Angeles, an area of heavy gang and drug concentration, prosecutors in the late 1980s charged only one in four dealers with gang membership.[3]

A third explanation blames structural changes in employment opportunities; these changes have left large numbers of people challenged to find new income sources, and many have turned to what one pundit called "illegal entitlements." In this view, those who commit property crimes—along with those who trade in illegal substances—reasonably account for a substantial portion of the vast increase in prison populations. Controlling offense data for new prisoners support the income-supplementing explanation: the percentage of people in prison for property offenses more than doubled since 1982. But, at the same time, incidents of property crime peaked in 1980; indeed, the decline in property crime pushed down the overall crime rate.

More recently, as both print and electronic media have started again to headline annual federal reports about long-term drops in crime (still falling since 1980) and as elected and appointed officials have started to take credit for the trends, the explanation for bulging prisons centers on the remarkable array of longer and stiffer sentences now doled out for a wide range of behavior that used to be punished differently, if at all. This explanation, tied to but different from the "moral

3   Davis, "Black Are Dealt Out." The low ratio is critical: gang membership designation allows prosecutors to demand longer, fixed sentences for dealers, and local law enforcement throughout California has conducted a census of gang membership so zealously that, in at least one city, according to Mike Davis, the police enumerated more gangsters between the ages of eighteen and twenty-five than were actually resident in their jurisdiction.

panic" explanation, proposes that while social deviance might not have exploded after all, active intolerance pays handsome political dividends. The explanation that new kinds of sentences (which is to say the concerted action of lawmakers) rather than crises in the streets produced the growth in prison is a *post facto* explanation that begs the question. Where did the punitive passion come from in the first place? While all the dominant accounts carry some explanatory power, there is a huge hole at their center. Who is being punished, for what, and to what end? If crime rates peaked before the proliferation of new laws and new cages, what work *does* prison do?

There are two major counter explanations for prison expansion. The first charges racism, especially anti-Black racism. The second focuses on the economic development and profit-generating potential that prisons promise, suggesting that *military* Keynesianism is giving way to, or complemented by, *carceral* Keynesianism. As with the dominant explanations, there is a great deal of truth in these claims. The statistical inversion, by race, of those arrested (70 percent white) to those put in cages (70 percent persons of color) quantitatively indicates that the system punishes different kinds of people differently; qualitatively, the stories of individuals and families caught up in the system graphically illustrate this uneven development. It is also true that communities and industrial sectors are increasingly dependent on prisons for governmental, household, and corporate income. But these explanations do not show us how prison—and the industrialized punishment system that is the heart of the prison-industrial complex—achieved such a central place in structuring the state and shaping the landscape, nor do they show us whether the state is a variation on the Keynesian theme or something new to globalization.

In my view, the expansion of prison constitutes a geographical solution to socioeconomic problems, politically organized by the state which is itself in the process of radical restructuring. This view brings the complexities and contradictions of globalization home, by showing how already-existing social, political, and economic relations constitute the conditions of possibility (but not inevitability) for ways to solve major problems. In the present analysis "major problems" appear, materially and ideologically, as surpluses of finance capital, land, labor, and state capacity that have accumulated from a series of overlapping and interlocking crises stretching across three decades.

The accumulation of surpluses is symptomatic of "globalization." Changes in the forces, relations, and geography of capitalist production during the past thirty years have produced more densely integrated "sovereign" (nation-state) political economies, exemplified by supranational trade regions such as NAFTA and supranational currencies such as the euro. However, interdependence is not a precursor to universal equality. Quite the contrary, as Neil Smith argues, the trend toward equalization rests on a deep foundation of differentiation: if the whole world is available as site or resource for capitalist production, intensive investment in some places to the detriment of others is caused by and produces "uneven development."[4] The disorderly effects of "globalization" are part and parcel of uneven development, and the expansion of prison in the United States is a logical, although by no means necessary, outcome of dynamic unevenness. But if economics lies at the base of the prison system, its growth is a function of politics, not mechanics.

Why 1968? Historicizing Crime, Keynesianism, and Crises

I have said that the "moral panic" underlying prison growth achieved formal US-wide recognition in Nixon's 1968 "law and

---

4 Neil Smith, *Uneven Development: Nature, Capital and the Production of Space*, second ed., New York: Basil Blackwell, 1990.

order" campaign. Mid-sixties radical activism, both spontaneous and organized, successfully produced widespread disorder throughout society. The ascendant right's effort to gain the presidency used the fact of disorder in persuading voters that the incumbents failed to govern. The claim was true insofar as it described objective conditions. But in order to exploit the evidence for political gain, the right had to interpret the turmoil as something it could contain, if elected, using already-existing, unexceptionable capacities: the power to defend the nation against enemies foreign and domestic. And so the contemporary US crime problem was born. The disorder that became "crime" had particular urban and racial qualities, and the collective characteristics of activists (whose relative visibility as enemies was an inverse function of their structural lack of power) defined the face of the individual criminal.

A broad-brush review of some major turning points in political radicalism highlights who became the focus of moral panic. Given that criminalization is most intensely applied to African Americans, it makes sense to start with the Black Power movement. Black Power became a popularly embraced alternative to assimilationist civil-rights struggle in 1964, after the Democratic Party publicly refused to seat the Black Mississippi Freedom Democratic Party (MFDP) at the national convention. The delegation represented women and men who had engaged in deadly struggles with white-power southern elites in order to gain the vote. While antisystemic bullets did not replace reformist ballots with the emergence of Black Power, the MFDP experience convinced many activists who had worked within legal and narrowly (electoral) political systems that tinkering with the racial structure and organizational practices of the US state would not make it something new. In response to the plausible impossibility that Black or other subordinated people could ever sue for equality within the framework of constitutional rights, below-surface militancy popped up all over the landscape.

Until the 1960s, virtually all riots in the United States were battles instigated by white people against people of color, or by public or private police (including militias and vigilantes, also normally white) against organizing workers of all races. But, from the 1965 Los Angeles Watts Riots forward, urban uprising became a means by which Black and other people held court in the streets to condemn police brutality, economic exploitation, and social injustice. Radical Black, Brown, Yellow, and Red Power movements fought the many ways the state organized poor peoples' perpetual dispossession in service to capital.[5] Radical white activists—students, wage workers, welfare rights agitators—added to domestic disorders by aligning with people of color; they also launched autonomous attacks against symbols and strongholds of US capitalism and Euro-American racism and imperialism.

Indeed, growing opposition to the US war in Vietnam and Southeast Asia helped forge one international community of resistance, while an overlapping community, dedicated to anti-colonialism and anti-apartheid on a world scale, found in Black Power a compelling renewal of historical linkages between "First" and "Third World" Pan-African and other liberation struggles. At the same time, students and workers built and defended barricades from Mexico City to Paris: no sooner had the smoke cleared in one place than fires of revolt flared up in another. The more that militant anti-capitalism and international solidarity became everyday features of US anti-racist activism, the more vehemently the state and its avatars responded by, as Allen Feldman puts it, "individualizing disorder" into singular instances of criminality that could then be solved via arrest or state-sanctioned killings rather than fundamental social change.[6] With the state's domestic war-making in mind, I will briefly examine another key aspect of the legendary year.

---

5   The colors refer, respectively, to African, Latino (especially Chicana/o and Puerto Rican), Asian American, and Native American groupings.

6   Feldman, *Formations of Violence*, 109.

Something Else about 1968

If 1967–68 marks the domestic militarist state's contemporary rise, it also marks the end of a long run-up in the rate of profit, signalling the close of the golden age of US capitalism. The golden age started thirty years earlier, when Washington began the massive build-up for World War II. Ironically, as Gregory Hooks has demonstrated,[7] the organizational structures and fiscal powers that had been designed and authorized for New Deal social welfare agencies provided the template for the Pentagon's painstaking transformation from a periodically expanded and contracted Department of War to the largest and most costly bureaucracy of the federal government. The United States has since committed enormous expenditure for the first *permanent* warfare apparatus in the country's pugnacious history.

The wealth produced from warfare spending underwrote the motley welfare agencies that took form during the Great Depression but did not become fully operational until the end of World War II. Indeed, the US welfare state bore the popular tag "military Keynesianism" to denote the centrality of warmaking to socioeconomic security. On the domestic front, while labor achieved moderate protections and entitlements, worker militancy was crushed and fundamental US hierarchies remained intact. The hierarchies map both the structure of labor markets and the socio-spatial control of wealth. Thus, white people fared well compared with people of color, most of whom were deliberately excluded from original legislation; men received automatically what women had to apply for individually, and, normatively, urban, industrial workers secured limited wage and bargaining rights denied household and agricultural field workers.

The military Keynesian or "warfare-welfare" state (to use

---

7 Gregory Hooks, *Forging the Military-Industrial Complex*, Urbana: University of Illinois, 1991.

James O'Connor's term[8]) was first and foremost, then, a safety net for the capital class as a whole in all major areas: collective investment, labor division and control, comparative regional and sectoral advantage, national consumer market integration, and global reach. And, up until 1967–68, the capital class paid handsome protection premiums for such extensive insurance. However, at the same time that Black people were fighting to dismantle US apartheid, large corporations and other capitals, with anxious eyes fixed on the flattening profit-rate curve, began to agitate forcefully and successfully to reduce their contribution to the "social wage." Capital's successful tax revolts, fought out in federal and state legislatures, provoked the decline of military Keynesianism.

Put broadly, the economic project of Keynesianism consisted of investments against the tide, designed to avoid the cumulative effects of downward business cycles by guaranteeing effective demand (via incomes programs, public borrowing strategies, and so forth) during bad times. The social project of Keynesianism, following from the central logic that full employment of resources enhances rather than impedes the production of new wealth, was to extend to workers (unequally, as we have seen) protections against calamity and opportunities for advancement. In sum, Keynesianism was a capitalist project that produced an array of social goods that had not existed under the preceding liberal (or laissez-faire) capitalist state form.

Keynesianism's economic project, severely weakened by capital's tax revolt, encountered its first round of dismantling in the early 1970s, but the social project took the rap for all the anxiety and upheaval that ensued. Part of the postwar civil rights struggle had been to extend eligibility for social welfare rights and programs to those who had been deliberately excluded. The individualization of *this* disorder (from the 1965

---

8   James O'Connor, *The Fiscal Crisis of the State*, New York: St. Martin's, 1973.

Moynihan report on the pathological Black family, through the 1980 Reagan presidential campaign) increasingly starred an unruly African American woman whose putative dependency on the state, rather than a husband, translated into criminality.

Crisis and Surplus

To sum up: there is a moral panic over "crime"—civil disorder, idle youth on the streets, people of color out of control, women and children without husbands and fathers, students who believe it is their job to change the world (not merely to understand it), and political alliances among organizations trying to merge into full-scale movements. In other words, there is a social crisis. And there is also an economic panic—capital disorder, or the profits crisis. These crises collide and combine into the crisis that prison "fixes."

The new state emerging from the crises, and materialized as the integument of the prison-industrial complex, is neither unexpected nor without roots. Rather, the US state (from the local to the national) can claim permanent ideological surplus in the realm of "defense." Indeed, from the genocidal wars against Native Americans to the totalitarian chattel slavery perpetrated on Africans, to colonial expansion, to the obliteration of radical anti-racist and anti-capitalist movements, the annals of US history document a normatively aggressive, crisis-driven state. Its modus operandi for solving crises has been the relentless identification, coercive control, and violent elimination of foreign and domestic enemies.[9]

---

9 Outside the scope of this essay is a discussion of two key themes. One concerns how the United States also built into the legal landscape a notably high tolerance for homicide, by defining "self-defense" so broadly that today the "average American" believes it is human nature to kill over property or insult as well as to remedy greater perceived wrongs; not surprisingly, the case law establishing aggressively violent standards consists exclusively of incidents in which white men killed white men. The law

Crisis and surplus are two sides of the same coin. Within any system of production, the idling, or surplusing, of productive capacities means that the society dependent on that production cannot reproduce itself as it had in the past, to use Stuart Hall's neat summary of Marx.[10] Such inability is the hallmark of crisis, since reproduction, broadly conceived, is the human imperative. Objectively, crises are neither bad nor good, but crises do indicate inevitable change, the outcome of which is determined through struggle. Struggle, like crisis, is a politically neutral word: in this scenario, everyone struggles because they have no alternative.

The economic panic deepened in the early 1970s, at the same time that radical political activists were assassinated, went to prison, disappeared underground, or fled into exile. In 1973, the federal government finished its five-year plan to decouple the dollar from gold and immediately thereafter devalued the dollar, shoving the United States into the 1973–77 global recession. The 1973 wage freeze was prelude to a twenty-five-year decline in ordinary people's real purchasing power, made instantly harsh as workers tried to buy necessities at inflated prices with devalued greenbacks. During the same period, money began its spectacular rise as *the* contemporary commodity (to echo Paget Henry's inflection), and interest brokering displaced productive investment as the means to make money make more of itself.

The mid-1970s recession produced many other kinds of displacements, related to the movement of dollars away from gold and capital away from production. Steep unemployment deepened the effects of high inflation for workers and their families.

---

therefore establishes norms that fix particular relationships among gender, race, citizenship, and power. See Richard Maxwell Brown, *No Duty to Retreat*, Norman: University of Oklahoma Press, 1991. The second key theme concerns violence differentials between nation-states and the role of victorious war-making in modelling civilian behavior in the United States. See Dane Archer and Rosemary Gartner, *Violence and Crime in Cross-National Perspective*, New Haven, CT: Yale University Press, 1984.

10   Stuart Hall et al., *Policing the Crisis*.

Big corporations eliminated jobs and factories in high-wage heavy industries (auto, steel, rubber), decimating entire regions of the country and emptying cities of wealth and people. Even higher unemployment plagued farmworkers and others who labored in rural extractive industries such as timber, fishing, and mining. Landowners' revenues did not keep up with the cost of money for a variety of reasons related to changing production processes and product markets, as well as seemingly "natural" disasters. Defaults displaced both agribusinesses and smaller growers and other kinds of rural producers from their devalued lands, with the effect that land and rural industry ownership sped up the century-long tendency to concentrate.

Urban dwellers left cities, looking for new jobs, for cheaper housing (given the inflated cost of houses and money), or for whiter communities, and suburban residential and industrial districts developed at the same time that city centers crumbled. Those left behind were stuck in space, lacking the social or financial mobility to follow capital, while at the same time international migrants arrived in the United States, pushed and pulled across territory and state by the same forces of equalization and differentiation that were producing the US cataclysm.

The sum of these displacements was socialized, in a negative way, by the state's displacement from its Keynesian job to produce equilibrium from profound imbalances. No central, strategic plan emerged to employ the state's capacities and absorb the national surpluses of finance capital, land, or labor. And why would there be, since the scale at which military Keynesianism operated—that of the nation-state—was approaching political-economic obsolescence in the late-twentieth-century round of globalization. Make no mistake: I do not mean "the state" was withering. Quite the contrary, the nation was being "prepped" for global developments by operators firmly ensconced in state institutions, such as the Federal Reserve Bank governors who, as Edwin Dickens argues, powerfully insisted that the state's capacity to discipline labor was politically and economically more important than the state's capacity to guarantee labor a decent share of surplus value.[11] The unabsorbed accumulations from the 1973–77 recession laid the groundwork for additional surpluses idled in the 1981–84 recession and again in 1990–94, as the furious integration of some worlds produced the terrifying disintegration of others.

Dateline California

California passed the trillion (million million) dollar Gross State Product (GSP) mark in 1997, a level nominally equal to the GDP of the entire United States in 1970. However, the wealthy and productive State's family poverty rate more than doubled between 1969 and 1995, rising from 8.4 percent to 17.9 percent of the growing population. Indeed, in 1995, California's national poverty ranking was eighth from the top, in company with historically poor states such as Louisiana, New Mexico, Mississippi, West Virginia, and Kentucky; with rich New York and Texas, where prisons have also expanded significantly, and with the classically bifurcated District of Columbia, which has both the highest per capita income and second highest poverty in the country.

Throughout the golden age of capitalism, California functioned as what Dick Walker calls a "principal engine of US economic growth" and used resources from defense-dependent prosperity to provide state residents with broadening opportunities.[12] An indicator of change to come was the 25 percent

---

11   Edwin Dickens, "The Federal Reserve's low interest rate policy in 1970–1972," *Review of Radical Political Economics*, 28.3 (1996): 115–125.

12   Richard Walker, "California rages against the dying of the light," *New Left Review* I/209 (1995): 42–74.

increase in children's poverty between 1969 and 1979. This abandonment of the least powerful members of society presaged the State's future broadening abdication of responsibility to remedy adversity and inequality. And, in fact, the child poverty rate jumped again, rising 67 percent between 1979 and 1995, to shape the future chances of one in four of the State's kids.

California's phenomenal rise in family and child poverty is a dynamic symptom of the displacements characterizing the 1970s, 1980s, and 1990s recessions—dynamic because the negative effects have compounded even in boom years. The surplusing of California's children goes hand in hand with the accumulation of other surpluses.

Finance capital. California experienced a dual shift in income. First, property income increased as a share of total income, the other principal components of which are wages and salaries. Second, interest income increased as a share of property income, the other components of which are dividends, rent, and profits. Productive capitals in the State started paying for equipment or factory expansion out of retained earnings (profits not paid out to shareholders as dividends). In these circumstances, finance capitals had to scramble for new profit-making opportunities and increasingly looked to money itself, rather than steel, cars, or aircraft, to do the job.

As a category of capital, finance capital is the most mobile, but the actual firms that specialize in matching borrowers with funds operate in particular political-economic geographies.[13] Spatial constraint is abundantly clear in the US realm of public

---

13 There are multi-State and multinational finance capital firms; but, deal by deal, they do their business in places, not in undifferentiated space. No matter how quickly value can be transferred between currencies and polities, each accounting moment occurs in, and by virtue of, a jurisdiction. Thus, when Leeson brought down Barings Bank (which had accumulated much lucre in the nineteenth century, lending money to US cotton plantations worked by slaves), he fled Singapore, not Barings, to evade punishment.

debt: all borrowing done at the State or municipal level is, by federal law, State-regulated. For California firms specializing in public-sector finance, the challenge to find governmental borrowers was further complicated because traditional infra-structural investment (school buildings, highways, and roads) had been deferred during the long 1970s recession, while there-after both State and local officials depleted reserves rather than ask short-tempered, wage-frozen taxpayers to approve new debt obligations. In sum, public-sector financiers had a crisis—growing pools of investable cash but shrinking outlets—that could only be resolved in the political arena, where decisions about the legitimate uses of public debt are made by voters, legislators, and clever interpreters of existing statute.

Land. California's patterns of land use have changed signif-icantly during the past thirty years. Most notably, since 1978 about 100,000 acres per year of irrigated farmland have been taken out of production. The fate of these idled farmlands stands as proxy for rural restructuring in general. The recession of the 1970s overlapped with a drought, huge increases in farm debt (taken on in part to irrigate land), and suburbanization brought on by the combination of white flight and the inability of wage earners of all kinds to afford houses in desirable urban areas.

Agribusinesses of varying sizes were forced out by debt—whether because their commodities were destroyed by early 1980s floods or priced out of global commodity markets due to the then-surging dollar—or quit in anticipation of adversity or an advantageous sale. Indeed, for some owners the surplusing of lands converted into cash because developers bought the farm: portions of inland counties once used almost exclusively for irrigated agriculture were developed into vast residential and commercial areas. However, there was not an acre-for-acre trade-off between farm disinvestment and suburban devel-opment. For other owners, whose lands lay outside the path of development, the surplus constituted crisis, in the form of both "fictitious" costs[14] and real costs (taxes, insurance, maintenance) necessary to maintain an under-producing asset. And finally, for rural monopolies or oligopolies, the crisis consisted of how to maintain unequal relations of power and control in places where increased productivity due to mechanization surplused both marginal land and many many workers, with the rural proletariat, rather than the long-disappeared small farmer, bearing the principal brunt of displacements. Indeed, surplus land and high unemployment can be guides for locating each other because in tandem they indicate that capital has reorganized in, or withdrawn from, an area. Such is the case with large areas of urban California.

Surplus labour. California's restructuring since the early 1970s included the reorganization, or the termination, of many capital-labor relationships that had been hammered out through struggle during the golden age. All kinds of workers experienced profound insecurity, as millions were displaced from jobs and industries by capital flight, by outsourcing, and by mechanization. Racist and nationalist confrontations heightened, driven by the common-sense perception that the state's public and private resources were too scarce to support the growing population and that therefore some people had to go. But actually, people came, as immigrants reconfigured the state's demographic composition. These twin movements of capital and labor produced a growing relative surplus population; workers at the extreme edges or completely outside restructured labor markets.

During most of the 1970s, California's increase in the labor force was roughly commensurate with the increase in available jobs, even though unemployment hit extremely high levels in the recession. But from 1980 onward, employments stopped keeping pace with the labor force—shortly before the number of prisoners started to shoot off the chart. The overall trend

---

14 The decline in the price at which the land might sell, especially compared to the rising price of suburbanizable plots.

is for labor-force growth to exceed employment growth by about 4 percent. The sum of the state's average annual number of unemployed persons, plus the average annual number of prisoners, is about one million. These million constitute the empirical minimum of California's relative surplus population, or surplus labor.

The reorganization of labor markets has expelled from the workforce modestly educated people in the prime of life who once might have gained their wages making and moving things. African American men are first among the dispossessed in this regard, although many kinds of workers are experiencing something close to permanent redundancy. Underemployment and worklessness are higher among men than women of similar demographic profile. The lower a person's income, the more likely she or he is to have been unemployed. In urban space, high unemployment rates correspond to areas with the greatest school dropouts, which in turn map onto areas that industries have abandoned, taking along their own jobs and local jobs dependent on the dollars circulated by the bigger firms. Of course, these dynamics are not simply the residual outcomes of "market forces" but, rather, the predictable results of capital abandonment facilitated by what Michael Tonry calls the State's "malign neglect."[15]

State capacity. As stated earlier, the Keynesian state came under sustained attack from powerful economic and political critics. Marx observed that tax struggle is the oldest form of class struggle. The tax revolt staged by California capitals in the late 1960s was answered by the legendary homeowners' (that is, labor's) tax revolt of 1978. And finally, starting in the early 1980s, the federal government reduced its participation in State and local government funding of social programs, thereby passing along to lower-scale jurisdictions the task of making up for federal tax cuts that had been granted to capitals and

---

15   Michael Tonry, *Malign Neglect: Race, Crime, and Punishment in America*, Oxford and New York: Oxford University Press, 1995.

rich individuals. California was left with the *technical* ability to do all kinds of things: raise money and spend it, pass laws and enforce them. But it lacked the legitimacy to renovate the old military Keynesian projects by, for example, putting inner city and rural youth to work, or expanding and improving educational opportunity, or buying firms that threatened to leave and making them community-owned cooperatives.

In this historical context, old markets for certain fractions of finance capital, land, and labor were dying, while new ones had not yet been born that might absorb the surpluses. For California, the outcomes of tax struggles translated into delegitimation of programs the state might have used to put surpluses back to work, while at the same time the state retained bureaucratic, fiscal, and legal apparatuses from the golden age. In other words, the massive restructuring of the state's tax base in effect surplused the Keynesian state's capacities. However, the state did not disappear, just as surplus workers or land or other idled factors of production do not disappear. Rather, what withered was the state's legitimacy to act as the Keynesian state. The state's crisis, then, was also a crisis for persons whose rights and entitlements would be surplused from the state: how absolutely would they be abandoned, and would their regulation take new forms?

The postwar pragmatic care once unevenly bestowed on labor was transferred, with an icing of solicitude, to capital. The state at all levels focused on capital's needs, particularly on how to minimize impediments and maximize opportunities for capital recruitment and retention. However, having abandoned the Keynesian full employment/aggregate guarantee approach to downturns, the power bloc that emerged from the 1980s onward faced the political problem of how to carry out its agenda—how, in other words, to go about its post-Keynesian state-building project in order to retain and reproduce victories. Capital might be the object of desire, but voters mattered. The new bloc, having achieved power under crisis conditions, consolidated around a popular anticrime campaign that revived Richard Nixon's successful law-and-order pitch. Thus, the state rebuilt itself by building prisons fashioned from surpluses that the emergent post–golden age political economy was not absorbing in other ways.

The Prison Fix

A final blow to "golden age" activism was the end of prisoners' rights movements. In concert with their counterparts elsewhere, California's radical prisoners framed their activism in terms of their economic, political, and racial lack of power, and challenged the class nature of the state's cage-based social control. But, at the same time, many prisoners fought in federal courts for reform; they used constitutional law to compel the State to improve prison conditions and to stop giving people indeterminate (that is, one-year-to-life) sentences. Federal court-ordered successes formed the basis on which California began to revise the purpose and design of the system. However, by changing its sentencing structure and pledging to remedy overcrowded and decrepit facilities, the State paved the way for expanding, rather than surplusing, its capacity to put people in cages.

The limit to any reform, as Angela Y. Davis and others consistently argue,[16] is the system itself: reform tends to strengthen institutions, especially those geared to social control. At first, California planned simply to replace decrepit facilities with small (500-person) new ones. However, that plan never materialized. Instead, new power blocs (which took office in 1982 using a strategy similar to Nixon's 1968 law-and-order campaign) used the improvement plans as a template for the "megaprisons" that have since been built.

---

16 Angela Y. Davis, *Women, Race, and Class*, New York: Vintage, 1981.

Once the State embarked on the prison construction project, the problem of funding surfaced immediately. In the flush of victory, the newly ensconced post-Keynesian power bloc persuaded voters that if crime was the problem (as electioneers had promised), prison was the solution and therefore voter approval of public debt was the means to the end. Voters did approve debt to start the building program and several rounds thereafter. However, the problem remained that those very voters had given themselves an enormous tax break in recent electoral memory and had since secured their residential perimeters by rejecting broad obligations and only voting for taxes and debt that would improve their exclusive locality. Therefore, State officials (both of the New Right and of the lapsed New Deal sort), guided by entrepreneurial California-based finance capitalists, figured out how to go behind taxpayers' backs. The California Public Works Board, an eminently Keynesian institution, was used to borrow money to build prisons. Previously, the Board's borrowing capacities were used only to raise money for housing, schools, hospitals, and other goods that would pay for themselves from homeowners' mortgage payments, local tax revenues, or fees. Prisons produce no income ... yet. And then they hired a technocrat from the State's welfare agency to run the expanding prison apparatus.

California's new prisons are sited on devalued rural land, most, in fact, on formerly irrigated agricultural acres. The State intended to put all the new prisons in the southern counties (the Southland) that produce nearly 70 percent of prisoners. However, political opposition, led by mothers of actual and potential prisoners, kept the State from putting a prison in Mexican American East Los Angeles. Landowners from the agricultural valleys spied an opportunity to unload sinking assets, and politicians from the area (which serves as the great tie-breaking region between the more "progressive" San Francisco-Oakland area and the conservative Southland) saw advancement if they could deliver the dollars to the agribusiness power brokers. The State bought land sold by big landowners. And the State assured the small, depressed towns now shadowed by prisons that the new, recession-proof, nonpolluting industry would jump-start local redevelopment, but in fact prisons have not produced the jobs or related improvements projected by prison boosters.

The Southland is an enormous area comprising eight of the State's fifty-eight counties. The greatest number of prisoners come from Los Angeles County, where they have been convicted in nearly two out of three cases of property or drug possession offenses. David Grant and his colleagues note that between 1985 and 1990, fully 25 percent of African American men who moved out of Los Angeles County were involuntary migrants in the prison system, as were 10 percent of the Black men who moved into the county.[17] While the percentage of women in prison is relatively small, the rate of increase in the number is actually higher than that for men, with again, drugs as the principal "controlling" offense. The ongoing destruction of postwar labor markets pushes people into new relations of competition, while the dismantling of the welfare state adds new stresses to the everyday life of the working and workless poor. And once in the industrialized punishment system, it is hard to stay out; administrative parole violations are now used so frequently that annually more than half the state's 110,000 parolees go back into cages without being convicted of new crimes.

The State has used its enormous capacity to raise money, buy land, and build and staff prisons. It also makes new laws that guarantee incarceration for more and more kinds of offenses, old and new. In fact, the flurry of law-making caused the California legislature to establish permanent committees (the Committees on Public Safety, or COPS) whose entire charge is

---

17   David M. Grant, Melvin L. Oliver, and Angela D. James, "African Americans: Social and Economic Bifurcation," in *Ethnic Los Angeles*, ed. Roger Waldinger and Mehdi Bozorgmehr, New York: Russell Sage, 1996, 379–413.

to review and recommend new criminal statutes. Nearly two thousand pieces of criminal law have been enacted in the past decade, and legislators from the dwindling Left to the firmly ensconced Right have all taken the lead on some piece of the new social product. Legislated justice micro-manages the courtroom and speeds up convictions and incarcerations (and the death penalty) by deskilling judges who otherwise might render different decisions than those mandated. Thus, the state produces, and is produced by, the industrialized punishment system, which is the core of the prison-industrial complex.

In the Long Run, We're All Dead

As I have already noted, California's State budget has grown since the 1970s, while voters have reduced their participation. An enormous, and growing, portion of revenue flows into the prison system, at a level nearly equal to general fund appropriations for the State's two university systems. One explanation for California's budget expansion is that the underlying conditions leading to the waves of tax revolts on the part of capital, labor, and the federal state have continued to be in flux, and therefore the state's definitive task—maintaining a general balance of power—has required big spending at the State level. This would suggest that the new power bloc's intervention, in the name of a small state apparatus, has not achieved hegemony and therefore, if and when relatively uncontested consent is secured, the State's apparatus might shrink. But an equally plausible explanation is that the new power bloc cannot rejig power in the form of the state with any greater cost efficiency than it has already exhibited. The "big stick" approach used by US capital to discipline labor requires an enormous, expensive industrial bureaucracy, as David Gordon has shown;[18] the

---

18 David Gordon, *Fat and Mean: The Corporate Squeeze of Working*

same appears to be true for the capitalist state in crisis.

How can the big state pay its way? Perhaps by selling off assets, such as public utilities and prisons. Many rightly worry that the privatization of prisons will further the civil deaths of those in custody and present grave dangers that might result in greater numbers of physical deaths and injuries as well. Capitals are, of course, trying to get a foothold in this lucrative market, where 95 percent of US prisons and jails are now publicly owned and operated. Alternatively, all prisoners might well be required to work in the public sector, both to pay their own costs and to make profit for the state, as was the case in prisons of the US South starting at the turn of the twentieth century. In such an eventuality, wide-scale slavery, under the provisions of the Thirteenth Amendment to the US Constitution, could be the big state's answer to tax struggle. We might think of public-sector slavery as the "crime tax," part of the "surplus labour tax," whose freeworld (non-prison) variation is workfare, or the "poverty tax." Thus, we return analytically to the class struggle inherent in tax struggle. But this return takes us to a new place, if we understand from the "surplus labor tax" that prisoners and other dispossessed persons are at the center (rather than under or marginal to) the contradictions by which the system moves.

In sum, military Keynesianism emerged from the profound crises of the Great Depression, when dislocations and reconfigurations of capital, land, labor, and state capacity restructured capital-labor relations and remapped the world, with California, in some key ways, first among first. Military Keynesianism came out of the same objective conditions that had produced Nazism and Fascism. In the current period of globalization, we see the demise of military Keynesianism and its successor militarist state rising on a firm foundation of prisons, peopled by the 2,000,000 and more who represent both the demise of

---

Americans and the Myth of Managerial "Downsizing," New York: Free Press, 1996.

golden-age capitalism and the defeat of alternative societies militantly pursued, throughout the golden age, by those who sought to make impossible the future we live today. But, before we're all dead, alternative global activism, matured by thirty years of mortal lessons, might rise to tear down the sturdy curtain of racism behind which the prison-industrial complex devours working men and women of all kinds.

10

In the Shadow of the Shadow State

> Organized philanthropy is playing a significant role in this age
> of tottering social standards, crumbling religious sanctions, per-
> verse race attitudes, and selfish and ulterior motives.
> —Ira De A. Reid, "Philanthropy and Minorities" (1944)

Even in today's world, Ira Reid's words still ring true, descrip-
tive of a scenario many contemporary social-justice activists
think is unique to our times. Yet, more than sixty years ago
the dimensions of organized philanthropy's "significant role"
in the African American community prompted Reid to write an
incisive analysis in which he noted two things. First, during a
period of about twenty years, both reformist and radical Black
groups had become increasingly dependent on foundation gifts
over membership dues. Second, both donors and recipients
acted on assumptions about each other *and* about the possibility for social change which, regardless of intent, reinforced the
very structures groups had self-organized to dismantle.[1] These
two obstacles—dependency and accommodation—did not
destroy the US midcentury freedom movement; activists took
down US apartheid in its legal form. Freedom was not a gift,
even if donations advanced the work for freedom. Our challenge is to understand these paradoxes in the early twenty-first
century, at a time when the US-led forces of empire, imprisonment, and inequality have even seized the word "freedom,"

---

1   Ira De A. Reid, "Philanthropy and Minorities," *Phylon* 5.3 (1944):
266–70.

using the term's lively resonance to obscure the murderous effects of their global military, political, and economic crusade.

Is there a nonprofit-industrial complex (NPIC)? How did it come into being? How is it powerful? In this essay I will work through these questions rather generally (one might say theoretically) and then illustrate how the mid-twentieth-century history is complicated in ways we can emulate, if not duplicate. And finally, I will offer a few suggestions about how organizations might think about funders and about themselves.[2]

The Nonprofit-Industrial Complex

During the past decade or so, radical thinkers have done a few turns on the term "military-industrial complex." Mike Davis's "prison-industrial complex"[3] was the first to gain wide use, in part because of the groundbreaking 1998 conference and strategy session "Critical Resistance: Beyond the Prison Industrial Complex." It is useful briefly to consider what these "-industrial complexes" consist of, and why they matter, by going back to President Dwight D. Eisenhower's 1961 farewell address to the nation, in which he introduced the concept "military-industrial complex." He warned that the wide-scale and intricate connection between the military and the warfare industry would determine the course of economic development and political decision-making for the country, to the detriment of all other sectors and ideas. His critique seems radical when we remember he was a retired general, an anti-communist

---

2   For explorations of specific instances and opportunities that current grassroots activists can use to strengthen and liberate our work, such that we are able to achieve nonreformist reforms on the road to liberation, see the contributions in *The Revolution Will Not Be Funded*, edited by Incite! Women of Color against Violence. Cambridge, MA: South End Press, 2007.

3   Mike Davis, "Hell Factories in the Fields: A Prison Industrial Complex," *The Nation* (January 1995): 229–34.

(speaking at the height of the Cold War), and an unabashed advocate of capitalism. But he spoke against many powerful tides. As a matter of fact, the United States has never had an industrial policy divorced from its military adventures (from the Revolutionary War forward), and the technical ability to mass-produce many consumer products, from guns to shoes, was initially worked out under lucrative contracts to the US military. However, in the buildup to World War II, and the establishment of the Pentagon in its aftermath, the production, delivery, and training for the use of weapons of mass destruction reconfigured the US intellectual and material landscape through the establishment of military bases, secure weapons research facilities, standing armed forces, military contractors, elected and appointed personnel, academic researchers (in science, languages, and area studies especially), pundits, massive infrastructural development (for example interstate highways), and so forth. Many taken-for-granted technologies, from the Internet to Tang-brand powdered citrus drink, were developed under the aegis of national security. The electoral and economic rise of the southern and western states (the "Sunbelt") ascended via the movement of people and money to those regions to carry out the permanent expansion and perfection of killing people on an industrial scale. In other words, without the military-industrial complex, presidents Nixon, Carter, Reagan, Bush I, Clinton, and Bush II would never have achieved the White House.

When activists started to use the term "prison-industrial complex," they intended to say as much about the intricate connections reshaping the US landscape as was suggested by the term "military-industrial complex." From "tough on communism" to "tough on crime," the consistency between the two complexes lies in how broadly their reach has compromised all sorts of alternative futures. The main point here is not that a few corporations call the shots—they don't—rather an entire realm of social policy and social investment is hostage to the development and perfection of means of mass punishment—from prison to postrelease conditions implicating a wide range of people and places. Some critics of this analytic framework find it weak because the dollar amount that circulates through the prison-industrial complex is not "big" enough to set a broader economic agenda. The criticism is wrong in two different ways: first, the point of the term "prison-industrial complex" is to highlight the devastating effect of industrialized punishment that has hidden, noneconomic as well as measurable dollar costs to governments and households; and second, the term's purpose is to show how a social policy based in coercion and endless punishment destroys communities where prisoners come from and communities where prisons are built. The connection between prisons and the military is both a not-surprising material one (some military firms have become vendors to prison systems, though most beneficiaries of prison and jail spending are individual wage earners—including retired military) and a not-surprising ideological or cultural one —the broad normalization of the belief that the key to safety is aggression.[4]

How does "nonprofit industrial complex" fit into the picture? Both the military- and the prison-industrial complex have reshaped the national landscape and consequently shifted people's understanding of themselves in the world—because norms change along with forms. Both the military- and prison-industrial complexes have led *and* followed other changes. Let's look at the state's role in these complexes. Importantly, part of the work the aggression agencies do is serve as the principal form of legitimacy for the intrigues of people who want to gain or keep state power these days. Why would they even need such cover? They and their ideologues have triumphed

---

4   See Ruth Wilson Gilmore, "Fatal Couplings of Power and Difference," in this volume, 132–153; Omer Bartov, *Murder in Our Midst: The Holocaust, Industrial Killing, and Representation*, New York and Oxford: Oxford University Press, 1996.

in promoting and imposing a view that certain capacities of the state are obstacles to development and thus should be shrunken or otherwise debilitated from playing a central role in everyday economic and social life. But their actions are contrary to their rhetoric. Strangely, then, we are faced with the ascendance of anti-state state actors: people and parties who gain state power by denouncing state power. Once they have achieved an elected or appointed position in government, they have to make what they do seem transparently legitimate, and if budgets are any indication, they spend a lot of money even as they claim they're "shrinking government." Prison, policing, courts, and the military enjoy such legitimacy, and nowadays it seems to many observers as though there was never a time when things were different. Thus, normalization slips into naturalization, and people imagine that locking folks in cages or bombing civilians or sending generation after generation off to kill somebody else's children is all part of "human nature." But, like human nature, everything has a history, and the anti-state state actors have followed a peculiar trajectory to their current locations.

During the past forty years or so, as the Sunbelt secured political domination over the rest of the United States, capitalists of all kinds successfully gained relief from paying heavily into the New Deal/Great Society social wage via taxes on profits. (The "social wage" is another name for tax receipts.) At the same time, they have squeezed workers' pay packets, keeping individual wages for all US workers pretty much flat since 1973, excluding a blip in the late 1990s that did not trickle down to the lowest wage workers but raised higher level salaries. These capitalists and their apologists hid the double squeeze behind their effective rhetorical use of issues such as civil rights and affirmative action to invoke, in the late 1960s and after, the "wages of whiteness"—which any attentive person should have figured wouldn't pay any better than they did at the close of Reconstruction a hundred years earlier.[5] While even white workers did not gain wage increases, the general southern strategy paid off, bringing Nixon to the White House and bringing "the government"—the weak social welfare state—under suspicion. From then until now, the agenda for capitalists and relatively autonomous state actors has been to restructure state agencies that had been designed under the enormous emergency of the Great Depression (the New Deal) and its aftermath (loosely, the Great Society) to promote the general welfare.

While neoconservatives and neoliberals diverge in their political ideals, they share certain convictions about the narrow legitimacy of the public sector in the conduct of everyday life, despite the US constitutional admonition that the government *should* "promote the general welfare." For them, wide-scale protections from calamity and opportunities for advancement should not be a public good centrally organized to benefit everyone who is eligible. Anti-state state actors come from both camps and insist that the withdrawal of the state from certain areas of social welfare provision will enhance rather than destroy the lives of those abandoned. Lapsed New Deal Democrat Patrick Moynihan called it "benign neglect," while Reagan heir George H. W. Bush called it "a thousand points of light." In this view, the first line of defense is the market, which solves most problems efficiently, and because the market is unfettered, fairness results from universal access to the same ("perfect") information individuals, households, and firms use to make self-interested decisions. And where the market fails, the voluntary, nonprofit sector can pick up any stray pieces because the extent to which extra economic values (such as kindness or generosity or decency) come into play is the extent to which abandonment produces its own socially strengthening

---

5 W. E. B. Du Bois, *Black Reconstruction in America, 1860–1880*, New York: Atheneum, 1992 [1935]; David Roediger, *The Wages of Whiteness*, New York: Verso, 1991.

rewards. That's their ideal: a frightening willingness to engage in human sacrifice while calling it something else.

In fact, for so large and varied a society as the United States, abandonment is far too complicated for any single ideologue, party, or election cycle to achieve; experience shows abandonment takes a long time and produces new agencies and structures that replace, supplement, or even duplicate old institutions. Many factors contribute to this complexity. One is that large-scale public bureaucracies are hard to take down completely, due to a combination of their initiative and inertia; another is the fear that a sudden and complete suspension of certain kinds of social goods will provoke uprisings and other responses that, while ultimately controllable, come at a political cost. Here's where nonprofits enter the current political economy.

As a "third sector" (neither state nor business), nonprofits have existed in what's now the United States since the mid-seventeenth century, when colonial Harvard College was incorporated. Today there are nearly 2 million nonprofits in the United States, including, along with educational institutions, hospitals, schools, museums, operas, think tanks, foundations, and, at the bottom, some grassroots organizations. While the role of some of these organizations has not changed significantly, we *have* seen increased responsibility on the part of nonprofits to deliver direct services to those in need of them. What also distinguishes the expansion of social-service nonprofits is that increasingly their role is to take responsibility for persons who are in the throes of abandonment rather than responsibility for persons progressing toward full incorporation into the body politic.

Jennifer Wolch developed the term "shadow state" to describe the contemporary rise of a voluntary sector involved in direct social services previously provided by wholly public New Deal/Great Society agencies.[6] Legislatures and executive

---

6 Jennifer Wolch, *The Shadow State: Government and the Voluntary Sector in Transition*, New York: The Foundation Center, 1990.

branches transformed bureaucracies basically into policing bodies, whose role became to oversee service provision rather than to provide it themselves. This abandonment provoked a response among organizations that advocated on behalf of certain categories of state clients: the elderly, mothers, children, and so forth.[7] It also encouraged the formation of new groups that, lacking an advocacy past, were designed solely to get contracts and the jobs that came with them. To do business with the state, the organizations had to be formally incorporated, so they became nonprofits. Thus, for different reasons, nonprofits stepped up to fill a service void.

The expansion of nonprofit activities structurally linked to public social services was not new, nor could it be said that when public services were on the rise the voluntary sector stayed home. To the contrary, for more than 100 years the relationship between public and voluntary had been a fairly tight one.[8] But for Wolch, the shadow state's specific provenance is the resolution of two historical waves: the unprecedented expansion of government agencies and services (1933–73), followed by an equally wide-scale attempt to undo many of those programs at all levels—federal, state, county, local.[9]

Anti-state state actors welcomed nonprofits under the rhetoric of efficiency (read: meager budgets) and accountability (read: contracts could be pulled if anybody stepped out of line). As a result of these and other pressures, nonprofits providing direct services have become highly professionalized by their relationship with the state. They have had to conform to

---

7   For a thorough analysis of the politics of health, see Jenna M. Loyd, "Freedom's Body: Radical Health Activism in Los Angeles, 1963–1978," Ph.D. dissertation, University of California, Berkeley, 2005.

8   See Reid, "Philanthropy and Minorities." See also Jennifer Klein, *For All These Rights: Business, Labor, and the Shaping of America's Public-Private Welfare State*, Princeton, NJ: Princeton University Press, 2003.

9   For a sense of the global dimension of this growth, see Lester M. Salamon, "The Rise of the Non-profit Sector," *Foreign Affairs* 73.4 (1994): 109–22.

public rules governing public money and have found that being fiduciary agents in some ways trumps their principal desire to comfort and assist those abandoned to their care. They do not want to lose the contracts to provide services because they truly care about clients who otherwise would have nowhere to go; thus, they have been sucked into the world of nonprofit providers, which, like all worlds, has its own jargon, limits (determined by bid and budget cycles and legislative trends), and both formal as well as informal hierarchies. And, generally, the issues they are paid to address have been narrowed to program-specific categories and remedies which make staff— who often have a great understanding of the scale and scope of both individual clients' needs and the needs of society at large —become in their everyday practice technocrats through imposed specialization.[10] The shadow state, then, is real but without significant political clout, forbidden by law to advocate for systemic change, and bound by public rules and nonprofit charters to stick to its mission or get out of business and suffer legal consequences if it strays along the way.

The dramatic proliferation of nonprofits in the 1980s and after also produced a flurry of experts to advise on the creation and management of nonprofits and the relationship of public agencies to nonprofits, further professionalizing the sector. High-profile professors of management, such as Peter F. Drucker, wrote books on the topic, and business schools developed entire curricula devoted to training the nonprofit manager.[11] As had long been the case, every kind of nonprofit from the largest (hospitals and higher education establishments) to the smallest sought out income sources other than public grants and contracts, and "organized philanthropy"

---

10   Robert W. Lake, "Structural Constraints and Pluralist Contradictions in Hazardous Waste Regulation," *Environment and Planning A* 24 (2002): 663–81; Robert W. Lake, "Negotiating Local Autonomy," *Professional Geographer* 13.5 (1994): 423–42.

11   Peter F. Drucker, *Managing the Nonprofit Organization: Principles and Practice*, New York: HarperCollins, 1990.

provided the promise of some independence from the rule-laden and politically erratic public-funding stream for those involved in social welfare activity.

While we bear in mind that foundations are repositories of twice-stolen wealth—*profit* sheltered from *taxes*—that can be retrieved by those who stole it at the opera or the museum, at Harvard or a fine medical facility,[12] it is also true that major foundations have put some resources into different kinds of community projects, and some program officers have brought to their portfolios profound critiques of the status quo and a sense of their own dollar-driven, though board-limited, creative potential. At the same time, the transfer to the baby boomer generation (those born between 1946 and 1964) of what by the year 2035 will be trillions of dollars of inherited wealth began to open the possibility for more varied types of funding schemes that nonprofits might turn to good use as some boomer heirs seek specifically to remedy the stark changes described in these pages.[13] Such initiatives and events encouraged grassroots social justice organizations that otherwise might have continued their work below the Internal Revenue Service and formal-funding radar to incorporate as nonprofits in order to make what they have consistently hoped to be great leaps forward in social justice.[14] In other cases, unincorporated grassroots groups receiving money under the shelter of existing nonprofits have been compelled to formalize their status because auditors have decided that the nonprofits who sponsor them have strayed outside the limits defined by their mission statements.

---

12   Teresa Odenthal, *America's Wealthy and the Future of Foundations,* New York: The Foundation Center, 1987.

13   Lester M. Salamon, "The Non-profit Sector at a Crossroads: The Case of America," *Voluntas: International Journal of Voluntary and Non-profit Organizations* 10.1 (1999): 5–23.

14   Robin Garr, *Reinvesting in America: The Grassroots Movements That Are Feeding the Hungry, Housing the Homeless, and Putting Americans Back to Work,* Reading, MA: Addison-Wesley Press, 1995. See also *Golden Gulag.*

The grassroots groups that have formally joined the third sector are in the shadow of the shadow state. They are not direct service providers but often work with the clients of such organizations as well as with the providers themselves. They generally are not recipients of public funds although occasionally they get government contracts to do work in jails or shelters or other institutions. They have detailed political programs and deep social and economic critiques. Their leadership is well educated in the ways of the world, whatever their level of formal schooling, and they try to pay some staff to promote and proliferate the organization's analysis and activity even if most participants in the group are unpaid volunteers. The government is often the object of their advocacy and their antagonisms—whether because the anti-state state is the source of trouble or the locus for remedy. But the real focus of their energies is ordinary people whom they fervently wish to organize against their own abandonment.

The "nonprofit industrial complex" describes all the dense and intricate connections enumerated in the last few paragraphs, and suggests, as is the case with the military-industrial complex and the prison-industrial complex, that something is amiss. What's wrong is not simply the economic dependencies fostered by this peculiar set of relationships and interests. More important, if forms do indeed shape norms, then what's wrong is that the work people set out to accomplish is vulnerable to becoming mission impossible under the sternly specific funding rubrics and structural prohibitions that situate grassroots groups both in the third sector's entanglements and in the shadow of the shadow state. In particular, the modest amount of money that goes to grassroots groups is mostly restricted to projects rather than core operations.[15] And while the activist

---

15 Robert O. Bothwell, "Philanthropic Funding of Social Change and the Diminution of Progressive Policymaking," *Non-profit Advocacy and the Policy Process: A Seminar Series* 2, Washington, DC: The Urban Institute, 2001, 67–81.

right (which has nonprofits and foundations up the wazoo) regularly attacks the few dollars that go to anti-abandonment organizations, it has loads of funds for core operations; as of the end of the last century, the right had raised more than $1 billion to fund *ideas*.[16] How core can you get? In other words, although we live in revolutionary times, in which the entire landscape of social justice is, or will shortly become, like post-Katrina New Orleans because it has been subject to the same long-term abandonment of infrastructure and other public goods, funders require grassroots organizations to act like secure suburbanites who have one last corner of the yard to plant.

What Is to Be Done?

Let's go back to the mid-twentieth century to think about what kinds of options people employed to make best use of the resources they had at hand. We saw that "organized philanthropy" caused problems even as it also produced opportunities. The dual obstacles to liberation occasioned by the vexed relationship between funders and "minority" organizations—dependency and accommodation—did not destroy the anti-apartheid movement. I suggest that part of what helped secure a better outcome was that Reid[17] and other critics pointed out what kinds of problems had materialized over the course of several decades, and people put their minds and hands to solving the problems without abandoning themselves. Thus, the problems were not absolute impediments, especially insofar as the recognition of them produced the possibility for some organizations—and their funders—to see

---

16 David Callahan, *$1 Billion for Ideas: Conservative Think Tanks in the 1990s*, Washington, DC: National Committee for Responsive Philanthropy, 1999.

17 Reid, "Philanthropy and Minorities."

each other differently and more usefully. More to the point, along the broadly interlocked social-justice front that swept across the country in the mid-century, the committed people took the money and ran. I don't mean they lied or stole, but rather that they figured out how to foster their general activism from all kinds of resources, and they were too afraid of the consequences of stopping to cease what they'd started. They combined flexibility with opportunity in the best sense, working the ever-changing combination toward radical goals. And they did not fool themselves or others into pretending that winning a loss—sticking a plant on a mound of putrid earth in a poisoned and flooded field—was the moral or material equivalent to winning a win. Here are snapshots of four cases that illustrate what I mean. These are not complete histories; those stories have been well written by many and should be read by activists who want to learn from the past in order to remake the future. If people living under the most severe constraints, such as prisoners, can form study groups to learn about the world, then free-world activists have no excuse for ignorance, nor should they rely on funder-designed workshops and training sessions to do what revolutionaries in all times have done on their own.

1949—Pacifist/anarcho-feminist organizing in the San Francisco Bay area. Pacifica Radio formed when a small group of white activists tried to figure out how to use radio for radical ends. They were inspired by radio's potential rather than daunted by its limitations. Their challenge was to make broadcast possible without advertising, because, in their view, commercial sponsorship would always compromise independent expression. To evade capitalist control they became a subscription, or listener-sponsored, organization that also, over time, combined foundation support with the dollars sent in each year from ordinary households. Without a single advertisement from that day until now, they have largely funded themselves from the bottom up.[18] Pacifica became a foundation that developed a small national network, and as it grew from the first station, its complexity made the straightforward goals of the founders a challenge to secure. In the late 1990s, the national board tried to sell off the network's main asset—the 50,000-watt KPFA station—using the then-prevalent logic of nonprofit management to veil their effort to limit independent expressive art and journalism. The fact that such a board came to direct the foundation was an outcome of the pressures to professionalize that all nonprofits have encountered during the period under review. The gargantuan efforts needed to fight back against the board and re-democratize Pacifica's governance forced the organization to confront its internal racial and gendered hierarchies.[19] Thus, a formidable means to amplify radical voices during the midcentury freedom movement developed from the grassroots, and success made it vulnerable to the structural constraints that squeeze even relatively mighty organizations that work today in the shadow of the shadow state.

1955—Urban antiracist activism in the Jim Crow South. In the folktale version, the Montgomery Bus Boycott started when Rosa Parks was too tired to move to the back of the bus. But, of course, we know the boycott was not a spontaneous event. Parks acted as part of a larger organization, and as one of a series of refuseniks who sat in the front of the segregated public from 1943 forward. How did a group of people concentrated in but not exclusively located in Montgomery, Alabama, manage to assault and scale apartheid's wall? The people who organized themselves had short-, medium-, and long-term goals to raise awareness, to involve the masses, and to desegregate the buses as a means to undo other aspects of apartheid. Three key

---

18 Lewis Hill, "The Theory of Listener-Sponsored Radio," *The Quarterly of Film, Radio and Television* 7.2 (Winter 1952): 163–69.

19 Iain A. Boal, draft statement of purpose, Coalition for a Democratic Pacifica, Berkeley, CA, December 29, 1999.

political formations were involved: the Dexter Avenue Baptist Church, the Women's Political Council, and the Montgomery Improvement Association. Each filled a different role, and all three were funded from the bottom up. The Women's Political Council—which comprised grassroots thinkers, including activist-scholars—crafted the plans and maintained a low profile during their execution. The Montgomery Improvement Association organized carpools that ensured boycott participants would be able to get to and from work and not lose their jobs or neglect their households. The Dexter Avenue Church served as a staging ground, and the place from which the principal rhetoric of equality as fairness emerged, in the form of thrilling speeches by the young Martin Luther King Jr. The collaboration by these groups evaded the obstacle of accommodation and worked relatively independently of the major African American organizations that were fighting for the same goal. And while the Dexter Avenue Church had no intention of disappearing, the other two organizations were flexible in their design and intended longevity, with the outcome rather than the organization the purpose for their existence.[20]

1956—Agricultural labor/antiracist activism. A third example is from the Agricultural Workers Organizing Committee (AWOC), a largely Filipino American and Japanese American grouping associated with the Congress of Industrial Organizations. The group began to organize in 1956 with the goal of reviving the type of radical agricultural organizing that had shut down harvests in California's Central Valley in 1933 and nearly succeeded a second time in 1938. They fought a hard battle; both state and federal law forbade farmworkers from organizing, and the *bracero* (or guest worker) program had undermined even illegal field organizing from 1942 onward. One of the techniques used by AWOC to get "buy in" from

---

20   Robin D. G. Kelley, *Race Rebels,* New York: The Free Press, 1996, and Robin D. G. Kelley, *Freedom Dreams,* Boston: Beacon Press, 2003.

workers was to require a large chunk of their meager wages to fund the organization's activities. In this view, when one owns something that one cannot sell—such as membership in an organization—one is more likely to participate in it. While AWOC did not succeed, its funding structure was adopted by César Chávez and Dolores Huerta when they started the United Farm Workers (UFW). Their work began as the *bracero* program ended, and while they still confronted legal sanctions against their work, they had the advantage of workers who, though migrant, were increasingly based in the region on a permanent basis.[21] Their campaigns powerfully combined the language of civil rights with that of labor rights,[22] and when the UFW reached beyond the fields for support they fashioned a variety of ways in which people throughout the United States and beyond could demonstrate solidarity, be it through writing checks, lobbying for wage and safety laws, forming coalitions in support of farmworkers, or refusing to eat grapes and other fruits of exploited labor.[23]

1962—Coffee-table politics. Many are looking for an organizational structure and a resource capability that will somehow be impervious to cooptation. But it is impossible to create a model that the other side cannot figure out. For example, imagine neighborhoods in which women come to have a political understanding of themselves and the world. They go to their neighbors and say, "Hey read this, it changed my life. I'll babysit your kids while you do." In this appealing model, the written works circulate while women care for each other's children and form a cooperative system, which does not have

---

21 Gilmore, *Golden Gulag;* Laura Pulido, *Environmentalism and Economic Justice,* Tucson: University of Arizona Press, 1996.

22 Marshall Ganz, "Resources and Resourcefulness: Strategic Capacity in the Unionization of California Agriculture, 1959–1966," *American Journal of Sociology* 105.4 (2000): 1003–62.

23 Pulido, *Environmentalism and Economic Justice*; Ganz, "Resources and Resourcefulness."

paid staff. Because of what they have learned, they go on to run for school board and lobby legislators, and ultimately exercise huge impacts on local, state, and national elections. Sounds like a great model, right? Yes, it does. It's also the origin of the New Right in California.[24] This is the movement that attempted to put Barry Goldwater in the White House, that put Ronald Reagan in the governor's mansion, Richard Nixon in the White House, and Ronald Reagan in the White House. This is the movement that has done the grassroots work that created the need for the shadow state to rise.

If contemporary grassroots activists are looking for a pure form of doing things, they should stop. There is no organizational structure that the right cannot use for its own purposes. And further, the example of the New Right points out a weakness in contemporary social theory that suggests the realm of "civil society"—which is neither "market" nor "state"—is the place where liberatory politics necessarily unfold. Michael Mann shows how quite the opposite happened in the Nazi takeover of Germany, arguing that a dense civil society formed crucial infrastructure for the party.[25] I argued earlier that "forms create norms," and it might appear that this last section is contradictory. Yes and no. Form does not mean blueprint, but rather the lived relations and imaginative possibilities emanating from those relationships. In a sense, form is a resolutely geographical concept, because it is about making pathways and places rather than searching endlessly for the perfect method and mode.

Grassroots nonprofits should uniformly encourage funders to move away from project-driven portfolios; if the results enjoyed by the activist right are any indication, $1 billion for ideas would go a long way toward regenerating the devastated

---

24 Lisa McGirr, *Suburban Warriors: The Origins of the New American Right*, Princeton, NJ: Princeton University Press, 2002.

25 Michael Mann, *Fascists*, Cambridge, UK: Cambridge University Press, 2004.

landscape of social justice. Funders who want to return their inherited wealth to the communities who produced it should reflect on whether they are building glorious edifices that in the end perpetuate inequality. Reid pointed out the mismatch between the gleaming physical plants that segregated colleges and universities built with foundation support and the weak curricula designed to produce a professional managerial class whose lifework would be to keep their people in check.[26]

Finally, grassroots organizations that labor in the shadow of the shadow state should consider this: that the purpose of the work is to gain liberation, not to guarantee the organization's longevity. In the short run, it seems the work and the organizations are an identity: the staff and pamphlets and projects and ideas gain some traction on this slippery ground because they have a bit of weight. That's true. But it is also the case that when it comes to building social movements, organizations are only as good as the united fronts they bring into being. Lately funders have been very excited by the possibility of groups aligning with unlikely allies. But to create a powerful front, a front with the capacity to change the landscape, it seems that connecting with *likely* allies would be a better use of time and trouble. Remembering that likely allies have all become constricted by mission statements and hostile laws to think in silos rather than expansively, grassroots organizations can be the voices of history and the future to assemble the disparate and sometimes desperate nonprofits who labor in the shadow of the shadow state.

---

26 Cathy Cohen, *Boundaries of Blackness: AIDS and the Breakdown of Black Politics*, Chicago: University of Chicago Press, 1999.

11

The Other California
(with Craig Gilmore)

Someone who one day found herself riding along one of the small east-west highways in California's southern San Joaquin Valley might be excused for thinking she was in the Third World.

Mile after mile of agriculture for export—tree fruits, tomatoes, nuts, melons, mega-dairies, and alfalfa—lines Garces Highway and the numbered roads that cross the Valley. The world's biggest cotton producer, J. G. Boswell, is at the intersection of Whitley Avenue and Highway 43 in Corcoran. The San Joaquin produces more grapes, peaches, tomatoes, nectarines, almonds, and pistachios than anywhere else in the world.

Most of the production takes place on what our visitor would see as plantations—huge plots of land owned by multinational corporations or prosperous families and farmed with state-of-the-art equipment and low-wage workers. She could look across hundreds and hundreds of acres without seeing any homes.

If our visitor stayed until nightfall, she would see another part of the Valley's peculiar landscape—huge facilities whose night lights can be seen for dozens of miles across the flat, mostly dark Valley landscape. These plants that clearly run 24/7, are not food processors or packers. They are prisons holding the strange fruit of California's globalized economy.

California has built twenty-three massive prisons in the last two decades, prisons that hold 4–6,000 people each. The majority of those new prisons are clustered in the southern San

Joaquin—the others scattered across other parts of the state's agricultural, timber, and mining lands.

Over the last ten years or so, small rural communities have organized to fight against the siting of prisons in their towns. The story of how the building of those prisons is part of globalization and how the fight against them relates to other struggles is the subject of this essay.

The Other California

Mr. R, a west Valley resident, put it this way in 1999:

> The other night I was listening to the news on television, and they were talking about the economy, and most notably they were talking about the economy here in California. Things are booming. Unemployment is down. Everything is great. And you know, I wondered how that washed here in Mendota, because in Mendota I feel like we live in the other California.

Mr. R. pointed out that Mendota, like a lot of Valley towns, had been "passed over" in the state's remarkable economic boom of the 1990s. Unemployment for the town's 8,000 residents hovers around 35 percent, and over half the town lives under the poverty line. The town's groundwater is saturated with salts and agrochemicals because of years of irresponsible irrigation and pest control practices in the fields around Mendota, forcing all residents to buy bottled water to drink and cook.

Mendota is not unique. In fact, there are many Valley towns with all these problems and more. Both Earlimart and McFarland, respectively just north and south of the Tulare/Kern County line along Highway 99, have epidemic cancer clusters among their children, caused, it appears, by pesticide exposure —direct spraying on kids in the fields with their parents, pesticide drift into residential neighborhoods and schools, and pesticide residues in the drinking water.

The accumulation of chemical fertilizers and pesticide over decades has poisonously polluted the water and soil. The water table is dropping rapidly as farms and new subdivisions pump more water from the aquifer than scarce rainfall can replenish. And the air quality is as bad as any in the country. Kern, Fresno, and Tulare counties rank as the third, fourth, and fifth worst air nationwide, according to the Environmental Protection Agency.[1]

While the state-wide unemployment rate ran around 5 percent through most of the 1990s, Valley counties averaged 12–16 percent, and towns within those counties suffered rates 2–3 times higher than that—in places as high as 50 percent. But that is not to say there is no wealth in the Central Valley. Fresno and Tulare Counties have ranked #1 and #2 in gross agricultural production worldwide for years, generating billions of dollars in agricultural income yearly. Fresno, Tulare, Kings, and Kern also rank high when assessed for capital investment: as we've noted, it costs a lot in machinery and irrigation to farm these bountiful acres.

In a sense, "globalization" is to urban California what "the farm crisis" is to rural parts of the state. To people in rural communities like Mendota's Mr. R, urban and suburban dwellers are a little late understanding something that's been going on for some time. The centralization of productive agricultural land in fewer and fewer hands, pressure to produce single crops that compete in a world market (even if consumed relatively nearby), a labor system that makes no allowance for needs other than maximizing profit, have defined facts of the state's agricultural economy for decades; and now those pressures are all the more intense.

---

1 For a brief but incisive overview of the Valley's current state, see Gray Brechin, "The Broken Promised Land," *Terrain* 33.2 (Summer 2002).

As farmland ownership becomes increasingly central-ized, one of the less visible casualties are the small towns that served small farmers as places to bank, to shop, to dine out, to get equipment repaired, and to socialize. Fewer farm owners means fewer customers with the income to support those towns. Greater mechanization in the fields means fewer farm workers spending even the little they are paid. The flipside of the farm crisis for these towns has been the emergence of regional shopping centers, financed with national or interna-tional capital and filled with national chains. Locally owned businesses are going under. Already frail, "rural communities" in Clyde Woods's words, "move from a permanent state of crisis toward social and fiscal collapse."[2]

Many farm towns suffering the loss of their business and tax base due to the forces outlined above turn to the state for help. For the last couple of decades, the state has offered prisons.

The Prison-Industrial Complex and Globalization

The counter-revolution of the capitalist entrepreneur today can only operate strictly within the context of an increase in the coercive powers of the state. The "new Right" ideology of *lais-sez-faire* implies as its corollary the extension of new techniques of coercive and state intervention in society at large.[3]

While California's prison-building boom of the last two decades has been what one state administrator called "the biggest prison building program in the history of the world," other US states and other countries are also building prisons at

---

2   Clyde Woods, *Development Arrested: The Blues and Plantation Power in the Mississippi Delta*, New York: Verso, 2000, 271. See also Walter Goldschmidt, *Small Business and the Community: A Study in Central Valley of California on the Effects of Scale in Farm Operations*, Washington, DC: US Government Printing Office, 1946.

3   Toni Negri, *Revolution Retrieved*, London: Red Notes, 1988.

a breakneck pace. That the "free trade" of the globalization era should bring with it massive increases in cages for the unfree is no coincidence.

Throughout the past twenty years [1982–2002] both critics and boosters of the new globalization predicted the demise of the state as a player of any importance. Contrary to the neoliberal propaganda coming from both major US political parties, the state has not withered away. Indeed, in many parts of the world, most notably in the United States, prisons and policing have provided a solid basis on which states are reorganizing themselves to help shape these times.

State budgets don't shrink, but human and environmental care does. The new relations of financing, production, and distribution we call globalization are necessarily also forces

SAN JOAQUIN VALLEY PRISONS

 Prison (13 state operated, 4 Federal, average population: 5,000 prisoners)

 Community Correction Facility (state prisoners, run by corporations or municipalities, average population: 500 prisoners)

• City

10 20 30 40 50 miles

NOTE: Map does not include state camps, juvenile facilities, or municipal jails.

that disorganize previous relations. All that was solid melts before our eyes. Structural adjustment names a wide variety of changes in how states act. As the state withdraws unemployment and health insurance, allowing rents and food prices to be driven up and wages driven down in the name of the free market, it expands policing and prisons.

The "creative destruction" of capital shatters communities whose means of reproducing themselves are poor and fragile due to decades of disinvestment, political disfranchisement, and social-spatial isolation. Capitalism is always changing (or "creating") in order to continue to grow by controlling the mixture of land, finance, materials and machinery, and labor. One sort of innovation involves making new kinds of products (cellphones or genetically modified organisms), or making old products seem new (fancier cars or colorless beer). Another kind of change (the "destruction" part) involves making old or new products under new circumstances. The quest for new circumstances signals that capital will reorganize its participation in the landscape. In some cases, capital's reorganization means capital flight, in which factories move from cities to suburbs, or from closed-shop to anti-union states, or from the United States to the market side of trade barriers in the industrialized world (such as France) or to labor-rich, money-poor Third World *maquiladoras* within free-trade zones. In other cases, capital's reorganization takes the form of more machines and fewer workers in the same place.

We don't have space to argue in detail all the connections between the prison boom and globalization, but there are a few points we'd like our readers to consider.[4]

---

4 For more detailed versions of the relations of prison growth to globalization, see Eve Goldberg and Linda Evans, "The Prison-Industrial Complex and the Global Economy," Oakland, CA: PM Press, 1998; Ruth Wilson Gilmore, "Globalization and US Prison Growth," in this volume, 199–223, and "Race and Globalization," in this volume 107–131; and Julia Sudbury, "Transatlantic Visions: Resisting the Globalisation of Mass Incarceration," *Social Justice* 27: 3 (Fall 2000): 133–49.

First, capital, with some kind of state connivance, has abandoned a generation of workers whose labor is not currently needed, people who are shut out of the kind of work their parents performed, and people (numbering around 2 million in the United States) who are more valuable to the system as prisoners than as workers. If, as Peter Linebaugh points out, "accumulation of capital means accumulation of the proletariat," then capital flight leaves behind it an abandoned, surplus proletariat: a workforce without work.[5] Places that have large numbers of surplused workers—inner cities, California Valley towns—also have surplus land: townscapes made derelict by the changes in the forces and relations of capitalist production outlined in this paragraph.

Second, as the state reinvents itself by developing in ways amenable to capital reorganization, corporations that made billions on projects financed with state debt (bonds) look for ways to maintain those lucrative flows of public money. The firms that designed and built schools, highways, canals, hospitals, and universities from the 1950s to the 1970s, and the banks that put the multimillion-dollar bond deals together to finance that construction, are now designing, building, and financing prisons.[6]

Third, the free flows of capital around the globe depend on the far less free movement of labor. What makes the movement of factories worth the cost is the fact that labor's movement is limited, and that limitation is enforced by policing and prisons. State coercion is also crucial in attempts by local capital (real estate, labor contractors, transport) to attract and retain multinational capital investment by using the local police and military to discipline the local labor force and keep wages as low as possible.

---

5   Peter Linebaugh, *The London Hanged: Crime and Civil Society in Eighteenth Century England*, London: Verso, 2003 [1992], 10.
6   See *Golden Gulag*.

Finally, places whose capacity to reproduce themselves—to feed and house and educate and enjoy themselves—has fallen sharply look desperately for help. Any group of desperate buyers finds sellers knocking soon enough. In California's San Joaquin Valley, where stories of Dust Bowl towns blowing away are still part of family lore among the Valley's Black and white Okie descendants, what's offered are toxic waste dumps, barely regulated power plants, waste-to-energy incinerators, and more prisons.[7]

Stopping Prisons, Reclaiming Place

What the government tries to do is to bring prisons into low-income barrios. They come to our barrios promising us all kinds of things; they tell us we will have employment, that our barrios will prosper.

But our experience tells us that this is not true.
—Juana Gutierrez, Madres del Este de Los Angeles

From Tehachapi to Tonopah, the landscape our alarmed visitor rides through suffers deepening devastations. From the planned nuclear waste dump at Yucca Mountain to the planned Delano II prison, governments and corporations dump toxic projects on the most vulnerable and least visible parts of the country.

In 1983, the California Waste Management Board hired a high-priced Los Angeles public relations firm to study where the state might locate waste incinerators. Cerrill Associates was

---

7 Rural California is not manufacturing running shoes or sportswear because the local agricultural powers don't want any competition in the local labor market. But the common notion that clothing makers have relocated to the global South ignores the explosive growth of Los Angeles as a world-class sweatshop center. It is no shock that LA County, with the highest concentration of hyper-exploited labor in the state, also has among the highest rates of arrest and conviction. Los Angeles provides a textbook example of the relation between policing and labor markets.

asked to study not geology or hydrology, neither air flow patterns nor earthquake faults. Rather, they were asked "to assist in selecting a site that offers the least potential of generating public opposition."

The Cerrill Report suggests that companies target small, rural communities whose residents are low income, older people, or people with only a high school education or less; communities with a high proportion of Catholic residents; and communities whose residents are engaged in resource-extractive industries such as agriculture, mining, and forestry.[8]

It might be coincidence that California's prison-building frenzy began the year Cerrill released its report and that the state's new prison towns match the criteria in that report—rural, poor, Catholic, agricultural, modestly educated.

However, the rural towns targeted for incinerators and prisons have not been so compliant as the Cerrill Report hoped. Resistance has sprung up in town after town, in the manner of urban activism springing from unanticipated kitchens and corners.

In California both the environmental-justice movement and activism to stop prison construction find roots in the work of the Madres del Este de Los Angeles (MELA). In 1985 a group of four women and two men began to organize to stop the state from building a prison in Chicano/Mexicano East Los Angeles. After nine years of organizing, the Madres forced the state to shelve the project. During those nine years, MELA also organized to stop an oil pipeline that was to cut through the barrio and a hazardous waste incinerator targeted for the neighboring town of Vernon.

You know how we did it? Knocking on doors and talking to the people. Telling them, "Join us." Especially women, talking to

---

8   Luke Cole and Sheila Foster, *From the Ground Up: Environmental Racism and the Rise of the Environmental Justice Movement*, New York: New York University Press, 2001, 71.

other women. Sometimes, men don't allow women to become involved in community problems. I would go door-to-door and ask women to come out. Some would. Some would not. Sometimes their husbands would say, "Don't go. That woman is crazy." But in the end even they became crazy, because they joined our marches. They saw the power of our marches and of our victories.[9]

Las Madres organized marches and protests every Monday for nine years, successfully fighting off the state and major oil companies. All evidence shows that the success of Las Madres drove the state to a strictly rural prison-siting strategy.

Towns all over rural California organize and fight back too.[10] What sparks those fights varies slightly from town to town, but like the Mothers of East LA, they begin with a small group, more women than men, wondering how the planned prison will affect their families and communities.

California's standard prison-siting practice follows this scenario. Department of Corrections representatives talk privately and quietly with town officials and leading businesspeople. If the town leaders like what they hear, they work with the state to push through site selection and such public meetings as are required by law. The Golden State's practices aren't unusual; indeed, the Encyclopedia of American Prisons warns that "[o]ne

---

9 Juana Gutierrez, comments during question and answer session at "Joining Forces: Environmental Justice and the Fight Against Prison Expansion," Fresno, CA, February 10, 2001.

10 There is a parallel struggle in the state's urban areas led mostly by the families of those arrested and imprisoned with significant organizational aid from long-time community activists. In Los Angeles, for example, Coalition Against Police Abuse, Mothers ROC, and Families to Amend California's Three Strikes have fought to end the endless roundup, and bring policing under community control. See Ruth Wilson Gilmore, "You Have Dislodged a Boulder," in this volume, 355–409. For more about rural prison siting, see Gilmore, *Golden Gulag*, and Tracy L. Huling, "Prisons as a Growth Industry in Rural America: An Exploratory Discussion of the Effects on Young African American Men in the Inner Cities," prisonpolicy.org.

of the most difficult and potentially adverse events in the site selection process is premature disclosure of a proposed project [a prison] resulting in negative community reaction."

The predictable "negative community reaction" is well founded. Prison peddlers sell their wares as recession-proof, clean industries, whose multimillion dollar payrolls and purchasing can lift any town from the economic doldrums. Most places do not, as a rule, start out by criticizing the ethical implications of basing an economic recovery on holding people in cages for part or all of their lives. Most US residents of all nationalities and races accept the propaganda put forth by elected and appointed governmental officials and all forms of media. Crime (communism) is a problem that can only be solved by prison (war)—even though the evidence shows (1) what counts as crime changes over time, and (2) places with more imprisonment have more of what's called "crime" than places with fewer humans in cages. On top of the moral wrong, it also turns out that prison towns haven't prospered from their new industries.

California's twenty-three new prisons offer prospective prison towns plenty of evidence. A few examples:

Corcoran has two massive prisons holding in sum 11,000 prisoners; the town's free-world population (that is, residents not locked in prisons) has remained fairly stable at just under 9,000 since before the first of the prisons was built in the late 1980s. Before the first prison opened, about 1,000 of Corcoran's residents lived in households whose incomes put them below the poverty line. Ten years later, after the state spent around $1 *billion* in Corcoran for the construction and operating costs of the two prisons, nearly 2,000 people lived beneath the poverty line. When the prison advertised two clerical positions with a starting wage of $17,000, about 800 people lined up waiting for the employment office to open so they could apply.[11]

---

11   Gilmore, *Golden Gulag*, and Mike Lewis, "Economic Lockdown," *Fresno Bee*, 9 January 2000.

Avenal is a town of 12,000, half of whom are in the state prison. The prison uses so much scarce water that the town has none to offer other prospective developers. And the prison's lack of positive effect on the town's retail trade is shown in the fact that sales tax revenues (a measure of local commercial activity) have declined to about 1/3 of what they were before the prison opened.

California built Tehachapi's first prison in the 1930s and substantially expanded it in the mid 1980s. In the decade following expansion, over 700 locally-owned businesses went out of business. The driving force? Big low-price "box stores" like Walmart, and national chains like McDonalds, located in regional malls and small towns, draining re-investment like leeches while providing low wages and no benefits. The low-wage, low-benefit "new jobs" brought in by these chains didn't make up for the jobs lost in destroyed locally owned businesses.

The prison industry works to reduce the risk that local opposition to a new prison can develop. In Tehachapi, the city council announced a new prison hospital project two days before Christmas and scheduled the council vote just two weeks later. In Mendota, the Federal Bureau of Prisons (BOP) published its 1,000-plus page Environmental Impact Statement (EIS), detailing the effects of a planned five-prison complex on the community, only in English. This, despite the fact that 95 percent of the town's 8,000 residents are Chicano, Mexicano, or Central Americanos, and most speak Spanish at home. The BOP held public meetings about the EIS in English without a Spanish translator. There is as much disinformation as information spread through the community, attempting to persuade that the prison will cost locals nothing and will provide jobs, local housing growth, more trade at local businesses, and so on. And finally, some who oppose the prison are threatened with loss of jobs and/or eviction.

While local fights look different from place to place, they have a few features in common.

First is that vital to anti-prison grassroots organizing is what Laura Pulido calls "place-based identities."[12] Such identities can be progressive or reactionary. The shared meaning of a place helps shape the ways that residents describe and understand themselves in the world. Place is a fluid creation of personal and group histories of struggles and work, of investments emotional and financial, of migrations in and out, of culture and change, of births and deaths. When residents ask what a prison means to their community, they are asking among other things what meanings sustain that community now, and what they're willing to fight to maintain or enhance.

A pillar of identity in many rural communities is the sense that the rest of the country neither knows nor cares about their struggles. As a result, many rural folks view with skepticism claims that "prisons are recession-proof, nonpolluting industries." As one Tehachapi activist noted: "When they told us how great the new prison would be for our town, I wondered, if it was that great, why wasn't LA or San Francisco getting it?" After their victory in the late 1990s stopping the proposed prison/hospital, Tehachapi activists took aim at the box stores and other national retail and fast-food chains which swept into town in the wake of prison expansion during the late 1980s.

In Farmersville, a tiny Tulare County town facing a proposal from a private prison company, the city council met opposition from both the local United Farm Workers (UFW) *and* local growers and ranchers—one of the few times that these traditional antagonists organized on the same side of an issue. A UFW march from the union headquarters connected with a

---

12 Laura Pulido's groundbreaking work on environmental justice has been crucial in developing the grassroots movement against prison construction and in developing links to the environmental-justice movement. "Place-based identities" is taken from "Community, Place, and Identity" in J. P. Jones et al., eds., *Thresholds of Feminist Geography*, Lanham, MD: Rowman and Littlefield, 1997. See also her other essays and her great book *Environmentalism and Economic Justice*, Tucson: University of Arizona Press, 1996.

march of high school students coming from the school in front of city hall. Whatever the differences between growers and the UFW, they agreed about the importance of maintaining local agriculture at the core of the town's economy.

Often the question of who's local and who's an outsider takes on great importance. During a public meeting about a proposed prison complex in Orange Cove, speaker after speaker began by establishing his/her link to the town. As in many agricultural towns, local growers live outside the city limits, and many prison boosters portrayed them as "outsiders," despite their having in many cases farmed in Orange Cove for generations. Those of us who come in to help local activists organize are inevitably labeled as "outsiders" as well, a term applied only rarely to the prison bureaucrats or even the national chain stores.

Prison boosters in Orange Cove played up the fact that the local growers were mostly white and mostly resided outside the town limits to suggest that the anti-prison movement was interested mostly in maintaining the low-wage, racially segregated agricultural labor market.

In struggle after struggle, the question of whose town it is comes to the front. Prison development highlights the questions both of who will benefit and who makes decisions—questions of economic justice and local democracy—all of which are framed within concerns about what the nature of life in the community will be or can be. The anti-prison movement strongly resembles the environmental-justice movement, and like it insists that the relations between land use and local democracy are essential. In other words, it is because communities appear to lack the power to resist toxic incinerators or prisons that they get them. And it is because they appear to lack the power to resist mass incarceration that they are arrested and imprisoned.

So, the goal becomes not simply to prevent a prison's siting and building, but through that process to help build local democracy and economic justice. To achieve that goal, activists must move beyond place-based identities toward identification across space, from not-in-my-backyard to not-in-anyone's-backyard. The challenge facing activists is to find the work which can expand senses of place and identity beyond simple localism and move toward a greater understanding of how our lives and our homes are connected globally in numerous ways.

It should be noted that there are competing ideas of how we are connected, and that a variety of political models of globalization compete in rural areas. It appears that organizers using anti-immigrant and racist models have made considerably more headway than the left in much of rural America.[13]

The concentration of prisons in rural areas creates the prospect that local politicians begin to identify incarceration with prosperity (or at least survival). As a result, votes for harsher sentences, less parole, and more behaviors criminalized, are less about public safety than about maintaining growth in the local industry. In rural California, that prospect is already a reality, as the state's powerful prison guards' union works tirelessly at the state and local levels to maintain a steadily increasing flow of new prisoners through control of the state's legislature and of county district attorneys.

Writing about the increasing disparities in income, wealth, and quality of life between rich and poor in the overdeveloped world, A. Sivanandan calls poor areas

> replica[s] of the Third World within the First. And it is that one-third society, asset-stripped of the social and economic infrastructure that give it some sense of worth and some sense of mobility, that provides the breeding ground for fascism.[14]

13 Joel Dyer, *Harvest of Rage: Why Oklahoma City Is Only The Beginning*, Boulder, CO: Westview Press, 1998.

14 A. Sivanandan, "La trahison des clercs," *Race and Class* 37.3 (1996): 65–70.

As rural California towns face their uncertain futures, they see a number of not-so-appetizing options: industrial agriculture, huge prisons, national retailers and food chains. Those fighting prisons find new allies and new alternatives. Central to the alternative vision is that local autonomy and local well-being can be achieved only through identification and alliance with the not-local. Or to put it another way, that globalization, considered as ever-stronger links between people separated by distance and culture, is inevitable. The question before us is what sorts of relations we can establish and who sets the terms for them.

One of the central tenets of our organizing has been to persuade people that security and prosperity won't come as a result of more policing or more imprisonment. Where we can make our case, we stop the growth of the prison-industrial complex in the literal sense of preventing the construction of more cages. Those cages link in an immediate and material way desperately poor urban and rural communities; people from the hyperpoliced poorest urban areas are locked away in rural prisons. That link provides activists a chance to connect life and death, day-to-day struggles in different places, and therefore to make connections among different places.

Conclusion

When we explain with stories and statistics that a new prison won't bring prosperity to a poor town, one question is asked at every meeting. "If prisons don't work, what will?" Our poorest urban neighborhoods and rural towns are ready for an answer to that question. The political challenge facing them and their allies resembles challenges facing peasants and workers in Southern Mexico, coastal Nigeria, Indonesia, or anywhere else people fight to get out from the yoke of globalization. The problem will not be solved by delinking from the rest of the globe, but rather by radically democratic redistribution of control over the material resources needed to maintain and improve their lives.

12

Restating the Obvious
(with Craig Gilmore)

Et puis, comme on trouve toujours plus de moines que de raison.

—Pascal[1]

Introduction

The announcement that fourteen alleged terrorists would be relocated from secret CIA prisons to the military prison at Guantanamo seemed to some a welcome move away from black ops and extraordinary renditions and, however haltingly, toward the rule of law. At the same time, the Bush administration proposed significant changes in court rules in order to allow secret testimony, the use of hearsay, and evidence obtained using so-called alternative interrogation techniques. "There's agreement on the goal," Texas Republican Senator John Cornyn said, "that we continue to comply with our international treaty obligations and all of our domestic laws, but at the same time not tie the hands of our intelligence officials."[2] Many legislators, including some Republicans, balked at the proposed revisions to rules of evidence and the unilateral redefinition of the Geneva Conventions' definition of torture. What

---

[1] "And then, since one always finds more monks than reason." Quoted in a dialogue from Fyodor Dostoevsky, *The Demons*, New York: Vintage, 1995, 61—where Blaise Pascal's original formulation from *Les Provinciales* is slightly altered.—Ed. note.

[2] Kate Zernicke, "White House Drops a Condition on Interrogation Bill," *New York Times*, September 20, 2006, nytimes. com.

ensued has been an extended public flap about whether the current government should be able to change what the state does legitimately—which means, practically and normatively, whether the government should change what the state *is*.

Although this particular public fight may have been extraordinary, significant changes in the state justified by wars—on terror or crime or drugs—have been commonplace throughout US history and have sped up during the last quarter century. Domestically, the war on crime has been changing the state in broad daylight. Let's start with some numbers to give a sense of the raw dimensions of this complex development. Since 1980, the number of people held in custody in the United States has grown tenfold, topping 2.3 million presently. In 1980, about 1 of every 800 people in the United States was in prison or jail; currently [2008] that number is about 1 of 130—not including the thousands held by the US Marshals and Immigration and Customs Enforcement (ICE). During the period of intense growth, which continues as we write, the racial composition of US prisons has changed: although absolute numbers are up across the board, a shrinking *percentage* of prisoners is white and upward of 70 percent are people of color. About 10 percent of prisoners are women of all races. The United States, comprising about 5 percent of the world's population, holds 25 percent of the world's prisoners and more than half the world's wealth.

The case of the Guantanamo 14 offers us a chance to pause and consider how legal protections under the law are not protections *from* the law, a point well illustrated by the unprecedented increase in numbers of people legally held in cages in the United States.

We propose that a key way to understand what the state has become, and a fundamental structure of the expansive neoliberal, or as we call it "anti-state state," is to consider the expanded use of cages as catch-all solutions to social and political problems. What are the ideological and material components of this extraordinary proliferation of cages and the policing, courts, belief systems, and pundits who make them seem so naturally a part of the contemporary landscape? Prisons are symptomatic and emblematic of anti-state state-building, and they are therefore concrete manifestations of a dour future for all insofar as they congeal within both novel and reworked state apparatuses a deadly present for many.

For some, prisons are an aberration, something to be talked away using a set of policy papers, rational alternatives, and lobbying days. For others, the state is a massive but simple cudgel of the corporations who rule the world, fading in importance as corporate power grows. Prisons in this view are simply a means by which public wealth is transferred to private hands. As milieu or tool the state in these views is characterized as rather statically insensate—a type of thinking that has roots in what Stuart Hall dubbed a "low-flying economism," which perpetuates the ideological misdirection neoliberal anti-state statism requires to grow and grow.[3] Following the lead of Stuart Hall et al.'s indispensable *Policing the Crisis*, we wish to raise the vantage point on prisons so that our view takes in the state's tricky, complicated, obvious yet often-caricatured central role in all aspects of the prison political economy.[4] If we follow the details (and not just the money, but that too) we'll see in greater specificity how the anti-state state has arisen and normalized extreme and exceptional relationships. The presumptions guiding popular acclaim for instituting the rule of law in Guantanamo belie a regrettably underdeveloped awareness of what's been happening in the domestic criminal system. There's a good excuse for this: what circulates about the growth in prisons, as we'll discuss below, is quite often more distraction than head-on analysis. As our brief caveat

---

3 Stuart Hall, *The Hard Road to Renewal: Thatcherism and the Crisis of the Left*, London: Verso, 1988.
4 Stuart Hall et al., *Policing the Crisis: Mugging, the State, and Law and Order*, London: Holmes and Meier, 1978.

agitor in the Guantanamo case suggests, and this essay aims to demonstrate, prisons and jails are central indefensible spaces: politically, socially, economically, morally, and ideologically they are what the growing neoliberal state is made of. They're big. They're horrible. They're tentacular. And they're not inevitable.

Stateless World, Hahaha

States matter not simply because of the goal-oriented activities of state officials. They matter because their organizational con-figurations, along with their overall patterns of activity, affect political culture, encourage some kinds of group formation and collective political action (but not others), and make possible the raising of certain political issues (but not others).
—Theda Skocpol, "Bringing the State Back In: Strategies of Analysis in Current Research"

The state is not univocal: the relations between state power, which is in a constant process of formation, and actors, social groups and local communities are highly diverse and complex.
—Béatrice Hibou, "From Privatizing the Economy to Privatizing the State"

A state is a territorially bounded set of relatively specialized institutions that develop and change over time in the gaps and fissures of social conflict, compromise, and cooperation. Analytically, states differ from governments: If states are ideological and institutional capacities that derive their legitimacy and material wherewithal from residents, governments are the animating forces—policies plus personnel—that put state capacities into motion and orchestrate or coerce people in their jurisdictions to conduct their lives according to centrally made and enforced rules. Through the exercise of centralized rulemaking and redistribution, a state's purpose (at whatever scale—municipal, county, national, and so on) is to secure a society's ability to do different kinds of things: such as tax, educate, support, connect, exclude, criminalize, segregate, equalize, make war, and make profits. As such, states interact with individuals and with other types of institutions (for example, religious, familial, corporate, union), while at the same time seeking to maintain, through consent or coercion, supremacy over all other organizational forms in the social order. A key feature of that supremacy lies in the state's singular control over who may commit violence, how, and to what end.

Modern states came into being during the long bloody process of staking out control of the planet's surface. Today's geopolitical structure is the residue of conflict—the material and ideological effects of domination and rebellion characterizing the massive dislocations of slavery, genocide, land theft, colonialism, imperialism, industrialization, urbanization, the Cold War, and capitalism. These conflicts, widely explained and resolved through perpetually redefining insiders and outsiders —and normalizing ways of seeing who is in or out—shaped the central contradictions of modernity, from racism to class struggle.

Indeed, the modern nation-state—organized through fictive and real blood-soil relationships of particular territorial residents ("nations")—consolidated in the late eighteenth century into the fundamental political and economic unit of the Earth's surface. At about the same time, the modern prison arose in the landscape as an easily reproducible, large-scale, impersonal yet individualized institution of total control.[5] The connection between the rise of the nation-state and the rise of the prison is located in the contradiction between mobility and immobility: when the conditions attending on a global system that

---

5 *Golden Gulag*; see also Erving Goffman, "Characteristics of Total Institutions" in Delos Kelly, ed., *Deviant Behavior*, New York: St. Martin's Press, 1984, 464–77.

requires constant motion (that is, capitalism) clash with challenges to maintain order, spatial fixes such as racialization and
criminalization temporarily settle things through complicating
insider-outsider distinctions with additional, rights-differenti-
ated hierarchical schemes.[6]

The racial state is a category of analysis taken up by a
number of theorists following the lead of sociologists Michael
Omi and Howard Winant.[7] The racial state signifies not simply
the rac*ist* state—the Jim Crow or Apartheid state—but, rather,
more generally the way the institutions comprising the state
develop and act, legislatively, juridically, and administratively,
through the establishment, regulation, and differentiation of
racial formations that through assertion as well as ascription (as Koshy argues) themselves change over time.[8] These
days in the United States, at all scales, the racial state operates
ironically (but without a hint of mirth) through the mode of
"colorblindness."[9] The state's management of racial categories
is analogous to the management of highways or ports or tele-
communication; racist ideological and material practices are
infrastructure that needs to be updated, upgraded, and modernized periodically: this is what is meant by racialization. And
the state itself, not just interests or forces external to the state,
is built and enhanced through these practices. Sometimes the
practices result in "protecting" certain racial groups, and other

6 "Race and Globalization," in this volume, 107–131; see also Donald
S. Moore, *Suffering for Territory: Race, Space, and Power in Zimbabwe*,
Durham, NC: Duke University Press, 2005; Barnor Hesse, "Im/Plausible
Deniability: Racism's Conceptual Double Bind," *Social Identities* 10: 1,
2004, 9–29.

7 Michael Omi and Howard Winant, *Racial Formation in the United
States*, New York: Routledge, 1986.

8 Susan Koshy, "Morphing Race into Ethnicity: Asian Americans and
Critical Transformations of Whiteness," *Boundary* 2, 28.1 (2001): 153–94.

9 Daniel HoSang, "Hiding Race," *Colorlines* 4.4 (2001): 6–9, arc.
org/ C_Lines/CLArchive/story4_4_03.html; Daniel HoSang, "The End of
Race in California? Ward Connerly, Multiculturalism, and the Politics of
'Racelessness,'" paper presented at the Western Political Science Association Annual Conference, Portland, Oregon, March 17, 2004.

times they result in sacrificing them. In any event, racialization is a key part of US governance, and the state's role as the sole determiner of legitimate violence has played a key part in management through racialization.[10]

Given the reach as well as the hesitations of the racial state, it is in the folds of the state's institutions—where inequality gathers its strength, speed, and stamina—that activists have sought and secured the energy to redirect social capacity and thereby social wealth. Many have remarked on how "color-blindness" works, on how politics and policies recode "color" (a standard though slippery proxy for race) to, for example, "urban" and "immigrant" in order to avoid the nasty stench of past outrage while perpetuating cruel practices and their predictably negative consequences into the future. But, oddly, in the case when such changes fall into the category of nonreformist reform, then redirection does not settle the matter but rather enlarges the scope of activity through which our everyday existences might be reconfigured. Nonreformist reforms —or what Avery Gordon calls "abolitionist reforms"—are systemic changes that do not extend the life or breadth of deadly forces such as prisons.[11]

How is such engagement possible? A useful way to think about the state's complexity in power-terms is to consider it as a contradictory set of institutions able to act with some autonomy and some impunity. Thus, the state is not only "not univocal," as Hibou says, but also fraught by intrastate antagonisms—put into play by the very kinds of forceful disputes and alliances constantly bringing the state into being as a centralizing structure in the first place. In other words, if states are the

---

10 For a discussion of an attempt to construct an anti-racist state, see Stefano Harney, *State Work: Public Administration and Mass Intellectuality*, Durham, NC: Duke University Press, 2002, especially chapter 1.

11 Avery Gordon, *Keeping Good Time*, Boulder: Paradigm Publishers, 2004. See also André Gorz, *Strategy for Labor: A Radical Proposal*, Boston: Beacon Press, 1968; Thomas Mathiesen, *The Politics of Abolition: Essays in Political Action Theory*, London: Martin Robertson, 1974.

residue of struggle, then the institutions comprising states are the same substance: partly realized and partly failed attempts to make general certain modes of social being whose underlying contradictions never fully disappear (more of this below). But in addition to the state's inner complexity, there is also the fact that at any historical moment, the people and ideas, parties and prejudices, interests and purposes that coalesce into "who" controls the state (the government) is a varied grouping. This formation, or "bloc" as some call it, achieves for a time general control of the state (if not thorough control of all state agencies) by appearing to be the "legitimate" steward of the public good.[12]

Legitimacy, then, is an important feature of the state—whatever it does can only be sustained if enough of the people whose opinions count (whether voters or rioters, investors or mothers) agree that the direction in which the society is going makes sense to them. Such sense need not be coherent or, even if coherent, demonstrable, but it needs to exist. Crime is the problem for which prisons are the solution is a version of such legitimating sense today, and it is virtually impossible to get through a meeting on prison reform (much less abolition!) without having somebody predict "but we'll always have prisons."

States make territories governable and predictably so, and they do it at a series of "removes" from the most local or immediate milieu. At different levels, states do different things, not only because of the rationalization of state-activity fought out over time (and continually revised—consider today's resurgent federalism that seemed, sixty-five years ago, to be decisively withering), but also because of the ways in which ordinary people's lives are enmeshed in a variety of overlapping and interlocking jurisdictions and political-economic scales. Thus,

---

12 The use of "bloc" follows Antonio Gramsci, *Selections from the Prison Notebooks*, New York: International Publishers, 1971; see also Hall et al., *Policing the Crisis.*

a local planning commission might help a community stop a prison but will have no sway over the municipal judge who sentences children of that community to long terms in cages; yet the judge might stand for election on the same ballot as the commission members, and the ballot might also contain language for approving certain kinds of taxes, debt, or other social-income-producing schemes to build prisons or parks.

The variety of political geographies, themselves differentiated and hierarchical, is cross-cut, materially and ideologically, by both elite and everyday understanding of what the state should be. Presently, the dominant if not consensual view of the state in the United States is what we have called the "anti-state state." The anti-state state is both producer and product of the prison and jail expansion; it gathers and deploys the wherewithal to normalize particular bureaucratic and fiscal capacities that put such spaces into motion as places.

A widely repeated tale runs in the opposite direction from what is actually happening. The fable tells us the state's in demise because tyrannical multinational corporations or free democratic societies don't find it useful anymore. The new end of history has been repeated from Thatcher and Reagan to Blair, Clinton, and Bush and by critics of globalization no less than by its boosters. One way to measure whether the state is shrinking or growing is to compare government spending as a percentage of the gross domestic product (GDP) in constant dollars. In the United States, state spending at all levels (federal, state, and local) has increased as a percentage of GDP by around 10 percent (from about 30 percent of GDP to about 33 percent) since the start of the prison-building boom.[13]

Although the state-as-economic-actor is not an invention of capitalism, there has never been a minute in the history of capitalism lacking the organized, centralized, and reproducible

---

13   Daniel Smelzer, "U.S. Government Spending as a Percentage of GDP," 2005, http://carriedaway.blogs.com/carried_away/2005/04/us_government_s.html.

capacities of the state. Those capacities did not merely preexist the struggles between capitalists and workers but, rather, in many instances came into being, or expanded, or shifted, as a result of the antagonisms inherent in a mode of production that requires inequality to thrive. The history of the United States is, in large part, the history of capitalists figuring out how to develop and use large-scale complex governmental institutions to secure their ability to get rich. A cursory study of any period in US history—the Civil War, the Progressive Era, the New Deal, the postwar New Frontier/Great Society—reveals examples of the ways that capitalists helped develop "the state" in order to disable monopolist adversaries, secure access to raw materials and new markets, murder indigenous people, outlaw or circumscribe worker organizing, or social- ize the cost of protections against calamity and opportunities for advancement in order to minimize vulnerability to wage demands. Workers of all races and conditions weren't gifted with concessions but, rather, won them through fighting hard, sometimes together and sometimes not.

The anti-state state's fable promising its own demise is a central part of the *rhetoric* of neoliberalism. As Peter Evans and others have argued, telling and retelling the story is part of the discourse of globalization, a crucial part of the current attempt to normalize market ideology in order to reshape and renew global domination. Ideology matters: the ways people think about the world, and understand themselves in it, define in large part what they do to endure or change the world. As Evans elaborates: "Today, the untrammeled hegemony of Anglo-American ideological premises is one of the most salient forces shaping the specific character of the current global economy, including the extent to which globalization is viewed as entailing the eclipse of the state."[14]

Central to our concerns here, and we would argue to the

---

14 Peter Evans, "The Eclipse of the State? Reflections on Stateness in an Era of Globalization," *World Politics* 50.1 (1997) 64.

project of state rebuilding more generally, is the way that the state's ability to erect barriers, enforce boundaries, patrol borders, and create enemies is rejigging the dynamic categories of poverty, race, and citizenship and imposing new threats on the life chances of the world's working people.

More specifically, the post–Cold War state is deriving considerable legitimacy and concrete impenetrability through its punishment-enabled growth and consolidation in the gaps opened by the dismantling of the Cold War welfare state. The general imperatives that are the motivating force for any state have not faded from the territory: defense, internal pacification, infrastructural coordination, and communication.[15]

How exactly is the state changing? The literature on states and globalization is enormous and some tendencies in the US model are clear. Although we see some programs such as welfare being eviscerated, it is a mistake to imagine that the state is simply withdrawing resources from the management of the poor. As Jamie Peck says of welfare reform: "In terms of the regulation of poverty and poor subjects, this is not less government but *different* government."[16]

How and why the state has turned to prisons and away from welfare as a means of managing the poor is beyond our scope here. It should be clear, however, that states have transformed the functions of certain agencies—such as welfare and housing. The agencies haven't disappeared: they do different things. Resources have been shifted from agency to agency, and agencies—from public student aid to income supports—have expanded their policing practices whatever their original social mandate. Twenty-five years ago, California spent 2 percent of the state budget on prisons. Today, it spends 8 percent. That increase signals a profound change in the state's

15 See Michael Mann, *States, War, and Capitalism*, Oxford: Blackwell, 1988.

16 Jamie Peck, "Geography and Public Policy: Mapping the Penal State," *Progress in Human Geography* 27.2 (2003): 224.

priorities—away from public education, away from health care, away from affordable housing and environmental protection—and toward prisons, jails, policing, and courts.

Very few people are against schools or health care. But to shift resources away from those departments, to lower their priority, residents whose opinions count need to be convinced. One commonly hears of politicians being afraid of voters—afraid to look soft on crime, for example. The fact is that it is often politicians or other employees of the state who create public opinion in the first place.

Mark Purcell and Joseph Nevins show that one of the key players in the creation of the hysteria over illegal immigration was the Western Regional Commissioner of the Immigration and Naturalization Service (INS), Howard Ezell. In addition to his many public statements fanning the flames of racist nativism, Ezell founded the not-for-profit Americans for Border Control—a solution to the problem that Ezell helped to create in the public's mind— to advocate for more funding for the INS, more Border Patrol agents. "So in everyday practice, certain factions of state actors engage key factions of the citizenry to produce expectations and pursue particular agendas."[17]

An important part of the legitimation of an expanded INS was to create fear in the minds of US residents. Part of that process was to change the ways certain people are seen. The creation and enforcement of new laws and the reimagining of peoples are mutually reinforcing. Thus, people are arrested because they are bad, and one knows they are bad because they've been arrested. "The goal of state violence is not to inflict pain; it is the social project of creating punishable categories of people."[18] Part of the infrastructure buildup along the

---

17 Mark Purcell and Joseph Nevins, "Pushing the Boundary: State Restructuring, State Theory, and the Case of U.S.-Mexico Border Enforcement in the 1990s," *Political Geography* 24 (2005), 217–18.

18 Carole Nagengast, "Violence, Terror, and the Crisis of the State," *Annual Review of Anthropology* 23 (1994), 122; see also Allen Feldman,

US-Mexico border has been renewed racist and nativist images of immigrants, or as Nevins calls the process, the "illegalization" of unauthorized entrants. In other words, the wall along the border was built to create fear and legitimize the state that built it.

Capitalists have always understood the usefulness of the state for their practices, and their constant groaning against "the state" is against particular ways that the social wage is collected rather than against the kinds of institutions necessary to negotiate and guarantee currency and trade, ensure open markets, raise tariffs, seize oil fields, build infrastructure, regulate competition, educate workers, support retirees, open or close borders, and so forth. The development of any state capacity is the outcome of struggle, and that struggle includes governmental actors who enliven and enforce the policies of their institutions and agencies. We can say that the state is a "relatively autonomous"[19] institution, whose economic role is complicated and to some degree doubles back on itself since its ability to perpetuate itself (via access to adequate resources) depends on how well it achieves legitimacy through guaranteeing economic capacities for certain workers or capitalists.

At the same time, state legitimacy is not the outcome of simply calculated economic benefit, and the appearance of benefits of other types can offset seemingly broadly held beliefs about what the state "should" do. Thus, for example, under today's neoliberal regimes, the "problem" of immigrants and nonimmigrant poor people is rhetorically posed as economic in nature—competition over scarce jobs or costly social welfare benefits—whereas the anti-state resolution of the problem— criminalization and incarceration—provides no economic security (or any other safety, for that matter) for most of those who are allegedly the proper objects of the state's care.

Formations of Violence: The Narrative of the Body and Terror in Northern Ireland, Chicago: University of Chicago Press, 1991.

19 Nicos Poulantzas, *State, Power, Socialism*, London: NLB, 1978.

Thus, the coincidence of the breathtaking incarceration of people of color, erection of border walls, uncontested stolen presidential elections, and international military excursions cannot be understood as simply the actions of a racist state or of a state acting in response to racist corporations or voters. In the struggle to produce its own legitimacy, the US state, through multiple governments, employs or delegates violence to name and resolve distinctions—and imprisonment is a machine and a purpose for these outcomes, while racism is the consequence of this interplay of relationships rather than the reason for which they developed. In the next section we will discuss the political economy of prisons, paying special attention to the multiplicity of elements and categories that add up to what has popularly come to be known as the prison-industrial complex (PIC).

The Political Economy of Prisons

A good theory in theory might be a bad theory in practice.
—Toni Negri

Ten years ago, nobody used the term "prison-industrial complex" to talk about the elaborate set of relationships, institutions, buildings, laws, urban and rural places, personnel, equipment, finances, dependencies, technocrats, opportunists, and intellectuals in the public, private, and not-for-profit sectors that synergistically make up the PIC. The term gained wide popularity after the historic 1998 "Critical Resistance: Beyond the Prison-Industrial Complex" conference and strategy session in California; but almost as rapidly it lost its meaningful breadth. By becoming too narrow, PIC became less accurate. The phrase, intended to resonate with rather than simply mimic "the military-industrial complex," has not fulfilled its potential to help people theorize adequately how the PIC shapes political and social life for everyone. As a result, it has yet to become a broadly useful tool in mobilizing opposition to the complex's continued expansion.

We must note that the hollowing-out of the term, and the skewed political vision thus implied, has often come from those who use the term with the most enthusiasm. Along the way, the meaning of "industrial" shrank to "profit" and the state disappeared behind the specter of immoral gain. In this view, the outcome of capitalist activity stands in for the complicated relationships that enable or change that outcome. This low-flying economism misses some key facts about where we are now.

Of those 1 of 130 US residents in prison, 95 percent are in institutions that are wholly public, and 100 percent of all prisons are publicly paid for. Of the prisoners who work (and fewer and fewer do), 97 percent work for the public agencies holding them in bondage. Prisoners' families indeed pay extra for everything: phone charges, soft drinks on visiting day, gifts, and cash. These poverty taxes have often been designed by public prison operatives in order to produce income for the agency; vendors come along to put the tax into practice, rather than as instigators. We're always happy to bash telephone companies, corporations who exploit anybody's labor, and private prison corporations. But those are not the principal players who have created the PIC and sustained its growth. Although campaigns against such adversaries might accomplish great things, shrinking or destroying the PIC is not one of them. In this context, it should be obvious that private prison firms and other corporations are opportunists slurping at the public trough rather than the prime movers behind this extraordinary period in US history.

Given that the United States has always been capitalist and always been racist, the question arises: why prisons now? Each element in the PIC is either an aspect of the state (a rule or a government agent or agency) or derives its power (or powerlessness) in relation to the state and its capacities. Because prisons and prisoners are part of the structure of the state, they enable governments to establish state legitimacy through a claim to provide social "protection" combined with their monopoly on the delegation of violence. The state establishes legitimacy precisely *because* it violently dominates certain people and thereby defines them (and makes them visible to others) as the sort of people who should be pushed around. In modeling behavior for the polity, the anti-state state naturalizes violent domination—as Archer and Gartner have demonstrated.[20] What's important is the transformation of relationships between and among the elements that make up the PIC, producing and projecting into the unforeseeable future a set of dependencies—in the form of domestic militarism—that rely on harming individuals and communities in the name of safety.

If, as many researchers have shown, the state's specific role as an economic player is changing rather than diminishing, then as Toni Negri predicted at the beginning of the current period of globalization and the PIC,

> the counter-revolution of the capitalist entrepreneur today can only operate strictly within the context of an increase in the coercive powers of the state. The "new Right" ideology of laissez-faire implies as its corollary the extension of new techniques of coercive and state intervention in society at large.[21]

---

20 Dane Archer and Rosemary Gartner, *Violence and Crime in Cross-National Perspective*, New Haven, CT: Yale University Press, 1984. The circulation of money through prisons might appear to function according to capitalist imperatives. Mostly it does not. The social expense, as James O'Connor named social wages squandered on prisons and policing, does not produce the means for producing more of anything. By contrast, because states are, by definition, in the work of redistribution, the fact that lots of people make their living from state income is not the reason we should raise our eyebrows and fists.

21 Toni Negri, *Revolution Retrieved: Writings on Marx, Keynes, Capitalist Crisis, and New Social Subjects (1967–83)*, London: Red Notes, 1988, 183.

Imprisonment—the involuntary loss of self-determination and mobility, and the consignment of human lives to cages—depends on coercion. As a result, although the political economy of prison crosses back-and-forth between the "public" and "private" (a line generally as depthless and invisible as an international boundary), it is always fully connected to the state while not wholly defining or motivating the state. The legitimacy for this unbroken connection derives, in part, from achieved consent concerning whose lives and bodies should be vulnerable to the destructive force of prisons. If the fiscal and bureaucratic capacities making mass imprisonment possible are strictly and unequivocally state capacities, and the ideological capacities are articulated through and by the state, then for analytical purposes, it is useful to think of the state in broad categories: in terms of actors, agencies, rules, bodies, and the contradictory crises through which change is generated.[22] The state, then, is not only site and weapon, it is both adversary and, in a few corners at least, ally—as the examples here demonstrate.

The Budget as Battleground

Changes in taxation necessarily lead to modifications in the logics of extraction and redistribution, and thus transform

---

22 This discussion of the political economy of the PIC leaves out an important sector—the nongovernmental organizations (NGOs) or the not-for-profit sector: foundations, think-tanks, activist organizations, service providers, intellectuals on all sides of the issues. The role of NGOs in the PIC deserves considerable study. According to Michel-Rolph Trouillot, "Haitians say in reference to NGOs: 'yo fè leta' (literally, 'they make the state') ... The same word can mean 'state' or 'bully' in Haitian." Michel-Rolph Trouillot, "The Anthropology of the State in the Age of Globalization: Close Encounters of the Deceptive Kind", *Current Anthropology* 42.1 (2001), 132. For more about NGOs and their relation to the state, see Jennifer R. Wolch, *The Shadow State: Government and the Voluntary Sector in Transition*, New York: The Foundation Center, 1990, and INCITE! Women of Color Against Violence, eds., *The Revolution Will Not*

modes of unequal accumulation or redistribution that legitimize the political.

—Béatrice Hibou, "From Privatizing the
Economy to Privatizing the State"

The era of the PIC and globalization has been in the United States a period in which the popularity of taxes dipped ever further. There is always considerable antipathy to handing one's money over to the state, but we can mark the election of Ronald Reagan as president as a time in which that tendency became even stronger. As with the panic around immigration, public emotions about taxes were fanned by state actors, none more important than Reagan himself. As a result, for much of the last twenty-five years, discussion of public spending has taken place as though it were a zero-sum equation: If we must spend more money here, we must spend less elsewhere (because we can't raise taxes).

It is in this period that the ideological mask of the new state makes its debut for a national audience. Too much state interference in our personal lives. Too much state interference in the economy. The state is a burden, a threat. We must shrink the state and restore liberty and markets. Although no doubt there were and are some true believers in this libertarian-lite rant, most of those who spout it, and all of those in power, have no intention of shrinking the state. Rather their intent has been and continues to be to remake the state to do other things. I have called this ideological construct "the anti-state state": a state that grows on the promise of shrinking.[23]

"The relative burden of taxes and the division of state expenditures between different social classes," argues James O'Connor "are the fundamental class issues of state finance." He continues: "Every important change in the balance of class

Be Funded: Beyond the Non-Profit Industrial Complex. Durham, NC: Duke University Press, 2017.

23   For more about the anti-state state, see *Golden Gulag*, Introduction.

and political forces is registered in the tax structure. Put another way, tax systems are simply particular forms of class systems."[24]

The difficulty in raising taxes is the threat of increasing delegitimation of the state, or at least of substantial state functions. That delegitimation has been a key part of the right's attempt to remake the state. Discredit those programs we want to change or destroy. Portray the rest as necessary and open only to the most technical discussion of means and methods, not of priority. The closure of discussions of alternatives to right policies in the 1980s was so successful it produced an acronym, generally credited to Tory Prime Minister Margaret Thatcher: TINA, or There Is No Alternative.[25]

Even if the state seems incapable of raising taxes to generate more income, there continue to be fights over how the money coming in will be spent. As the recent [2005] indictments of Congressman Randy "Duke" Cunningham and lobbyist Jack Abramoff show, some of that fighting is still happening the old-fashioned way, by bribing politicians. Other tactics also take place behind closed doors but might involve campaign contributions of money or labor in exchange for votes or access. There is also a fight for public opinion.

Anti-prison activists seeing the budget crisis that hit US states after the dot-com crash of 2000 tried to take advantage of the opportunity by educating those with a stake in public spending to demand cuts in prison spending. Here in California, the budget crisis continues into its sixth year. The results of our work are unclear. Apart from the Delano II prison, on the boards since the early 1990s and greenlighted by Governor Gray Davis at a time when there was no budget crisis (Davis inherited a surplus of hundreds of millions of dollars when he took office in 1999), California has neither built nor planned any new prisons since the budget crisis began—a

---

24   James O'Connor, *Fiscal Crisis of the State,* New Brunswick, NJ: Transaction Books, 2001 [1973], 162, 203.

25   See Hall, *The Hard Road to Renewal.*

substantial contrast to the twenty-two built in the previous two decades.

In the first year of the budget crisis, we helped teachers, students, and parents from the Bay Area organize a lobby day in the state capitol. Tens of thousands of teachers were sent pink slips that spring, giving them notice they would not be employed the following fall. We descended on the capitol with students asking legislators why the state was willing to spend hundreds of millions of dollars for a new prison but was laying off teachers.

Students from the University of California Students Association and groups from other state colleges and junior colleges demanded that funds be taken from the prison budget in order to avoid increases in student fees. They lost that fight: student fees at state universities were increased 40 percent and fees for junior colleges by 67 percent. Over 100,000 students were forced out of state community colleges because of that one year's fee increases.

Who was most hurt by the cuts in public school funding? By increases in college fees? By cuts to state health programs? The poor, people of color, and the state's substantial immigrant population.[26]

Back in 2003, Julie Falk argued that activists who hoped to shrink the prison system through the budget crisis were probably misled. Instead, she warned, prisons would simply become leaner and meaner, with more cuts to education and counselling programs. During California Governor Arnold Schwarzenegger's first year in office, it appeared that Falk was right. His solution to overspending in California prisons was to propose cutting the number of meals prisoners were served in a week.[27]

---

26 For more about Education not Incarceration, see ednotinc.org. For other coalitions working on California's prison budget politics, see the Coalition for Effective Public Safety at effectivepublicsafety.org and Californians United for a Responsible Budget at curbprisonspending.org.

27 Julie Falk, "Fiscal Lockdown, Part I," *Dollars & Sense* 248 (2003): 19–23, 45; "Fiscal Lockdown, Part II: Will State Budget Cuts Weaken

As we have argued elsewhere, the targeting of the overlapping categories of people of color, noncitizens, and the poor cannot be explained simply by the convenience of their lack of power.[28] Peter Evans argues that contemporary state managers, trying to secure state legitimacy, sacrifice "the capacity to deliver services that the affluent can supply privately for themselves (for example, health and education)." What the state promises to deliver is protection. "In turn, delivering security means devoting more resources to the repression of the more desperate and reckless among the excluded, both domestic and international."[29]

We can take Evans a couple of steps further. First would be to point out that by diverting resources away from education, health care, mental health services, and so on, the state is increasing the numbers of "the more desperate and reckless among the excluded." Or, as Tony Fitzpatrick puts it, "The contemporary state consists of a series of punitive responses to the chaos it has facilitated."[30] That chaos includes freeing racism from both state definition (as in Jim Crow laws) and state disapproval (civil rights laws, which have become so narrowly adjudicated as to be nearly unenforceable), as a result of which the proliferation of certain kinds of laws that do not specify "race" has resulted in the most enormous roundup of people of color in the history of the United States, and many poor white people have been caught at the margins. The people in prison, and their kin outside, lacking "services the rich provide themselves" are increasingly vulnerable to premature death

---

the Prison-Industrial Complex—Or Strengthen It?," *Dollars & Sense* 250 (2003): 32–35.

28 *Golden Gulag*; "The Other California," in this volume, 242–258; Rose Braz and Craig Gilmore, "Joining Forces: Prisons and Environmental Justice Organizing in California," *Radical History Review* 96 (2006): 95–111.

29 Evans, "The Eclipse of the State?", 84–85; see also *Golden Gulag*.

30 Tony Fitzpatrick, "New Agendas for Social Policy and Criminology: Globalization, Urbanism and the Emerging Post-Social Security State," *Social Policy & Administration* 35 (2001): 220.

sanctioned by the state through the policies of aggressive, iron-fisted abandonment.

Second, we would add that as in any protection racket, the protector requires the threat from which we need protection: gang members, meth labs, immigrants.[31] If they didn't exist, they would have to be invented. From Willie Horton to Mara Salvatrucha, politicians, bureaucrats, agencies, and unions heavily or exclusively representing police and prison guards have made certain that the public understand the need for protection from "people like that." These days, it is hard to distinguish the union representing California's prison guards—the California Correctional Peace Officers Association (CCPOA)—from Crime Victims United. Both campaign very effectively for more criminal laws and longer sentences and against any reform of the prison system that would reduce time served, all in the name of protecting public safety.

"He stole something. We don't know what it is yet."
Watermelon Man

Here's another example of the ideology of the anti-state state playing out in the realm of current policing policy.

So-called Broken Windows policing grew out of a magazine article from 1982 written by a couple of arch-conservatives, James Q. Wilson and George Kelling. William Bratton made the theory famous during his high-profile term as head of the New York Police Department, and now in his double role as head of the Los Angeles Police Department and as an international consultant, he is exporting Broken Windows policing around the world.

---

31 Charles Tilly, "War Making and State Making as Organized Crime," in Peter B. Evans, Dietrich Rueschemeyer, and Theda Skocpol, eds., *Bringing the State Back In*, Cambridge: Cambridge University Press, 1985, 169–91.

One of the central tenets of Broken Windows policing is that long-term crime reduction depends on neighborhoods in which people are in the streets, know each other, and take some responsibility for their neighbors and neighborhoods. This belief is not unique to the conservatives who espouse Broken Windows policing.[32] Indeed, looking at the model in a wider context, we can see how the ideology of Broken Windows plays into the fable of the disappearing state and the related celebration of the public sphere as a sort of third space, neither market nor state.

Broken Windows policing aims to remove not only broken windows and graffiti but also the people who are, as Fred Moten puts it, themselves broken windows: those who make others uncomfortable, those who spend too much time in the streets. As Bernard Harcourt and Joe Domanick remind us, much of the practice of Broken Windows—rounding up the usual suspects, checking for their outstanding warrants, keeping them off the streets and on the defensive—is not new to the policy. In fact, most of what is new is the name and the justification—both for increasing the number of involuntary encounters with police and the level of police aggression in those encounters.[33]

Broken Windows advocates argue that the only way to achieve neighborhoods in which neighbors reduce crime by hanging out and knowing each other is, like any other anti-state state project, by hiring more police, and arresting, convicting, and incarcerating more people. In this scheme, we get to depend on each other more only if we first depend on the state, and on an even more punitive version of the state, first.

---

32 See Bernard Harcourt, *Illusion of Order: The False Promise of Broken Windows Policing*, Cambridge, MA: Harvard University Press, 2001, and the many essays by Dina Rose and Todd Clear and their colleagues.

33 Joe Domanick, *To Protect and to Serve: The LAPD's Century of War in the City of Dreams*, New York: Simon and Schuster, 1994; Harcourt, *Illusion of Order*.

What the research of Dina Rose and Todd Clear and their colleagues shows is that saturation policing—arresting, convicting, and imprisoning too many people from a neighborhood—actually has negative impacts on the crime rate.[34] Why? Because taking so many people out of a neighborhood—and returning many of them years later after the horrors of prison—disrupts the very neighborhood ties that Broken Windows purports to strengthen.

Although Chief Bratton campaigns to hire more police in Los Angeles, his consulting firm and its competitors and colleagues are selling US-style policing across the globe. He and his former boss, ex-New York City mayor Rudolph Giuliani, have helped seed such projects as Mano Dura ("Strong Hand") in El Salvador and Honduras. Mano Dura, a near cousin of Broken Windows, is also Zero Tolerance policing. Police stop "the suspicious" in Central America—often those with tattoos—and arrest and detain at every opportunity. The crackdowns on youth in those countries have led to massive overcrowding in prisons, the reemergence of death squads, and what appears to be the state-organized mass murder of alleged gang members in prisons.[35] El Salvador will host the new International Law Enforcement Academy, which, depending on who you listen to, will either help to modernize and depoliticize Latin American police forces, making it an important tool in the move toward democracy, or it will be the School of the Americas II, where police (and military) will share lessons of social cleansing, mass arrests, and deportations that stay carefully within

34 See Dina Rose and Todd Clear, "Incarceration, Social Capital and Crime: Examining the Unintended Consequences of Incarceration," *Criminology* 36 (1998): 441–80.

35 Tom Hayden, "Homies Were Burning Alive," 2004, libertad condignidad.org; Elana Zilberg, "Fools Banished from the Kingdom: Remapping the Geographies of Gang Violence between the Americas (Los Angeles and San Salvador)," *American Quarterly* 56.3 (2004): 759–79. For more about Mano Dura and crackdowns in both the United States and in Central America, see both homiesunidos.org and libertadcondignidad. org.

contemporary human rights boundaries. Globalization? Yes. The eclipse of the state?

What About the State-as-Ally?

The massive economic dislocations of globalization, combined with anticipatory tax revolts waged by banks and corporations in the late 1960s, and by a segment of workers (especially aging homeowners) in the late 1970s, threw California's social wage—its general fund—into deep imbalances that are still to be worked out. The result, as we noted earlier, has been the proliferation of "zero-sum" rhetoric around state spending, as though a political entity and a household were identical in their ability to produce income. The result in the shift of spending to prisons and policing and courts and jails, and away from postsecondary education and social welfare programs, has hit public service workers hard and put many who are not direct participants in the prison-industrial complex—teachers, nurses, clerical staff, and others—on the defensive.

But even direct participants have seen the writing on the wall. Several years ago, a career teacher in the California prison system reached out to several anti-prison activists and organizations to try to sound the alarm over what, in his view, was happening inside the system that would in the end not only jeopardize his job but also accelerate prison growth. Everybody knows that education, along with employment and strong emotional support (family, friends, community groups) enable people who have been to prison to overcome the devastation of that experience, as well as the causes that may have made them vulnerable to it (such as drug dependency), and to stay in the free world. The expansion of the California Department of Corrections, initiated by political elites but maintained by the CCPOA—which became the state's largest political contributor—minimized to the point of near-extinction meaningful education, health, and other rehabilitative programming inside.

The teacher, a member of the Service Employees International Union (SEIU), decided that enough was enough. As a member of the California State Employees' Local 1000, he worked hard to persuade his State Council, the local leadership, and the rank and file to consider what might seem unthinkable: to work with anti-prison activists to shrink the system. After many false starts, a coalition developed including the SEIU state council and SEIU Local 1000 that significantly shifted the terrain of battle at the state level. Why? Because the state employees declared their willingness to do battle with the guards, not only for a share of California's social wage but also because their complexity as an organization, representing more than half a million workers in many different public sectors (cities, counties, as well as the State of California), told the union that what was ultimately at stake is the future of public service and the kinds of social well-being public workers such as themselves might be able to offer both to prisoners and to people in the free world. They also concluded that opportunities for workers with their skills—instructors, health care providers, locksmiths, secretaries—could readily translate into other kinds of public jobs, and it was only the guards, with their single specialty, whose motive to expand the state prison system and whose vision for the future could not be tempered by alternative visions of future workplace opportunities. Given that total California SEIU membership outnumbers that of the guards' union by an order of magnitude (500,000 vs. about 50,000) it seems possible that the ongoing alliance between anti-prison activists and the union holds great promise.

In the early 1970s, James O'Connor theorized that public-sector workers and their clients might find the contradiction between them not antagonistic at all, and a shift in solidarity would change the ground of political activism especially with respect to the state. Odd that such a shift seems to be proceeding on the most antagonistic grounds imaginable—prison—and it is exactly that oddity to which activists should pay attention. Indeed, about a decade ago Paul Johnstone argued that it is in the public sector (along with the low-wage private sector—such as Justice for Janitors) that true social-movement unionism has grown and flourished, while in the ranks of the old labor aristocracy membership decline and many unions' capitulation to double-tiering has weakened the unionism that flourished briefly during the Golden Age of American Capitalism.[36] What's the dynamic here? How do the members of public-sector and low-wage unions overlap with the communities most impacted by criminalization, and what is the possible basis for invigorating organizations already attuned to understanding labor struggles as not merely workplace, "bread-and-butter" issues to oppose the proliferation of cages? How might organizers develop outreach to organized public-sector health, welfare, and education workers whose frontline experience working with people vulnerable to criminalization may well hold as rich a potential for nonreformist reform strategies as was found among SEIU prison workers?

Fanon tried to convince his readers to think hard about the many ways that people in conditions of crisis can be understood categorically—that is, as classes or groups—and in so thinking to look beneath the surface and ask what the possibility might be for cooptation, on the one hand, and differential alignment, on the other.[37] Fanon, like Du Bois before him, examined how various groupings cohere internally and connect externally—what calls them to identify in some ways but not in others, how those relationships might change, and to what end.[38] This is the great challenge for anti-prison activists who can engage

36 Paul Johnstone, *Success While Others Fail: Social Movement Unionism and the Public Workplace*, Ithaca, NY: ILR Press, 1994.

37 Frantz Fanon, *The Wretched of the Earth*, New York: Grove Press, 1963.

38 W. E. B. Du Bois, *Black Reconstruction in America, 1860–1880*, New York: The Free Press, 1992 [1935].

the state in surprising ways, and in particular expand the repertoire of such engagements beyond the narrow, technocratic rehearsals of "experts" at hearings. Marx wrote that ideology becomes a material force when it grips the masses; and broadly based public-sector unions might be a way to proliferate active understanding of prison as a machine that produces premature death for prisoners and their kin rather than safety for the types of vulnerable communities who have gained a measure of *real* security through social movement unionism and other innovative organizing.

Conclusion

> Gramsci was interested in what he called an autonomous state life, one in which the transformation of politics transformed the state. Yet it was also one in which a transformed state transformed politics.
>
> —Stefano Harney, *State Work: Public Administration and Mass Intellectuality*

If, as we have argued, the state is remaking itself using the newly vast prison system's coercive powers on some parts of the population to produce consent among others, there are implications for political activists.

Those already struggling against police and prisons need a clearer and deeper picture of why the state does what it does to their family members and neighbors. Thinking about state violence, and especially racist state violence, as an aberration to be reformed away misses the way that states work and the work that states do. Many activists in Critical Resistance warn us not to think of the prison system as broken. Rather, they insist, we should imagine it is working and think about what that means. The political implications demand an understanding of why the system does work this way, and of how, as Gramsci argues, we can change the state enough to make real changes in it—or what we have been calling nonreformist reform.

For those involved in other social justice work, we would suggest that there is great risk in not incorporating some analysis of how the state is becoming or has become a "penal state."[39] It is not clear that the growth of the prison system will reach some natural plateau. If the state seems to require more enemies, who will be next? And where will the funds be found to pay for the next rounds of increased staff of Border Patrol, Marshalls, prison guards, police, Immigration and Customs Enforcement, not to mention the prisons, jails, and border fences yet to be built? The prison buildup is a key, perhaps *the* key, political attack on the political ground created in the New Deal and Civil Rights eras.

Our opposition has mastered the Gramscian puzzle of changing the state to change politics and changing politics to change the state. We have to go deeply into the state in all its aspects —its legitimacy, the ideological apparatuses it wields to normalize the everyday horror of mass incarceration, its budget process, its inner contradictions, its intrastate antagonisms and frictions. All of these places are sites where activists can set their feet to fight the fight. And the sites are, as well, locations where we meet others struggling to piece together lives torn apart by poverty, illness, undereducation, war, long-distance migration, flight. Here, where we fight, is where the state is.

---

39 Peck, "Geography and Public Policy."

13

Beyond Bratton
(with Craig Gilmore)

The modern police system was designed to keep the marginalized in their place and to warn the poor of a fate worse than poverty.

—Tony Platt, "Obama's Task Force on Policing: Will It Be Different This Time?"

#BlackLivesMatter (BLM) exploded into US and global consciousness by way of the Ferguson uprising against the police who killed Michael Brown. Founded when Trayvon Martin's killer went free, BLM came together to name and undo a general pattern: the state's central role in the destruction of Black lives.[1] As Tony Platt notes, the police dispense warnings to contain exclusion, abandonment, and change—using forms of speech, including killing, to make the message crystal clear.[2]

Among the crises police interventions contain are legitimation crises, during which the foundations of the racial-capitalist state apparatuses shake and crack. The lack of consensus about what the state should be or do requires greater coercion of some of that state's subjects. In the turn to neoliberalism, for example, the Thatcher and Reagan regimes manufactured legitimation crises designed to refashion the state—massively

---

1 Alicia Garza, "A Herstory of the Black Lives Matter Movement," *Feminist Wire*, October 2014, feministwire.com.

2 Tony Platt, "Obama's Task Force on Policing: Will It Be Different This Time?," *Social Justice: A Journal of Crime, Conflict, & World Order*, February 28, 2015, socialjusticejournal.org.

slashing the social wage by cutting welfare benefits, public education and public housing, and smashing public and private unions, all the while lowering taxes on the rich and on corporations and increasing spending on the military, police, and prisons.[3]

The institutional result of rhetorical but not real state shrinkage, with its attendant devolution of obligations to more local levels or to parastate actors (such as charter schools or nonprofits), we have long called the "anti-state state."[4] What's most notable about the phenomenon is that those who seek to seize or maintain appointed or elected state office by campaigning against government exercise "relative autonomy" to consolidate power by strengthening—not dismantling—certain aspects of the state.[5] It doesn't get cheaper, and it doesn't, in the aggregate, shrink. However, the purpose and outcome of the anti-state state's crisis-fueled practice is to facilitate upward transfer of wealth, income, and political power from the relatively poor and powerless to the already rich and powerful.

The relatively powerless are not without social capacity and have fought to maintain, extend, and redefine access to health care, income, housing, public education, and life itself in urban and rural contexts. This ongoing struggle spans multiple regimes of accumulation and the policing apparatuses appropriate to them. Indeed, from the origin of professionalized policing in the early twentieth century, when Progressivism and Jim Crow arose as an interlocking system of benefit and exclusion, through the gendered racial and regional hierarchies of the New Deal, and on to the courtroom and legislative triumphs of the civil rights movement, the location of the "thin blue line"

3   Stuart Hall, *The Hard Road to Renewal: Thatcherism and the Crisis of the Left*, London: Verso, 1988; Neil Smith, *The New Urban Frontier: Gentrification and the Revanchist City*, New York: Routledge, 1996.

4   Ruth Wilson Gilmore, *Golden Gulag*; "Restating the Obvious," in this volume, 259–87.

5   Nicos Poulantzas, *State, Power, Socialism*, London: New Left Books, 1978.

has moved but never disappeared as a prime organizing—or disorganizing—principle of everyday life. In recent decades the rise of the anti-state state has depended on increased criminalization to mark the poor as ineligible for as well as undeserving of social programs. Under regime after regime, the politics of race define techniques and understanding, even though racial categories and hierarchies—at any moment solid—are not set in concrete.[6] If, therefore, as Stuart Hall painstakingly argued, race is "the *modality* in which class is lived," then mass criminalization, and the policing it depends on, is class *war*.[7]

Post-Ferguson, the #BlackLivesMatter uprisings and broad-based organizing have pushed some aspects of US policing to the brink of a legitimacy crisis. Complex and militant work against police violence since the shooting of Michael Brown challenges the normal support upon which police organizations depend. Mainstream media raise questions—long-standing among activists from Ida B. Wells to Angela Y. Davis—about the racism inherent in the purpose and use of saturation policing, mass criminalization, and mass incarceration as alleged "solutions to crime." Left-liberal magazines such as *The Nation* and *Rolling Stone*—not noted for deep or systemic critiques of US criminal justice—have gone so far as to call for the abolition of the police.[8]

But even in the face of mainstream criticism and so-called "bipartisan" calls for reform, has police legitimacy actually melted into air? Are we in the midst of structural change? If

---

6 A. Sivanandan, *A Different Hunger: Writings on Black Resistance*, London: Pluto Press, 1982.

7 Stuart Hall, "Race, Articulation, and Societies Structured in Dominance," in *Sociological Theories: Race and Colonialism*, Paris: UNESCO, 1980, 341 (emphasis added).

8 José Martín, "Policing Is a Dirty Job, but Nobody's Gotta Do It: 6 Ideas for a Cop-Free World," *Rolling Stone*, December 16, 2014; Michael Denzel Smith, "In Order to End Police Brutality, We Need to End the Police," *The Nation*, February 25, 2015. Not all the talk of abolishing police has come from liberals. See, for example, Mariame Kaba, "Summer Heat," *New Inquiry*, June 6, 2015.

so, how and to what end does the anti-state state deploy ideological and material resources toward, around, or through the institutionalized forces of organized violence? How in particular have the police and their patrons responded to widespread condemnation of police violence and militarization, and have they offered solutions that threaten neither the power of the police nor the status of their patrons?

Police Violence/Police Legitimacy

Police homicides prove police violence in general, and police tanks emblematize police militarization in general—yet they are not the whole sordid violent tale. The righteous outrage against police murders and extra-heavy equipment enables a strange displacement (often unintended, yet also often cynically coopted) of political focus away from the necessarily systemic character of organized violence. This displacement results in partial containment of expansive, international grassroots work to weaken, in order to undo, contemporary police legitimacy. In other words, the techniques and ideologies of saturation policing and mass criminalization remain too frequently unacknowledged except at the margin, where minor tweaks (body cameras, a few dozen sentence commutations) focus energy and resources, ultimately changing little. What are the preconditions for individual killings and industrialized killing equipment? They include stop-and-frisk, widespread arrests, the issuance of massive numbers of citations, and the political culture of perpetual enemies who must always be fought but can never be vanquished. These preconditions, and the violence enabled and required to maintain them, will not change if an officer or two is indicted and a few tanks are dismantled for scrap metal.

Transfers and convergences between military and police have a long history. While dramatic objects such as Mine Resistant

Ambush Protected (MRAP) vehicles command attention, what matters more in terms of police legitimacy and power are more subtle objects such as standard-issue handguns or out-of-sight capacities such as computerized profiling. The United States not only dominates the planet militarily, it is also the world's principal manufacturer and purveyor of military equipment. The Department of Defense's 1033 program (dating from 1997) enables a tiny fraction of surplus warfare matériel to remain active. The corporations that sold military equipment to the Pentagon don't get paid again when the Pentagon funds the transfer of such surplus to police. To kill, police use ordinary weapons—guns, batons—and weaponize ordinary things—hands, forearms, flashlights, trash bags, vans.

Any focus on military-police interdependence might usefully drill down through both equipment and ideology to reveal the underlying strategies and practices that rebuild rather than weaken legitimacy even or perhaps especially in a long moment of crisis. If the principal use of tanks and armor is to deliver a visual message through news and social media that those who demonstrate against police killing and other outrages are dangerous, then what is obscured behind that implicit narrative? What, in other words, do police organizations do to secure their foundational role? Both capitalization and institutional change provide insights, as the rest of this essay will demonstrate.

The Los Angeles Police Department (LAPD) has long been at the vanguard of increased use of machinery in place of putting more cops on the street with guns and clubs and radios. Whether the equipment was first designed for or acquired from the military or not, this process is "capitalization." Take the helicopter, now an almost clichéd symbol of high-tech policing: the LAPD purchased its first one in 1956—more than four decades before the Department of Defense's 1033 program began.[9]

---

9   For a good overview of the current LAPD air force, see Hamid Khan, "LAPD Helicopters Flying Overhead Don't Deter Crime. They

The LAPD's capitalization intensified in the wake of the 1965 Watts rebellion. In the aftermath of Watts, the LAPD started the country's first special weapons and tactics (SWAT) team, which in its first deployment stormed the LA headquarters of the Black Panther Party for Self-Defense at 41st and Central in December 1969. The department also purchased more helicopters and other weaponry, cars, and vans, and it acquired state-of-the-art upgrades in communications hardware and intelligence-gathering infrastructure. But even before 1965, "in the days when the young Daryl Gates was driver to the great Chief William Parker, the policing of the ghetto was becoming simultaneously less corrupt but more militarized and brutal."[10] That trend intensified post-1965, as Gates's LAPD repressed Watts through the "the paramilitarization of the police and the destruction of the community's radical fringe."[11]

Gates had deep ties to Parker, and his own years as chief were marked by both intensely modernized technology and thoroughly racist ideology, implemented by a succession of new programs such as Operation Hammer and new divisions such as Community Resources Against Street Hoodlums (CRASH), whose motto was "We Intimidate Those Who Intimidate Others."

The 1992 LA uprising, coming on the heels of Mike Davis's *City of Quartz* and after years of tireless organizing by the Coalition Against Police Abuse, produced a legitimation crisis for the LAPD.[12] Gates resigned from a lifetime appointment as

---

Antagonize Minorities," *Guardian*, March 12, 2015. Well-known depictions of the LAPD's choppers include Kid Frost, "East Side Story" (Virgin Records, 1992); Ice Cube, "Ghetto Bird," *Lethal Injection* (Priority, 1993); Red Hot Chili Peppers, "Police Helicopter," *Red Hot Chili Peppers* (EMI Records, 1984).

10 Mike Davis, *City of Quartz: Excavating the Future in Los Angeles*, London: Verso, 1990.

11 Davis, *City of Quartz*, 294.

12 João Costa Vargas, *Catching Hell in the City of Angels: Life and Meanings of Blackness in South Central Los Angeles*, Minneapolis: University of Minnesota Press, 2006.

chief of the LAPD two months after the rebellion. Attempting to regain some of its legitimacy, the city replaced him with Willie L. Williams, the first Black department head and the first chief to come from outside the department. Four years later, Bernard C. Parks became LA's second Black chief of police. Like Williams, he served only one term.

To replace Parks, Mayor James Hahn recruited former New York Police Department (NYPD) commissioner William Bratton. When Bratton took over, the LAPD had not significantly improved its reputation in Black LA since the days of Parker and Gates. Joe Domanick remarked that the LAPD's South Central style "wasn't policing, it was anti-insurgency run amok. Sheer brutality, suppression and force—those were the only things the LAPD thought people in South LA understood, and those were the only things the LAPD itself understood."[13]

Bratton's political strategy to rebuild police power in Los Angeles involved two key approaches. The first consisted of intensive outreach to the old civil rights leadership and the press to emphasize the new LAPD's commitment to protecting poor people of color, and especially Black people, from violent crime committed by Black people. The second focused on significantly increasing the size of the police force, which Bratton justified by arguing that the LAPD's militarized history was the result of too few officers trying to police too much territory. By extension, according to Bratton, trigger-happy strong-arm policing resulted from feelings of vulnerability to street gangs on the part of thin-on-the-ground police personnel. Thus, to end police brutality Bratton's force required more police, and to achieve it the LAPD worked hard to transition the mainstream civil rights agenda away from opportunities for advancement and protections from calamity and toward support of criminalization.

---

13 Quoted in John Buntin, "What Does It Take to Stop Crips and Bloods from Killing Each Other?," *New York Times*, July 10, 2013.

More cops don't arrive without adequate funding to pay for them. In 2004, Bratton gambled that city voters would approve Measure A, an attempt to raise sales taxes to hire 1,260 to 1,700 more police. The measure was defeated by an unusual but not unprecedented electoral alignment of two increasingly well-organized factions—anti-tax West Valley conservatives and anti-police people of color concentrated in South Central Los Angeles.

Bratton's outreach to the civil rights establishment paid more immediate dividends. While he achieved some success among the leaders of Black LA's biggest churches, his most import-ant recruit was noted civil rights attorney Connie Rice, former co-director of the National Association for the Advancement of Colored People Legal Defense Fund's LA chapter and co-founder of the Advancement Project (AP). As Rice tells the story, Bratton "persuaded me to put my complaints away and come inside the department, and I did. He gave me a parking space and a badge, and I haven't left."[14]

Community Policing Reborn

In the decade-plus that Attorney Rice has had her badge and parking place, working closely with former chief Bratton and his successor, Charles Beck, she and her colleagues at the AP have built programs that Rice assures us have eliminated the possibility of "another Rodney King riot" in Los Angeles.[15] Launched with a report called "A Call to Action: A Case for a Comprehensive Solution to LA's Gang Violence Epidemic," the AP plotted a long-term "Violence Reduction Strategy" to attack the "ten root conditions of violence" through providing

---

14 Connie Rice, remarks at "Bridging the Great Divide: Can Police-Community Partnerships Reduce Crime and Strengthen Our Democracy?," John Jay College, September 4, 2014.

15 Rice, Remarks.

services in five broad areas: "prevention, intervention, suppression, reentry and the equitable distribution of resources."[16]

The plan focused more narrowly on two targets: gang violence and domestic violence toward children. The strategy of suppressing gangs while strengthening families (rather than vice versa) embraced Moynihan's racist manifesto of blame, pretending that the patriarchal family might be free of violence if sufficiently "strong" while maintaining that street organizations, strong or not, could be a source of nothing but violence. The equitable distribution of resources took a backseat to gang suppression.

A dizzying number of new state and parastate agencies, tools, and initiatives has sprung from "A Call to Action," including Urban Peace, the Urban Peace Academy, the Mayor's Gang Reduction and Youth Development zones, the LA County Regional Gang Violence Taskforce, the Community Safety Scorecard, and, finally, the Community Safety Partnership (CSP).

Following Chief Bratton's penchant for hot-spot policing, the AP called for concentrating more violence-prevention resources in "the highest need communities."[17] As the five-year report makes clear, resources for gang suppression flow more easily to those neighborhoods than funds for job creation, programs like rent control, or subsidies that might enable struggling households to stabilize themselves.

The crown jewel of the new programs—the one that will prevent any more "Rodney King riots"—is the CSP, lauded by the AP as the "Future of Suppression."[18] According to the AP, the new "strategic suppression" will replace "a counterproductive, overbroad suppression approach." The strategy? "CSP is unique for both HACLA (Housing Authority of the City of Los Angeles) and LAPD in its recognition that safety

---

16 Advancement Project, "A Call to Action: Los Angeles' Quest to Achieve Community Safety," Los Angeles, 2013, 5ff.

17 Advancement Project, "A Call to Action," 44.

18 Advancement Project, "A Call to Action," 39.

cannot be achieved through traditional policing, but instead requires *collaboration* among all stakeholders."[19]

In remarks at Bridging the Great Divide, an exclusive policing conference held in New York City in September 2014, Rice detailed some of the CSP's mechanisms. The first order of business was to break down the "negative perception of law enforcement by the community." Toward this end, the LAPD selected new squads, each with exclusive responsibility to patrol one of four public housing projects. Each squad is teamed with Gang Intervention Experts, former and generally older gang members (OGs) now on the AP payroll. Their role is to facilitate relationship-building between the police and the policed in order to "lower the level of perceived bias" among the policed.

According to Rice, the police and their retired gangster guides started with grandmothers in the housing projects, apologizing for acts of police violence against the elders' families and asking what needs the residents might have. Deteriorating eyesight? Diabetes? No computers for the grandkids to do their homework? The LAPD delivered 800 pairs of bifocals, arranged a medical van from the University of Southern California to do onsite diabetes screening, and bought and gave away $300,000 worth of tablet computers.

The goal of that largesse was to build trust.

Rice and others promote CSP as a new model that solves the legitimation crisis of US policing, and many see it as a seductive alternative to the militarization that has so damaged that legitimacy. "If you serve the community," says Rice, "the community will get to know you, and they will get to trust you; and if they trust you, maybe they'll pick up the phone when there's a crime ... Just maybe the community would back the police for a change."[20] However, the fact that officers of the LAPD, LA Sheriff, and other LA County agencies kill an Angeleno almost

19   Advancement Project, "A Call to Action," 39 (emphasis added).
20   Rice, Remarks.

once a week significantly undermines CSP's ability to gain the trust of residents of the housing complexes.[21]

The Velvet Glove

The attempt to manage a police legitimation crisis through community-based policing is not new at all. The classic analysis of such campaigns remains *The Iron Fist and the Velvet Glove*, first published in 1975:

> Massive spending on military hardware, by itself, would not only fail to stop rising crime rates and urban discontent, but would probably serve to further alienate large sectors of the population. This approach stressed the need for police to develop closer ties to the communities most heavily patrolled by them. The emphasis began to be placed less on paramilitary efficiency and more on insuring popular consent and acquiescence.[22]

In the 1970s, the LAPD rolled out community policing models in which "developing more intimate relations with people in the community" was a central goal, particularly in "poor and Third World communities" where police were central to maintaining order despite "increasing militancy and resistance to the police" in those neighborhoods.[23]

Across the United States, community policing experiments flowered. According to Platt and others, most community policing projects shared two common factors: "One is to give people more responsibility in policing themselves—to bring people into active participation in the policing process. The

---

21   Youth Justice Coalition, "Don't Shoot to Kill: Homicides Resulting from Law Enforcement Use of Force within LA County, 2000–2014," 2014.

22   Tony Platt et al., *The Iron Fist and the Velvet Glove: An Analysis of the U.S. Police*, Berkeley: Center for Research on Criminal Justice, 1975, 54.

23   Platt et al., *The Iron Fist and the Velvet Glove*, 57.

other is to encourage greater daily contact between the police and neighborhoods they patrol ... Theoretically, with people's trust and participation, the job of the police will be less difficult."[24] While the community police experiments of the 1970s went far beyond earlier police efforts at public relations and crisis management, by attempting to enlist community members as extensions of the police web, two points stand out. First, the new relationships did nothing to disturb existing relations of coercive power and control. "From [the LAPD's] perspective, it is useful to decentralize police *functions* without decentralizing police *authority*."[25] Second, while the velvet glove's purpose was to soften the image of late 1960s and early 1970s militarized police, community policing spread across the country at virtually the same time as SWAT teams; thus, to be effective, the velvet glove—then as now—clothed an iron fist. Thus, for example, since the LAPD created SWAT teams in 1967, the use of those forces has risen from about 3,000 operations a year in the 1980s to about 40,000 a year.[26]

Counterinsurgency

If CSP's emphasis on building relationships among specially detailed police and the housing projects they patrol isn't new, does it still provide an alternative to military policing?

No, it does not. In fact, the most notable innovations in the CSP model directly incorporate up-to-date military counterinsurgency tactics.

---

24   Platt et al., *The Iron Fist and the Velvet Glove*, 63.

25   Platt et al., *The Iron Fist and the Velvet Glove*, 58.

26   Stephen Graham, *Cities under Siege: The New Military Urbanism*, London: Verso, 2010. The study Graham cites is Peter Kraska's *Militarizing the American Criminal Justice System: The Changing Roles of the Armed Forces and the Police*, Lebanon, NH: Northeastern University Press, 2001. For more on SWAT, see Joe Domanick, *To Protect and to Serve: The LAPD's Century of War in the City of Dreams*, New York: Pocket Books, 1994.

The importation of US military technique to domestic inner-city policing itself has a long and complex history, as many scholars have demonstrated. For example, Nikhil Singh shows the long articulation of late-nineteenth-century US imperial methods of insurgency suppression with changes in the structure and organization of domestic forces of organized violence.[27] Laleh Khalili describes how military/policing practices imported from the Philippine-American war to the United States grew out of the US military experience fighting indigenous peoples in the colonization of the West.[28]

Platt and Takagi write of the "increasing militancy and resistance" to racist police violence—the broad range of activity and activism that put into crisis not only police legitimacy but by extension the racial-capitalist state. To suppress spontaneous or consolidated opposition, the military techniques imported are generally those actively in use elsewhere. Seen in this light, the CSP resembles, not surprisingly, counterinsurgency campaigns operated by the US military in Iraq and Afghanistan. Stephen Graham argues: "'High-intensity policing' and 'low-intensity warfare' threaten to merge."[29] Indeed, they *have* merged.

CSP practice follows, nearly to the letter, the steps outlined by David Kilcullen, whom Khalili has dubbed "the counterinsurgency guru." The first move is to coopt women.

---

27   Nikhil Pal Singh, "Critical Theories of Modern Policing," paper presented at Resisting Arrest conference, Department of Social and Cultural Analysis, New York University, April 11, 2015. See also Nikhil Pal Singh, *Exceptional Empire: Race and War in US Globalism*, Cambridge: Harvard University Press, forthcoming; and Stuart Schrader, "Policing Empire," *Jacobin*, September 5, 2014, jacobinmag.com.

28   Laleh Khalili, "Lineaments of Settler-Colonialism in Counterinsurgency Confinement," paper given at The Scope of Slavery: Enduring Geographies of American Bondage, Harvard University, November 8, 2014. See also Laleh Khalili, *Time in the Shadows: Confinement in Counterinsurgencies*, Stanford: Stanford University Press, 2013.

29   Graham, *Cities under Siege*, 96.

These ideas are operationalized in the Female Engagement Teams in Afghanistan. Their mission is described as "non-lethal targeting of the human terrain" to "enable systemic collection of information from the female population in a culturally respectful manner to facilitate building confidence with the Afghan [or South Central] population."[30]

Cops in South Central, like the military in Afghanistan or Iraq, work to win the hearts and minds of the grannies through the provision of goods and services—precisely the goods and services that the neighborhood has been starved of, thanks to the organized abandonment carried out by neoliberal firms and warfare states. Resources become, then, not the stuff of life but the difficult-to-refuse inducements used to secure cooperation with the occupying army or police. Over the course of half a century, the LAPD has moved from Vietnam War anti-insurgency ("anti-insurgency run amok") to Iraq counterinsurgency. Khalili describes Kilcullen's predecessor John Paul Vann's impact on US strategy in Vietnam as:

a rupture that framed—and continues to shape—the metanarrative of counterinsurgency … The story begins with a lumbering, conventional, and conservative counterinsurgent military using its firepower and technical prowess to bomb an unequal enemy into submission, all the while stoking native hostility not only with the force of arms but also its naïve racism. Then arrive unconventional—in both senses of the word—thinkers and military men, rebels who anger the bureaucracy around them, who, against their racist colleagues … look for more humane ways of acquiring local allegiances through virtuous behaviour, humility, and the provision of security (and resources and social goods.)[31]

30   Khalili, *Time in the Shadows*, 198.
31   Khalili, *Time in the Shadows*, 41–42.

The unconventional thinkers and military people are Bratton and Rice. The strategic hamlets are South Central housing projects. The reaction to overwhelming racist police violence produces, again, a velvet glove, but we must not ignore the fact that the glove remains a military-issue combat glove. Or that CSP, like the community policing initiatives of the 1960s and 1970s and like Vietnamization, does not reduce police or military violence.

Rather, the new policing programs are intended to reduce "increasing militancy and resistance" in reaction to such violence —not only police killings but all of the violence on which mass criminalization depends. A large part of Bratton's cleverness has been to reinvigorate discourses of Black pathology, arguing that the numbers of Black people arrested, imprisoned, and killed by the police are not disproportionate. Rather, they are proportionate to the concentration of crime in Black neighborhoods and to Black victimization. Stopping and interrogating, arresting, and incarcerating so many Black people, Bratton argues, is the way to protect Black people. Gil Scott-Heron saw through an earlier iteration of organized violence targeting Black people, commenting on the benefits of Nixon's no-knock law for Black people: "No Knock, the law in particular, was allegedly legislated for Black people rather than, you know, for their destruction."[32]

Bratton and Rice are poised to lead the police through the current crisis of legitimacy toward a new, however temporary, stage of increased police power and prestige. The CSP velvet glove sheathes a centralized and high-tech iron fist. In other words, there's no movement whatsoever to shift power away from the police. Quite the opposite: the provision of necessary goods and services through the police—now often justified only as a means to reduce crime or violence—will further weaken what remains of the social welfare state and the neighborhoods that most depend on public services.

---

32 Gil Scott-Heron, "No Knock," *Free Will* (Flying Dutchman/RCA, recording, released August 1972).

Devolution and Police Power: Organized Abandonment and Organized Violence in Racial Capitalism's Neoliberal Turn

> A recurring problem, and not just limited to the issue of housing, is the lack of tools and resources available to municipalities when faced with a problem whose origin is global. Increasingly, conflicts specific to an urban area are caused by phenomena that exceed the formal powers held by municipal governments.
> —Ada Colau and Adrià Alemany, *Mortgaged Lives: From the Housing Bubble to the Right to Housing*

> I love the police because politicians are afraid of them.
> —Connie Rice

Why does the racial-capitalist state ever change? What accounts for variations? For convergences? To enhance their ability to extract value from labor and land, elites fashion political, economic, and cultural institutions. They build states. Tweak them. Aggrandize and devolve them. Promote and attack stories about why things should either persist or change. But even during periodic waves of abandonment, elites rely on structures of order and significance that the anarchy of racial capitalism can never guarantee.[33]

At the same time, non-elites are never passive pawns. Ordinary people, in mutable diversity, figure out how to stretch or diminish social and spatial forms to create room for their lives —including building states to safeguard and more universally advance the general good, as happened in the US South among Black people during Reconstruction and during other

---

33　Clyde Woods charted this process across 130 years of Lower Mississippi Delta history. Woods extended these theoretical and analytical insights to policing in Los Angeles—a topic to which he turned his formidable intellectual energy late in his too-brief career. See Clyde Woods, *Development Arrested: The Blues and Plantation Power in the Mississippi Delta*, introd. Ruth Wilson Gilmore, London: Verso, 2017 [1998].

revolutionary times in modern history.[34] In nonrevolutionary conjunctures, some use elites' methods and join with dominating forces to get what they want, while others compel change from the ground up. Usually struggles combine top-down and grassroots efforts—part, as C.L.R. James remarked, of the exhaustive conservatism that underlies revolutions.[35] That said, in the long aftermath of the so-called golden age of US capitalism (c. 1938–1970), the increased vulnerability of workers and their communities, broadly defined across society and space, has resulted from purposeful abandonment organized by elites, as racial capitalism makes and consolidates the neoliberal turn.

The pattern of racial capitalism's contemporary class war in the overdeveloped world (imprecisely, the global North) closely resembles what international financial institutions have longer demanded of the so-called developing world (loosely, the global South): limited states run by technocrat executives on behalf of local and transnational oligarchs and firms.[36] "Devolution"— the name for structural adjustment in richer, inequality-riven polities—consists of offloading to increasingly local state- and non-state institutions the authority to allocate or withhold shredded social welfare, further restricting protections from calamity and opportunities for advancement. Municipalities encounter new obligations as unfunded mandates or tied to narrowly targeted funding streams. Therefore, devolution in

---

34   See W. E. B. Du Bois, *Black Reconstruction in America*, New York: Atheneum, 1992 [1935].

35   C. L. R. James, *Modern Politics*, San Francisco: PM Press, 2013 [1961].

36   See, for examples, Robert S. Browne, "Africa's Economic Future: Development or Disintegration?," *World Policy Journal* 1: 4, 1984, 793–812; Robert S. Browne, "Africa and the International Monetary Fund: Conditionality, a New Form of Colonialism?," *Africa Report* 29: 5, 1984, 14–18; Bobby M. Wilson, *America's Johannesburg: Industrialization and Racial Transformation in Birmingham*, Lanham, MD: Rowman and Littlefield, 1996; Beverly Silver and Giovanni Arrighi, *Chaos and Governance in the Modern World System*, Minneapolis: University of Minnesota Press, 1999.

action is a set of institutionalizing practices—a regime that, veiled by the rhetoric of "less government," specifically prevents the hands of the vulnerable from extracting the social wage from ever-deeper, tax-resistant pockets.

The social wage is public revenue (taxes and use fees) plus the deposits (gifts or bequests) stored in foundations and other tax-exempt, nongovernmental institutions. "Welfare state" indicates a broad range of institutional, legal, and moral frameworks that temper racial capitalism's tendencies (monopoly and poverty) by downwardly redistributing a significant chunk of surplus money (and other resources such as public education, housing vouchers, and sometimes cheese). Neoliberalism's delegitimation and dismantling of welfare state capacities reallocates racial capitalism's accumulation crisis by taking resources from institutions, programs, streets, households, and lives, throwing all into permanent crisis.

Crisis, then, is organized abandonment's condition of existence *and* its inherent vice. To persist, systematic abandonment depends on the agile durability of organized violence. For example, by the year 1980, California's diverse economy was bigger than that of any of the other forty-nine US states and all but a handful of the world's nation-states. Throughout the next thirty years, through several booms and busts, the gross state product nearly doubled. Every bust destroyed jobs—shaking up households, communities, and productive regions and dropping more and more people into poverty. Every boom deepened inequality while padding the ranks of the very rich.

As capital strolled or ran away from paying a significant percentage of the state treasury's receipts, the sweep of Golden State policy shifted dramatically, bringing to an end the expansive Cold War–justified social investment in people, infrastructure, and innovation. Abandonment-induced anxieties about the future encouraged voters to punish elected officeholders by instituting tax limits and term limits—which, unsurprisingly if ironically, guaranteed that individual political ambition could only be realized through capitulation to the biggest checkbooks rather than the general desires of potential district voters.[37] These, combined with fiscal, procedural, and policy shifts, shredded protections from calamity and raised the sticker price on opportunities, all the while ideologically recasting public goods such as education, for example, as an individualized instrument. Worldwide today, wherever inequality is deepest, the use of prisons as a catchall solution to social problems prevails—nowhere as extensively as in the United States, led by California where, in turn, Los Angeles dominates.

The racial-capitalist state's institutional capacities changed because, in the aggregate, capital succeeded in burdening workers and their communities with the costs of both downturns and surges in economic activity. By contrast, for a few prior decades the rising strength of workers had, again in the aggregate, compelled capital to smooth fluctuations by paying both higher wages and, important for this discussion, a significant indirect—or social—wage through taxes on profit. But now, states' rights, once the bulwark of US apartheid, have returned with a vengeance.

Thus, as we have seen in the case study, what Rachel Herzing terms "the Bratton brand" of policing developed in the context of ideological as well as institutional crises.[38] Capitalism saving capitalism from capitalism creates vulnerabilities and opportunities precisely because the intertwined imperatives of organized abandonment and organized violence are so thoroughly destabilizing. The motion affects everybody and everything.

In other words, racial capitalism's contemporary self-saving modality—cut costs and evade regulation by starving the welfare state and smashing regulatory and other barriers to rapid accumulation—has put all public agencies on notice by

---

37 Michan Connor, "Uniting Citizens after Citizens United: Cities, Neoliberalism, and Democracy," *American Studies* 54.1 (2015): 5–27.

38 Rachel Herzing, "Resisting the Bratton Brand: Lessons from the US," Institute of Race Relations, 2011, irr.org.uk.

raising the anti-state hue and cry. As a result, in the general context of organized abandonment, all state actors, fighting their redundancy or seeking state power, try to expand their agency's scope and durability. Both the relative autonomy of the state and interinstitutional competition within states help us understand how this unfolds. The constant invocation of oligarchs' demands ("do more with less") belies behind-the-scenes scheming for comparative advantage that permeates what Toni Negri characterized in 1980 as "the crisis of the crisis-state."[39] Superficial instrumentality underlies institutional ambitions. The ruse is to appear compliant—act and sound anti-state— while achieving security toward the goal of absolute growth, in the process developing and sustaining the anti-state state.

Given the default legitimacy of "organized violence" in the range of obligations, responsibilities, and privileges characterizing the modern state, it might seem self-evident that in a time of abandonment police would come out well—compared with education or health or housing. But in fact, even the domestic agents of organized violence have consolidated and grown by relegitimizing themselves institutionally and ideologically, certainly before 9/11 but even since then.[40] Such success takes a lot of work because institutional competition within states draws on varying constituencies who, at least in theory, might come together to achieve different outcomes.[41]

---

39   Toni Negri, "The Crisis of the Crisis-State," *Revolution Retrieved: Writings on Marx, Keynes, Capitalist Crisis and New Social Subjects (1967–1973)*, London: Red Notes, 1988, 177–98.

40   For an overview of this shift, see the Policing Futures Institute volume: Joseph Andrew Schafer et al., *Policing 2020: Exploring the Future of Crime, Communities, and Policing*, Washington, DC: United States Department of Justice/Federal Bureau of Investigation, 2007.

41   James O'Connor, *The Fiscal Crisis of the State*, Piscataway, NJ: Transaction, 2001 [1973]. Certainly, the case study alludes to such a failed possibility, and many organizations around the country have tried to build on the kinds of insights put forward by O'Connor, the late Dr. Eddie Ellis, and others. See, for example, California Prison Moratorium Project, "How to Stop a Prison in Your Town," n.d., curbprisonspending.org.pdf.

Much to the dismay of libertarians who embrace devolution as a route to shrinking government absolutely rather than merely rescaling it, the dollar cost of the "anti-state state" hasn't diminished much, if at all. While attacks rage on non-discretionary spending (social security, medicare, and other entitlements), discretionary costs associated with the production and management of mass criminalization manifest most dramatically. Criminal justice spending has risen across the board, with most cost devoted to uniformed and civilian personnel, in the wake—not ahead—of decades-long drops in all kinds of crime.[42]

In addition, police departments have revised and expanded their remit, as the Los Angeles case study demonstrates.[43] The practice of agencies imitating institutional competitors in order to secure scarce dollars or secure reputational legitimacy is not new. Analytically, what's important is the interplay of fiscal, bureaucratic, and ideological capacities, as we explain in the next section.

Structure and Flow

Interinstitutional competition and copying is hardly a feature specific to devolution. The contemporary dynamic brings to mind a—perhaps *the*—major change that occurred during and after World War II, at a time of state aggrandizement. To prevent the Department of War's normal postwar dismantling, military elites and industrial and political members of their

---

42 As Platt and Takagi note, police personnel and equipment spending increased in the 1960s and 1970s, and the LAPD committed enormous resources to developing the first comprehensive computerized data management system. Tony Platt and Paul Takagi, "Intellectuals for Law and Order: A Critique of the New 'Realists,'" in Tony Platt and Paul Takagi, eds., *Crime and Social Justice*, New York: Macmillan, 1981, 32–34; LAPD website: lapdonline.org.

43 Schafer et al., *Policing 2020*.

bloc figured out how to use fiscal and bureaucratic capacities, developed for New Deal social welfare programs, to grow rather than wither the department.[44] They built and expanded bases, hired uniformed and civilian staff, promoted mass post-secondary education, established the Gunbelt, oversaw one of the biggest population relocation projects in the United States, and churned trillions of dollars through public and private research, development, manufacturing, and think-tank outfits—including universities—that together produced not only vast industrialized capacity for war-making but also the ideological and public relations methods to promote and naturalize this remarkable transformation.[45]

The military-industrial complex is the short name for all of these activities, relationships, people, and places, and one of its achievements was the creation of the Sunbelt—a political-economic region that produced a string of presidents: Johnson, Nixon, Carter, Reagan, Bush, Clinton, Bush. After Johnson, most candidates ran on anti-state platforms, and, having won, they all set about making the state bigger while destroying individuals, institutions, and initiatives that might improve working people's lives and hopes: radical anti-capitalist organizations, full employment, public-sector unions, the short-lived "peace dividend," welfare rights, prisoners' rights, open immigration, public education, peace itself.

In the closing decades of the twentieth century, prison, policing, and related agencies of state and local governments have demonstrated patterning similar to that of the Department of War in the late 1940s. As we have seen, there's a more detailed history of police/military interaction. But for our purposes here the pattern of achieving legitimate stability is what matters.

---

44 Gregory Hooks, *Forging the Military-Industrial Complex: World War II's Battle of the Potomac*, Champaign: University of Illinois Press, 1991.

45 Ann Markusen, Peter Hall, Scott Campbell, and Sabina Deitrick, *The Rise of the Gunbelt: The Military Remapping of Industrial America*, Oxford: Oxford University Press, 1991.

Police, prisons, and jails have consolidated their numbers, relevance, status, and capacity—sometimes competitively, but always with combined growth.

In other words, devolution creates its own intrastate struggle for dominance; in the same way that capitalist firms concentrate while extending their reach, so do institutions patterned on the capitalist imperative to grow or die. Certainly, the rise of the voluntary sector, as Jennifer Wolch demonstrates in *The Shadow State*, shows how ordinary people built the capacity to withstand some aspects of organized abandonment and meet basic needs. A good deal of the contemporary social justice not-for-profit sector is heir to the desire—whether altruistic, cynical, or desperate—to demand or provide services externalized from the state.[46] In such a context it isn't a foregone conclusion that in current practice, whatever legitimacy the police and military might have in theory, they automatically will withstand pressure to shrink.[47] Rather, they make themselves ideologically and practically indispensable.

Indeed, while the postwar Pentagon successfully imitated fiscal and bureaucratic forms intended for social welfare agencies in order to expand its war-making abilities, today's crisis-driven agencies—including the Pentagon—strive to absorb their institutional rivals' missions in order to survive and thrive. Since the late 1970s, for example, the US Department of Education has punitively monitored selective service (military draft) registration, as well as certain kinds of drug convictions. What's more, it has its own SWAT team to bust alleged financial aid fraudsters. Federal and local housing authorities ration eligibility for shelter based on criteria unrelated to the need for affordable rent.

---

46 Jennifer Wolch, *The Shadow State: Government and Voluntary Sector in Transition*, New York: Foundation Center, 1990. For an elaboration on these themes, see "In the Shadow of the Shadow State," in this volume, 224–241.

47 Schafer et al., *Policing 2020*.

So it is with the police and military: police organizations are increasingly participants in social services as both coordinating forces and primary providers, at the same time that the Pentagon has developed its latest counterinsurgency doctrine to recast soldiers as door-to-door diplomats in camouflage.[48]

Thus, while organized violence gives police a modicum of institutional durability, that platform, combined with the bureaucratic and fiscal capacities required of contemporary departments, has enabled the people in blue to seize new opportunities to manage organized abandonment—to administer all aspects of pacification, as has happened in the capitalist workplace and related institutions during this period.[49] Who is better positioned for such a role in the ambience of organized-abandonment-related crises than the police, whose professional hubris in recent years, beyond the hosannahs of heroism, rests on the expensive and expansive development of technocratic expertise: logistics, big data, CompStat, so-called predictive policing? This, then, shows us the larger context for our case study, by pointing to where the police intersect not only with rival agencies, but also articulate with shadow state formations that might have arisen in opposition to policing but now slurp at a single trough.

But even the opportunism—if it can be thus styled—isn't cut from whole cloth. Rather, the precedent for the case study has decades-long roots that snake forward from the time the rate of profit in US capitalism began to fall and *de jure* US apartheid came apart. We have already referred to the Sunbelt presidents

---

48 U.S. Army/Marine Corps, *Counterinsurgency Field Manual*, Chicago: University of Chicago Press, 2007. See also Joint Chiefs of Staff, *Counterinsurgency*, Joint Chiefs of Staff Joint Publication 3–24, November 22, 2013; Khalili, *Time in the Shadows*.

49 See David Gordon, *Fat and Mean: The Corporate Squeeze of Working Americans and the Myth of Managerial Downsizing*, New York: Free Press, 1996; Samuel Bowles and Arjun Jayadev, *Guard Labor: An Essay in Honor of Pranab Bardhan*, University of Massachusetts Amherst, Department of Economics Working Papers no. 2004–15, 2004, ideas. repec.org.

who established the Law Enforcement Assistance Administration and spread it through significant federal subventions for policing and prisons.[50] They also made widespread if patchy attempts to develop snitch culture as a condition of minimal local development dollars, especially the Weed and Seed program—surely a preview of federal, state, and foundation-funded "community reinvestment" cash currently trickling down.[51] Remaining traces of the long transition from state aggrandizement to anti-state devolution show quite starkly how the social wage remains centrally controlled even as it appears that localities choose how to participate in various aspects of public life. Participation in design, scope, and consequence is not open to democratic process, while at the same time both categorical and procedural constraints determine possibilities within narrowly defined funding allocations (underwritten by private foundation dollars) and the preferences of the most powerfully organized municipal agencies.

In 2011, the administration of California's Democratic governor Jerry Brown rolled out a "Realignment" program for the adult criminal justice system. Realignment follows to the letter devolution's underlying principles, and in California's case it recapitulates an earlier round that involved the care (and sometimes custody) of persons with mental health problems. The vast criminal justice project shifts authority for control and custody of people with particular conviction profiles from Sacramento to the state's fifty-eight counties, accompanied by a rhetoric of "closer to home" that seems amenable to something

---

50 Naomi Murakawa, *The First Civil Right: How Liberals Built Prison America*, Oxford: Oxford University Press, 2014; Marie Gottschalk, *Caught: The Prison State and the Lockdown of American Politics*, Princeton: Princeton University Press, 2014; Judah Schept, *Progressive Punishment: Job Loss, Jail Growth, and the Neoliberal Logic of Carceral Expansion*, New York: New York University Press, 2015.

51 See the Urban Strategies Group, "A Call to Reject the Federal Weed and Seed Program in Los Angeles," Labor/Community Strategy Center, 1992.

like more democracy. But as we have seen, the anti-state state is forcefully organized by centralization—ranging from strengthened and technocrat-heavy executive branches to mandatory minimums, through strong central command of police departments to categorical exclusion of millions of people from many aspects of normal life due to criminal records. California is also in the process of funding and building $2 billion in new prison capacity, and the counties are competing for state grants (initially funded by new state debt) to expand jail capacity. At the same time, the Golden State hosted a test run for the new, US-wide "bipartisan consensus on criminal justice reform," which purports to return to schools money long since diverted to prisons. The first year's implementation produced about a dollar per student, and even that paltry amount requires school districts to be organized to acquire the resources that police and sheriffs are already prepared to absorb into their budgets.

Ideologically, which is to say both in thought and in everyday culture, the experience and normalization of the twin processes, devolution and centralization—patterned as they are by the sensibility of permanent crisis—shape structures of feeling and therefore to a great extent determine the apparent range of socially as well as politically available options. That dynamic, in turn, sheds light on why certain tendencies in scholarship and advocacy have risen to prominence in the dense context of many kinds of analysis and many varieties of advocacy. When Connie Rice dismisses a worry about police delivering social welfare to benefits-starved residents, claiming that "it's what the community asked for," we can see beyond the shadow of a doubt that the shadow state has been absorbed into the repressive function of the anti-state state, and neither devolution nor a new round of deliberate state growth will undo the relationships so firmly established—as naturalized as the Pentagon's role in many aspects of everyday industry, workforce development, land use, and knowledge production.

Conclusion

In May 1961, local Alabama law enforcement allowed Ku Klux Klan members in Montgomery and Birmingham to beat Freedom Riders and burn one of their buses, provoking the Kennedy administration's Justice Department to intervene. Rather than relying on Ku Klux Klan violence to discourage and discipline Freedom Riders, which would invite federal troops, Democratic Mississippi Governor Ross Barnett changed the plot. He effectively told the plantocratic state's paramilitary wing (the Klan) to stay home by promising that differently uniformed officers would take care of matters using arrest and imprisonment—in local jails and at the Parchman Farm state prison plantation. Seven decades of organizing against white mob violence protected by law enforcement and the courts, growing out of Ida B. Wells's proto-#BlackLivesMatter advocacy, had finally managed to crack the legitimacy of a certain kind of terror regime. In other words, Governor Barnett agreed to protect the Riders from mob violence but did so by enforcing Mississippi's laws, including segregation laws and long sentences.

> Well, we didn't have much trouble with the freedom riders. When they didn't obey the officials here in the City of Jackson in Hinds County, we just simply put them in jail, and when the jails were all filled and the mayor's chicken coops down on the fairground were all filled, there were thirty-two of them left, and it was my happy privilege to send all of them to the State Penitentiary at Parchman and put them in maximum security cells. We put them in maximum security cells so they would be protected, you see. You haven't heard of any more freedom riders in Mississippi.[52]

---

52 Ross R. Barnett, oral history interview, May 6, 1969, jfklibrary .org.

The shift from state-sanctioned mob violence to arrest and incarceration is one mark of the transition from US apartheid. While the rural and urban Black freedom struggle created the crises that compelled the transition, the movement's interdependent ideologies and tactics ran up against counter-revolutionary forces that regrouped behind a blue line they could move at will. Eventually massive expansion and capitalization of local law enforcement, community policing, and accelerated criminalization produced a temporary stasis.[53] The legitimacy of the badge replaced the discredited Klan hood.

Yet the onslaught of police killings suggests as well that turning the extralegal into the legal, more than half a century later, internalized in police forces certain aspects of non-state organized violence that erupt with regularity in the context of the crisis state. How often do police killings happen? Twice a week? Once every twenty-eight hours? Or, as the *Guardian* newspaper shows for the year 2015, once every eight hours—all, we might say, in a day's work.

The Bratton brand developed out of the need, variously understood, to deal with and contain long-standing opposition to police killing and other police violence. Just as Mississippi's Barnett shifted practices during Jim Crow's death throes, such reforms are not only about policing. Mississippi passed right-to-work laws and cut income taxes the same year that the Freedom Riders arrived. As a result, it welcomed some of the first companies fleeing strong union states and made nice with the federal government in order to position the Magnolia State to receive a steady flow of Gunbelt-directed federal dollars.

"Bipartisan consensus" around police reform has emerged and flourished in the precise nexus of organized abandonment

---

53 See Platt and Takagi, "Intellectuals for Law and Order"; Murakawa, *The First Civil Right*; Khalil Gibran Muhammad, *The Condemnation of Blackness: Race, Crime, and the Making of Modern Urban America*, Cambridge: Harvard University Press, 2011.

and organized violence. The specificities of the contemporary anti-state state do not stop with reinvigorated rights for states and localities. Rather, by recasting obligations and responsibilities of various levels of the state in a state of permanent crisis caused by the withdrawal of the social wage coupled with the withering of the paycheck, Bratton, Rice, and their ilk become the Tancredi of the racial state, insisting that: "If we want things to stay as they are, things will have to change."[54] To whom, against whom, can one carry one's petition or raise one's fist?

Sparked by police murder, in the context of racial capitalism's neoliberal turn, the post-Ferguson movement may therefore be understood as protests against profound austerity and the iron fist necessary to impose it.[55] The movement's central challenge is to prevent the work from facilitating another transition in regimes of racist policing and incarceration, displacement, and disinvestment through formal but not transformative reforms.[56] James Kilgore, one of the first to write about police humanitarianism, recently warned how the "bipartisan consensus on criminal justice reform" is actually a move toward what he, following Tariq Ali, calls the "extreme center."[57] The extreme center of the United States is far to the right, especially when it comes to vulnerable lives. The truth of the matter is that a few high-profile sentence commutations, coupled with new offers such as body cameras, training books, even the occasional indictment or end to military-surplus weapons transfer, will not de-weaponize the various capacities, reaches, and effects of the Bratton brand, as mass criminalization—and the

---

54　Giuseppe Tomasi di Lampedusa, *The Leopard*, New York: Pantheon, 2007 [1960], 28.

55　Ed Vulliamy, "The Rebellion in Baltimore Is an Uprising against Austerity, Claims Top US Academic," *Guardian*, May 2, 2015.

56　Ruth Wilson Gilmore and Craig Gilmore, "Restating the Obvious," in this volume, 259–287. See also Woods, *Development Arrested*.

57　James Kilgore, "Obama, Mass Incarceration and the Extreme Center," *Counterpunch*, July 21, 2015, counterpunch.org.

straight-up human sacrifice it relies on, from Trayvon Martin to Sandra Bland—enables racial capitalism's death-dealing austerity.[58]

---

58   Ruth Wilson Gilmore, "The Worrying State of the Anti-Prison Movement," in this volume, 449–453; Marie Gottschalk, "The Folly of Neoliberal Prison Reform," *Boston Review*, June 8, 2015; Kay Whitlock and Nancy Heitzeg, "Moneyballing Justice: 'Evidence-Based' Criminal Reforms Ignore Real Evidence," *Truthout*, March 29, 2015.

14

From Military-Industrial Complex to Prison-Industrial Complex
An Interview with Trevor Paglen

Trevor Paglen [TP]: The phrase "prison-industrial complex" recalls the phrase "military-industrial complex." As far as I know, President Dwight D. Eisenhower coined the term "military-industrial complex" in 1961 during his farewell speech as he was leaving office. In that speech, Eisenhower warned the country of a rising military-industrial complex, which he described as being a great danger to the country. Can you tell us a little bit about this "military-industrial complex?"

Ruth Wilson Gilmore [RWG]: Eisenhower was a general in the Army for his entire adult career, other than his eight years as President, so he had a deep sense of the relationship between the military and politics. He could see that in the aftermath of World War II, the military had become extremely powerful in American politics.

Whenever I reflect on this, I'm surprised that the military's newfound political power worried him so much, but it did. It worried him for a few reasons. First, he saw that the national economy was becoming guided by big military contractors. This also meant that the Pentagon was only going to rise with its power relative to other agencies. Remember that Eisenhower was a Republican, he wasn't a big-government kind of guy. He believed in free enterprise. It wasn't that he was worried about what the Pentagon was doing in terms of squeezing the welfare state to death. Instead, Eisenhower was worried that the combination of the welfare state and the Pentagon would kill the entrepreneurial spirit that he thought made America great. He worried that our society and economy would become dependent on these huge amounts of government and military spending.

By the time Eisenhower delivered his farewell speech, the military was already receiving a huge chunk of the government's annual budget. Because of that, it had become responsible for a large part of the nation's economy. In Eisenhower's view, that meant that the broad range of possibilities that he imagined (however sentimentally) made America great would be restricted. He worried that this transformation of our society and economy meant the loss of a certain kind of freedom, as he imagined it.

I don't get romantic about Dwight Eisenhower, but it's interesting that a guy who made his life going to war with everyone still imagined freedom in terms of "freedom to" rather than "freedom from." Being free meant more than being free "from communism" or being free "from totalitarianism." At the end of the day, he seemed worried that the freedom to try something new—and fail—would disappear. That's what worried him about the military-industrial complex (MIC).

TP: In the first ten or fifteen years after the end of World War II, there was also a huge amount of paranoia in American politics. There were the McCarthy Hearings, the "bomber gaps," and "missile gaps." There was widespread paranoia about communism and the Soviet Union. The nuclear arms race was also going forward at an incredible rate. The threat of nuclear war was very much a part of everyday life. Do you think that Eisenhower was also concerned about an environment that combined paranoia and fear with nuclear weapons?

RWG: Eisenhower was very afraid of the nuclear age: he couldn't even say the word "nuclear age." Because, for him, it meant that warfare from then on would be something that he didn't know about. I think it is true that Eisenhower had some concern about the kinds of political power that the military had. He was dismayed about the growth and stabilization of the Pentagon in the postwar years as its own agency. The Pentagon did not exist before 1947. That's one of the hardest things to get people in the United States to understand these days. The Pentagon and the Defense Department as we know them are relatively new things in American history.

On the other hand, I don't want to seem to be nostalgic for the "good old days" of hand-to-hand combat or something. War-making in the United States was increasingly industrialized in the nineteenth and early twentieth centuries. Long before the nuclear age, questions like "how can we kill more people with fewer shooters?" and "how can we make weapons more efficiently?" were constantly asked. If you study the Civil War for fifteen minutes, you see that the fortunes of the post-bellum robber barons came from the Civil War. They made money off the Union, selling everything from boots to guns. They even sold things that the Union never took delivery of. And that's how they got their start. If you look back earlier in the nineteenth century, certain innovations like the manufacture of steel came into existence because the British government threw a lot of money into innovations in steel production. They wanted to clad the hulls of their boats or lay the rails for trains. Over the entire history of the modern world, the relationships between capitalism, innovation, and war-making are tightly connected. In a sense, when Eisenhower sings his lament in 1961, he's suggesting that we've arrived at a certain break, but it's hard to see exactly what the break was other than the fact that we'd arrived at nuclear capability.

TP: People still talk about the military-industrial complex. Where is it now, how has it changed, and how important is it to the United States?

RWG: There are a couple of things that I'd like to talk about a little bit. One is that when Eisenhower lamented the development of this complex, he focused his attention on two areas: he was talking about the government, on the one hand, and a certain faction of big business, on the other. After that speech a lot of people, from the sixties to the nineties, analyzed what the other components of the MIC were. Because, obviously, those two institutions, however powerful they may seem, couldn't have that kind of power if there weren't other forces enabling them.

The MIC really consisted of a whole shift in the relationship between a certain part of the federal state and a certain faction of capitalists. But it also represented a change in the fiscal and political relationship between the Northeast, on one hand, and the former "hinterlands," the Southwest, on the other. One of the major achievements of the MIC was to push a whole lot of capital out of the Northeast and spread it across the South, the Southeast, and the West. It had never been there before, and that money shifted the political balance of the country. It shifted a lot of political power away from the Northeast.

There's a reason why all of the presidents in your lifetime have come from the South. And that is related to the MIC. There was a big investment of money into the South, and this also meant a huge influx of people to these areas out of the Northeast and Midwest. The rise of the MIC also shifted the political makeup and class and education of the regions into which the new people moved. It displaced a whole lot of people, Black and not Black, and at the end of the day, turned the country into the place from which Ronald Reagan, Richard Nixon, the Bushes and so forth could rise.

Taking a step back and looking at the MIC, it's important to see it as the "complex" that it is. It's not just the business and military interests. We have all the people who are dependent on these expenditures of public money for the military. This includes all the people in all the towns that got the military bases and people who work at the bases. All the people in the academy who get federal grants and contracts to do classified and unclassified research and development. All of the intellectuals in the quasi-public nonprofits like the RAND Corporation that write reports for the military. Of course, you also have people like Lockheed, Boeing, the generals and Joint Chiefs of Staff, and so forth. All of those people make up the MIC. The MIC seems at first to be something that's really between the Pentagon and the corporations, but it's much more. It's a complicated process, hence the word "complex." And people depend on the MIC from local levels all the way through the central state.

The MIC has had a huge cultural effect on this country. I do think—and I absolutely believe this—that one of the key cultural effects of the MIC has been to constantly refresh, renew, and reinvigorate the cultural violence that holds this country together. There's an assumption in this country that says, "When in doubt, attack." That's how people live their everyday lives. We have a permanent warfare mentality. We assume that our neighbor is threatening us and that we should harm them if they come over the fence. People in the United States talk about self-defense as, "I ought to kill someone who I think is threatening me," and then we say, "That's just human nature." It's not human nature—it's American culture. We also say that we ought to kill people who have harmed other people. Our society is constantly chanting, "Kill, kill, kill, kill, kill."

The MIC, on top of having certain kinds of political and economic effects, renews, reinvigorates, and refreshes a culture of violence that presumes people ought to kill one another all the time, whether or not war is declared. To have this kind of MIC, you have to justify it by having a society that always imagines itself at war with someone else.

TP: So, how did the term "prison-industrial complex" come out of this idea of the MIC?

RWG: The person who gets credit for coining the phrase "prison-industrial complex" is Mike Davis, who published an article in the mid-1990s with "prison-industrial complex" in the title.[1] But all through the 1990s, people were throwing around variations on that phrase.

In the 1980s and 1990s, the US prison system hit record high after record high, year after year. More and more states and counties built more and more prisons, passed more and more mandatory minimum sentencing laws, and these massive prison systems and severe sentencing laws became totally normal. At that point a lot of people were able to see that it had all of the complexities of the MIC, and began talking about a prison-industrial complex (PIC).

What I find useful in terms of thinking about the PIC is that like the MIC, there are all sorts of people and places that are tied in, or want to be tied in, to that complex. There are people who are dependent on the PIC voluntarily, and people dependent on it involuntarily. As with the MIC, there are boosters who want to build prisons, and there are all kinds of employees —uniformed and not. There are all the intellectuals—I'm one of them—who make a living off it, most of whom want to make it either bigger or better. Most want to make it better, these are the reformists. There are people who are politically dependent on its growth.

To this day, it doesn't matter what anybody says in any poll, what the soccer moms say, or what any "likely voters" say, every politician will say "I can't be soft on crime." It doesn't matter what anyone in the public says. So we're making a segue here from the political and economic to that kind of cultural dimension that the PIC has created, or has recreated, I should say. The PIC has shifted folks' conceptions of problems and what the solutions to problems should be.

Our society has completely normalized extreme punishment

---

1   Mike Davis, "Hell Factories in the Field: A Prison-Industrial Complex," *The Nation* 260.7 (February 20, 1995): 229–34.

through torturous circumstances, which is what putting people in cages is. Criminalization produces an endless supply of enemies, like the "threat of communism" used to, and "radical Islam" does now. The MIC and PIC are very similar—you can go point by point and show the ways that they line up with each other. There's also an actual material connection between what General Electric, for example, does with developing its products for warfare, and what it does with developing technologies for surveillance and control. One of the big ironies is that when communism fell, a lot of people on the left were saying that we could take all that money from the MIC and convert it to peacetime uses like "fighting crime." That sort of mentality made me very sad at the time.

TP: So the prison-industrial complex and the military-industrial complex are related to each other in some very strong ways. Prisons have been around for about 200 years, but "prisons" and the "prison-industrial complex" are not necessarily the same thing. Can you speak a little bit about the origins of the PIC?

RWG: In the 1950s and through the 1960s and 1970s, you had a huge number of revolutions going on. Colonized peoples were kicking the French out of Algeria, the United States out of Vietnam, and so forth, all over the world. Here at home, there were also the beginnings of a revolution: everything from the civil rights movement to the anti-war movement to groups like the Black Panthers getting together and saying "we're not going to take this anymore." People around the world were trying to liberate themselves from the institutions of colonialism, racism, and capitalist oppression. In my view, the origins of the modern PIC emerge out of the contexts of those struggles. More specifically, I think that the origins of the modern PIC are in what we might call the counterrevolution: the reaction to these struggles.

I find it hard to accept arguments that suggest a lot of guys woke up one morning and said, "Hey, I have an idea, let's be mean to Black people," and got all their friends on the phone and went into a smoke-filled room and got busy. And that Black people were just walking around minding their own business and then all of the sudden they got snapped up in the dragnet. Especially because, the morning before, these guys were already being mean to Black people.

I like to think about it this way: in the 1950s and 1960s, there really were people struggling on radical and reformist fronts, struggling for example to get rid of American apartheid. People were fighting really, really, hard and dying a lot in this struggle. The problem that the United States faced was that even though they could demonize this or that little group, there was enough of a positive response to anti-racist or anti-colonialist struggle that the state couldn't really contain it. They really didn't know where it was going to go. There really was disorder in the streets—and not all of it was following a political agenda, not all of it was fleshed-out in many years of study groups. Some of it was spontaneous and erratic and some of it was spontaneous and really great. And so the state's response was, "What do we have? We lost Jim Crow. Culturally, we still have racism, so we don't have to worry about it too much, but legally Jim Crow is no longer a weapon. What do we have left in the arsenal? Well, we have all the lawmaking that we can do. And we do have the cultural idea that there's something wrong with 'those people': the colonized or the victims of apartheid." During this time, we saw the conversation around race change from "they're just not smart enough" to "they're not honest enough." "Crime" became the all-purpose explanation for the struggles and disorder that were going on.

These efforts to explain political struggles and anti-state sentiments as "crime" didn't work overnight: it took some time. Even when the Rockefeller drug laws came in 1973, people around the country were taken aback. Even in Texas, a notoriously bad place to get caught with drugs, people were saying, "Look at New York, those people are really crazy. They're going to send people away for life for this kind of bullshit."

A lot of people explained these new, very extreme, anti-drug laws by saying that Rockefeller wanted to be President and that these drug laws were his last hurrah. By later in the 1970s, you see that the shift was working. The moment of openness from the late 1960s to the early 1970s was over. People in general could not engage or empathize with activists anymore. I think it had to do with the fall of Saigon and the long depression of the 1970s. There were a lot of events that narrowed people's willingness to understand the things that were going on in the 1960s. There were real conditions that allowed the strategy of criminalization to work. By the late 1970s, the idea that poor people, brown people, and activist people were "criminals" had pretty much solidified.

There were some real problems in the 1960s and 1970s, as there are now. Racism and oppression, economic insecurity and depression, for example. People wanted those problems solved. The state didn't say, "We're going to solve this problem by giving income guarantees to everyone in low-income communities." Instead, it said, "We're going to solve this problem by putting everyone in prison for part or all of their lives for doing things that we didn't used to put people in prison for." In the 1970s, the state started coming in and re-arranging social relations. Pretty quickly, it became normal that more and more people were taken away and punished. But people also started demanding those kinds of surveillance and control in their own neighborhoods. It's kind of astonishing to imagine the huge shift that had taken place since the 1960s. There used to be a whole lot of suspicion about what cops and courts were up to —Jim Crow was dead in its grave, but not cold yet. By the early 1980s, community organizations were saying, "We really want more police here."

So during this time period society went from being suspicious of the police and the courts to placing all their trust in them. At the same time, the numbers of people in prison started going through the roof, and "crime" became a national concern. Before the 1970s, crime had been a local issue. "Crime" became a national obsession. Now we're at the point where it seems completely natural to have massive prisons and huge numbers of people in them. These ideas about "crime" and prisons that were very new in the 1970s have become common sense. In only a few years, it has become very hard to imagine a society without mass incarceration.

I'll use myself as the universal anecdote. I didn't grow up in a family that was deeply hostile to cops, but no one would even think of calling the cops for any reason. I mean, there was a motorcycle cop who sat on the street looking for people driving through stop signs, and we used to go over there and chat with the cop, so it wasn't like, "Don't go over there, the Antichrist is over there," or something. But no one would ever, ever, ever, call the police, and if you saw a policeman going to someone's house, you'd assume that the policeman was there to tell them that someone was dead. That's what they were good for: bringing very bad news. It's just amazing how the prison system has changed the traditional ways that people would check each other.

In my generation, there were always old ladies hanging out on the block looking out of windows and if they saw you messing up, they'd tell your grandmother. And they would do it; it would never occur to them not to. So you'd get in trouble and you wouldn't do it again, or you'd do it more stealthily the next time. Some people will say, "You can't blame the PIC for the breakdown of traditional relationships of sociability and responsibility, because this generation is different—they have guns." Well, there *are* more guns. And the guns are easier to conceal, and are more lethal, and are harder to evade. But when I grew up everyone had guns as well. My dad had a rifle and I think he had a pistol as well, but I didn't know where it was. I guess there's the whole "crack epidemic," but I really wish that I'd be alive a hundred years from now to see what they say about it in the future. I'd like to know that. In the 1950s and 1960s people had plenty of legal drugs—mostly alcohol—that caused plenty of lethal behavior. People who say that the difference between now and then has to do with drugs don't really convince me because alcohol was always plentiful. In every situation where someone I know of died horribly (if it wasn't a car crash), it was alcohol related, someone got drunk and beat his wife to death or whatever. What's different now?

One thing that's happened culturally over the last twenty years is that everyone is taught from childhood, "Don't talk to your neighbors, talk to the cops," or, "Don't talk to your parents, talk to the teacher who will talk to the cops." People are taught to get as quickly as they can to someone in uniform. We're taught that doing so is the only safe way to deal with problems. And people believe it. They don't know what else to believe. Everyone is so saturated with police culture and the culture of incarceration that they don't think to do anything else. And if someone like me says, "Why don't you talk to your neighbor?" the answer is, "Because I don't want to get shot."

TP: So, if all of these cultural and economic changes related to the rise of the PIC are new, then are prisons the same thing now that they used to be? What's the same and what's different between a state prison in the nineteenth century and a prison in the twenty-first century?

RWG: Well, if you're taking a bunch of men and a smaller number of women and putting them in cages for some or all of their lives, then you're doing the same thing. But what's different comes from the middle term in the phrase "prison-industrial complex." All aspects of punishment have been industrialized in more recent history, and *only* punishment has been industrialized. The idea of "correction" is out the window. All that's left is punishment. What's different between 1949 and 1989 is that by 1989 in California prisons, the buildings were designed to make punishment as efficient as possible. That's it. That's what it says in the law starting in 1977, effective in 1978.

Let's look at a particular building. In 1949, the purpose of San Quentin was allegedly to figure out ways to help the men and women in prison become self-reliant. It was to make them literate and to give them the things that they need to make it on the outside. Now, we know that this "correction" went to different people in different ways, based on how much the wardens liked them, what color their skin was, where they were from, and so forth. But allegedly, the building was for "corrections." Same building, same cages as now, but a whole lot of employees' time was taken up on behalf of prisoners. I don't want to make it seem like there were some "good old days" for prisoners, because I don't believe that, but the system wasn't completely and efficiently devoted to pure punishment, and nobody minded. Nowadays, it's all about punishment, there's very little in the way of "corrections."

TP: It's obvious to everyone that the prison system is racist. It would be hard to find a single person, even within the government, to say that that isn't true. This might seem like a naïve question, but how and why is race such a huge factor in this system?

RWG: Here's the way it works, I think. If we look at prisons in the United States over time, we'll always find that Black people are disproportionably represented in prisons in the Southeast. Almost anywhere where there are Black people, there are more Black people in prison than there are as a percentage of the population. Same thing goes for Latinos and Latinas in the South and Southwest and so forth.

Up until the early 1870s, prison was a place for white, working class guys to go. That's also true before the Civil War— prison wasn't a place where you wasted scarce public resources punishing or correcting some Black person, or brown person, or red person. You sent white people there, so they would learn, in the words etched on the oldest New Jersey state prison in Trenton, "fear of the law, and [how to] be useful." There were other ways to deal with people of color. In thinking about the PIC today, a lot of people will compare it to the convict lease system in the South, which was created after the Civil War.

In the South after the Civil War, starting around the 1870s, the industrialists of the South were really worried. They were worried about having a labor shortage, because now that the slaves were free, there was really no incentive for the former slaves to work, and a lot of them didn't like the industrialists and they wouldn't work for them unless they were compelled to. The Thirteenth Amendment had outlawed slavery, but fortunately for the industrialists there was an exception in the amendment: slavery was abolished "except as a punishment for a crime." Well, the industrialists got together and said, "Could we please have some crimes—turn these people into criminals so that we can have them back in our clutches and put them back to work?"

After the Civil War, we see the proliferation of laws controlling the movement of people—first there was a series of laws passed to control the movement of Black people called the "Black codes," but then there were laws passed that didn't have "race" in the wording of them, but which had the same effect. So, in the 1870s and 1880s, it was illegal to move around and it was illegal to stand still. You were either a vagrant or you were loitering. Either way, they could grab your ass, put you in chains, and lease you out to the industrialists.

Through these kinds of conspiracies, the white planters produced a whole system in the late nineteenth and early twentieth century that criminalized all kinds of people, but predominantly Black men. By criminalizing Black men and throwing them into prisons, the men could be made to work in mines, fields, railroads, and so forth—for no pay. The only cost to the industrialist was the lease that they paid to the state and the horrible food that they fed to their prisoners/slaves. It was really a death sentence, because lots and lots of those prisoners died. The convict lease system was a racist system designed to compel people who had labored without compensation under slavery to keep laboring without compensation.

The convict lease system actually ended because working-class white people got tired of competing with criminalized Black people for jobs. Around that time, Jim Crow emerged from the South as a way to control Black people, while allowing working-class white people to participate in local government and a local economy. Jim Crow laws started slowly and then took off like wildfire.

If we fast-forward to the last part of the twentieth century, what's the same and what's different? Well, what's marginally the same is that a lot of the people who are arrested, tried, convicted, and sentenced are people of color. And everyone who's not a person of color is a poor white person. At the time of conviction, about half of prisoners were working steadily, which means half were not. These are people with rocky employment records. Maybe half are literate, half are not. We're talking about modestly educated men and women who work in jobs making, moving, growing, and taking care of things. That's who gets taken to prison. But unlike the convict lease system, the difference between the latter half of the nineteenth century system and the latter half of the twentieth century is that there isn't a huge demand for their labor. We don't have a place that just went through the destruction of a Civil War. We don't have the complete rejigging of the economy from, in the case of the South, slavery to capitalism. So that doesn't explain why all these people are going to prison.

If the people who are caught up and sent into prison are not caught up and sent there in order to have their labor exploited —and they're not—then what else do we know about them? Well, for them to be raw material for the PIC, they've got to be as good as dead. You have to have a cultural attitude where people think, "Black people? They ain't nothing. Muslims? They're all terrorists. Poor white people? They're all speed addicts. Women? They're all welfare queens." And so on.

So there's got to be already something in place, which is to say, the founding racism of this country. You have to have such pervasive racism that you can have 2.2 million people in prison and almost nobody except little rag tag organizations like Critical Resistance says, "Wait a minute, this isn't right!" That's what racism does, and it creates the conditions for racism to proceed. In the logic of racism, there is this parasitic category of people—"criminals"—whose relatives and people like them are probably also parasites, so better we relieve ourselves of that burden by locking them away and putting the kids in foster care so that we can save ourselves.

The whole system wouldn't be possible without racism, but racism has been renovated. It's not the same old racism, even though it requires white supremacy to work, anti-Black racism to work, and it requires thinking and acting on those thoughts. Racism makes it possible to become so detached from another human being that another person with a different skin color might not even seem human.

TP: It seems that both of these phenomena, the MIC and the PIC, really bring up a fundamental question about the role of government or the state. They suggest questions like "what is the purpose of government?"

RWG: The one thing we didn't talk about is the relationship between the bureaucratic capacities of the state and what the state actually does. "What's within the realm of the state in terms of what it can do legitimately, and what it can do materially?"

Legitimately, the state can raise money. Materially, it can staff an office, or it has an office full of people who can do things with the money it raises. But, can it legitimately raise money for just anything? How does that legitimacy shift from time to time?

For some people, it's always legitimate to claim that the state's primary responsibility is defense. That it's only sometimes legitimate to claim—and what I mean by legitimate is that you can make a political statement and get anywhere with it—that the state equally has a principal responsibility for welfare. If you went out and did a survey on my block tonight, you'd find most people saying that, "No, the state doesn't have a responsibility to provide welfare." Those people have never read the first sentence of the Declaration of Independence, which has welfare in it.

After World War II, we see a big shift happen around what the legitimate functions of the government are. Before 1947, the Department of War was a relatively marginal part of the government—it only really gained real power during times of war. But after World War II and the beginning of the Cold War, the newly formed Department of Defense and the Pentagon become some of the most powerful institutions in the government. In order to achieve that kind of power, the entire society had to be mobilized, culturally and economically, against the "threat" of communism. And so we really see a dramatic change in how our society thinks about the legitimate functions of government. This is what Eisenhower was talking about in his warning about the MIC.

When we get into the 1970s and 1980s, and the era of the PIC, we see a similar shift. Certain bureaucratic capacities of the state lost legitimacy and others gained new legitimacy. Let me give you an example: the California State Public Works

Board was established in 1946 in order to build homes for veterans, hospitals, schools, and other big projects. Until the 1980s, no one even dreamed to use the Public Works Board to build prisons. That's an example of what I mean.

You can also see what I'm talking about in the changes in the internal structures of the Department of Corrections and how it became much bigger and more complicated. The planning department grew and so did the construction department. They eventually hired an investment banker to figure out how to do everything more cheaply. They hired a guy named Gomez, and he was the first guy who hadn't come up through the prison system. What he brought with him was the ability to deal with large numbers of people effectively.

These shifts in what the state does and how the shifts occur goes back to that laundry list we talked about—the questions "What is the MIC?" and "What is the PIC?"

15

Prisons and Class Warfare
An Interview with Clément Petitjean/Période

Clément Petitjean [CP]: In *Golden Gulag*, you analyze the build-up of California's prison system, which you call "the biggest in the history of the world." Between 1980 and 2007, you explain that the number of people behind bars increased more than 450 percent. What were the various factors that combined to cause the expansion of that system? What were the various forces that built up the prison-industrial complex in California and in the United States?

Ruth Wilson Gilmore [RWG]: Let me say a couple of things. I actually found that description of the biggest prison building project in the history of the world in a report that was written by somebody whom the state of California contracted to analyze the system that had been on a steady growth trajectory since the late 1980s. So it's not even my claim, it's how they themselves described what they were doing. What happened is that the state of California, which is, and was, an incredibly huge and diverse economy, went through a series of crises. And those crises produced all kinds of surpluses. It produced surpluses of workers, who were laid off from certain kinds of occupations, especially in manufacturing, not exclusively but notably. It produced surpluses of land. Because the use of land, especially but not exclusively in agriculture, changed over time, with the consolidation of ownership and the abandoning of certain types of land and land use. It also produced surpluses of finance capital—and this is one of the more contentious points that I do argue, to deadly exhaustion. While it might appear, looking globally, that the concept of surplus finance capital seemed absurd in the early 1980s, if you look locally and see how especially investment bankers who specialized in municipal finance (selling debt to states) were struggling to remake markets, then we can see a surplus at hand. And then the final surplus, which is kind of theoretical, conjectural, is a surplus of state capacity. By that I mean that the California state's institutions and reach had developed over a good deal of the twentieth century, but especially from the beginning of World War II onwards. It had become incredibly complex to do certain things with fiscal and bureaucratic capacities. Those capacities weren't invented out of whole cloth, they came out of the Progressive Era, at the turn of the twentieth century. In the postwar period they enabled California to do certain things that would more or less guarantee the capacity of capital to squeeze value from labor and land. Those capacities endured, even if the demand for them did not. And so what I argue in my book is that the state of California reconfigured those capacities, and they underlay the ability to build and staff and manage prison after prison after prison. That's not the only use they made of those capacities once used for various kinds of welfare provision, but it was a huge use. And so the prison system went from being a fairly small part of the entire state infrastructure to the major employer in the state government.

So the reason that I approached the problem the way I did is because I'm a good Marxist and I wanted to look at factors of production, but also to make it very clear—and this has to do with being a good Marxist—that these factors of mass incarceration, or factors of production, didn't have to be organized the way they were. They could have become something else. Therefore I begin with the premise that prison expansion was not just a response to an allegedly self-explanatory, free-floating thing called crime, which suddenly just erupted as a nightmare in communities. And indeed, in order to think about crime and its central role in California's incarceration system, I studied, like anybody could have, what was happening with crime in the late 1970s and early 1980s. And not surprisingly, it had been going down. Everybody knew it. It was on front pages of newspapers that people read in the early 1980s, it was on TV, it was on the radio. So if crime did not cause prison expansion, what did?

CP: So what was happening more specifically in California? How did those surpluses come together to create this mass prison system?

RWG: Well, they came together politically. In a variety of ways. During the 1970s, the entire US economy had gone through a very long recession. It was the time when the United States lost the Vietnam War, when stagflation became a rule rather than an unimaginable exception—which is to say there was both high unemployment and high inflation. In that context, throughout the United States, people who were in prison had been fighting through the federal court system concerning the conditions of their confinement, the kinds of sentences that they were serving, and so forth. Many of these lawsuits were brought by prisoners on their own behalf. They slowly made their way through the courts. Eventually, in California but in many other states too, in the late 1960s and again in the mid-1970s, the federal courts told the state prison system: "Do something about this, because you're in violation of the Constitution." At first it might seem that the Vietnam War, stagflation, and the violation of prisoners' constitutional rights are unrelated. But indirectly, building prisons and using crime became a default strategy to legitimize the state that had become seriously delegitimized because of political, military, and economic crises. Prison expansion became a way for people in both political parties to say: "The problem with the United States is there is too much government. The state is too big. And the reason people are suffering from this general economic misfortune is because too much goes to taxes, too much goes to doing things that people really should take care of on their own. But if you elect us, we will get rid of this incredible burden on you. There is something legitimate we can do with state power, however, which is why you should elect us: we will protect you from crime, we will protect you from external threats." And people were elected and re-elected on the basis of these arguments, even though everybody knew that crime was not a problem. It's pretty astonishing to me. I lived through this period and went back and studied it later. I found in the California case—and I currently have students who are studying other states—we keep coming across similar patterns: economic crisis, federal court orders, struggles over expansion, increased role of municipal finance in the scheme of prison expansion.

In California, people who had come up through the civil service, working in the welfare department, or working in the Department of Health and Human Services, eventually were recruited to work on the prison side because they had the skills to manage large-scale projects designed to deliver services to individuals. And they brought their fiscal and bureaucratic capacities over to the prison agency in order to help it expand and consolidate. We actually see the abandonment of one set of public mandates in favor of another—of social welfare for domestic warfare, if you will. And I can't say, nor should anybody, that the reason all this happened was because a few people who had bad intentions distorted the system. Rather, we can see a systemic renovation in the direction of mass incarceration: starting in the late 1970s, when Jerry Brown, a Democrat, was governor of California, as he is now; then taking off enormously in the 1980s under Republican regimes; but never going down. It didn't make any difference which party was in power. And the prison population did not begin to go down until elaborate and broad-based organizing combined with a long-term federal court case (again!) compelled system shrinkage in the last several years.

CP: In the book, you argue that prisons are "catchall solutions to social problems." Would you say that the rise of the prison-industrial complex illustrates, or means, deep transformations of the American state and marks the dawn of a new historical period for capitalism, one where incarceration would be not only the legitimate but the only way of dealing with surplus populations?

RWG: Honestly, fifteen years ago, I would have said yes. Now, I say, "Pretty much, but not absolutely yes." Because it's almost worse than the way you framed the question. Rather than mass incarceration being a catchall solution to social problems, as I put it, what has happened is that that legitimizing force, which made prison systems so big in the first place, has increasingly given police—including border police—incredible amounts of power. What has happened is that certain types of social welfare agencies, like education, income support, or social housing, have absorbed some of the surveillance and punishment missions of the police and the prison system. For example, in Los Angeles, a relatively new project, about ten years old, focuses on people who live in social housing projects. Their experience has been shaped by intensive policing, criminalization, incarceration, and being killed by the police. Under the new project they have opportunities for health, tutoring for children, all kinds of social welfare benefits if and only if they cooperate with the police. In the book *Policing the Planet*, my partner and I wrote a chapter that goes into rather exhaustive detail about that case.[1]

CP: Would you say that those shifts herald a new historical period for capitalism?

---

1 "Beyond Bratton," in this volume, 288–317.

RWG: This is a tough question, as you know, for a bunch of reasons. One is that we've all learned to lisp: everybody used to say "globalization," now it's "neoliberalism," and people are more or less talking about the same thing. My major mentor in the study of capitalism is the late great Cedric Robinson, who wrote an astonishing series of books, but the one that completely changed my consciousness is *Black Marxism*. Robinson argues that capitalism has always been, wherever it originated (let's say rural England), a racial system. So it didn't need Black people to become racial. It was already racial between people all of whose descendants might have become white. Understanding capitalism this way is very productive for me when thinking about the present. One issue is what's happening with racial capitalism on a world scale. A second issue has to do with particular political economies, especially those that are not sovereign, like the state of California: how does political-economic activity re-form in the context of globalization's pushes and pulls? Certainly, California's economy continues to be big. It moves up and down a little bit, but if it were a country, it would be in the top seven largest economies. However, the mix of manufacturing, service, and other sectors has changed over time. There's still a lot of manufacturing in the state, although it tends to be more value-added, labor-intensive lower-wage manufacturing, sweatshops, and so forth. And far less steel, and producer goods, and consumer durables.

How, then, should we analyze in order to organize in places like California, New York, and Texas, with their various and variously diverse economies, characterized by organized abandonment and organized violence? How can we generalize from the racist prison system to a more supple perception of racial capitalism at work, to understand and intervene in places where states no less than firms are constantly trying to figure out how to spread capital across the productive landscape in ways that will return profits to investors as quickly as possible? The state keeps stepping in while pretending it's not there. And here I'm not talking about private prisons, which are an infinitesimal part of mass incarceration in the United States, nor of exploited prisoner labor, which also doesn't explain much about the system's size or durability (which, as we've already seen, is vulnerable). Rather, I am talking about how unions that represent low- to moderate-wage public-sector workers, which have a high concentration of people of color as current and potential members, might join forces with environmental-justice organizations, biological diversity/anti–climate change organizations, immigrants' rights organizations, and others to fight, on a number of fronts, group-differentiated vulnerability to premature death—which is what in my view racism is. And if that's what racism is, and capitalism is from its origins already racial, then that means a comprehensive politics encompassing working and workless vulnerable people and places becomes a robust class politics that neither begins from nor excludes narrower views of who or what the "working class" is.

CP: In the book, you develop a critical perspective strongly influenced by David Harvey's critical geography. What does this perspective reveal specifically about mass incarceration?

RWG: I became a geographer when I was in my forties because it seemed to me, at least in the context of US graduate education, that it was the best way to pursue serious materialist analysis. There are so few geography PhD programs in the United States. And I'd been thinking that I was going to train in planning because it seemed the closest to what I wanted to do: to put together "who," "how," and "where" in a way that did not float above the surface of the earth but rather articulated with the changing earth. I actually stumbled into geography. I happened to come across Neil Smith at a Rethinking Marxism conference and was really taken by his work; not only had I not thought about geography, I hadn't taken a geography course for three decades, since I was thirteen. So at the last minute, instead of mailing my application to the planning department at Rutgers, I mailed it to the geography department. And the rest is kind of history. Enrolling in geography brought me into the world of Harvey's historical-geographical materialist way of analyzing the world. I took very seriously what I learned from David, what I learned from Neil and a few other people, and tried to build on it, having already had a long informal education with people like Cedric Robinson, Sid Lemelle, Mike Davis, Margaret Prescod, Barbara Smith, Angela Davis, and many others. And I think that had I not been trained in geography, or beguiled by geography, maybe, I would not have thought as hard as I did about, for example, urban-rural connections —their co-constitutive interdependencies. And I know I wouldn't have thought in terms of scale—not scales in the sense of size, but in terms of the socio-spatial forms through which we live and organize our lives, and how we struggle to compete and cooperate. And I certainly would not have conceptualized mass incarceration as the "prison fix" had I not read David's *Limits to Capital* and thought about the spatial fix as hard as I could. We're colleagues, now, David and me. We enjoy working together and debating toward the goal of movement rather than having the last word.

CP: Can you elaborate on what you mean by "prison fix" compared to Harvey's "spatial fix"?

RWG: What I mean in my book is that the state of California used prison expansion provisionally to fix—to remedy as well as to set firmly into space—the crises of land, labor, finance capital, and state capacity. By absorbing people, issuing public debt with no public promise to pay it down, and using up land taken out of extractive production, the state also put to work, as I suggested earlier, many of its fiscal and organizational abilities without facing the challenges that were already mounting when the same factors of production were petitioned for, say, a new university. The prison fix of course opened an entirely new round of crises, just as the spatial fix in Harvey displaces but does not resolve the problem that gave rise to it. So in the case of communities where imprisoned people come from, we have the removal of people, the removal of earning power, the removal of household and community camaraderie, you name it—all of that happened with mass incarceration. In the rural areas where prisons arose, we can chart related destabilizations: rather than, as many imagine, rural prison towns acquiring resources displaced from urban neighborhoods, the fact is the two locations are joined in a constant churn of unacknowledged though shared precarious desperation—which was the basis on which some of the organizing I described above took form. In other words, infrastructure materially symbolized by the actual prison indicates the extensively visible and invisible infrastructure that connects the prison and its location by way of the courts and the police, the roads for families to visit and goods and incarcerated people to travel, back to the communities of origin expansively incorporating the entire intervening landscape. One of the things I tried to do in the book, framing it with two bus rides, was to give people a way of thinking about what I've just said that's more viscerally poignant. Thinking about the movement across space and the movement through space gives us some sense of the production of space.

The purpose of *Golden Gulag* was not to make people say, "Oh my God, we've all been defeated!" but rather to say, "Wow, that was really big, and now I can see all the pieces. So perhaps instead of thinking there's nothing to be done, what I recognize is there's a hundred different things that we could do. We can organize with labor unions, we can organize with environmental-justice activists, we can organize urban-rural coalitions, we can organize public-sector employees, we can organize low-wage, high-value-producing workers, who are vulnerable to criminalization. We can organize with immigrants. We can do all of these things, because all of these things are part of mass incarceration." And we did all that organizing!

CP: That's a perfect transition to another set of questions about organizing against mass incarceration. Are there resistance movements within prisons comparable to what happened in the 1970s, with the 1971 Attica uprising, for instance?

RWG: My area of expertise doesn't happen to be on that. Orisanmi Burton is someone who is doing fantastic research on that question. Of course, one of the things that's happened in California prisons, particularly the prisons for men, is that their physical design, as well as the design of their management system, were deliberately aimed by the Department of Corrections, starting in the late 1970s, to undermine the possibility of the kind of organizing that had characterized the period from the early 1960s to the mid-1970s. Especially the ones called 180s, or level 4: those are the high-security prisons. They're not panopticons, but prisoners can't evade being under surveillance. There have been not only automatic lockdowns, but also the reduction of education and other in-prison programs, even places where people in prison can gather, such as day rooms, classrooms, gyms, places where prisoners could do the time with some however-modest ongoing sense of self. All the design changes were intended to undermine prisoner organizing and solidarity.

One hugely notorious thing that happened in the California system in the late 1970s, that may or may not have happened in other systems, is that the Department of Corrections was experimenting with ways to keep prisoners from developing solidarity with each other and against the guards. In the early 1970s, California prisoners had notoriously declared, "Every time a guard kills one of us, we're going to kill one of them until they stop killing us." And there were seven incidents over some years. A guard killed a prisoner, prisoners killed a guard.

Not necessarily the guard who killed the prisoner, but somebody died because somebody died. So the department, right before its big expansion began, was trying to figure out what to do. And it came up, not surprisingly, with a solution that was designed to foster interprisoner distrust. The managers declared that certain categories of prisoner belonged to certain ethnic or regional gangs and then fomented discord between the gangs. In a time when desegregation was becoming the law of the land, the Department of Corrections started segregating people in prisons according to the gangs and then to racial and ethnic groups. This is all well-documented, there are case files and lawsuits, and an incredible archive, still to be thoroughly read and written about. And there were countless hearings about this practice throughout the 1990s. I sat through hours of testimony, in which the Department insisted, and still has to this day: "No, we were just responding to what objectively existed." Whereas others who testified, including former prison wardens, said: "No, this didn't exist: you made it. You created it."

What the Department "created" led to development of something called the Security Housing Unit (SHU), which is effectively a prison within the prison. The first one in California opened in 1988 and the second in 1989. In the latter, called Pelican Bay State Prison, people in the SHU had staged several hunger strikes beginning in 2013. And some of the people in that unit, segregated according to their alleged gang affiliation, some of whom had been in that prison within the prison for more than twenty years, had accepted and projected the rigid ethnic, racial, and regional differences as meaningful and immutably real. But as they were trying, as individuals, to sort out a way for them to get out of the prison in the prison and go back to the general prison population, they became increasingly aware of what had happened historically, a dire reform of which they were the current expression. And so in recent years, these people in four "gangs" eventually declared that the only way to solve the problem inside was, to use their word, to end the hostility between the races. Which is an astonishing thing. I've been inside a lot of prisons, including Pelican Bay. And the transformation of consciousness from what I learned from interviewing people in prisons for men about their conditions of confinement in the early 2000s compared with the organizing and analysis that emerged in the last five or so years is astonishing.

I also want to add something about the prisons for women. In the prisons for women, the level of segregation was never as high—to the extent, for example, that they had not separated out people who were doing life on murder and people who were doing a year on drugs. Whereas in a prison for men people are segregated according to custody level (what they are serving time for having done) plus segregated in a number of other ways including race and ethnicity. And so, in part because of the social and spatial organization of the prisons in the period that featured the crackdown on organizing in prisons for men, there was a high and growing level of organizing among the people in prisons for women. So during the last fourteen or fifteen years, as the state of California was trying to build fancy new so-called "gender responsive" prisons for women —to allow mothers to be locked up with their kids, for example —people inside those prisons, however they identified in terms of gender, wrote and signed, "Don't do this for us, because that's just going to expand capacity to lock people up. It's not going to make our lives better." Three thousand people did that organizing in prisons for women, and their self-determination and bravery occurred at great personal risk to themselves because locked-up activists are wholly at the mercy of guards and prison managers.

CP: What about the organizing outside of the prisons? And in particular in communities directly affected by mass incarceration?

RWG: The organizing outside has been quite rich and varied over the years. In my experience, people who at the outset started doing work on behalf of one person in their family or even maybe two people in their family, thinking this was an individual, or the largest scale, a household problem, came to understand through their experiences—working with others, mostly women, most of whom were mothers—the political dimensions of what they originally encountered as a personal, individual, and legal problem. That's one kind of organizing that has persisted for many years now, twenty-five years or more. There's also the organizing that we, meaning the groups Critical Resistance and California Prison Moratorium Project, helped to foster between urban and rural communities, under a variety of nominal issues which I described earlier: biological diversity (we took up on behalf of the lowly Tipton kangaroo rat) but also environmental justice (air quality, water quality, for instance). We managed to develop and wage campaigns bringing people together across diverse issues and diverse communities in rural and urban California, so that they could recognize each other as probable comrades rather than presumed antagonists. And that has happened over and over again.

Going back to the fact that the number of people in prisons in California has gone down in recent years: the public explanations for that, the superficial or above-the-surface explanation, is that in 2011 the state of California lost yet another lawsuit, *Brown v. Plata*, also called "Plata/Coleman," and was ordered to reduce the number of people held in the Department of Corrections' physical plant (thirty-three prisons plus many camps and other lockups). The federal lawsuit demonstrated that approximately one person in prison a week was dying of an easily remediable illness because of medical neglect. During the two decades between the beginning of the legal campaign and its resolution, some of the original litigants had long since died. Ultimately, the right-wing Supreme Court of the United States (the court that handed George W. Bush the presidency in the year 2000) could not deny the evidence. There were just too many bodies. In its final judgment that court agreed with lower court rulings, affirming that California could not build its way out of its problem.

But the question that few people who have followed this story ever asked themselves is: "How come California, which had been opening a prison a year for twenty-three years, suddenly slowed down to almost a halt and only opened one prison between 1999 and 2011?" And the answer is all that grassroots organizing I described earlier. We stopped them building new prisons. We made it too difficult. And we showed in our campaigning that whenever the department built a new prison, allegedly to ease crowding, the number of people in prison jumped higher than the new buildings could hold. The new relationships on the ground, organized by prison abolitionists —though the vast majority of participants themselves were not necessarily abolitionist—compelled these courts, which had never summoned any of us as serious witnesses for anything, to say that California could not build its way out of its problem and that it had to do something else. So now a lot of anti–physical plant expansion activity in California has shifted to jails, not prisons. (Jail is where someone is held pending trial or if their sentence is only a year or less. Prison is where someone is sent to serve a sentence for a year and a day or more.) The jails are now expanding because once California complied with the Supreme Court ruling, the state, in order to reduce the number of people it locks up, made resources available to the lower political jurisdictions—the counties— to do whatever they wanted in exchange for retaining people convicted of certain crimes locally rather than sending them to state custody. (This adjustment is called "Realignment.") The counties could have taken those resources and said to convicted people, "Go home and behave yourselves." They could have taken the resources and changed guidelines for prosecutors so there would be fewer convictions. They could have put

the resources into schools or health care or housing. But—
and this gets back to the nagging question of state capacity
and legitimacy—a little more than half of the state's fifty-eight
counties have thus far decided to build new jails. And then
we see in reverse the phenomenon I discussed earlier, about
welfare-state agencies absorbing surveillance and punishment
agencies. The sheriffs, who run the jails, now insist that they
need more and bigger jails for reasons of health: "We have to
supply mental health care and counseling to troubled people.
We need to deliver social goods, and the only way we can do it
is if we can lock people up." So the new front is fighting against
"jails-instead-of-clinics," "jails-instead-of-schools," and so on.
The work brings new social actors into the mix, and, as we
discussed earlier, it enables the broadest possible identification
of purpose in class terms.

To give you a few other examples of the kinds of solidarity
that we managed to bring into action over time in California,
there was a prison that was supposed to have opened in 2000
but we slowed it down. We didn't manage to stop it, but as I
said, after opening a prison a year up to 1998, there were none
opened between 1999 and 2005. That prison was scheduled
for construction by a member of the Democratic Party who
had just been elected governor, and he was paying back the
guards' union, who had given him almost a million dollars
to help with his campaign. So then we got busy and organized in as many different ways as we could. And one of the
ways we could organize, it turned out, was with the California state employees' association, which is part of an enormous
public-sector union in California. And they represent all kinds
of workers in the prisons except the guards, because the guards
have their own stand-alone union. And much to our surprise,
the members of the state employees' union were willing to
go up against the guards and oppose that prison. When they
finally agreed to meet with the abolitionists, they said: "Look.
The guards get whatever they want. What we do, as secretaries,

schoolteachers, locksmiths, drivers, mechanics gets squeezed more and more. We see the lives of the people in custody getting worse and worse, with no hope for getting back to a normal life when they get out—as most people do. And the union that we're part of represents people who work in the public sector, in housing, health care, so on and so forth, in the cities and counties as well as at the state level. So if we recognize who our membership is and what they do, there's no reason for us to support this prison. Even if we might lose a few members who would have the jobs in the new prison, there's more to our remit, as a public-sector union." That completely surprised me, and for a heady political moment we had half a million people throughout California calling for a prison moratorium. It's hard to keep those kinds of political openings lively, but it lasted long enough to interrupt the relentless schedule that the prisons in California had been on since the early 1980s.

CP: From an outsider's perspective, it seems that the Black Lives Matter movement gave a new impetus to debates around prison abolition in radical circles. What does it say about the history of the abolition movement? What's the current balance of forces? What do strategic debates look like?

RWG: It's true that #BlackLivesMatter has got people thinking about and using the word "abolition." That said, the abolition that they have helped put into common usage is more about the police and less about the prisons, although of course there is a connection between the two. It's been amazing to me and many of my comrades to see left-liberal politicians, or magazines like *The Nation* or *Rolling Stone*, seriously ask whether it is time to abolish the police. The ensuing debates tend to be the obvious ones: insofar as abolition is imagined only to be absence—overnight erasure—the kneejerk response is, "that's not possible." But the failure of imagination rests in missing the fact that abolition isn't just absence. As W. E. B. Du Bois showed in *Black*

Reconstruction in America, abolition is a fleshly and material presence of social life lived differently. Of course, that means many who are abolition-friendly falter at what the practice is. All the organizing I've described in our conversation is abolition—not a prelude, but the practice itself. There was a recent attack on abolitionists by some historian who decided, without studying, that abolitionists are a deranged theology. He knew a little, for example, about the *Brown v. Plata* case, but zero about the on-the-ground moratorium organizing that realized the Plata/Coleman theory ("overcrowding") as sufficient cause for which the remedy would not be more of the same. Abolition is: figuring out how to work with people to make something rather than figuring out how to erase something. Du Bois shows, in exhaustive detail, both how slavery ended through the actions and organized activity of the slaves no less than the Union Army, and, since slavery ending one day doesn't tell you anything about the next day, what the next day, and days thereafter, looked like during the revolutionary period of radical Reconstruction. Abolition is a theory of change, it's a theory of social life. It's about making things.

CP: What does the central role of mass incarceration in maintaining the status quo imply in terms of class-struggle strategies? Do anti-incarceration struggle and abolition organizing play a more strategic role today?

RWG: Here's a way of thinking about that in the US context. In the United States today, there are about 70 million adults who have some kind of criminal conviction—whether or not they were ever locked up—that prohibits them from holding certain kinds of job, in many types of job. In other words, it doesn't make any difference what you allegedly did: if you've been convicted of something, you can't have a job. So just take a step back and think about that for a second, just in terms of sheer numbers. If we add the number of people who are effectively documented *not* to work, with the additional 7 or 8 million migrants who are not documented *to* work, the sum equals about 50 percent of the US labor force—mostly people of color, but also 1/3 white. *Half the US labor force.* So it seems that anti-criminalization and the extensive and intensive forces and effects of criminalization and perpetual punishment have to be central to any kind of political, economic change that benefits working people and their communities, or benefits poor people, whether or not they're working, and their communities. This should be a given, but often it's not. In part that's because "mass incarceration" has unfortunately but for understandable reasons come to stand in for "this is the terrible thing that happened to Black people in the United States." It *is* a terrible thing that happens to Black people in the United States! It happens also to brown people, red people ... and a whole lot of white people. And insofar as ending mass incarceration becomes understood as something that only Black people must struggle for because it's something that only Black people experience, the necessary connection to be drawn from mass incarceration to the entire organization of capitalist space today falls out of the picture. What remains in the picture seems like it's only an anomalous wrong that seems remediable within the logic of capitalist reform. That's a huge impediment, I think, for the kind of organizing that ought to come out of the various experiments in worker and community organizing that can produce big changes. Everything is difficult in the United States right now, for all the obvious reasons I won't waste space on. That said, I look with hope for all indications of ways to shift the debate and organizing. The answer for me is to consider in all possible ways how the preponderance of vulnerable people in the United States and beyond come to recognize one another in terms not just of characteristics or interest, but more to the abolitionist point and purpose.

PART IV

ORGANIZING FOR ABOLITION

16

You Have Dislodged a Boulder: Mothers and Prisoners in the Post-Keynesian California Landscape

Now that you have touched the women, you have struck a rock, you have dislodged a boulder, and you will be crushed.
—Women's political chant, Anti Pass-Law Movement, South Africa 1956[1]

Introduction

Mothers Reclaiming our Children (Mothers ROC) is a Los Angeles-based multiracial group that began to organize in November 1992 in response to a growing crisis: the intensity with which the state was locking their children, of all ages, into the criminal justice system.[2] At the outset, the ROC consisted

---

1 Quoted in Angela Y. Davis, *Women, Culture, and Politics*, New York: Random House, 1989, ix–x.

2 A note on terms: When "State" is capitalized, it refers to California; in lower case, "state" refers to the political-geographic category, which I will discuss at a number of scales: US federal, California, Los Angeles County, Los Angeles City, and so forth. The state is not a monolith; the conflicts, coordinations, and compromises within and between various scales of the state are the subject of a different segment of this project [a version of this essay forms the core of Chapter 5 of *Golden Gulag*]. However, I do wish to underscore here that readers who find structural analysis debilitating might (ironically) find reassurance in the indisputable fact that "agency" figures in state practices just as in grassroots movements. What's different, of course, are the all-important attributes of

of only a few mothers and others, women and men, led by founder and president Barbara Meredith and lifelong activist Francie Arbol. The initial project was to mobilize in defense of Meredith's son, an ex-gangster, who had been instrumental in the historic Los Angeles gang truce. The ROC lost his case but gained the makings of a movement. By the spring of 1993, when the LA Four went to trial, Mothers ROC had developed a network throughout greater Los Angeles and achieved recognition as an organization devoted to action rather than to commentary.[3]

The Mothers ROC mission is "to be seen, heard, and felt in the interest of justice." To achieve this goal, Mothers ROC convenes its activism on the dispersed stages of the criminal justice

---

power—including legitimacy, as well as initiative and immunity. On legitimacy, see James O'Connor, *The Fiscal Crisis of the State*, New York: St. Martin's, 1973; on initiative and immunity, see Gordon Clark, "A Theory of Local Autonomy," *Annals of the Association of American Geographers* 74 (1984):195–208. The power blocs in Sacramento that have mustered great political and ideological energies on behalf of constructing the country's biggest prison system are not "the state"—but they have effectively brought about widespread, secular changes in how "the State" deals with criminal and judicial issues, captured the resources (five billion dollars plus debt service in fiscal year 1997), and developed the bureaucratic and architectural structures to maintain and augment the project. By seizing and developing this area of state capacity, the bloc, whose membership is not constant, has changed the state as a whole while creating a bureaucratic class-fragment that protects and advances its own interests (on the seizure of state power, see Eric Hobsbawm, "Gramsci and Marxist Political Theory," in *Approaches to Gramsci*, ed. Anne Showstack Sassoon, London: Writers and Readers, 1982. The state remains, institutionally, "a contradictory object and subject of struggle" (see Alain De Janvry, *The Agrarian Question and Reformism in Latin America*, Baltimore: Johns Hopkins University Press, 1981).

3 The LA Four were the young African American men charged with the widely televised beating of white truck driver Reginald Denny on April 29, 1992, the first day of the uprising. Opposition to the LA Four trial centered on the ideological use of the case to justify acquittal of the four Los Angeles Police Department officers for the televised beating of Rodney King. Reginald Denny himself objected to the railroading of his assailants and also to the state and media's deliberately ignoring the dozens of Black people who saved him.

system.[4] The group extends an unconditional invitation to all mothers struggling on behalf of their children, and it reaches its audience in various ways. The primary method is leafleting public spaces around jails, prisons, police stations, and court-houses to announce the group's existence and purpose. When distributing flyers and business cards, members try to engage people in conversations to explain further what Mothers ROC (whose members are known as ROCers) is and does. ROCers give talks and workshops at elementary and secondary schools, colleges and universities, churches, clubs, and (with decreasing frequency) carceral institutions. They also appear on regional and local radio and television programs. Using these means, Mothers ROC has established a presence at many locations throughout the political geography of the penal system.

ROCers have attracted hundreds of mothers who want to fight on behalf of their own children in the system. Many were already performing in solitude the arduous labor of being on the outside for someone—trying adequately to switch among the many and sometimes conflicting roles required of caregiv-ers, waged workers, and justice advocates. Some attend one meeting and never return, and others persist whether their per-son's case loses or wins. Often newcomers bring someone to the meeting for moral support—marriage or other partner, relative, child, friend from church or neighborhood—and that person

---

4   A note on method: The formal research for the project was conducted from January to December 1996. It was preceded and supplemented by the author's membership in the organization since shortly after its found-ing in 1992. I participated as a member in normal fashion as described in the text of this article. Because everyone in the group is expected to share any special knowledge or expertise, I was called upon several times to present research reports at workshops (as have other scholar-activists over the years). I did in-depth interviews with twelve members of the group, eleven of whom have or have had persons in custody; the interviews were topic-driven and open-ended but always included questions about how the member arrived at the organization, what her/his evaluation of its activities are, and where it could or should be headed. All names in this article are pseudonyms.

also becomes active. Usually, twenty-five women and men participate in each weekly gathering. Most of them learned about the ROC from one of the outreach practices noted above or from an acquaintance who had direct contact with a member. The rest, however, were guided to the organization by their persons in custody. Among the tens of thousands awaiting trial or doing time in the juvenile detention camps and centers and in the county jails throughout the Southland, knowledge of Mothers ROC circulates by word-of-mouth, and a standard part of the message is that the women are willing to help with even apparently hopeless cases.

The ROC's principle is printed on every flyer: "We say there's no justice. What are we going to do about it? ... EDUCATE, ORGANIZE, EMPOWER." Mothers ROC makes no judgment about the innocence of charged persons whose families turn to the group. The group does not provide services to mothers but rather helps them learn how each part of the system works and, as we shall see, to grasp the ways in which crisis can be viewed as an opportunity rather than a constraint. In the process, which can be thought of as cooperative self-help, the mothers transform their reproductive labor as primary caregivers into activism; the activism expands into the greater project to reclaim all children, regardless of race, age, residence, or alleged crime. Experienced ROCers team up with newcomers to call on investigators and attorneys. They research similar cases and become familiar with the policies and personalities of prosecutors and judges. In addition, ROCers attend each other's hearings or trials. They also observe courtroom practices in general and monitor individual officers of the court or state's witnesses believed to promote injustice.[5] The group's periodic demonstrations outside courthouses and police stations bring public attention to unfair practices. Finally, ROCers

---

5 Officers of the court include judges, prosecutors, prosecution and defense attorneys, bailiffs; untrustworthy witnesses include police and jailhouse informants who trade time for testimony.

sponsor monthly legal workshops with activist attorneys and request research reports from scholar-activist members to help mothers become familiar with the bewildering details of the system in action.

Never an exclusively Black organization, Mothers ROC presumed, at first, that it would appeal most strongly to African American women because the state seemed to concentrate its energies on taking their children. However, the sweeping character of the State's new laws, coupled with the organization's spatially extensive informational campaigns, brought Chicanas, other Latinas, and white women to Mothers ROC for help. Today, the group consists of Black, brown, Asian American, and white women along with some men. Most participants currently have persons in custody. People come to meetings from all over Los Angeles County, western San Bernardino and Riverside Counties, and northern Orange County. Their loved ones are in detention throughout California.

Mothers ROC self-consciously identifies with other Third World activist mothers, the name deliberately invoking South African, Palestinian, and Central and South American women's struggles. As we shall see, the organization is neither spontaneous and naive, nor vanguard and dogmatic, but rather, to use Antonio Gramsci's formulation of a philosophy of praxis, "renovates and makes critical already-existing activities" of both action and analysis to build a movement.[6]

From Military Keynesianism to Post-Keynesian Militarism

The stories I will tell about Mothers ROC are evidence of how people organize against their abandonment and disposal within oppositional spaces delimited by gender, race, class, and violence. The crisis that Mothers ROC encounters is not

---

6 Antonio Gramsci, *Selections from the Prison Notebooks*, New York: International Publishers, 1971, 330–1.

unique to the group or the communities they represent. Rather, the crisis emerges from the objective conditions produced by changes in the forces, relations, and geography of capital accumulation in California. These changes, in turn, have produced surpluses of land, labor, finance capital, and state capacity.[7] Since the early 1980s, power blocs have resolved great portions of these surpluses into the state's enormous, costly, and profitable prison system. In expanding and coordinating across scales, its capacities to monitor, coerce, and punish, the state itself is in process of restructuring its own scale, form, and purpose. I call this restructuring the transition from military Keynesianism to post-Keynesian militarism.[8]

During the "golden age" of US capitalism (1944–1974), the rapidly growing economy both generated and was partly dependent on the now legendary military-industrial complex that Dwight D. Eisenhower spoke of with alarm during his final presidential address.[9] In turn, the motley array of welfare-state bureaus that had developed in the interstices of national sectoral, racial, and class conflict during the Great Depression provided the model for the Pentagon's postwar evolution into a major fiscally and politically insulated institution of the central state.[10] New Deal agencies also achieved uneven measures of postwar success as the modes through which the state deployed

---

7 The theoretical and empirical elaboration of these surpluses and their transformation into prisons make up another segment of the project from which the present work is excerpted. Important here is the concept of crisis nicely summarized by Stuart Hall and Bill Schwarz: "the social formation cannot reproduce on the existing basis of social relations." Stuart Hall and Bill Schwarz, "State and Society 1880–1930," in Stuart Hall, *The Hard Road to Renewal*, London: Verso, 1988, 96.

8 See "Globalization and US Prison Growth: From Military Keynesianism to Post-Keynesian Militarism," in this volume.

9 See Fred J. Cook, *The Warfare State*, New York: Macmillan, 1962; Andrew Glyn, Alan Hughes, Alain Lipietz and Ajit Singh, "The Rise and Fall of the Golden Age," in *The Golden Age of Capitalism*, eds. S.A. Marglin and Juliet Schor, New York: Oxford University Press, 1990, 39–125.

10 Gregory Hooks, *Forging the Military-Industrial Complex*, Chicago: University of Illinois Press, 1991.

programs to guarantee some measure of aggregate consumer demand.[11] At the same time, more collective forms of social investment—the highways, roads, and schools that constituted the major share of publicly-owned infrastructure from 1947–1993[12]—provided foundations for capital accumulation as well as for the social and spatial mobility of certain segments of the population. The intertwined sum of these parts constitutes the basic armature for military Keynesianism—or what O'Connor calls the "welfare-warfare state."[13]

Although the *welfare state* is being dismantled, its "organized abandonment,"[14] while signaling fundamental changes in power relations and policies, hardly means that "the state" itself is about to disappear. The state still systematizes relations between capital and labor.[15] However, new and reorganizing power blocs that have led the assault on income guarantees and other provisions against individualized calamity have also invoked the default-legitimacy of government—defense—to promote both continued federal military might (against "international terrorists") and increased domestic policing might (against "urban terrorists").[16]

---

11   Linda Gordon, *Pitied But Not Entitled: Single Mothers and the History of Welfare*, New York: Free Press, 1994.

12   Edward M. Gramlich, "Infrastructure Investment: A Review Essay," *Journal of Economic Literature* 32 (1994): 1176–96.

13   O'Connor, *The Fiscal Crisis of the State*; see also Mike Davis, *Prisoners of the American Dream*, New York: Verso, 1985, and Michael Mann, *States, War and Capitalism*, Oxford: Blackwell, 1988.

14   David Harvey, *The Limits to Capital*, London: Verso, 2006 [1982], 397.

15   Aijaz Ahmad, "Issues of Class and Culture: An Interview with Aijaz Ahmad," *Monthly Review* 48.5 (1996):10–28.

16   The fundamental policy change is the shift from a "bastard Keynesian" regime (Joan Robinson's phrase, cited in Lynn Turgeon, *Bastard Keynesianism: The Evolution of Economic Thinking and Policymaking since World War II*, Westport, CT: Greenwood Press, 1996) to one defined by monetarist theories of the state's proper role in cycles and growth. For monetarists, the state's economic intervention should be limited to control of the money supply via interest rates; all other state interventions keep the business cycle from hitting its "natural" lows—and highs.

The project to incapacitate—or cage—the domestic security threat has resulted in California's fifteen-year, five-hundred-percent increase in prisoners. Crime peaked in 1980, before the prison expansion movement began. Since 1988, the State legislature has passed more than twelve hundred new pieces of criminal legislation.[17] Notable among the types of laws are two tendencies: one, introduced with the Street Terrorism Enforcement and Prevention (STEP) Act of 1988, targets youths who may or may not be members of gangs.[18] The law requires local jurisdictions throughout the State to identify, by name, all suspected gangsters. The second, exemplified by the Three Strikes Law of 1994, extends the already well-established power for prosecutors and judges to punish defendants' past behavior and

---

Importantly, income guarantees keep wages artificially high and therefore interfere with workers' ability to maximize utility by making rational choices about when and where to enter or exit the labor market. Because in this system of equations, high wages cause inflation, then the antidote to inflation must be unemployment. The rightward drift of the Phillips curve since the mid-1950s suggests a "natural" rate of unemployment that has climbed from about two percent to six percent (Stuart Corbridge, "Plausible Worlds: Friedman, Keynes and the Geography of Inflation," in Ron Martin, Stuart Corbridge and Nigel Thrift [eds.], *Money, Power and Space*, Oxford: Basil Blackwell, 1994, 63–90). Economist Anwar Shaikh has demonstrated the weakness of the alleged causal relation between wages and inflation; his research shows that prices for basic commodities in relation to gold did not change over nearly two centuries—until currency went off the gold standard. See Anwar Shaikh, "Inflation and Unemployment." Paper presented at the Brecht Forum in New York, 1996; see also *The Current Economic Crisis: Causes and Implications*. Detroit: Against the Current Pamphlet, 1983 (reprinted 1989). However, the "elegance" (i.e., simplicity) of the monetarist view—"too many dollars chasing too few goods"—is difficult to refute in a soundbite or two.

17   See Peter W. Greenwood, C. Peter Rydell, Allan F. Abrahamse, Jonathan P. Caulkins, James Chiesa, Karyn E. Model, and Stephen P. Klein, *Three Strikes and You're Out: Estimated Costs of California's New Mandatory-Sentencing Law*, Santa Monica: The Rand Corporation, 1994; Legislative Analyst's Office, *Judiciary and Criminal Justice*, Sacramento: Legislative Analyst's Office, 1996.

18   See also California State Task Force on Youth Gang Violence, *Final Report*, Sacramento: California Council on Criminal Justice, 1986.

present offenses. Both kinds of laws "enhance"—or lengthen —sentences for crimes already on the books, and like many relatively new federal and state laws around the United States, both carry mandatory minimum sentences for certain kinds of offenses.[19]

In my view, a summary description of the state criminal system is this: it has become increasingly Fordist—indeed, in my view, the "punishment industry" is better understood as *industrialized punishment* when approached from a perspective that evaluates how the state accumulates and organizes the raw materials of offenses and transforms them into durable prisoners in durable cages.[20] For California, as for much of the United States, the purpose of prison has become incapacitation —which means, quite simply, holding convicts for the term of their sentences in such a manner that they cannot commit other crimes.[21] This stark time-space punishment disavows the

---

19   Mandatory minimum sentencing is called "truth in sentencing" by its supporters—in a perversion of the prisoners' rights movement of the 1950s–70s when those condemned to open-ended sentences for a wide variety of convictions sought to have sentencing standardized so that local parole boards would have less power to act capriciously in individual cases. For more on mandatory minimums from a critical perspective, see the Families Against Mandatory Minimums (FAMM) newsletters. For a view of the federal situation with respect to drugs, see Dan Baum, *Smoke and Mirrors: The War on Drugs and the Politics of Failure*, Boston: Little, Brown, 1996.

20   See also James Austin, *America's Growing Correctional-Industrial Complex*, Washington, DC: The National Council on Crime and Delinquency, 1990; Nils Christie, *Crime Control as Industry*, New York: Routledge, 1993; Mike Davis, "The Prison-Industrial Complex: Hell Factories in the Fields," *The Nation* 260.7 (1995): 229–34.

21   See Paul Butler, "Racially Based Jury Nullification: Black Power in the Criminal Justice System," *Yale Law Journal* 105.3 (1995): 677–726; Norval Morris and David J. Rothman (eds), *The Oxford History of the Prison: The Practice of Punishment in the Western World*, New York: Oxford University Press, 1995; Paul C. Rosser, "Justice Technology and Architecture," *Corrections Today* (April 1983): 122–23; Paul Silver, "Crossroads in Correctional Architecture," *Corrections Today* (April 1983):118–19.

penal system's earlier responsibility for, or concern with, rehabilitation[22]—or the latter's negative avatar, recidivism. Under statewide pressures to achieve efficiencies and economies in the context of expected growth, the California criminal justice system has internalized and specialized functions and services that, in scale and scope, follow organizational structures of what Chandler terms "the modern industrial enterprise."[23]

Gender, Power, Race, and Space

Huge and powerful structural adjustments are not simply determinant of all social processes and outcomes. The rapid expansion of prisons *also* derives from the political, social, and ideological operations of the US racial state.[24] Racism alone does not, however, adequately explain for whom, and for what, the system works. The state's attempt to produce a geographical solution (incarceration) to political-economic crisis is informed by racialized contradictions that are also gendered. These contradictions, in all of their everyday messiness, and the attempts by mother-activists to resolve them, are the subject of

22 Eric Cummins, *The Rise and Fall of California's Radical Prison Movement*, Stanford: Stanford University Press, 1994.

23 Alfred Chandler, *Scale and Scope*, Cambridge: Harvard/Belknap, 1990. See also David Ashley and Melvin Ramey, *California Prison Capital Cost Reduction Study*, University of California Office of the President, 1996; California Department of Finance, *A Performance Review: California Department of Corrections*, Sacramento: California Department of Finance, 1996; Legislative Analyst's Office, *Judiciary and Criminal Justice*, and Legislative Analyst's Office, *The New Prison Construction Program at Midstream*, Sacramento: Legislative Analyst's Office, 1986. The tendency to internalize and specialize spans the branches of government so that, in the California Department of Corrections, no less than in the State Legislature, no less than in the county courts, similar and coordinated processes are evident. See also R. Bernard Orozco, Principal Consultant, California Joint Legislative Committee on Prison Construction and Operations, interviews with author, June 27, 1995 and July 23–24 and 27, 1996, Sacramento.

24 Michael Omi and Howard Winant, *Racial Formation in the United States*, New York: Routledge, 1986.

this essay, which coheres around three major themes that all have to do with breaking boundaries.

The first theme centers on how African American practices of social mothering produce a group of diverse women working toward common goals.[25] The second theme explores how outreach projects successfully permeate the organization of highly (if not "hyper"[26]) segregated social space and, in some measure, start a process of spatial reorganization. The final theme concerns mobilizing the symbolic power of motherhood to challenge the legitimacy of the changing state. As we shall see, Mothers Reclaiming Our Children refuses to be bound and isolated by the normative limitations of California's gender, class, and race hierarchies. While the organization does not model utopia, it does enact both the possibilities and the difficulties of organizing across the many boundaries that rationalize and reinforce apartheid America.[27]

Free Gilbert Jones: The Early Political Geography of Mothers ROC

Mothers suffer a special pain when their children are incarcerated (lost to them). It was from this pain and suffering that

---

25   By social mothering I mean the collective practices of "bloodmothers," "othermothers," and "community othermothers" who cooperate to raise, guide, and protect the children of actual and "fictive kin" and, by extension, the children of the extended community. See Patricia Hill Collins, *Black Feminist Thought*, Boston: Unwin Hyman, 1990, 115–39. The expression fictive kin is quoted by Collins from Carol B. Stack, *All Our Kin: Strategies for Survival in a Black Community*, New York: Harper, 1974.

26   See Nancy Denton, "Are African Americans Still Hypersegregated?," in Robert Bullard, J. Eugene Grigsby III, and Charles Lee (eds.), *Residential Apartheid: The American Legacy*, Los Angeles: University of California at Los Angeles/Center for African American Studies, 1994.

27   Douglas Massey and Nancy Denton, *American Apartheid*, Cambridge: Harvard University Press, 1993. See also Leela Fernandes, *Producing Workers: The Politics of Gender, Class, and Culture in the Calcutta Jute Mills*. Philadelphia: University of Pennsylvania Press, 1997.

Mothers ROC was born! We are an organization of Mothers (and others) whose children have been arrested and incarcerated. We fight against the police abuse, the false arrests and convictions, and the unfair treatment throughout the Justice System. We educate ourselves and our young about the workings of the Criminal Justice System.

—1995 Flyer, Mothers Reclaiming Our Children

Nobody disputes that on November 29 1991 the Los Angeles Police Department shot George Noyes to death at the Imperial Courts public housing project, outside the homes of his mother and grandmother. The still-raging controversy concerns whether he was armed, whether he was kneeling, and whether he was begging for his life. According to members of the George Noyes Justice Committee, he was executed by a notoriously brutal policewoman. According to LAPD, he was a gangster run amok. No charges have ever been filed in the case.

The killing provoked the beginning of a grassroots rearrangement of power throughout South Central Los Angeles, producing along the way both the LA Gang Truce and Mothers Reclaiming Our Children. Formerly an active gang member, George had recently moved to Sacramento to get out of the life. He died while home for the Thanksgiving holidays. For his family members and friends who began organizing, the nature of George's violent end epitomized their collective experience and dread of the LAPD.[28]

---

28 Helicopters are the premier symbol of Los Angeles's capitalized, militarized police force; choppers pulse and hover overhead day and night, coordinating motorized ground forces from a superior and flexible vantage point—mobilely panoptic, although lacking the stealth Bentham envisioned. For a fine representation of the "feel" of chopper surveillance, see John Singleton's uneven "Boyz 'n the Hood." Bear in mind that LAPD invented the Special Weapons and Tactics (SWAT) Team specifically to police politically organized Black people. See Walton E. Bean, *California: An Interpretive History*, second ed, New York: McGraw-Hill, 1973; Mike Davis, *City of Quartz: Excavating the Future in Los Angeles*, New York:

Two of the dead man's cousins, Gilbert and Jocelyn, and their mother Barbara initiated the work of figuring out how those most vulnerable to state violence could begin systematically to shield themselves from it. Family, neighbors, and visitors at Imperial Courts, including George's mother, grandmother, siblings, aunt, and cousins began to testify among themselves about what they had seen, what they had heard, and how the death could only be explained as murder. Such practice is typical wherever poor people are harassed, hurt, or killed by police.[29] The political problem centers on what to do with the energy that fears and traumas produce. Does the state's discipline work? Does it terrorize everyone into silence by dividing the "good" from the "bad," by intensifying anxieties that lead to premature deaths due to alcoholism and drug addictions (including cigarettes), heart disease, suicide, crimes of passion, and other killers of the urban working and workless poor?[30]

In order to persuade as many residents as possible that the death concerned them all, the family formed the George Noyes Justice Committee. The committee started meeting at Imperial Courts in the all-purpose room to figure out ways to fight the wrongful death. To mark the moment further, Barbara, Gilbert, and Jocelyn decided to walk the neighborhood. They started with the three South Central public housing projects and asked the gangs to declare a one-day truce, so that all of George's family and friends—who lived scattered about the area—could attend the funeral. Los Angeles has a steady history of making and remaking itself along highly segregated lines and material

---

Verso, 1990; Raphael Sonenshein, *Politics in Black and White*, Princeton: Princeton University Press, 1993.

29 For examples, see Stuart Hall, Chas Critcher, Tony Jefferson, John Clake, and Brian Roberts, *Policing the Crisis: Mugging, the State, and Law and Order*, New York: Holmes and Meier, 1978, and Frances Fox Piven and Richard A. Cloward, *Regulating the Poor*, New York: Vintage, 1971.

30 See Michael Greenberg and Dona Schneider, "Violence in American Cities: Young Black Males is the Answer, But What Was the Question?," *Social Science Medicine* 39(2) (1994):179–87.

pressures and limits that did not originate with gangs, but which keep certain kinds of people stuck in specific deindustrialized areas.[31]

The dangers of the pilgrimage were many: Gilbert was a well-known gang-member who could not pass the streets freely. His sister, Jocelyn, and mother, Barbara, could not identify themselves as George's or Gilbert's relatives without simultaneously revealing their familial connections to, and therefore exposing themselves as, potential enemies. And finally, since neither Jocelyn nor Barbara lived in the public housing projects, residents might easily view them as outsiders making trouble in locations intensely surveilled through a number of means including helicopters, on-site security, caseworkers from income assistance programs, and periodic LAPD raids.[32]

To reassure residents that she was not an "outside agitator" but rather a grieving aunt, fearful mother, and good sister, Barbara started holding meetings for women, especially mothers, at Imperial Courts. She explains:

> I believed we had to start taking care of our children. The police would not think they could get away with shooting our children down in cold blood if we took better care of them. So I started [what eventually became] Mothers ROC at Imperial Courts. We would meet once or twice a week. We talked about grooming, about how to brush and braid your daughter's hair. How your children should look when they leave your house. How they should talk to the police, to strangers, to each other. It seemed to me it was up to us to change things by doing what we already knew how to do. Our mothers had taught us everything. And

---

31 See B. Marchand, *The Emergence of Los Angeles*, London: Pion Ltd, 1986; Melvin L. Oliver, James H. Johnson, Jr., and Walter C. Farrell, Jr., "Anatomy of a Rebellion: A Political-Economic Analysis," in Robert Gooding-Williams (ed.), *Reading Rodney King/Reading Urban Uprising*, New York: Routledge, 1993, 117–41; Edward W. Soja, *Postmodern Geographies*, New York: Verso, 1989.

32 Davis, *City of Quartz*.

our grandmothers, and our aunts, and the ladies next door. They all taught us so we could have a better life. So we have to teach our children for them to have a better life. I think we let them down because we stopped teaching them and talking to them … My [late] husband and I both worked all day, every day, so our kids could have the things we never had. We thought it was the right thing to do, to work hard and to make our children's lives easier than our lives. But we didn't make their lives easier, we made them harder. And now we have to teach them, and let them teach us where we went wrong.

Born on the eve of World War II, Barbara grew up in Louisiana enmeshed by formal and informal community networks of family and friends.[33] She married a career military man, lived on bases around the US including Alaska, and eventually settled in Los Angeles where she was widowed as her four children reached adulthood. While many African Americans in Los Angeles achieved modest prosperity during the defense boom of World War II, their segregation from good jobs started at the war's end, and every subsequent recession has hit the community with lasting severity. When the old heavy industries (steel, tire, auto, and to some degree oil) cut workers or closed plants, and the waterfront delaborized, direct loss of those jobs, in combination with the disappearance of jobs reliant on that industrial core, left the city's Black working-class men without access to alternative, high-wage, local, industries.[34]

Many women from the "stranded communities"[35] who were

---

33 See for example, bell hooks, *Yearning*, Boston: South End Press, 1990, Chapters 5 and 6.

34 See David Grant, Melvin L. Oliver, and Angela D. James, "African Americans: Social and Economic Bifurcation," in Roger Waldinger and Mehdi Bozorgmehr (eds) *Ethnic Los Angeles*, New York: Russell Sage Foundation, 1996, 379–412; Oliver et al., "Anatomy of a Rebellion"; Nelson Peery, *Black Fire*, New York: The New Press, 1994; Soja, *Postmodern Geographies*.

35 Jacqueline Jones, *The Dispossessed: America's Underclass from the Civil War to the Present*, New York: Basic Books, 1992.

concentrated in the projects enthusiastically welcomed Barbara's meetings. They could talk about themselves, their hopes and disappointments, their interrupted life-plans. As many as sixty mothers and daughters (and sometimes young sons, but rarely any boys more than four or five years old) might attend one of the sessions, and they eagerly put themselves to the tasks of doing each other's hair and staging fashion shows while talking about their loved ones who had died violently, who were in prison, or who had simply disappeared. According to Barbara, most of the women were engaged in the informal economy, selling legal goods or providing lawful services for unreported income.[36] At the same time, concern about joblessness —their own, their children's fathers', their children's, and especially their sons'—dominated the discussions that did not focus on grooming, nutrition, or violently premature deaths. The women reported from experience what scholars prove again and again: in the United States, certain types of people have access to certain types of jobs. For Black people looking out from the jail-like complex of the Courts, the landscape of legitimate work is an expanse of big, empty factories, minimum wage service jobs in retail or home health care, unreliable, slow, and expensive public transportation, and bad schools leading, in terms of education and skills, nowhere.[37]

Before Barbara had become deeply involved with the women, but after she had held an organizational meeting to propose her strategy for action, she, Jocelyn, and Gilbert achieved the one-day truce for George's funeral. As they walked and talked with people in the three projects and along the streets between them,

---

36 See Heidi Hartmann, "The Family as the Locus of Gender, Class and Political Struggle: The Example of Housework," *Signs* 6.3 (1981): 366–94, and *How Are Women Faring in the New Economy? Keynote address at Women Work*, New Brunswick, NJ: Rutgers Institute for the Study of Women, 1996.

37 See also Holly Sklar, *Chaos or Community? Seeking Solutions, Not Scapegoats, for Bad Economics*, Boston: South End Press, 1995.

they emphasized how everyone could relate to a family who had lost a loved one to police violence. Rodney King's beating in March of that year provided a ready and politically-charged referent that even extremely hostile listeners could recognize, and it transformed highly segmented groupings into a provisional "we" who might mediate the gang-controlled divisions of Los Angeles's streets. Little by little, the older male gang members began to acknowledge their collective power and what it could mean for Rodney King, for George Noyes, for many others, and for themselves should they decide to allow everyone free passage through the streets of South Central for one day.

The men also agreed to a truce in the name of grieving mothers. They extended their common-sense notion of the gangs as "families" and thereby recognized a central familial figure's claim on their care. "Mother" became, in name, George's mother, for whom Barbara, her sister, was a stand-in. Barbara's ability to speak from her heart, to express a mother's pain at losing a child, and to acknowledge her own son's gangster status without glorification or shame touched men for whom George's death was, at least at first, of minimal importance. On behalf of Barbara, of George's mother, of "mothers," the men agreed to redirect their power and to instruct the gangs to police their streets and themselves in order for the dead man's family to gather for a big, peaceful funeral.

Thus, Barbara forged an alliance among women in the projects, in spite of her own outsider status, by appealing to a power achieved through coordinated maternal practices; they made critical the activities of mothering as necessary, social, and consequential by doing, as a group, what they already knew how to do as individuals.[38] At the same time, she, Gilbert, and Jocelyn persuaded the gangs to rearticulate South Central's divisions and to shift their everyday capacity to act as

---

38 Collins, *Black Feminist Thought*.

extralegal "shadow states" by realigning their practices from small-scale "inter-state" rivalries to an area-wide alliance.[39]

Both groups—mothers and gangs—quite rapidly developed a process of identification focused, at the outset, on realizing a common interest—a non-violent funeral for a man many of them did not know. But while they came together in the name of children and of mothers, their goal became actionable in the context of their more general interest to struggle against the conditions that required so much organizing to precede such a homely affair as a burial. The everyday brutality that provoked Barbara and her children to bring this particular funeral to the foreground of consciousness provided material and symbolic shape for what was to follow. The interest embodied by those who attended, or who enabled, George's peaceful service gave way to a sense of purpose not bounded by a gravesite or a day. The developing identity of purpose cast the spatially unified legal state as the legitimate object of resistance and opposition against which to organize future actions.

---

39 Wolch developed the "shadow state" concept to theorize state-sanctioned non-governmental organizations (NGOs); I use it here to emphasize how gangs constitute, as Diego Vigil and others have argued, not only superior marketing forces for illegal substances but also territorially centralized rule-making bodies for a mosaic filling in vast regions that the legal state has abandoned except in the form of militarized occupation and social-services-based surveillance. The point is not to romanticize gangs but rather to emphasize that all social formations—even stranded communities in deindustrialized urban centers—develop some means for maintaining order; sometimes it is necessary to look beneath the surface of apparent *disorder* to grasp the logic of a particular system of order. Further, as Tilly argues, war-making, state-making, and organized crime are distinct with reference to those who produce and enforce the "law" but not so different in terms of actual practices, relations, and outcomes. See Jennifer Wolch, *The Shadow State: Government and Voluntary Sector in Transition*, New York: The Foundation Center, 1989; James Diego Vigil, "Youth Gang Subcultures in a Changing Los Angeles." Paper presented at the Conference of Ford Fellows, October 1996, Irvine, CA; Léon Bing, *Do or Die*, New York: HarperCollins, 1991; Charles Tilly, "War Making and State Making as Organized Crime," in Peter B. Evans, Dietrich Rueschemeyer, and Theda Skocpol (eds), *Bringing the State Back In*, Cambridge: Cambridge University Press, 1985, 169–91.

The next stage of organizing followed shortly after George's December 9 funeral. During the services, mothers and others who spoke in his memory called for a rally to protest the police murder. At the same time the Imam of a nearby independent mosque offered his house of worship as a sanctuary where the gangsters could work to extend the truce across time and space. The gang reconciliation first embraced the rally: more than five hundred people turned out at the 108th Street Station to accuse the police of murder and to announce the end of the community's passivity, vulnerability, and complicity with respect to the brutal treatment too-often doled out by the hands of the law.[40]

Gilbert and a number of other gang members, inspired by the turn of events, continued the peacemaking process, each day bringing in more people from a wider and wider region of South Central. Word went out through all sorts of networks alerting Black gangsters everywhere to the possibilities of the historic moment. Barbara attended every meeting at the mosque and continued to hold the self-help discussion groups at the Courts, where women from other projects would sometimes show up to see what was going on. Gang members from the truce meetings would come to report their progress, and women other than Barbara would also attend meetings at the mosque to monitor the proceedings. The George Noyes Justice Committee also continued to meet with the objective of finding an opening in fortress LAPD through which they could successfully lob their charges of wrongful death.

---

40 Frank Donner, *Protectors of Privilege*, Berkeley: University of California Press, 1990. Notably, attendees at the rally—or "coming together" as many participants termed it—included survivors from prior generations' social movements, such as the Black Panther Party for Self Defense. Thus, the "coming together" commingled community members, who were developing their political consciousness in that particular moment of powerfully focused anger and grief, with activists representing theoretical tendencies and traditions that were forged in earlier struggles against state and state-sanctioned violence.

In the middle of February 1992, just as a Justice Committee fundraising dance at the Imperial Courts all-purpose room was about to end, LAPD showed up at the door to arrest Gilbert. They charged him with taking ten dollars during an armed robbery that allegedly occurred outside the building moments earlier. The problem of justice for George immediately widened to include his cousin Gilbert. Barbara, convinced that the purpose of her son's arrest was to stop the work she and her children had started, began to organize on his behalf as well.

While Gilbert was in custody, fighting for his freedom, the Los Angeles Uprising (April 29–May 2) significantly shifted the prevailing political mood of the city. Three days of "multicultural riots"[41] produced both new unities and new divisions. The uprising began in the afternoon after a Simi Valley jury acquitted the four LAPD men who had beaten Rodney King, who had apparently committed several misdemeanors. Millions had viewed the LAPD 4 in action because the beating, videotaped by eyewitness George Holliday, had been extensively and intensively broadcast for more than a year.[42] Several hours before the verdict became public knowledge, the peacemakers of the Los Angeles gang worlds had signed the truce. Indeed, the riots did not produce the truce; rather, the truce, Mothers Reclaiming Our Children, and the uprising were all expressions of the same objective conditions that characterized relations between the state and stranded Black, brown, and other poor communities throughout deindustrializing Los Angeles.

Like the LAPD 4's trial, Gilbert's also changed venue. But, unlike the movement of the officers' trial to Simi Valley, where they would be more likely to have a jury of their peers (police or

---

41   Mike Davis, "Uprising and Repression in L.A.," in Robert Gooding-Williams (ed.), *Reading Rodney King/Reading Urban Uprising*, 142–154.

42   Ruth Wilson Gilmore, "Terror Austerity Race Gender Excess Theater," in this volume; Gooding-Williams (ed.), *Reading Rodney King/ Reading Urban Uprising*; Haki R. Madhubuti, *Why L.A. Happened*, Chicago: Third World Press, 1993.

retired military), the state re-sited Gilbert's case from Compton —where seating a Black jury is quite easy—to the Long Beach courtroom of a notoriously "anti-gang" judge. Despite the testimony of numerous witnesses who were with him at the time of the robbery, the jury found Gilbert guilty, and despite further testimony at the sentencing hearing by former Governor Jerry Brown, Congresswoman Maxine Waters, and others concerning his peacemaking achievements, the judge bound the young man over to the custody of the California Department of Corrections (CDC) to serve seven years for a ten-dollar robbery.

For Barbara, the injustice in both the LAPD 4 and Gilbert's cases made clear that the object of struggle was not only the Southeast station house of the LAPD Southern Division. It was the state, at many levels, that took her son away, just as it was the state, at many levels, that enabled the police to take her nephew's life. The CDC assigned her son to Susanville, a prison located more than five hundred miles from Los Angeles, near Reno, Nevada, where the White Aryan Brotherhood reputedly dominated the prisoner population. This assignment terrorized the family on two accounts: first, they feared that his notoriety as a Black gang peace activist would bring him into conflict with the Aryans. Second, Barbara had suffered a heart attack during the fall of 1992, and she was not able to make the long journey to visit him. Mothers ROC launched a successful political campaign to have Gilbert moved closer to home, and he spent about half his time in Tehachapi, about one hundred fifty miles north of home, and was released on parole after serving three years and eleven months.[43]

---

43 Prisoners are "unitized"—which is CDC jargon for "segregated." While individual wardens have power over the social organization of their prisons, the general policy is to keep prisoners in each facility separated by "race." California Department of Corrections demographic analyses use four basic categories: White, Black, Latino, Other. "Others"—Asian-Pacific Islanders and Native Americans—are not housed separately but are distributed among the three principal groups, such that e.g., Samoans are usually Black, Filipinos are Latino, people of Chinese, Hmong, Lao

The project to "Free Gilbert Jones" also marks the beginning of the formal organization of Mothers ROC. In alliance with a number of other South Central mothers, many of whom had children in custody as a result of the uprising, Barbara started to hold regular sidewalk protests downtown at the main Los Angeles County Courthouse and at Parker Center—the LAPD headquarters. During this phase, in November 1992, Los Angeles activist Francie Arbol met Barbara through the intervention of an LA-based writer/activist who had been impressed both by Gilbert's accomplishments and by Barbara's eloquent persistence. Together, Francie and Barbara founded Mothers ROC.

From Imperial Courts to the State Courts

The formation of Mothers ROC as a political group seeking justice coincided with the restructuring of a disbanded communist tendency that had organized in several US cities in the 1950s. An African American revolutionary founded the small party. His consciousness of race and class oppression developed while he rode the rails as a teenage laborer during the Great Depression and further evolved while he served in the Pacific Theater during World War II.[44] The group was renowned in radical Los Angeles circles for grassroots, issue-oriented organizing with non-party folks.

---

or Vietnamese descent might be White or Latino but not Black, Native Americans are usually Latino but sometimes Black (author's interview with R. Bernard Orozco, 1996). According to the testimony of some prisoners, "unitizing" helps produce and reinforce animosities, keeps internal hierarchies intact, and discourages any kind of substantive cross-racial organizing on behalf of, e.g., prisoners' rights (see Eric Cummins, *The Rise and Fall*). Certainly, letters from prisoners to organs such as *Prison News Service* demonstrates how ignorant many are, as members of racialized groups, of each other's sentences, prospects, and perspectives.

44 Peery, *Black Fire*, and *Black Radical: The Education of an American Revolutionary*, New York: The New Press, 2007.

Francie Arbol joined the party as a teenager in the 1960s. She always worked on both workplace and community-based issues arising from exploitation and injustice, while raising her two daughters—mostly alone—on a bookkeeper's wages. She brought to Mothers ROC a systematic analysis of social structures and political economy, cast in colloquial terms, and a keen sensibility for how to get things done. Unafraid to engage in spirited debate, she also carries through on any project the group decides to pursue regardless of her opinion of it.

When Francie and Barbara sat together to plan the contours of an action-oriented group of mothers, they met in the garage office of the disbanded party's ongoing community organization, the Equal Rights Congress (ERC). The office is about a mile north of the infamous intersection where Reginald Denny and the LA Four had their fateful encounter, and seventy-five blocks northwest from the site of George Noyes's murder. The garage sits on property belonging to the Society of Friends, and the living room of the small front house became Mothers ROC's regular meeting place. The house has long been a location for activists to meet, a surprisingly pacific oasis amid a neighborhood in constant flux. People who live in South Central, as well as those from outlying communities, are not afraid to go there because the house is not "of" any particular group's turf.

By linking Mothers ROC to the other projects of the ERC, Barbara and Francie started out with amenities others struggle long to acquire: an office, a telephone, one of the world's oldest copiers, and a convenient meeting place on neutral ground. They announced a regular Wednesday evening meeting beginning in November, and someone has been there to greet mothers on a weekly basis ever since, regardless of weather or holiday schedule. African American mothers came—six, then ten, then twenty, then twenty-five or more. They came to talk about the injustice of the LAPD case compared with that of the LA Four; they came to talk about their own children's cases;

they came because there was someone, at last, they could talk with about what concerned and frightened them most.

Who did not come? Most of the women who so enthusiastically participated in Barbara's mothering sessions down at Imperial Courts did not make the journey north. Mothers ROC's central premise did not change. Barbara has always been consistent in her invocation of collective mothering as the practice from which activism springs. However, the outright politics of the formal organization seems to have deterred some, especially given its dedication to confronting the state head on. This aspect seemed dangerous to people who, as noted earlier, live intensively policed lives. Francie's role discouraged others who will not trust white people as a matter of course. And, finally, some came and left because rumors that communists controlled the new group spread rapidly, thanks to the inadvertently strategic intervention of two Black policemen.

According to the story that circulated widely through the organization and beyond, the two policemen called on the mother of an LA Four defendant to warn her that her son's case would go much better if she disassociated herself from "those communists" in Mothers ROC. The purpose of the visit is open to dispute: some say the police were trying to break up the group, and others say they were trying to help a struggling Black woman, known personally to one of them, who did not understand the consequences of her activism.[45]

---

45 A recurring irony in Mothers ROC cases—especially African Americans'—is how frequently the (extended) family knows or is related to a police, probation, parole, or corrections officer (the frequency is related, of course, to the historical battle by Black people to procure access to state jobs, which became a relatively secure labor market niche until the attack on government size launched in the past two decades). The irony has been quite useful in helping mothers take a systemic, rather than individualized, view of their struggle. Knowing, as they do, that their friend/relative is not a bad person and probably not a racist (although anti-Black racism among Black people is not uncommon), they then have to figure out another explanation for what is happening to their children, in which they can account for people "like" themselves on the other side. See, for

The news provoked a crisis in the ROC. Some women wanted Francie expelled; others, including the mother in question, quit. Barbara and Francie held special meetings one weekend at several locations in the city and county, where they fielded questions and engaged in fiery debates about communists, racism, and justice.

Francie candidly discussed her reasons for having become a communist and also described how the party had, in her experience, outlived its usefulness. She also refused to quit the ROC and made clear to those who planned to flee her influence that if she was the biggest problem in their lives, they would not have joined the ROC in the first place. The brutality of policemen, the menace of prosecutors, and the meanness of judges with respect to their children were not responses to communism. But could the specter of communism make things worse? Barbara reminded the group that its purpose did not preclude any kind of person from joining and being active—as long as they worked toward the goal of justice for the children.

The debates followed an intricate pattern, demonstrating the rich complexities of common sense in this particular time and place.[46] The systematic critique of state power with respect to criminalized children required the mothers also to question the authority of the state's representatives—police, judges, prosecutors, and other lawyers. If communism was bracketed the mothers would agree in one voice that their problem was, indeed, state violence and systemic injustice. Yet, when confronted by the post-1989 fact of a (former) communist in their midst, many of the women absolutely embraced the state's definition of *the* collective enemy for whom Francie, a tiny Anglo activist, was a stand-in. Most of the women had

---

comparison, Daniel Guérin, *The Brown Plague: Travels in Late Weimar and Early Nazi Germany*, Durham, NC: Duke University Press, 1994.

46 Gramsci, *Selections*; Stuart Hall, "Gramsci's Relevance for the Study of Race and Ethnicity," *Journal of Communication Inquiry* 10.2 (1986):5–27.

attended elementary school during the Cold War buildup in the 1950s, and the lessons they learned—whether lining up for civil defense drills or studying the geography of "the free world"—informed their current evaluation of possibility and danger. Further, the connection of communism with atheism sits ill with women for whom, as we shall see, God and prayer are vital sources of guidance and strength.

What Barbara and Francie and their allies had to do was help the women see and say that their own children—not the "communists"—were "the enemy" now.[47] Even if the policemen represented authentic African American anti-communist fears rather than the designs of the county prosecutor, the outcome would not change. The ROC's children already labored under the greatest liability—that of having been designated "human sacrifice"[48] in the ongoing drama of a state struggling and restructuring in the context of its own delegitimation at the "end of history." Others versed in radical traditions spoke up during the agonizing debates, but the heat stayed mainly on Francie, who stalwartly took it. Francie was not the only Anglo in the group at the time, but the combination of her whiteness, her radical roots, and her refusal to yield—plus her blunt confrontational style—kept her downstage center during the crisis.

The crisis resolved into a truce among those who stayed, forcing the group to mature quickly into an organization *for* itself despite substantial internal differences. The process heightened suspicions but also enhanced everybody's sense of political identity. That is, while disagreeing with the "politics" figured by Francie and others, the women enacted an alternative political vision by remaining in the fight *as* the ROC. They made clear to all who inquired that *mothers,* not some hidden cadre of white or Black communists, openly and deliberately

47 Gilmore, "Terror Austerity Race Gender Excess Theater."
48 Wilmette Brown, *No Justice, No Peace: The 1992 Los Angeles Rebellion from a Black/Women's Perspective,* London: International Black Women for Wages for Housework, 1992.

set the agendas for action. Severance of the ROC from the ERC gave symbolic emphasis to the organization's insistence on autonomy, even though the meeting place, office, and telephone number did not change.

In this period, the group's actions, formerly centered on the Gilbert Jones and LA Four cases, became generalized so that the ROC could act quickly and consistently on new cases. The ROC set up the systems of court monitoring, legal workshops, and outreach activities described at the beginning of this paper. The workshops became primary centers for people to learn about topics such as self-representation, sentence enhancement, and related issues. One crucial area emerges consistently in the workshops: the assumption that a private attorney is preferable to a public defender is rooted in US common-sense assumptions that "you get what you pay for." The fact that working people, including the mothers, "pay" for all the public defenders via taxation is invisible in this schema. However, *in* the ROC, automatic distrust of public defenders has gradually given way to a view of how sectoral growth in industrialized punishment produces both overworked public defenders and a concomitant expansion of unscrupulous private lawyers looking to make a sure dollar.[49]

The shift in membership—from the proto-formation at Imperial Courts to the fully-fledged Mothers ROC poised to

---

49 Many new Mothers tell the same story—they mortgage the house or sell the car in order to pay a lawyer whose contract, it turns out, is only to take the case through the most routine rounds of court filings and appearances. Further, the question of mortgaging or selling has its own racialized contradictions. Oliver and Shapiro show the ways that, for Black people, residential apartheid and lender redlining effectively limit access to (as well as growth of) the fundamental source of US household wealth: home equity. In the case of the ROCers who mortgage, they leverage lower-than-average equity at higher-than-average loan costs in order to—at best—maintain the status quo (a loved one kept out of prison) rather than to "invest" in the future in the form of education or other potentially remunerable family or personal development. Melvin L. Oliver and Thomas M. Shapiro, *Black Wealth/White Wealth: A New Perspective on Racial Inequality*, New York: Routledge, 1995.

do battle in the state courts—represented a change in the social position of the women as a group. Nearly all current ROCers perform waged work in the formal economy, and if they do not, it is because they are disabled (generally by ailments of poverty and stress such as heart disease and cancer) or they are retired. Many are homeowners who live in modest stucco or frame bungalows or condominiums. They are keenly conscious that they have *something* to lose.[50] The structure of Mothers ROC gives them a framework for hope as well as for action, and it provides the basis for an expansion of their attention from seeking remedies in the courtroom (law) to exposing and changing the ways the system operates (politics).

One State + Two Laws = Three Strikes

[W]hen the woes of the poor press most dangerously upon the rich, then an age searches most energetically to pierce the future for hope.

—Peter Linebaugh[51]

Every Mothers ROC meeting is framed by prayer. At the beginning and end of each session the group holds hands in a circle and asks for protection and guidance. The women who lead the prayers have a gift for preaching. Their invocations set and summarize the seemingly endless agenda of reclaiming the children within a material context of spiritual hope realized through human action. Prayer helps span the visible and invisible social distances among ROCers for whom, in most cases, organized religion is a vital aspect of life. Prayer also demonstrates the power of attentive listening for group-building. Anyone in the

---

50 A. Sivanandan, *A Different Hunger*, London: Pluto Press, 1982.

51 Peter Linebaugh, *The London Hanged*, Cambridge: Cambridge University Press, 1992, 65.

group may comment affirmatively on the leader's devotional trajectory, and such encouragement of the speaker encourages the collectivity. And finally, by emphasizing the difficulty and urgency of the situation that has brought them together, prayer renews and strengthens the mothers' provisional unity. Individual differences, which occasionally produce incidents, need not become persistent organizational impediments—in a church or in the ROC.

The group meditation on power and powerlessness establishes the scene in which mothers are able to identify with each other. In 1994, the FBI recorded 11,500,000 arrests by federal, state, and local law enforcement. In 1995 the number increased to 14,500,000.[52] Arrest and incarceration are common in the US, yet those who are touched by law enforcement are so segregated in many different ways that the experience of confrontation with the legal system does not produce collective oppositional activities. In the ROC and elsewhere, the similarity of mothers' stories can produce a sense of commonality, but there are no guarantees that such a sensibility will serve as the basis for collective action. Within a social order of wide and deep inequality—most forcefully expressed as racial inequality—mothers are cautious because they know not all children are equally vulnerable to the law's harsh punishments.

When Pearl Daye's thirty-one-year-old son called from the police station to say he had been arrested for allegedly shoplifting a package of razor blades from a discount drugstore, she was confused—he had a steady job—and distressed—he had not been in any kind of trouble for more than eight years. Going to the station to post bail, Pearl found it set at an absolutely unattainable $650,000 because the Los Angeles County District Attorney's office charged Harry Daye with a third-strike felony rather than a petty theft misdemeanor. Suddenly, then, the African American man who seemed to have successfully

---

52 Statistical Abstract of the United States 1994, 1995.

put his life in order faced a mandatory minimum sentence of twenty-five years to life without possibility of parole.

As Pearl related the compounding events of Harry's arrest and accusation at her first Mothers ROC meeting, she often had to pause because of the almost unendurable anxiety of retelling and revealing seemingly unbelievable adverse family circumstances to strangers. However, the roomful of women recognized the Dayes' drama as neither bureaucratic error nor bad dream, but rather as an increasingly ordinary conflict between families like theirs and the law. The plot had already become so familiar, one year into implementation of California's Three Strikes Law that, at certain moments, a number of women, as though they were a chorus, recited with Pearl what the Public Defender and others had told her—especially the (street name of the) guaranteed sentence: "Twenty-five to ... without."

Harry Daye faced the death of freedom because, at that time, the Los Angeles County District Attorney's written policy was to enforce the Three Strikes Law vigorously. Such vigor includes charging defendants to ensure the longest possible prison sentences, regardless of the current character of the defendant's life. Harry's alleged petty theft constituted what California law designates a "wobbler"—an offense that can be classified and punished as either a misdemeanor or a felony. Three strikes and other minimum-mandatory-sentence laws, conventionally portrayed to work with a machine-like disregard for individual circumstance, actually explicitly allow prosecutors and judges to use discretion "in the interest of justice." However, throughout California—especially in the southern counties where most prisoners are produced—the practice of prosecutorial or judicial discretion in favor of second or third "strike" defendants is so rare as to be newsworthy.[53]

Pearl ended her introductory testimony to Mothers ROC

---

53 See, for example, Tom Gorman, "Lawyer Fired Over '3 Strikes' Switches Sides." *Los Angeles Times*, April 25, 1996, A-3.

with an observation about the entire system: "The way I see it there are two laws, one for the Black, and one for the white." Leticia Gonzales, a Chicana whose husband had started a "twenty-five to ... without" sentence some months earlier disagreed. "No. I think there is one law for the people of color, and another law for the white." By this time, everyone was talking. Francie Arbol proposed another structure: "Poor people, and rich people." But poor versus rich failed to explain the State versus O.J. Simpson: Why was the Los Angeles County District Attorney's office spending so much time and money to convict one Black defendant?[54] Therefore, the distinction could not be rich versus poor. At the same time, because virtually all the prisoners anyone in the room knew or could imagine were people of modest means from working-class families, the money question could not simply be dropped. Anti-Black racism seemed to explain a great deal but could not account for all of poverty, powerlessness, and vulnerability before the law.

In the year or so before Pearl Daye brought her case to the ROC, Latino (mostly Chicano and Mexicano) prisoners surpassed African Americans as the largest group, in absolute numbers, in CDC custody.[55] The unevenness in outcome for people of color lies in the offense with which defendants are charged. For example, in Los Angeles County, white defendants are far more likely to have charges reduced from felonies to misdemeanors or dropped completely, while people of color are more likely to have the harshest possible charge leveled against them.[56] Both federal and California laws allow radi-

---

54   The Simpson criminal trial had not been resolved during this discussion, but even his acquittal and the aftermath supported the ROCers' sense that a Black man's trial is completely unlike a white man's trial.

55   Between 1977 and 1982 the number of white prisoners increased fifty percent while Black prisoners doubled, producing nearly equal absolute numbers between the two groups; from that time forward, Black prisoners exceeded all other groups until 1994, when the steady increase in Latino incarceration shifted the balance.

56   Vincent Schiraldi and M. Godfrey, *Racial Disparities in the Charging of Los Angeles County's Third "Strike" Cases*, San Francisco:

cally different treatment of people who have done essentially the same thing. Such police, prosecutorial, and judicial power, which, since its introduction in the early 1980s, has remained fundamentally impervious to challenges based on "equal protection" and other constitutional principles, provides both the means and the encouragement for application of substantively different rules and punishments to various kinds of defendants.[57]

It is not surprising, then, that the ROCers had a hard time developing a brief characterization of how the law discriminates against and among those who are most vulnerable to the system. The law's ability to wobble makes routinely unequal punishments possible. At the same time, the wobble makes developing a common-sense definition of how such inequality is achieved and reproduced on a case-by-case basis very difficult indeed. Everyone who spoke—nearly everyone in the room—had no doubt that the system operates on a dual track. But how is each defendant routed?

Leticia Gonzales could match Pearl's story horror for horror. Her husband had been tried and convicted for shoplifting a pair of pants during the Christmas shopping rush. She is convinced that either nobody took anything, or that somebody else, who looks like her husband, took the things. "Why would he take some pants? He could buy them. And at Christmas, there are guards everywhere around at the stores. He's not stupid." However, since in his deep past he had been convicted on two counts of robbery, the petty theft of a pair of inexpensive trousers became, in his case, robbery, sending him down for "twenty-five to ... without."

Leticia heard about the ROC from her husband who heard in the county jail. She was afraid to come to the meeting at

Center on Juvenile and Criminal Justice, 1994. See also Sylvia Nasar, "More Men in Prime of Life Spend Less Time Working," *New York Times*, Dec 1, 1994, A–1.

57   See, for example, Paul Butler, "Racially Based Jury Nullification."

first, because she did not know anybody, lived down in San Pedro, and was afraid she might not be welcomed. Much to her surprise, the group, still composed predominately of African Americans, did welcome her, and as the months went by, more and more Latinas showed up at the door. Mothers of sixteen-year-olds charged with murder. Wives of second and third-strike defendants. Grandmothers of kids charged under the STEP Act. Indeed, the Black and brown cadres of *abuelas* began to hold occasional caucuses—after the manner of the grandmothers of Argentina's Plaza de Mayo—to discuss their unique problems, which often centered on their status as undocumented primary caregivers to their children's children.

The number of Latinas attending meetings increased as the Los Angeles County prosecutor extended vigorous enforcement of California's one thousand two hundred new pieces of criminal legislation to brown as well as Black defendants. The night of Pearl Daye's first visit, the ROC'S debate about the law's unequal application continued well into the evening and spilled out onto the sidewalk after the regular meeting came to a close. The crucial issue in resolving the question had to do with maintaining organizational solidarity. Finally, one of the women proposed this solution: There are, as Pearl had said, two laws—one for Black people and one for white people. Given how the prosecutors had started charging more and more brown and other poor defendants under the new laws, especially Three Strikes, then perhaps the explanation could be put this way: You have to be white to be prosecuted under white law, but you do not have to be Black to be prosecuted under Black law. The resolution satisfied that evening's debaters as it provided a way to recognize the extension of prosecutorial practices without displacing the African Americans' indisputable experience of the most intensive application of the laws.

Not long after discovery of the Black/white law solution, a local power broker came calling on the ROC. The African

American man, who had made a small fortune running secured (locked-down) drug rehabilitation units for the State, wanted the ROC's blessing to build a private (owned by him) prison in the neighborhood where the State would send selected prisoners to serve the final year of their sentences. He assured the women that the prison would be run in accordance with community wishes, since the city would not grant a provisional use license without community approval. This visit crystallized, for many ROCers, the dynamic contradiction in the system they had taken on. If the ROC is right, then the prison is unnecessary. If the prison comes in, accompanied by "jobs" then part of the ROC's critique—poverty—will seem to have been addressed by expanding the specific object of the ROC's opposition—cages.

As the unabashed profiteer explained how much good the prison would bring to South Central, the ROCers listened closely. Then, in an orderly show of political passion, each one told him why, from her perspective, the ROC would never endorse the facility. His claim that somehow the community could control the inner workings of a prison because of its location struck them as ludicrous; they had learned that distance is not simply measured in miles and that the prison would not be a neighborhood or community facility, but rather a State facility run according to State rules. His promise that perhaps their own children could be in the prison elicited, at first, an emotional moment of hope on the part of some mothers, who drive fifteen-year-old cars four hundred miles round-trip on Saturdays to see their sons. But the record of failures in many of the campaigns to have children moved closer to their families indicated that the people in the proposed South Central prison probably would not come from the area. The ROC told him, over and over, that they would not remedy the disappearance of jobs at GM, Firestone, and Kaiser by putting half the population into prisons so the other half could make good money minding them. They sent him on his way, somewhat bruised by their blunt words.

The visit provoked the members to ask themselves what else they should be doing to stop the prison from going up in South Central. They reasoned that the prison would go up somewhere—the power broker assured them of that—and so protesting at the local level would not solve the problem. Clearly, the ROC had to expand its activities to a scale adequate to the challenge. At the next meeting they decided to take on the brutal Three Strikes Law in order to build a Statewide coalition of people who would be likely to help fight the expansion of prisons as the State's all purpose solution to social problems involving the poor. That project, inaugurated in January 1996, built slowly over a year, eventually culminating in a "Three Strikes Awareness Month," during which time teach-ins, radio and television appearances, and leafletting outside courthouses raised consciousness of the legislation's scattershot effect. While the scale of activity has grown, so have uneasinesses and antagonisms as the ROC enters a new phase of organization, in which 4167 South Normandie Avenue may remain the symbolic, but not necessarily the political, center of the group.

Situating Mothers ROC: Some Strategic Historical Comparisons

We think organizations have to be the first step toward a social movement.
—Myles Horton, founder, Highlander Center[58]

Mothers Reclaiming Our Children is part of a rich history of oppositional struggle and may be compared with several kinds of twentieth-century movements whose systems, organizations, and/or practices resonate with the Los Angeles grass-

58 Myles Horton and Paulo Freire, *We Make the Road by Walking*, Philadelphia: Temple University Press, 1990, 124.

roots women's understanding of social conditions and their approach to social change. As with Mothers ROC, the organizations briefly examined in this section mingle reformist and radical ideologies and strategies; in the vision and substance of their political projects, they pose challenges to the oppressive system in question and to the dominant structures of antisystemic movements. I believe such complexity expresses an organic relation between these struggles and the specific context of the crises from which they emerge. Here, I differentiate specificity from a narrow conception of localism. Thus, by organic I mean situatedness. In this move I follow Gramsci and gloss Haraway.[59] The way conflict emerges in a social structure is not inevitable, even though it may be understood at a higher level of abstraction to be an expression of a fundamental antagonism—such as class conflict. What happens at the local level has everything to do with forces operating at other scales, and my interest lies in reconciling the micro with the macro by showing how the drama of crisis "on the ground" is neither wholly determined by, nor remotely autonomous from, the larger crisis. I do not wish to ascribe intentions or dimensions to groupings where evidence indicates otherwise; rather, I wish to draw out the ways in which practical questions of method, argument, and/or structure powerfully engage crisis on the material and ideological stages where the conditions of crises unfold.

For Mothers ROC, then, three major conditions of existence —and categories of analysis—form the heart of the group's specific response to crisis. These consist of the embeddedness of African American and other working-class mothers in a world only minimally circumscribed by home; the problem of organizing the unorganized in the US according to strategies other than singular, insular identities (e.g., occupation, race, parental

---

59   Donna Haraway, "Situated Knowledges: The Science Question in Feminism and the Privilege of Partial Perspective," in *Simians, Cyborgs and Women*, New York: Routledge, 1991, 183–201.

status); and the potential power of "motherhood" as a political foundation from which to confront an increasingly hostile state.

Women whose paid labor is crucial to the household economy, and who are normatively measured in the dominant discourse and the gross domestic product according to their performance in the gender-segmented labor market, embody different roles with respect to production, reproduction, and politics than women who evade such material and ideological constraints.[60] Such difference in the United States is further structured by race.[61] During the Progressive Era, African American "club" women who organized around issues of gender and work could not echo, on behalf of their sisters, the rhetoric of home and dependency espoused by white women reformers.[62] While immigrant European working-class women ordinarily had to engage in waged labor, the standards by which white feminist/gender politics—dominated by native elites—strove to produce the "True" and then the "American" woman rested on the expectation that all such women should, at the earliest economic opportunity, become dependent, full-time homemakers.[63] The gendered economic power of anti-Black racism made such an expectation for African American women impossible, since there was no likelihood that their own paid labor would soon become redundant or that their mates could ever gain a reliable family wage.[64]

---

60   Eileen Boris, "The Power of Motherhood: Black and White Activist Women Redefine the Political," *Yale Journal of Law and Feminism* (Fall 1989): 25–49.

61   Barbara Jeanne Fields, "Slavery, Race and Ideology in the United States of America," *New Left Review* 181 (1990): 95–118.

62   Boris, "The Power of Motherhood"; Paula Giddings, *When and Where I Enter: The Impact of Black Women on Race and Sex in America*, New York: William Morrow, 1984; Gordon, *Pitied But Not Entitled*.

63   Hazel Carby, *Reconstructing Womanhood*, New York: Oxford University Press, 1987; Nancy Fraser and Linda Gordon, "Contract Versus Charity: Why is There no Social Citizenship in the United States?," *Socialist Review* 22.3 (1992): 45–67.

64   Mariarosa Dalla Costa and Selma James, *The Power of Women and the Subversion of the Community*, London: Falling Wall Press, 1972;

African American club activists' politics focused on ways to ameliorate working-class women's daily experiences within and between home and work, with the church typically serving as a semi-public arena where such women could gather in relative safety to organize for social change.[65] Efforts centered on life's everyday details and included lessons in such areas as grooming, literacy, and better housekeeping for wage or for family. Club women used recognizable household relations to build women's political consciousness. The self-help lessons constituted strategies through which the most vulnerable members of the workforce could make themselves stronger against everyday assaults on their integrity—assaults typified by employer rape no less than paltry wages.[66] Activists insisted that Black women must expect to act on a stage where no sturdy legal or customary curtain shielded the private from the public realm. The legacy of slavery, the reality of Jim Crow laws, and the discipline of lynching suspended any illusion that Black women might either withdraw from the labor market—and the coercive social controls determining when and where they enter it—or turn to the state for protection or relief.[67]

Leopoldina Fortunati, *The Arcane of Reproduction: Housework, Prostitution, Labor and Capital*, Brooklyn: Autonomedia, 1995; William Julius Wilson, *The Truly Disadvantaged*, Chicago: University of Chicago Press, 1987.

65 Giddings, *When and Where I Enter*; Cheryl Townsend Gilkes, "Dual Heroisms and Double Burdens: Interpreting Afro-American Women's Experience and History," *Feminist Studies* 15.3 (1989): 573–590, and *Black Women's Work as Deviance: Social Sources of Racial Antagonism*, Wellesley: Wellesley College Center for Research on Women, 1979; Charles H. Long, *Signification: Signs, Symbols, and Images in the Interpretation of Religion*, Philadelphia: Fortress Press, 1986; Albert Raboteau, *A Fire in the Bones: Reflections on African-American Religious History*, Boston: Beacon Press, 1995, and *Slave Religion*, New York: Oxford University Press, 1978; Dorothy Sterling (ed.), *We Are Your Sisters*, New York: W.W. Norton, 1984; James Melvin Washington, *Frustrated Fellowship: The Black Baptists Quest for Social Power*, Macon, GA: Mercer, 1986.

66 Angela Y. Davis, *Women, Race, and Class*, New York: Vintage, 1981.

67 Davis, *Women, Race, and Class*; Giddings, *When and Where I Enter*; Ralph Ginzburg, *100 Years of Lynchings*, Baltimore: Black Classic

In this historical context, motherhood functioned through and as an attribute of the woman-as-laborer, enacted as collective or social rather than individualized practice.[68] Club women included mothering lessons among their outreach projects because they rightly viewed the collective future of the race as depending on the children's successful preparation to participate in severely restricted, highly unstable job markets. In other words, the club women's specific conception of the politics of motherhood required good housekeeping to include, as a matter of course, deliberately raising children to survive in racially-defined, conflict-riven lives. These lives would be shaped by a constantly "changing same"[69] of negative contingencies—exemplified by the nation's territory-wide, multiscalar accumulation of both Jim Crow laws and *de facto* segregation practices in the early twentieth century.[70] Most children might learn strictly to labor in whatever niche constituted their generation's market enclave.[71] At the same time, however, the constant restructuring of labor markets—most notably during wartime—meant that mothers were also educating their daughters and sons in ways of thinking that might lead to more radical consciousness of what change *without*

Press, 1988; Jacqueline Jones, *Labor of Love, Labor of Sorrow*, New York: Random House, 1985; Sterling (ed.), *We Are Your Sisters*; Deborah Gray White, *Ar'n't I a Woman? Female Slaves in the Plantation South*, New York: Norton, 1985.

68 Collins, *Black Feminist Thought*; Temma Kaplan, "Female Consciousness and Collective Action," *Signs* 7.3 (1982):545–66; White, *Ar'n't I a Woman?*

69 LeRoi Jones (Amiri Baraka), "The Changing Same (R&B and New Black Music)" (1966), in *Black Music*, New York: Morrow, 1970.

70 W. E. B. Du Bois, *Black Reconstruction in America*, New York: Atheneum, 1992 [1935]; Frances E.W. Harper, *Iola Leroy*, Boston: Beacon Press, 1987 [1892]; Carol Marks, *"Farewell: We're Good and Gone" the Great Black Migration*, Indianapolis: Indiana University Press, 1989; Clyde Woods, *Development Arrested: The Blues and Plantation Power in the Mississippi Delta*, new ed., introd. Ruth Wilson Gilmore, London: Verso, 2017 [1998].

71 Paul Willis, *Learning to Labor: How Working Class Kids Get Working Class Jobs*, New York: Columbia University Press, 1977.

progress meant, given the material and ideological positioning of Black people in the racial state.[72]

While it may appear that the type of organizing club women espoused falls simply and squarely into Booker T. Washington's Tuskegee model of cooperative apartheid, it also opened new possibilities for women to enlarge their scope of activity through emphasizing rather than minimizing Black women's visibility in the world. Although dangerous, visibility also provided Black women with peculiarly exploitable access to potentially political audiences because of their regular passage through public space. For example, women were often in the vanguard protesting state and state-sanctioned terrorism—in part because men were the ordinary victims of lynching and police brutality.[73] Similarly, the Montgomery Bus Boycott—popularly viewed as a founding moment of the post–World War II civil rights movement—gained structure and strength from a church-based organization of women who built the scaffolding from which to dismantle US *de jure* apartheid around the issue of public transportation for African American domestic and other workers.[74] For both the immediate Montgomery audience and for viewers of newsreels shown on televisions and in movie theaters across the United States, the boycott produced an unfamiliar and compelling image of urban Black women walking in groups to and from the job, their apparent cheerfulness belying the fearful conditions in which they confronted the most readily perceivable ways in

72 Chester Himes, *If He Hollers*, New York: Thunder's Mouth Press, 1986 [1945], and *The Quality of Hurt: The Autobiography of Chester Himes*, New York: Doubleday, 1971; George Lipsitz, *A Life in the Struggle: Ivory Perry and the Culture of Opposition*, Philadelphia: Temple University Press, 1987; Woods, *Development Arrested*.

73 Carby, *Reconstructing Womanhood*; Vron Ware, *Beyond the Pale: White Women, Racism and History*, London: Verso, 1992.

74 Robin D. G. Kelley, *Race Rebels: Culture, Politics and the Black Working Class*, New York: Free Press, 1994; Fred Powledge, *Free at Last? The Civil Rights Movement and the People who Made It*, Boston: Little Brown, 1991.

which US racism divides class and gender. In these women, foes recognized unanticipated adversaries; allies, by contrast, recognized, through the women's actions, how familiar *practices* of everyday life might be rearranged in order to take on previously unimaginable tasks.[75]

Organizing is always constrained by recognition: How do people come to actively identify in and act through a group such that its collective end surpasses reification of characteristics (e.g., identity politics) or protection of a fixed set of interests (e.g., corporatist politics) and, instead, extends toward an evolving, purposeful social movement (e.g., class politics)?[76] This question has particular importance when it comes to the age-old puzzle of organizing unorganized US workers, especially when the fundamental criterion for identification is not limited by a worksite or occupational category. US labor history is dominated by worksite- and occupational-movement building, with group boundaries established by employers or by skills. These boundaries, of course, negatively organize— and even disorganize—the excluded because US worksites and occupations are historically segregated by both gender and race.[77]

---

75   Aldon D. Morris, *The Origins of the Civil Rights Movement: Black Communities Organizing for Change*, New York: The Free Press, 1984.

76   Gramsci, *Selections*; Hall, "Gramsci's Relevance," and "Cultural Identity and Diaspora," in Jonathan Rutherford (ed.), *Identity: Community, Culture and Difference*, London: Lawrence and Wishart, 1990; Doracie Zoleta-Nantes, personal conversation with author, 1995.

77   Dorothy Sue Cobble, "Making Postindustrial Unionism Possible," in S. Friedman et al. (eds), *Restoring the Promise of American Labor Law*, Ithaca, NY: ILR Press, 1994, 285–302, and *Dishing it Out: Waitresses and Their Unions in the Twentieth Century*, Chicago: University of Illinois Press, 1991; Paul Johnston, *Success While Others Fail: Social Movement Unionism and the Public Workplace*, New York: ILR Press, 1994; Ruth Milkman, *Gender at Work*, Champaign-Urbana IL: University of Illinois Press, 1987; David Roediger, *The Wages of Whiteness: Race and the Making of the American Working Class*, New York: Verso, 1991; Howard Wial, "The Emerging Organizational Structure of Unionism in Low-Wage Services," *Rutgers Law Review* 45 (1993): 671–738; Woods, *Development Arrested*.

In a few instances, US labor movements have broadened their practices by engaging in a class rather than corporatist approach. Whereas most such efforts resulted in failure—crushed by the capitalist state's coercive and ideological apparatuses—some attempts along this way produced surprising results.[78] When the Communist Party attempted to organize workers in the relatively new steel district of Birmingham, Alabama during the 1930s, it ran into a sturdy wall of racism that prevented the CPUSA from forging a movement in which whites could recognize themselves and Black people as equally exploited workers rather than as properly unequal Americans. However, the organizers who traveled the urban mills and rural mines seeking out industrial laborers discovered an unanticipated audience for their arguments among predominately Black sharecroppers. The Sharecroppers' Union adapted the CP analysis to their own precarious conditions, and the group grew rapidly, forming a network of cells in urban and rural locations throughout the region. One needed neither to be a sharecropper, nor employed, nor Black to participate in the union. Upwards of six thousand millworkers and miners, in addition to dispossessed farmers (busy or idle), found common cause in a social movement through their understanding of their collective "equality"—which was, at that time, their individual interchangeability and disposability on northern Alabama's agricultural and industrial production platforms.[79] State forces eventually crushed the movement, yet the submerged remnants of the union, according to its indigenous leadership, formed the

---

78   Melvyn Dubofsky, *We Shall Be All: A History of the IWW*, Champaign-Urbana, IL: University of Illinois Press, 1969; Phillip Foner, "The IWW and the Negro Worker," *Journal of Negro History* (1970): 45–64; Wial, "The Emerging Organizational Structure of Unionism in Low-Wage Services."

79   In the United States, the word "equality" seems often to connote an upward leveling. In *The Arcane of Reproduction*, Fortunati helpfully points out that other forms of "equality" (e.g., slavery) have analytical weight that requires political and organizational attention.

already-existing regional foundation for intra-wartime organizing and postwar anti-racist activism.[80]

In the current period, Justice for Janitors (JfJ) is an innovative labor movement in which neither worksite nor occupation
has served as a sufficient organizational structure in the low-
wage service industry. Learning from history, JfJ's strategy is to
exploit the otherwise inhibiting features of the labor market by
pursuing a "geographical" approach to organization.[81] In the
massive layoffs of the late 1970s and early 1980s, firms broke
janitorial unions that African Americans and others had painstakingly built under the aegis of the Congress of Industrial
Organizations (CIO) during and after World War II.[82] Industry
subcontracted maintenance and, thereby, negated labor's hard-
won worksite-by-worksite agreements.

The ensuing proliferation of small, easily reorganized janitorial service contractors has made actual employers moving
targets and, thus, rendered traditional forms of wage bargaining
impossible to carry out and enforce.[83] Further, janitors working
under the new arrangements, often at less than minimum wage,
are not the same people who fought wages up to ten dollars or
more per hour by 1980.[84] Thus, in addition to pressing employers for contracts, JfJ's solution is to organize both the actual
market for janitorial services *and* the potential labor market
for janitors. This areal approach limits employers' flexibility

---

80   C. L. R. James et al., *Fighting Racism in World War Two*, New
York: Monad Press, 1980; Robin D. G. Kelley, *Hammer and Hoe: Alabama
Communists During the Great Depression*, Chapel Hill, NC: University of
North Carolina Press, 1990; Nell Painter, *The Narrative of Hosea Hudson*,
Cambridge: Harvard University Press, 1979.

81   Johnston, *Success While Others Fail*; Wial, "The Emerging Organizational Structure of Unionism in Low-Wage Services."

82   See James et al., *Fighting Racism*.

83   The companies that now hire janitors can disappear overnight,
thanks to no fixed capital or other constraints holding them in place.
Therefore, labor lacks the leverage it had when, for example, janitors
negotiated contracts directly with the former employers (owners of hotels,
restaurants, office buildings, factories, and so forth) who are now clients.

84   In 1980 dollars.

because it is their actual and potential *clients* who agree to do business only with unionized contractors. The solution also requires that labor organizing be community organizing as well, as was the case with the CPUSA's work in 1930s greater-Birmingham. To appeal to former janitors in target areas and to potential janitors wherever they may be, JfJ proposes a bottom-up strategy to develop comprehensive regional plans that include but are not reducible to setting minimal standards for wages that employed individuals (janitors or not) can expect to pull down.[85]

The divisions between home and work, private and public, on the stage of capitalist culture constitute for many the normative limits to particular kinds of conflict. When the political dimensions of breaches in those limits become apparent in crises, new possibilities for social movements unfold. As we have seen, Black working-class women politicized the material and ideological distance between their paid and unwaged labor by traversing the streets. More recently, janitors around the US have taken their

---

85 Eric Parker and Joel Rodgers, *The Wisconsin Regional Training Partnership*, 1995 (manuscript in author's possession); Wial, "The Emerging Organizational Structure of Unionism in Low-Wage Services"; see also Elizabeth Faue, *Community of Suffering and Struggle: Women, Men and the Labor Movement in Minneapolis, 1915–1945*, Chapel Hill, NC: University of North Carolina Press, 1990, and Woods, *Development Arrested*. According to a presentation given by a JfJ organizing committee in Los Angeles in March 1993, organizing has, in some cases, stretched back to immigrant janitors' towns of origin in Mexico and El Salvador. Insofar as it is common for people from a particular region to migrate to both the same area and labor-market niche as their friends and families who precede them, JfJ started to work backward along the migratory path in an attempt to incorporate the wider-than-daily labor market into the movement's sphere of influence. During this same presentation, when challenged by a Sandinista cadre who asked an apparently simple question ("What became of the people who used to be janitors?"), JfJ acknowledged their organizing had not extended to the former workers. JfJ pledged to expand its Southern California scope of activity and reach out to former janitors in the community who are, as noted above, mostly African Americans in a project that might well revive submerged knowledges from earlier labor and anti-racist struggles.

clandestine exploitation public on a number of fronts, combining community-based organizing with front-line, public sphere militancy led by immigrants who gained experience as oppositional subjects of, for example, Salvadoran state terrorism.[86]

In Argentina, under the fascist military government (1977–1983) the Madres of the Plaza de Mayo defied the expectation that women should not meddle in affairs of the state—which is to say the male, or public, sphere—by organizing on the basis of a simple and culturally indisputable claim that mothers ought to know where their children are. The fascists' nightly raids to kidnap teenage and adult children, most of whom were never seen again, effectively coerced neighbors, who had not yet been touched, to avert their eyes and keep their mouths closed. However, a cadre of mothers, who first encountered each other in the interstices of the terrorist state—waiting rooms, courtrooms, and the information desks of jails and detention centers—eventually took their quest into the Plaza de Mayo. There, with the eyes of the nation and eventually the world on them, they demanded both the return of their disappeared and the identification and punishment of those who had perpetrated the terror. The mothers dressed for recognition, wearing head scarves made of diapers on which each had written or embroidered the name(s) of her disappeared.[87]

---

86 Laura Pulido, "The Geography of Militant Labor Organizing in Los Angeles," Paper delivered at the meetings of the Association for Economic and Social Analysis, December 7, 1996, University of Massachusetts, Amherst.

87 Martin Anderson, *Dossier Secreto: Argentina's Desaparecidos and the Myth of the "Dirty War."* Boulder, CO: Westview, 1993; Marguerite Guzman Bouvard, *Revolutionizing Motherhood: The Mothers of the Plaza de Mayo*, Wilmington, DE: Scholarly Resources, Inc., 1994; Nora Amelia Femenia, "Argentina's Mothers of the Plaza de Mayo: The Mourning Process from Junta to Democracy," *Feminist Studies* 13.1 (1987): 9–18; Jo Fisher, *Mothers of the Disappeared*, Boston: South End Press, 1989; Matilde Mellibovsky, *Circle of Love Over Death: The Story of the Mothers of the Plaza de Mayo*, Willimantic, CT: Curbstone Press, 1997; Emma Sepúlveda (ed.), *We, Chile: Personal Testimonies of the Chilean Arpilleristas*, Falls Church, VA: Azul Editions, 1996.

The Madres' fundamental position, echoing and echoed by similar movements in such places as South Africa, Palestine, and El Salvador, was and is that children are not alienable.[88] In order to make this position politically material in the face of continuous terror, the Madres permanently drew back the curtain between private and public, making "maternal" activism on behalf of children a daily job conducted as openly and methodically as possible. The Madres' persistence, both before and after the official admission that the children had died horribly, transformed the passion of individual grief into the politics of collective opposition. Betrayed in the early years by state and church officials alike, by military, police, bureaucrats, and priests, the Madres learned to suspect institutions as well as individuals, and as their analysis became enriched by experience, they situated their disappeared in the context of political-economic crisis. Thus, when a re-democratized Argentina emerged, they did not return to hearth and home but rather expanded their political horizons. Currently [1999], their politics focus on the effects of the country's structural adjustment program, which has widened and deepened poverty and reduced opportunities for young people.[89]

As we have seen, Mothers ROC does its work in a political-economic climate as hostile, and often as bloody, as that which formed each group we have briefly examined. The ROC's solutions to the problems constituting the daily struggle to reclaim their children draw from the structural features of radical self-help, from the strategies of organizing on every platform where conflict is enacted, and from the argument that mothers should extend their techniques as mothers beyond the veil of traditional domestic spheres. In a word, they enact

---

88 Barbara Harlow, *Barred: Women, Writing and Political Detention*, Hanover: Wesleyan University Press/University Press of New England, 1992; Maria Teresa Tula, *Hear My Testimony*, Boston: South End Press, 1994.

89 Fisher, *Mothers of the Disappeared*; Calvin Sims, "The Rock, Unyielding, of the Plaza de Mayo," *New York Times*, March 2, 1996, 4.

the "consciencization" of motherhood.[90] The solutions are grounded in, but not bounded by, local conditions. Indeed, the organicism of Mothers ROC has to do precisely with its attention to the specific sites and scales of power that produce prison geographies *and* to the ways those sites and scales might be exploited for oppositional ends.

Conclusion: From the Crisis of Place to the Politics of Space

A small, poor, multiracial group of working-class people, mostly prisoners' mothers, mobilize in the interstices of the politically abandoned, heavily policed, declining welfare state. They come forward, in the first instance, because they will not let their children go. They stay forward, in the spaces created by intensified imprisonment of their loved ones, because they encounter many mothers and others in the same locations eager to join in the reclamation project. And they push further, because from those breaches they can see, and try to occupy, positions from which to collectively challenge the individualized involuntary migration of urban "surplus population" into rural prisons.

"Arrest is the political art of individualizing disorder."[91] Again and again, such individualization produces fragmentation rather than connection for the millions arrested in the US each year, as each person and household, dealing with each arrest, must figure out how to undo the detention—which appears to be nothing more than a highly rationalized confrontation between the individual and the state. The larger disorder is then reified in the typologies of wrongdoing such as gang activity;

90 Paulo Freire, *Pedagogy of the Oppressed*, New York: Seabury, 1970.

91 Allen Feldman, *Formations of Violence*, Chicago: University of Chicago Press, 1991, 109.

alternatively, the larger disorder is mystified as "crime," which, like unemployment, is alleged to have a "natural" if changing rate in a social formation.[92] ROCers gradually but decisively refuse both the individualized nature of their persons' arrests and the "naturalness" of crime, of poverty, of the power of the state.[93] They arrive at their critique through action. Action crucially includes the difficult work of identification—which entails production, not discovery, of a "suture or positioning."[94] Through the socially and spatially complex processes of identification that are attentive to racial, class, and gender specificities as well as commonalities, the ROCers transform themselves and the external world.

By enlivening African American practices of social mothering, the ROCers engage a broadening community in their concern for the circumstances and fate of prisoners. That social opening provides avenues for all kinds of mothers (and others) to join in the work as the enormous labor confronting each mother tends to encourage all both to accept and extend help. I make no claim for "social mothering" as an exclusively or universally African American cultural practice; it is neither. However, Barbara Meredith's common-sense invocation of mothering as collective action makes possible the group's integration of mothers with similar or quite different maternalist assumptions.[95] In other words, techniques developed over

---

92 See, for examples, Peter W. Greenwood et al., *Three Strikes and You're Out*; James Q. Wilson and Richard Herrnstein, *Crime and Human Nature*, New York: Simon and Schuster, 1985.

93 See also David Anderson, *Crime and the Politics of Hysteria*, New York: Times Books, 1995; Charles Derber, *The Wilding of America: How Greed and Violence are Eroding our Nation's Character*, New York: St. Martins, 1996; Carol Stabile, "Media's Crime Wave: Legitimating the Prison Industrial Complex." Paper delivered at *Behind Bars: Prisons and Communities in the United States*, George Mason University, 1996.

94 Hall, "Cultural Identity and Diaspora"; see also Peter Jackson, "Changing Ourselves: A Geography of Position," in R. J. Johnston (ed.), *The Challenge for Geography*, Oxford: Basil Blackwell, 1993, 198–214.

95 Kaplan, "Female Consciousness and Collective Action"; see also

generations on behalf of Black children and families within terror-demarcated, racially-defined enclaves, provide contemporary means to choreograph interracial political solidarity among all kinds of "mothers" losing their loved ones into the prison system. These mothers and others can and do identify each other in the small "public" spaces between their socially segregated residential living places and the "unitized" carceral quarters in which their children are caged. Some members are shy about jumping into the process, and others come to the ROC for help on their individual case only; but all who persist practice the "each one teach one" approach.[96]

The process of integrating different kinds of mothers and others into the ROC involves extensive outreach designed to permeate the social organization of space. These projects also catch people in the "betweens" of segregated lives: at work, for example, or on the bus. Such areal permeation, similar to (and literally overlapping) the Justice for Janitors Los Angeles crusade, raises a more general problem of identification. The ROCers easily recognize each other in the spaces of the criminal justice system. Outside those areas, what constitutes resemblance? If we are not all Black, and if all activists are not

---

Mark Traugott (ed.), *Repertoires and Cycles of Collective Action*, Durham, NC: Duke University Press, 1995.

96   A recurrent theme in discussions among many of the shyer mothers is their avowal of and explanation for their own unfitness. They refute the dominant explanations—they don't take drugs, rely on welfare, or work in the sex industry. But what lingers is a doubt whether they, as women (and men) who might have trouble reading or who have been afraid to stand up to the law, can ever be fit mothers for loved ones caught in a system in which book-knowledge and various types of intimidation—intellectual as well as physical—feature centrally in outcomes of cases. Many ask me to accompany them to meetings with officials because they feel stronger knowing that I know all the *words*—as well as the demographics, statistics, history, etc. As they teach each other what they learn, all of the ROCers gain confidence; indeed, those who cannot read well flourish by using their substantial memories to chart and compare cases (compare with "Decorative Beasts," in this volume, on the boys in the California Youth Authority).

mothers, and if all prisoners are not (young) children, then who are we? Poor people who work. As a community of purpose, Mothers ROC acts on the basis of a simple inversion: We are not poor because our loved ones are in prison; rather, our loved ones are in prison because we are poor. It follows that outreach should target working poor people and their youth. Class, then, constitutes the context for this analysis and action but cannot displace or subsume experiential issues of race: poor people of color have the most persons in prison.[97]

Nor does gender disappear on two accounts; first, women who work to support their families and to free their loved ones encounter each other as laborers with similar triple work-days—job, home, justice. In addition, mothers who reject the disposal of their children and ask why they themselves should not be compensated for struggling against the state raise a challenge to both their children's and their own devaluations from the vantage of reproductive labor.[98] The communist organizational and analytical influences in the ROC help keep these overdetermined antagonisms in the foreground of activism. As a result, Mothers ROC is building an alliance that women and men may enter from a number of positions and where they stay because the group's primary purpose retains clarity— even as members repeatedly clash when trying to produce an

---

97 See also Stuart Hall, "Race, Articulation and Societies Structured in Dominance," in *UNESCO Sociological Theories: Race and Colonialism*, Poole, England: Unesco, 1980, 305–46.

98 Dalla Costa and James, *The Power of Women and the Subversion of the Community*; Fortunati, *The Arcane of Reproduction*; Paddy Quick, "Capitalism and the Origins of Domestic Labor," *Review of Radical Political Economics* 24.2 (1992): 1–7. Compare Catherine MacKinnon's stridently clear exposition of gender displacement/subsumption in *Toward a Feminist Theory of the State*, Cambridge: Harvard University Press, 1989. The integrations are, of course, fragile; everything is at risk, and old structures and habits of inequality easily fill social spaces left vulnerable by uncertainty. For example, at a number of Mothers ROC meetings, men who have not been active in the organization will often steamroll discussions when the ROCers are trying to figure something out; and the ROCers let it happen, reenacting other relations of love, respect, and fear.

adequately comprehensive account of the world in which they struggle. In the context of shared antagonism, the activists "discover"[99]—which is to say, they *produce*—the values they share; in turn, that collective work produces community solidarity, or political integration, enabling further action. Solidarity increases with increased knowledge concerning the complexity with which the state and its allies conduct the imprisoning project. The alliance tends toward a scale of resolution at which, for example, any individual police precinct house ceases to be the total presence of the state and shrinks back toward its systemic position—the neighborhood outpost of what the ROCers characterize as a military occupation that will require a political movement to dismantle it.[100] As Mothers ROC seeks a wider regional membership, it also seeks to locate itself in a wider community of activism, reaching out nationally and internationally to organizations like itself.[101] Such movement heightens the potential for connections between Mothers ROC and women throughout the global workforce who struggle daily against the actual processes and effects of worldwide structural adjustments.[102]

---

99   Kaplan, "Female Consciousness and Collective Action."

100   Markusen and Yudken's analysis of the Cold War economy must be extended to the domestic warfare economy. See Ann R. Markusen and Joel Yudken, *Dismantling the Cold War Economy*, New York: Basic Books, 1992; see also Fanon's *The Wretched of the Earth*. At the same time that Mothers ROC has expanded, the LA gang truce has done so as well. By mid-1996, the LA truce included a number of Eastside and Westside Chicano and other Latino gangs. The Fourth Anniversary T-Shirt (1996) features a drawing of Malcolm X and Emiliano Zapata, the legend beneath their representations reading, simply, "X y Z." Also note, gangs engaged in peacemaking have, on a national basis, changed their moniker from "gangs" to "street organizations."

101   For example, a fairly recent newcomer to Mothers ROC is an immigrant Salvadoreña who works nights as a janitor; as noted above, core cadres among militant labor organizers in Los Angeles include Salvadoreña refugees who are experienced in dealing with state terror and with challenging state legitimacy.

102   According to the United Nations International Labour Organization, women do two-thirds of the world's work, receive five percent of the

The ineluctable salience of gender structures is the means through which Mothers ROC critically deploys the ideological power of motherhood to challenge the legitimacy of the changing state. All prisoners are somebody's children, and children are not alienable.[103] The racial and gendered social division of labor requires mothers of prisoners to live lives of high visibility; ROCers turn that visibility to a politically charged presence, voice, and movement against injustice, such that their activism becomes the centerpiece of their reproductive—and socially productive—labor.[104] As with mothers' movements in Latin America, South Africa, and Palestine, Mothers ROC's frontline relation to the state is not as a petitioner for a share in the social wage, but rather as an antagonist against the state's form and purpose with respect to the life chances of their family members and those like them. The insistence on the rights of mothers to children and children to mothers is not a defense of "traditional" domesticity as a separate sphere, rather it represents political activation around rising awareness of the ways that the working-class "domestic" is a site saturated by the racial state.

Coda

The organization of space can indeed define relationships between people, activities, things and concepts.

—David Harvey[105]

---

income, and own one percent of the assets. Activist Margaret Prescod of the Wages for Housework Campaign interprets these figures as illuminating both sexism and racism on a global scale. See "Terror Austerity Race Gender Excess Theater," in this volume.

103 See Drucilla Cornell, *The Imaginary Domain: Abortion, Pornography and Sexual Harrassment*, New York: Routledge, 1995.

104 See Fisher, *Mothers of the Disappeared.*

105 David Harvey, *The Condition of Postmodernity: An Enquiry into the Origins of Cultural Change*, Cambridge: Basil Blackwell, 1989, 216.

In Volume 1 of *Capital,* Marx takes great pains to explain how the capitalist mode of production depends on social and spatial qualities that, in turn, are the potential grounds for undoing exploitation. Cooperation, in his view, is a necessary feature of production processes that are organized into detailed divisions of labor; the many workers who must congregate in a factory to produce goods constitute a fundamental social unit capable of rising up and expropriating the expropriators. In other words, the constrained cooperation among employee workers can become political cooperation among the class "workers." A significant body of anti-colonialist, feminist, anti-racist, and communist/workerist theory expands upon Marx's insight and finds the material of political action in the folds of contradiction—at "points of production" not limited to locations where commodities are made.[106] Such work, in making revisions to Marxist orthodoxy, also provides a dynamic analytical and organizational model for the production of social justice. By organizing surplus labor into cages, the state also pulls into its spheres of operation prisoners' mothers and other caregivers who, finding each other in the interstices of the system, can cooperate against the state's catch-all solution to social problems involving the poor.

The magnitude of imprisonment suggests the magnitude of possibility. And yet the magnitude starts small, over and over again. Gilda Garcia's testimony exemplifies the socio-spatial constraints of everyday life for ROCers and their families:

---

106 For examples, see Dalla Costa and James, *The Power of Women and the Subversion of the Community*; Fanon, *The Wretched of the Earth*; Fortunati, *The Arcane of Reproduction*; Michael Hardt and Antonio Negri, *Labor of Dionysus: A Critique of the State-Form*, Minneapolis: University of Minnesota Press, 1994; Harvey, *The Limits to Capital*; Sidney J. Lemelle, "Ritual, Resistance, and Social Reproduction: A Cultural Economy of Iron-Smelting in Colonial Tanzania 1890–1975," *Journal of Historical Sociology* 5.2 (1992): 161–82; Negri, *Revolution Retrieved*, and *The Politics of Subversion*, Cambridge: Cambridge University Press, 1989; Robinson, *Black Marxism*.

And then she [the public defender] said, "The reason the prosecutor can add the extra time is because your son was within 500 feet of a school when he was picked up." My son went to bring his little brother home from school! That's why he was at the school. *La migra* waits by schools to catch people without Green Cards, and they detain anybody who looks like us. Anybody. We sent our son because he doesn't have a job, so if they stop him we don't lose any money. We're just making it. We can't afford to miss work just because INS needs to look good to … I don't mean any offense, but … they need to look good for the white people. They don't care about us, that we have jobs. It's all a show. But in the morning, as soon as my husband and I drive away to work, the [city] police are on our street, starting stuff, making our kids mad, telling them they are going to get them. One day I went back because I forgot something, and the police were there, outside of their cars. I asked them "What is wrong? What do you want here?" And this one cop, his name is _____ [knowing laughter in the room], told me, "We're going to get your son," and he called my son names. He told me my son was in a gang. But see, I know he isn't in a gang because the gang they said he was in is in another neighborhood. My son could not live with us and be in that gang. I have relatives in that gang who have an auto body shop, and sometimes my son does some work for them to make a few dollars. But he could never join that gang because of where we live. Everyone knows that.

The political geography of the state's industrialized punishment system determines the scale of everyday struggle for Mothers ROC, which in turn is determinant of their concepts of motherhood. They discover that the scale of the body, at which disorder is individualized, requires multiple forms of political care. Their techniques of mothering, in and as Mothers ROC, extend past the limits of household, kinship, and neighborhood, past the limits of gender and racial divisions of social space, to embrace the political project to reclaim children of all ages whose mothers are losing them, at a net of fifty-five Statewide per business day, into the prison system.

Mothers Reclaiming Our Children has evolved from a self-help group that formed in response to a crisis of place—a police murder in South Central Los Angeles—to a political organization trying to build a powerful movement across the spaces of domestic militarism. The forces that control and contain poor working people, and especially people of color, in prisons, in segregated neighborhoods, and in low-paying jobs have particular ideological and political reaches. For the ROC successfully to oppose the disposal of their children, they organize to challenge the full reach of the powers arrayed against them. This involves building alliances of and as multiracial groups that can reproduce solid centers of activism throughout and across the "nested scales" of the rising prison state.[107] The means toward that end consist of renovating and making critical ideologies of motherhood and techniques of mothering—derived from particular African American traditions—and extending them within the context of class struggle against state-organized (or at least state-complicit) structural adjustments that characterize the current period.

The South African women's political chant from which Mothers ROC derives its name presents a succinct image of contradiction in action: From woman, to rock, to boulder, the singers predict their resolute consolidation into a force set in motion ("You have dislodged a boulder") by the very power they must crush.

---

107   Neil Smith, "Geography, Difference, and the Politics of Scale," in Joe Doherty, Elspeth Graham, and Mohammed Malek (eds.), *Postmodernism and the Social Sciences*, New York: St. Martin's, 1992.

17

Forgotten Places and the Seeds of Grassroots Planning

The Mix

Forgotten places are not outside history. Rather, they are places that have experienced the abandonment characteristic of contemporary capitalist and neoliberal state reorganization. Given the enormous disorder that "organized abandonment"[1] both creates and exploits, how can people who inhabit forgotten places scale up their activism from intensely localized struggles to something less atomized and therefore possessed of a significant capacity for self-determination? How do they set and fulfill agendas for life-affirming social change—whether by seizing control of the social wage or through other means? In this essay I will conceptualize the kinds of places where prisoners come from and where prisons are built as a single—though spatially discontinuous—abandoned region. I will then present three exemplary facets of the process I am trying to think through by doing and writing, in order to highlight the potential of certain kinds of research. Here indeed is where scholars can make a difference: not because we have technical expertise (although that matters) but rather because we have the precious opportunity to think in cross-cutting ways and to find both promising continuities and productive breaks in

---

1 David Harvey, *The Limits to Capital*, Chicago: University of Chicago Press/Midway Reprints, 1989, 303.

the mix of people, histories, political and economic forces, and landscapes that make up forgotten places.[2]

Why prisons and prisoners? I didn't turn to the topic because I was driven as a scholar to answer some pressing questions. Rather, the issue hailed me in the early 1990s, when I started to work with some prisoners and their families and persisted as I pursued a PhD in geography and employment in academia. The entire world of premature death and criminalization was not at all new to me: I've had family members who have done time, some of us have been harmed by others, and one of us has been killed. In short, the problem already, to paraphrase Hall, bit into my existence.[3] But with sometimes surprising intensity during the past decade and a half, my lifelong activism has been mixed into and fixed on the places prisoners come from and the places where prisons are built. In the United States, these people and locations are among the most vulnerable to the "organized abandonment" that accompanies globalization's large-scale movements of capital and labor, and as such they are subject to many other processes that accumulate in and as forgotten places. Here's a chicken-egg conundrum: I don't know whether I think we can find important lessons for making change by studying the margins because I'm a geographer or whether I became a geographer because of how I already thought about contradictions and interfaces. What geography enables is the combination of an innate (if unevenly developed) interdisciplinarity with the field's central mission to examine the interfaces of the earth's multiple natural and social spatial forms.

---

2   Fred Moten, *In the Break: The Aesthetics of the Black Radical Tradition*, Minneapolis: University of Minnesota Press, 2003; Cedric J. Robinson, *Black Marxism: The Making of the Black Radical Tradition*, London: Zed Press, 1983; see also Gillian Hart, *Disabling Globalization: Places of Power in Post-Apartheid South Africa*, Berkeley: University of California Press, 2002.

3   Stuart Hall, "Race, Articulation and Societies Structured in Dominance," in *Sociological Theories: Race and Colonialism*, Paris: UNESCO, 1980.

Greenberg and Schneider's "marginal people on marginal lands" suggests the conceptual continuity of forgotten places that I wish both to broaden and specify.[4] People in these locales, exhausted by the daily violence of environmental degradation, racism, underemployment, overwork, shrinking social wages, and the disappearance of whole ways of life *and* those who lived them, nevertheless refuse to give up hope. What capacities might such people animate, and at what scales, to make the future better than the present? What does *better* mean? How do people make broadly contested sensibilities—indeed *feelings*—the basis for political struggle, especially when their social identities are not fixed by characteristics that point toward certain proven patterns (or theories) for action? In terms of prisons and prisoners the goal is double: to find relief for all from the expanding use of cages as all-purpose solutions to social and economic problems and to use the extreme (marginal) case to figure out how social justice activists might reinvigorate an organizational movement after it has spent several decades underground, undertheorized, or under cover of the not-for-profit sector.[5]

Forgotten places, then, are both symptomatic of and intimately shaped by crisis. I use *crisis* in the sense summarized by Stuart Hall and Bill Schwarz: it occurs when "the existing social formation can no longer be reproduced on the basis of the pre-existing system of social relations."[6] Crises are territorial and multiscalar; they overlap and sometimes interlock.[7] At the

4 Michael Greenberg and Dona Schneider, "Violence in American Cities: Young Black Males Is the Answer, But What Was the Question?," *Social Science and Medicine* 39.2 (1994): 179–87.

5 Incite! Women of Color against Violence, *The Revolution Will Not Be Funded*, Cambridge, MA: South End Press, 2007.

6 Stuart Hall and Bill Schwarz, "State and Society, 1880–1930," *The Hard Road to Renewal*, London: Verso, 1988, 96.

7 See Walter Rodney, *How Europe Underdeveloped Africa*, Washington, DC: Howard University Press, 1972; Frantz Fanon, *The Wretched of the Earth*, New York: Grove Press, 1961; Edward Soja, *Postmodern Geographies*, New York: Verso, 1989.

outset of my studies I learned everything I could about what was happening in urban areas because that was where most prisoners came from. But since they were sent away to new rural prisons it seemed necessary to learn about what drove the lockups' location and proliferation.[8] In the early 1990s, Thomas Lyson and William Falk edited *Forgotten Places*, a volume on uneven development in rural America.[9] Inspired by the editors' framework, I read closely the arguments they and their colleagues—especially Ted Bradshaw—had made, and I tried to connect their insights with my own and others' research on abandoned urban locales.[10] My goal was to connect rural and urban in a nonschematic way.

Especially at a time when urban and rural appear to be self-evidently and perhaps irreconcilably different (as in the "red state"/"blue state" distinction that has come to stand in for real descriptions *or* explanations of US intranational geopolitics), it seemed important to consider not only how they are connected—an old question for geographers—but also how they are objectively similar. What are the material and ideological linkages that make urban and rural—in some areas of the United States as well as elsewhere—more continuous and

---

8 I have written an entire book about this, but the work is far from done. See *Golden Gulag*.

9 Thomas A. Lyson and William W. Falk, eds., *Forgotten Places: Uneven Development in Rural America*, Lawrence: University of Kansas Press, 1993.

10 Ted K. Bradshaw, "In the Shadow of Urban Growth: Bifurcation in Rural California Communities," in Lyson and Falk, eds., *Forgotten Places*, 218–256; Robert Gooding-Williams, *Reading Rodney King/Reading Urban Uprising*, New York: Routledge, 1993; Laura Pulido, "Rethinking Environmental Racism: White Privilege and Urban Development in Southern California," *Annals of the Association of American Geographers* 90: 1, 2000, 12–40; Manuel Pastor Jr., "Common Ground at Ground Zero? The New Economy and the New Organizing in Los Angeles," *Antipode* 33.2 (2001): 260–89; Neil Smith, *The New Urban Frontier: Gentrification and the Revanchist City*, New York: Routledge, 1996; Cindi Katz, *Growing up Global: Economic Restructuring and Children's Everyday Lives*, Minneapolis: University of Minnesota Press, 2004.

less distinct than ordinarily imagined? There are problems with such an approach. One set of them is broadly subjective: What about the self-perception of communities in different kinds of locales, the ways they view other kinds of communities across social and spatial divides, and their understanding of those divides? Another set is material: Given that, place by place, past and present pathways and trajectories for capital and labor are often significantly different, can we usefully—even in theory—combine disparate sites into singular objects of scholarly and political action when the decisive motion of productive factors shaping social, political, economic, and physical space might seem necessarily to leave entirely distinctive topographies in their wake?[11] In short, to make connections raises a number of challenges, which are addressed in the examples given in this chapter.

Urgency and not mere curiosity is involved in scaling up the object of analysis by articulating urban with rural. The urgency has to do with the imperative to understand how ordinary people who lack resources but who do not necessarily lack "resourcefulness" develop the capacity to combine themselves into extraordinary forces and form the kinds of organizations that are the foundation of liberatory social movements.[12] Granted the difficulties, where might we find the ground for considering at least some urban and rural forgotten places together—as a single, though spatially discontinuous, abandoned region? There are precedents for such political-theoretical ambitions in many kinds of internationalism, of which Pan-Africanism is a long-standing and by no means outmoded example.[13] Perhaps the twentieth century's most widely

---

11 See Cindi Katz, "On the Grounds of Globalization: A Topography for Feminist Political Engagement," *Signs* 26.4 (2001): 1213–34; Katz, *Growing up Global*.

12 Marshall Ganz, "Resources and Resourcefulness: Strategic Capacity in the Unionization of California Agriculture, 1959–1966," *American Journal of Sociology* 105.4 (2000): 1003–62.

13 Sidney Lemelle and Robin D. G. Kelley, ed., *Imagining Home:*

lived and influential example was the meeting of nonaligned states in 1955 in Bandung, Indonesia, where debate and planning, rhetoric and material analysis brought the Third World into self-conscious being.[14]

Toward a Unified Concept of Forgotten Place

In previous writing I have used the concept of "gulag" to talk about the places prisoners come from and the places where prisons are built, and I think it works quite well as an indicator and analytical guide. However, it also seems to carry within it a conclusion that is quite the opposite of the actual material and ideological end toward which I have studied prisons so thoroughly: it does not enable description of what else is out there, beyond *its* margins. What concept might get at the kinds of forgotten places that have been absorbed into the gulag yet exceed them?

Class, Culture, and Nationalism in the African Diaspora, New York: Verso, 1994; Brent Hayes Edwards, *The Practice of Diaspora: Literature, Translation, and the Rise of Black Internationalism*, Cambridge, MA: Harvard University Press, 2003; Robinson, *Black Marxism*.

14   There is plenty of criticism about the Third World as an actual political-economic anti-dependent formation, and I do not dismiss the critics' learning and insights. However, "Third World" as a condition of existence and category of analysis has been very powerful for over half a century, and nonalignment (or perhaps more precisely, *differential* alignment) continues to be acted out as a countertrend to US hegemony on a global scale. I should also like to add that *third* need not indicate a transcendent category (in the sense that fascists deployed the term), a blurry cosmopolitan space, or the defeatist-triumphant "third way" of Giddens-Blair Britain. (See Michael Mann, *Fascists*, Cambridge: Cambridge University Press, 2004; Edward Soja, *Thirdspace*, Oxford: Blackwell, 1996.) There are threes, and there are threes: in some cases, *third* is deployed to suggest completion or resolution (as in bad dialectics), in others, *third* opens up the possibility for freshly viewing relationships in the world without succumbing to displacement-as-closure (as in good dialectics; see, for example, Denise Ferreira da Silva, *Toward a Global Idea of Race*, Minneapolis: University of Minnesota Press, 2007; Moten, *In the Break*).

In the summer of 2002, I had the good fortune to help conceive of and then attend an amazing workshop called "Globalization and Forgotten Places," organized by Yong-Sook Lee and Brenda Yeoh at the National University of Singapore. The group convened to share research and to look for theoretical and methodological assistance to refine our objects of study, analyze them, and think through what might be done about them. As should be evident from the previous discussion, we looked abroad, not because intranational theories and methods are necessarily threadbare, but rather because it struck us, as it has so many others, that if globalization is indeed *globalization*, we might usefully find convergences at many levels—not solely in the realm of capital concentration or information networks or other typically studied categories. In other words, to take seriously the thinking and actions of generations of internationalists who wish to globalize liberation is in part to take comparison seriously. Comparison is often imagined narrowly to be a statistical or institutional exercise (looking at organizations, practices, outcomes); and while it is indeed a method for discovering crucial distinctions within and between the similar, comparison is also a means for bringing together—or syncretizing—what at first glance seems irreconcilable.

One concept that captured my attention was *desakota*, a Malay word, meaning "town-country," that was brought into economic geography by Terry McGee to designate and think about places that are *neither* urban *nor* rural.[15] McGee's interest was to characterize regions in Indonesia and other southeast Asian countries where settlement, economic activity, politics, demographics, and culture belie categorization as "either/or"—ambiguous places in the dominant typology of settlement and sector. This kind of thinking derives from the

---

15 Terry McGee, "The Emergence of Desakota Regions in Asia: Expanding a Hypothesis," in N. Ginsburg, B. Koppel, and T. G. McGee, eds., *The Extended Metropolis: Settlement Transition in Asia,* Honolulu: University of Hawai'i Press, 1991, 3–25.

anti-colonial and anti-racist work of Third Worldist scholars; from Du Bois to Rodney, from Nkrumah to Sivanandan and Hall, the goal has been to compare political, economic, territorial, and ideological valences that distinguish and might unite disparate places shaped by external control or located outside particular developmental pathways (for whatever combination of reasons).[16]

So far, so good; but is the concept mobile? I think it works provisionally for California, but not without some adjustment (as any migration requires). A modified concept of *desakota* might give us a way to think the-city-and-the-country (and embrace the "Third World") somewhat freshly without advancing yet another theoretical novelty that stands in for political analysis but is actually only a luxurious evasion of politics.[17] However, freshness is required precisely because inadequate concepts and methods have, as Hart and Sitas note in their work on and with South African relocation townships, "trapped a large chunk of scholarship into an iron cage of instrumental knowledge and policy recommendations ... sharply at odds with emerging realities."[18]

---

16   W. E. B. Du Bois, *Black Reconstruction in America, 1860–1880*, New York: Free Press, 1935; Rodney, *How Europe Underdeveloped Africa*; Kwame Nkrumah, *Consciencism*, New York: Monthly Review Press, 1964; A. Sivanandan, *A Different Hunger: Writings on Black Resistance*, London: Pluto Press, 1982; and *Communities of Resistance: Writings on Black Struggles for Socialism*, London: Verso Press, 1991; Stuart Hall, "Africa Is Alive and Well and Living in the Diaspora," Unpublished manuscript, 1976 [now in *Selected Writings on Race and Difference*, ed. Paul Gilroy and Ruth Wilson Gilmore, Durham, NC: Duke University Press, 2021, 161–194]; Stuart Hall, "Cultural Identity and Diaspora," in Jonathan Rutherford, ed., *Identity: Community, Culture, Difference*, London: Lawrence and Wishart, 1994, 222–37.

17   Ruth Wilson Gilmore, "Public Enemies and Private Intellectuals," in this volume, 78–91; Laura Pulido, "FAQs: Frequently (Un)asked Questions about Being a Scholar-Activist," in Charles R. Hale, ed., *Engaging Contradictions: Theory, Politics, and Methods of Activist Scholarship*, Berkeley: University of California Press, 2008.

18   Gillian Hart and Ari Sitas, "Beyond the Urban-Rural Divide: Linking Land, Labour, and Livelihoods," *Transformation* 56 (2004), 31.

Desakota indicates a mix that in the California case encompasses the strange combination of sudden settlement changes —urban depopulation along with the establishment of megaprisons on formerly agricultural lands—and the regular circulation of people throughout the entire region without any necessary relation to the formal economy, to the distinct and overlapping political jurisdictions, to the prisons, or even to each other: visitors, prisoners, workers. In addition, *desakota* helps us situate the rural-and-urban forgotten in a relational as well as linked context. It raises for our consideration how dwellers in the more urban areas combine deep rural roots with participation in formal and informal economies and even subsistence farming,[19] while many of the more rural dwellers work in what are ordinarily thought of as more urban economic sectors and do periodic or annual circular migrations within and beyond the region. The quality of having been forgotten that materially links such places is not merely about absence or lack. Abandoned places are also planned concentrations— or sinks—of hazardous materials and destructive practices that are in turn sources of group-differentiated vulnerabilities to premature death (which, whether state-sanctioned or extralegal, is how racism works, regardless of the intent of the harms' producers, who produce along the way racialization and therefore race). Thus, California *desakota* is a mix, a region composed of places linked through coordinated as well as apparently uncoordinated (though by no means random) forces of habitation and change. Hart and Sitas's arguments concerning the formation and possible futures of South African relocation townships help deepen this understanding, in part

---

19 Daniel Flaming, *Poverty, Inequality, and Justice*, Economic Roundtable, Los Angeles, June 2006, www.economicrt.org. Los Angeles County, which was the premier agricultural county in the United States for more than half of the twentieth century, was until August 2006 home to a fourteen-acre inner-city farm made up of independent gardens, one of the largest in the United States. South Central Farmers, "What We Are About," 2006, www.southcentralfarmers.com.

because voluntary and involuntary movements, layering pre-vious rounds of dispossession, domination, and development, make a particular grounding for politics in relation to capital, the multiple scales of the state, and the rest of society; indeed, the point is that these contradictions at the margin are resolved in and as *desakota* spaces.[20]

In other words, people in forgotten places who lack social or economic mobility, or who simply don't want to move away, act within and against the constraints of capital's changing participation in the landscape and the government's multisca-lar and sometimes contradictory struggle to relegitimize state power through the ideology and practices of an anti-state state in the ambient atmosphere of neoliberalism.[21] People in forgotten places also act within the institutional and individ-ualized constraints defined by racialization, gender hierarchy, and nationality, and the complex potential mix of these possi-bilities has produced its own academic specialties old and new: the various branches of the social sciences, area studies, ethnic studies, gender studies, cultural studies—the latter three dedi-cated to the study of disabling (in the sense of both debilitating and undoing) constraints.[22]

Constraints does not mean "insurmountable barriers." How-ever, it does suggest that people use what is available to make a place in the world. In my research I have found that the con-straint of crisis becomes a central element in whole ways of life—that having been forgotten is part of a syncretic culture of "betweenness"—of *desakota* considered not simply as a pecu-liar spatialization of the economic but also as cultural, social, and political.[23] While the syncretic is no more amenable to

---

20 Hart and Sitas, "Beyond the Urban-Rural Divide."
21 Gilmore, *Golden Gulag*; "Restating the Obvious," in this volume, 259–87. "In the Shadow of the Shadow State", in this volume, 224–41.
22 Hart, *Disabling Globalization*.
23 Clyde Woods, *Development Arrested*, New York: Verso, 1988 [2017, new ed. with introd. by Ruth Wilson Gilmore]; Clyde Woods, "Life after Death," *Professional Geographer* 54.1 (2002): 62–66.

change than whatever one can imagine that is not syncretic, the awareness of being "neither/nor," which is to say the awareness of imminent and ineluctable change that comes with abandonment in new ways and at new scales, opens up the possibility for people to organize themselves at novel resolutions.

Practical Syncretism

Syncretic, which traces its long English-language usage to observations of surprising religious intermixture, is a term that had a lot of academic cachet about twenty-five or thirty years ago—in studies of religion and other aspects of contact culture—but was less used as *hybrid* became popular in the 1980s and 1990s. *Syncretic* appeals more to me than *hybrid* because it avoids suggesting technical intervention (other than perhaps, in the poetical sense, as in Jerome Rothenberg's *Technicians of the Sacred*).[24] More importantly, it downplays any presumption of prior purity and instead emphasizes a more active and general practice through which people use what they have to craft ad hoc and durable modes for living and for giving meaning to—interpreting, understanding—life. Indeed, Brackette Williams has long argued that *all* cultures are contact cultures.[25] In any event, *syncretism* denotes qualities key to crafting the kinds of motivated methodologies that enable the continuum of scholarly research as political experimentation.[26]

24　Jerome Rothenberg, ed., *Technicians of the Sacred: A Range of Poetries from Africa, America, Asia, Europe, and Oceania*, New York: Anchor, 1969.

25　Brackette Williams, "A Class Act: Anthropology and the Race to Nation across Ethnic Terrain," *Annual Review of Anthropology* 18 (1989): 401–44.

26　As a result of heinous practices carried out at the expense of people's lives and well-being, researchers rightly hesitate before conducting "human experiments," and US higher education has developed complicated apparatuses to safeguard human subjects from inhumane protocols. That said, all politics are experimental; the question is not whether but how experiments proceed ethically and practically.

If we see in a syncretic approach to research and activism provisional resolutions—some more lasting than others—to contradictions and challenges, then we might imagine that the concept is charged at the outset by a particular kind of questioning. Syncretism has a purpose, and asking questions that enable it is part of the challenge of doing research well. This thinking flies in the face of some academic disciplining, even in avowedly interdisciplinary formations. The either/or boundary drawing that secures academic practices and jobs is not inherently useless; it is silly to suggest that the powerful forces of the liberal arts and professions, organized for good, for not-so-good, and for straight-up evil over the last two centuries, could be characterized as thoroughly weak today. But as universities on a global scale struggle through what seem to be endless crises of accumulation of enough students, endowments, and prestige, the retreat into disciplines, no less than the formal (but frequently not real) embrace of "interdisciplinarity," seems to foreshadow if not prove widespread irrelevance, which is exactly (although not exclusively or uniquely) what the activist scholar is *not* about.

The syncretic compels us to think about problems, and the theories and questions adequate to them, in terms of what I have called their stretch, resonance, and resilience. With a focus on questions, let's take each in turn.[27]

- *Stretch* enables a question to reach further than the immediate object without bypassing its particularity—rather than merely asking a community, "Why do you want *this* development project?" one asks, "What is development?"
- *Resonance* enables a question to support and model nonhierarchical collective action by producing a hum that, by inviting strong attention, elicits responses that do not necessarily adhere to already-existing architectures of sense

---

27 From Ruth Wilson Gilmore, "Scholar-Activists in the Mix," in this volume, 92–103.

making. Ornette Coleman's harmolodics exemplify how such a process makes participant and audience a single, but neither static nor closed, category.[28]

- *Resilience* enables a question to be flexible rather than brittle, such that changing circumstances and surprising discoveries keep a project connected with its purpose rather than defeated by the unexpected. For example, the alleged relationship between contemporary prison expansion and slavery falls apart when the question describes slavery in terms of uncompensated labor, because very few of the 2.2 million prisoners in the United States work for anybody while locked in cages. But the relationship remains provocatively stable when the question describes slavery in terms of social death and asks how and to what end a category of dehumanized humans is made from peculiar combinations of dishonor, alienation, and violent domination.[29]

If we assume that identities are changed through action and struggle, what sort of political-economic and cultural projects can draw enthusiastic participation from both rural and urban residents and forge among them a new vision? The term *desakota* highlights the structural and lived relationship between marginal people and marginal lands in both urban and rural contexts and raises the urgent question of how to scale up political activity from the level of hyperlocal, atomized organizations to the level of regional coalitions working for a common purpose, partly because their growing understanding of their sameness trumps their previously developed beliefs in their irreconcilable differences. Insofar as regions are economic as well as cultural and geopolitical units of analysis, this essay will, by depicting a combination of experimental and ethnographic

28 Jennifer Rycenga, "The Composer as a Religious Person in the Context of Pluralism," PhD diss., Graduate Theological Union, 1992.

29 Orlando Patterson, *Slavery and Social Death,* Cambridge, MA: Harvard University Press, 1982; Avery F. Gordon, "Abu Ghraib: Imprisonment and the War on Terror," *Race and Class* 48 (2006): 42–59.

insights, identify ways in which research combines with the actions of everyday people to shift the field of struggle and thus reorganize both their own consciousness and the concentration and uses of social wealth in "forgotten places."

The Process in the Territory

Joining Forces: Stretch

Politically, a solid but supple mix of aims and people is hard to achieve, and very often its categorical contingencies (some will do X but not Y; others will support A but never B) make it far too brittle to withstand the wear and tear of sustained and purposeful practical movement. A tiresomely overdeveloped take on leftist politics argues that the twentieth-century failure of solidarity to endure in the long run should be laid at the door of something the critics call "identity politics." What they seem to mean is anti-racist politics or anti-sexist politics; and often what they really mean, given the examples they choose, is that Black people or women of all races interrupted and messed up class politics in favor of "militant particularism." That is a pretty silly view for a number of reasons, most of which are well grounded in the evidence of what happened to whom and why. It is also a stupid view, given that capitalism has regularly encountered its "sternest negation" from peoples organized according to a number of principles at once, including anti-racism and anti-colonialism.[30] A more useful critique of identity complicates its subjective qualities (noting, for example, that class is also an identity rather than an ontology), shows how the complexity operates (as in Hall's exquisite "Race is ... the modality through which class is lived"[31]), and

---

30 Robinson, *Black Marxism*.

31 Stuart Hall, "Race, Articulation, and Societies Structured in Dominance," in UNESCO, ed., *Sociological Theories: Race and Colonialism*, Paris: UNESCO, 1980, 305–340.

reveals the contradictory ways in which identities fracture and reform in the crucibles of state and society, public and private, home and work, violence and consent.[32]

In other words, if race *is* the modality through which class is lived, but not voluntarily, then the official codes, habits, and institutions, and the military, immigration officers, and other police who maintain order (sometimes through producing a mess to be endlessly fixed up), have a lot to do with the production and reproduction of ways of being in the world.[33] It is frightfully unpopular to talk about how top-down identity ascription operates, or even that it is meaningful. A decade ago, during a seminar on the politics of reproduction, the brilliant Nuyorican scholar-activist Caridad Souza rolled her eyes and whispered to me, "If one more of these workshop-feminists says 'agency' I'm going to choke her." Within seconds someone uttered the offending word; eschewing nonproductive violence, Souza soon quit academia's ranks. The point here is not that "agency" is an unimportant concept but rather, as I have argued elsewhere, that it is too often used as if it designated an exclusive attribute of oppressed people in their struggle against an opponent called "structure."[34] Such a dichotomy doesn't stand up to how the world actually works. Structures are both the residue of agency[35] and animated by agential capacities,

---

32   See, for example, M. Jacqui Alexander, "Not Just (Any) *Body* Can be a Citizen: The Politics of Law, Sexuality, and Postcoloniality in Trinidad and Tobago and the Bahamas," *Feminist Review* 48 (1994): 5–23; Michael Omi and Howard Winant, *Racial Formation in the United States*, New York: Routledge, 1986; Barbara Ransby, *Ella Baker and the Black Freedom Movement: A Radical Democratic Vision*, Chapel Hill: University of North Carolina Press, 2006; Robin D. G. Kelley, *Freedom Dreams: The Black Radical Imagination*, Boston: Beacon Press, 2002.

33   Claire Jean Kim, "The Racial Triangulation of Asian Americans," *Politics and Society* 27.1 (1999): 105–38; Wendy Brown, *States of Injury*, Princeton: Princeton University Press, 1994.

34   Gilmore, *Golden Gulag*.

35   Jim Glassman, "Rethinking Overdetermination, Structural Power, and Social Change: A Critique of Gibson-Graham, Resnick, and Wolff," *Antipode* 35.4 (2003): 678–98.

while the modes in which ordinary people organize to relieve the pressures that kill them and their kin are, or become, structural—especially insofar as they draw from, and operate through, relationships that can only be called structural as well (familial, religious, cultural, and so on).[36] Racialization works—vertically *and* horizontally—through the contradictory processes of structure-agency. Change certainly makes more sense when perceived this way (see Du Bois for a detailed exposition of structure-agency dialectics in the post–Civil War South).[37] Here, then, we stretch in a couple of directions, both in terms of generalization (to think of key concepts such as structure and agency in relation to each other) and in terms of what we must think about to think at all well.

In February 2001, a group of people trying to figure out how to stop construction of a prison in Delano, California, organized Joining Forces, a conference for environmental-justice and anti-prison activists. The purpose for the meeting was to develop strategies for mixing issues, understanding, and campaigns throughout the *desakota* of California's prison region. While it did not for them bear the Malay name, the region theorized in this chapter was becoming increasingly visible to the conference organizers, in part because they had taken seriously the scholarship of Mary Pardo, Laura Pulido, myself, and others; they had learned about the workings of environmental law and environmental justice; and they were persuaded that the only way to stop the prison would be to build an extensive coalition whose convergence centered on principles other than "Not in My Backyard."[38]

---

36 See for example Leela Fernandes, *Producing Workers: The Politics of Gender, Class, and Culture in the Calcutta Jute Mills*, Philadelphia: University of Pennsylvania Press, 1997.

37 Du Bois, *Black Reconstruction*.

38 Mary Pardo, *Mexican American Women Activists*, Philadelphia: Temple University Press, 1998; Laura Pulido, *Environmentalism and Economic Justice: Two Chicano Struggles in the Southwest*, Tucson: University of Arizona Press, 1996; Ruth Wilson Gilmore, "Globalisation

In addition, some of the conference organizers had traveled in the area surrounding the proposed prison in the preceding couple of years, retracing my earlier research path and also following the spatial patterns laid out by United Farm Workers campaigns and emergency relief, by environmental-justice cases, and by whoever serendipitously contacted the tiny, all-volunteer California Prison Moratorium Project via its website or answering machine. They had learned from grassroots activists in small towns (many of whom thought of themselves, not as activists at all, but rather as concerned citizens, residents, parents, farmers, farmworkers, immigrants, schoolchildren) that attention to what created the continuity of urban and rural—what we might call here its structural betweenness—was crucial to understanding prison proliferation.[39] The organizers had held a miniconference of urban and rural organizers a year earlier and had learned that unlikely organizations and alliances could be created through persuasively appealing to a shifting range of subjectivities differentially located in the wider *desakota*'s political, productive, and problem-riddled landscapes.

The conference featured a series of panels in which activists talked about how they had come to encounter, identify, understand, and solve the problems where they lived. To build a coalition, the conference organizers wanted to establish that

---

and US Prison Growth: From Military Keyne-sianism to Post-Keynesian Militarism," in this volume, 199–223; Ruth Wilson Gilmore, "'You Have Dislodged a Boulder': Mothers and Prisoners in the Post Keynesian California Landscape," in this volume, 355–409; Luke W. Cole and Sheila R. Foster, *From the Ground Up: Environmental Racism and the Rise of the Environmental Justice Movement*, New York: New York University Press, 2001; Robert D. Bullard, *Dumping in Dixie: Race, Class, and Environmental Quality*, Boulder, CO: Westview Press, 1990; Rose Braz and Craig Gilmore, "Joining Forces: Prisons and Environmental Justice in Recent California Organizing," *Radical History Review* 96 (2006): 95–111.

39   California Prison Moratorium Project, *How to Stop a Prison in Your Town*, Oakland: California Prison Moratorium Project, 2006; "The Other California", in this volume, 242–58.

prisons constitute environmental harms for both the places where prisoners come from and the places where prisons are built: prisons wear out people and places, and that exhaustion has lethal consequences. There were lunchtime breakout sessions organized topically and an open microphone plenary, so that individuals and organizations who had found their way to the conference but hadn't been placed on the formal agenda could speak. The final segment was a planning workshop in which conference participants broke into groups and tried to brainstorm alternative outcomes to life-harming situations (prisons, toxic waste, and so on) that could be realized given what the participants already had some idea of how to do or control.

In the first part of the program, each speaker described what their group did and how they had achieved success. A group of immigrant farmworkers, mostly indigenous Mixtec speakers from Oaxaca in south central Mexico, had forced Chevron to clean up the murderous toxic wastes that poisoned their *colonia* outside Fresno. An East Los Angeles group of mostly Mexicana women with green cards had stopped a state prison in their neighborhood and, tracing the roots of school-leaving that make children vulnerable to criminalization, had also stopped environmentally harmful industrial production and transport in their community. An East Palo Alto group of people who had been in prison had organized a community-based, non-cop-controlled live-work-treatment facility to help people stay away from prisons and other death-dealing institutions and materials. As these activists spoke, what became increasingly clear was the ways in which they had all encountered, and tried to prevail against, the state-sanctioned and/or extralegal production or exploitation of their own group's vulnerability to premature death. A coalition of anti-prison and environmental activists brought suit under the California Environmental Quality Act, charging that the proposed prison would harm Delano in a number of ways not dealt with in the official environmental analysis that could, nevertheless, be partly understood in terms of environmental justice. In stretching both the object and the analysis from their parochial struggles to the entire range of struggles represented in the room, conference attendees began to recognize that—*objectively* —they and their places shared a family resemblance that needed further investigation.

The cooperation that came out of the conference might be viewed as multicultural organizing in today's dominant lexicon of cooperation and difference; or it might be viewed as something else. In 1970s and 1980s Britain, in response to the various forces unleashed by Enoch Powell's 1968 "Rivers of Blood" speech, various postcolonials of different generations living in the metropole came together as Black—not African, *Black*—Britain. A bottom-up politics of recognition in the face of threatened annihilation enhanced a syncretic rescaling of identity for these people, even though the novel category directly conflicted with the statistical identities that had officially divided them.[40] In the United States today, *white* people suffering from a concentration of environmental harms in some rural communities have learned to call what is happening "environmental racism" without imagining that they are somehow excluding themselves from the analysis, and instead feeling whiteness peel away in the context of their vulnerability. This stretched understanding of racism enables vulnerable people to consider the ways in which harmful forces might be disciplined and harms remedied (rather than areally redistributed—or concentrated out of sight). Race does not disappear; in some instances, reworking race reveals its structural essence to be residue rather than destiny. At least potentially, such a stretch evades (if it cannot quite preclude) any imagined necessity for *desakota* countercoherence to pattern itself according

---

40 Neil Smith and Cindi Katz, "Grounding Metaphor: Towards a Spatialized Politics," in Michael Keith and Steve Pile, eds., *Place and the Politics of Identity*, New York: Routledge, 1993, 67–83.

to logics of victim and punishment rather than to tend toward the pleasure of life-affirming political and cultural practice.

Indeed, it was for the future that the conference participants gathered, laboring in triple shifts (work at the job, work at home, work for justice). But lest the reader say, "A-ha! What you've described is what the workshop-feminists mean by 'agency,'" I'd like to take the analysis a bit further. That is, if these participants found a provisionally syncretic identity by comparing their efforts and aims, they also had to re-form the ambitions of their organizations and struggle with mission statements, funding streams, and other boundaries that have enabled many groups working for justice to achieve formal/legal recognition of the legitimacy of their characteristics and objectives. The structures they have come to inhabit in the shadow of the "shadow state"[41] enable certain kinds of creativity and achievement but stifle other kinds of association. As a result, organizations become competitive and use comparison to create distances rather than alliances with other organizations. This is a product of many connected practices and the result of specialization and professionalization in oppositional political work.[42] That such narrowing occurred *in response to* capital's twentieth-century counterrevolution— which was downright murderous and ultimately resulted in the criminalization of entire generations and communities and practices—goes much farther than the postulation of some prior sentimental or uncritical attachment to an extraeconomic "identity" in explaining the brittleness of political mixes in the present moment. Organizations *became* "legal" under the rules of the Internal Revenue Service to pursue justice, whereas earlier they had *used* "the legal" as a tool to pursue justice.

The people who met at the Delano conference and in similarly ad hoc gathering places (such as prison parking lots and seasonal workplaces) are at once way out on the edge and

---

41   Gilmore, "In the Shadow of the Shadow State."
42   Ibid.

keenly aware of what they have to lose: they have endured Jim Crow, Japanese American internment, farm fascism,[43] NAFTA. Their marginality is not simply metaphorical but rather a feature of a spatial dilemma. Their consciousness is a product of vulnerability in space coupled with unavoidable and constant movement through space (an inversion, if you will, of gated communities and full-service suburban malls, but based in related conditions and logics). Indeed, the *desakota* region is all about the movement of resources—whether transfers of meager social wealth from public sectors (welfare to domestic warfare) or migration of persons (voluntarily or not) intraregionally or across supraregional spaces to amass remittances that, once sent, counter the apparently unidirectional concentration of wealth. Indeed, all this movement makes the *desakota* a region of dynamic betweenness—not in dominant development's terms of "catching up" or "falling behind," but rather in the sense that it is the shadow, echo, enabler, and resolution of "globalization." Also, because of their constant motion (which is not the same as "mobility"), people who live in the "between" have a strong sense of it as simultaneously a temporary and a fixed reality. At a general level, they share a sense of possibility based in the necessity for change (which they enact through irregular migrations through the region), and their frequent changes of place demand—objectively and subjectively—a respatialization of the social. This, rather than any automatic recognition based in racial or ethnic categories, forms the basis for syncretizing previously separate political movements. They don't transcend, they mix; and it takes a lot of debate, strangely hostile at first because based in narrowly defined ascriptions of difference, for the mixing to happen among such disparate actors as long-distance migrants from

43 Paramilitary squads working for wealthy agriculturalists murdered labor organizers to discipline farmworkers in Depression-era Central California; see Carey McWilliams, *Factories in the Field: The Story of Migratory Farm Labor in California*, Hamden, CT: Archon Books, 1939.

indigenous Mexico, African Americans, immigrant women in male-dominated Mexican American households, and so on. All their learning is based in skepticism as well as reflection, as is the case with all strong scholarly inquiry, and the outcome is as good as its ability to be reproduced throughout the region and to produce the conditions for new and useful outcomes.

The Mismeasure of Man: Resonance

In the mid-1980s, when prison expansion was the latest thing, designed to secure the ideological legitimacy of the advancing neoliberal anti-state state by dispersing that state's sturdy presence via the proliferation of cages throughout its expanding gulag,[44] locations willing to take on these monstrosities in the hope of jobs were awarded significant signing bonuses in the form of "mitigation" funds that could be used to make local infrastructural improvements. At the same time, given the rhetorical urgency with which the claim for endlessly increasing cages was made, federal and state environmental review requirements were sometimes waived—thus further developing the public's perception that "crime" was the paramount harm that any individual or family might encounter. By the early 1990s, however, once the anti-state state found itself on firm footing, communities throughout the *desakota* region looking for industries of last resort found themselves back where they had long been—as petitioners of rather than partners in the prison boom. That meant the bonuses evaporated, as did most other demands host towns might make. Representatives of these communities' local development bodies might easily identify with the words of an industry-seeking mayor of Ladysmith, a South African relocation township, who declared to his constituency: "[W]e go kneeling to beg. It is difficult to beg a person and put conditions."[45]

---

44 Gilmore, *Golden Gulag.*
45 Gillian Hart, *Global Competition, Gender, and Social Wages in*

A prison is a city that weighs heavily on the place where it is. The thousands of people who live and work there make environmental and infrastructural demands on the surrounding area that are not offset by the prison's integration into the locality's economic, social, or cultural life. A prison is a political weight that, in a lightly populated jurisdiction, can reconfigure legislative representation by plumping up a district's size because prisoners (who cannot vote) are counted where they are held,[46] and it can tip the electoral balance as well because relatively well-paid prison staff can and do support or oppose local candidates even though they do not live in the district. A prison is also heavy in part because it is a "dead city,"[47] built and staffed for the singularly unproductive purpose of keeping civilly dead women and men in cages for part or all of their lives. James O'Connor rightly designates spending on prisons and other policing functions as "social expense"—nonproductive outlays that do not, under any mode of accumulation, enhance the present or future capacity of a place to grow and prosper the way "social investment" does.[48] Besides wages, a prison's biggest expenditures are for utilities, which are not locally owned. What do prisons produce besides wave after wave of unhappy involuntary residents? An extremely poor yield of local jobs, mostly because competitive wages enlarge the labor market across space and skill[49]; the negative effects of anticipatory investment *and* disinvestment in residential and

South Africa, 1980–2000, Paper 13. United Nations Research Institute for Social Development, Social Policy and Development Programme, 2002, 23.

46 Peter Wagner, "Importing Constituents: Prisoners and Political Clout in New York," 2002, www.prisonpolicy.org/importing.

47 See Mike Davis, *Dead Cities*, New York: New Press, 2003; Lewis Mumford, *The City in History*, New York: Harvest Books, 1968, chapter 1.

48 James O'Connor, *The Fiscal Crisis of the State*, New Brunswick, NJ: Transaction, 1973.

49 Gregory Hooks, Clayton Mosher, Thomas Rotolo, and Linda Lobao, "The Prison Industry: Carceral Expansion and Employment in U.S. Counties, 1969-1994," *Social Science Quarterly* 85.1 (2004): 37–57.

retail real property; no retail activity; few new residents, lots of traffic as workers come and go; the destruction of both prime agricultural land and endangered-species habitat; and sewage.[50] No wonder the bended knee has difficulty straightening out.

Because the residents of prospective prison towns lack political and economic clout (as is true of all localities that turn to industries of last resort), it is not surprising that even as the evidence has accumulated putting the lie to prisons as economic engines, the normalization of prisons as an unending need has caused the urgency-fueled mitigation-dollar largesse to evaporate. Yet prison boosters and prison-department public relations personnel have continued to insist that lockups are good for local economies: recession proof and environmentally friendly. Ironically, however, as the urgency of the rhetoric about the need for prisoners has diminished and prisons have been viewed more as being—although public and nonproductive—just like any other industry, it has become easier to criticize the practice of environmental review waiver. From the early 1990s onward, environmental reviews have been produced for state and federal lockups in *desakota* California fairly consistently.[51]

The Federal Bureau of Prisons (FBOP), no less than the California Department of Corrections (CDC), has been on a long-term building binge—famously because of Reagan-era

---

50   California Prison Moratorium Project, *How to Stop a Prison in Your Town*; Gilmore, *Golden Gulag*.

51   Environmental reviews are not always done, as was recently the case for a significant expansion to the federal prison in Lompoc. Also, the political model for claiming urgency to evade responsibility is currently being reinvigorated by the state legislature and governor, who have agreed to waive environmental review in a proposed multibillion-dollar Sacramento delta flood control project. They are using the New Orleans–Katrina abandonment disaster to weaken state statutes under the guise of responsibly facing up to imminent danger. In the early years of World War II, two big cotton growers in the region that is now *desakota* California used a similar set of arguments to get the Army Corps of Engineers to build them a couple of dams that guaranteed both free water and fertile bottomland to their empires. Norris Hundley Jr., *The Great Thirst: Californians and Water, 1770s–1990s*, Berkeley: University of California Press, 1992.

(1980s) and Clinton-endorsed (1990s) drug laws carrying mandatory minimum sentences, but also because starting in the mid-1980s the FBOP began planning to lock up more and more immigrants who the Department of Justice forecast would be convicted of crimes.[52] The expanded federal capacity is not part of the Immigration and Customs Enforcement (ICE) detention centers; rather, it exemplifies the general trend by the anti-state state to use criminalization to "solve" problems, particularly the problem of how the rhetoric of "state-lite" can be coordinated with what is actually happening: the constant evolution of a bigger and more coercive state apparatus run by a strong executive branch (which includes policing and prisons). In 2000 the FBOP published its third Criminal Alien Requirements III (CAR) Request for Proposal for sites in California. A number of towns submitted letters of intent asking to be considered. Some towns withdrew from consideration after they learned from other towns or through their own diligence that the wear and tear of a federal prison would far outweigh any imagined benefit.

One city manager produced his own study, which he shared with a group of my undergraduates who had decided to find out why a town would first embrace and then reject the prison solution.[53] His data and analysis made it obvious to him that the meager benefits would accrue elsewhere, where prison employees lived and shopped. In fact, he tried to form a strategic tax alliance with the nearby larger city that would claim most prison employee residence and consumption, but the last thing the larger city was going to do—especially in an age of devolution and boundary tightening—was open the door to other petitioners hoping for a share in the social wage.[54]

---

52 The politics of forecasting is an urgent topic for social justice.

53 Davin McHenry, "Shafter Abandons Plans for Prison," *Bakersfield Californian*, February 10, 2001.

54 Gilmore, *Golden Gulag*; Angus Cameron, "Turning Point? The Volatile Geographies of Taxation," *Antipode* 38.2 (2006): 237–58.

The FBOP decided to look more closely at two Fresno County towns that stayed in the running—Orange Cove and Mendota. In both towns the elected and appointed leadership were united in their boosterism. The FBOP got to work on the Environmental Impact Statement, which turned out to be a thousand pages of a stylistic hodgepodge of technical description and evaluation that concluded Mendota would be the preferred location. During this time, organizers tried to spread the news that economic benefits would not be forthcoming from a prison, while other harms might ensue. However, constituting audiences to make the argument proved very difficult. The environmental review process provided both topic and method to reach people. Since environmental reviews look at a range of impacts—in theory raising concerns before harms occur—and since they require public comment, they are potentially useful means for publishing findings that would not reach people—vertically or horizontally—by other means.

In his classic analysis of racist science, *The Mismeasure of Man*, Stephen Jay Gould reworked a number of experiments and scrutinized the underlying evidence that supported an array of biological justifications for the political, social, and economic marginalization of certain of the world's people.[55] The book had a second life a few years before the author's untimely death, when Herrnstein and Murray's heinous *Bell Curve* commanded front-page coverage in newspapers, book reviews, magazines, and other opinion-producing media.[56] Gould put the basic scientific practice of redoing experiments to practical political use. From his exploration of cranial capacity to his later demolition of Herrnstein and Murray's cheap statistics, Gould used the resonance of already produced knowledge—including its origins as well as its circulation—to highlight

---

55 Stephen Jay Gould, *The Mismeasure of Man*, New York: W. W. Norton, 1981.

56 Richard Herrnstein and Charles Murray, *The Bell Curve: Intelligence and Class Structure in American Life*, New York: Free Press, 1994.

the intentionally destructive purposes occasioning the original research. He could reach audiences because of his status as a Harvard professor who wrote books (such as *Mismeasure*) for popular consumption. People invited him to speak. He demolished Herrnstein and Murray and others wherever he went.

The environmental review allowed for a modest version of Gould's labor. Taking the environmental review apart piece by piece, a patient researcher could get to the bottom of the data (often with no more technical assistance than a glossary and a calculator) and choose a few high-profile areas to challenge. The next step was to help a number of people speak to the issues in the required public comment periods, both orally at hearings and in writing. The public comment at hearings enabled organizers to meet the few members of the Mendota community who knew about the prison; most supported it and a few were in opposition. At that time, it was already possible to present to city officials proof that their claims for the prison would not be realized. Those nonreturns were in, and people from throughout the region could come to testify that a prison would not provide the benefits that the review had enthusiastically insisted it would.

After one of the hearings, I approached the city manager, and we had a reasonably cordial conversation in which I told him that he knew very well that the prison could not and would not do what he and other city leaders claimed. He replied that he knew but he'd been hired, at a generous salary, to bring the town a prison. Unlike that off-the-record exchange, liable to he-said-she-said dismissal, the authors of an environmental review[57] must address the concerns and criticisms of every letter and oral statement. As a result, it became possible to get

---

57 In this case, a consulting firm with a long-standing FBOP contract that seems to get by with minimal research and maximum Web-based cursory data collection and analysis, as activists in places around the United States have reported at conferences and meetings.

into the official record written acknowledgment that prisons are not economic engines or otherwise fiscally benevolent. And through publishing—that is, making available—both research and critiques of research in a publicly accessible place, we could persuade the county rural redevelopment agency to deny Mendota money to build water infrastructure for the prison, on the basis of the conclusion that the residents would not get jobs or other benefits. The city was instructed by redevelopment to come back with a development plan that would actually help the town's 95 percent Latino residents, who were a mix of second- and third-generation Chicanos, Mexicans, Salvadorans, and other Central Americans—some with green cards and even more without documents authorizing them to work. The boosters did not reflect the full demographic, only the Anglo and Chicano power elite. The divisions within the community highlight the complex processes of racialization and the fact that mutual political recognition between groups may produce fractures as well as identification.

Both the thousand-page English-language document and the hearings—in which translation was not available and Spanish testimony was not transcribed—became the focus of a sustained campaign because 90 percent of the city's households used Spanish as the primary language. The problem of language resonates in many ways throughout *desakota* California. In a number of other campaigns against locally unwanted land uses (incinerators, toxic dumps) or on behalf of life-enhancing infrastructure (such as wells drilled deeply enough to bypass the pesticide-poisoned upper aquifer), communities have fought against their linguistic exclusion from the decision-making process. In many places (as has been true throughout US history from west to east), English is not the primary language.[58] In addition, certain kinds of technical prose obscure

---

58 Presuming that even people who have developed the psychological habits of the bended knee are not permanently so configured, some scholarship that seeks to intervene does so by combining writing and images.

the contents and consequences of land use changes. In South Central Los Angeles, a site that was home to a fourteen-acre urban garden had been slated to be used for toxic waste. Organizers fought against the dump, mobilizing around multiple themes, including the fact that the reports were unreadable. In fact, the reports were barely literate by any measure, perhaps less because of jargon than because of the way these extensive documents merely fulfilled the law in letter but not in spirit. The documents' militant illiteracy suggests that a narrowly technocratic solution (for example, hiring an ecologist for every community) will not solve the larger problem of civic engagement when the anti-state state's purpose is to minimize such engagement. For Mendota, the FBOP eventually drafted a ten-page Spanish-language "executive summary" of the report that focused entirely on the alleged benefits of the prison for the community.

A young organizer from the region canvassed Mendota door to door, eventually meeting several people who agreed to host a house party to discuss the environmental review. They had been organizing among farmworkers and therefore were aware of both risks and opportunities. A surprising number of people came on a weekday evening, and they crowded into a tiny living room with food to share and kids too young to leave at home. The discussion led by two organizers met at first with mild interest as people passed around the short Spanish-language summary. But when one of the organizers pulled the

---

For example, the Real Cost of Prisons Project supplements a series of workshops with three comic books that lay out the dollar and other costs of prisons to prison towns, the costs of prisons to women and their children, and the real cost of the war on drugs. See www.realcostofprisons. org; Kevin Pyle and Craig Gilmore, *Prison Town* (documentary comic book), Northampton, MA: Real Cost of Prisons Project, 2005; Susan Willmarth, Ellen Miller-Mack, and Lois Ahrens, *Prisoners of a Hard Life: Women and Their Children* (documentary comic book), Northampton, MA: Real Cost of Prisons Project, 2005; Sabrina Jones, Ellen Miller-Mack, and Lois Ahrens, *Prisoners of the War on Drugs* (documentary comic book), Northampton, MA: Real Cost of Prisons Project, 2005.

thousand-page document from behind his back, the room's atmosphere changed. Everyone started talking and trading stories about how the same thing had happened in a friend or relative's town. Communication networks in *desakota* California work according to a variety of logics, with constantly shifting workplaces, parishes, supratown union locals, and kin groups all contributing to the richness of exchange. Convinced that a wrong had been perpetrated as it habitually was against people like themselves, they collectively composed a letter of protest. It was written out in Spanish by hand on ruled theme paper signed by dozens of households—all vulnerable to eviction or employment reprisal from prison proponents—and sent to Washington, DC.

The FBOP refused to honor the demand that the full environmental review be translated, insisting that it could not "be translated because it is *scientific* material." Wouldn't they be surprised in Salamanca! Their refusal was based in what Gould had spent a good deal of his life debunking: racist science that both encourages and justifies the sacrifice of human lives. Such science—which is ahistorical in willfully ignorant as well as methodologically negligent ways—seeks to make both reasonable and inevitable the concentration of locally unwanted land uses where people are most vulnerable to them. The natural and social-science practices that underlie the building of the anti-state state deliberately ignore the cumulative effects of atmospheric and other toxins, as well as the cumulative impacts of debilitating social policies and economic policies,[59] whether these policies and outcomes be pesticide drift, expensive or poisoned water, the hunting down of immigrants, bad schooling, racial profiling, intensive policing, or incinerators spewing dioxin.

One afternoon not long ago, the adults who mobilized against the prison rode buses and vans back from a day in the

---

59   Braz and Gilmore, "Joining Forces."

fields and marched, with their children, from the high school to a park for a rally. Many of these people live lives that circulate throughout *desakota* California and beyond. Most of them are immigrants without documents, but in spite—or because—of that vulnerability they are willing to participate in the mix and even rally side by side with growers whose opposition to the prison is not yet tempered by an anti-NIMBY consciousness. Indeed, much to everyone's surprise, they have been willing to keep fighting even though construction has begun at the now controversial site. Like the participants in the 2001 conference, these women, men, and young people are simultaneously looking for and creating a guide to action through embodied political experimentation—to theorize or map or plan their way out of the margins.

The Charrette: Resilience

Industries of last resort materially congeal displacement and defer real resolutions of economic, social, and technological problems to other places and times. Such deferral is not respectful but rather exploitative, and those who live in the shadows of such industries, as prisoners or workers or residents, become what a reformed white-supremacist lifer named himself and the white and of-color others who took part in a prison rebellion several years ago: a convict race.[60] In today's intransigent rebiologization of difference, race has been again characterized as being in the blood—the genetic determinant of life chances. Yet at the same time the social processes of racialization—carried out through warfare against Third World immigrants, Muslims, African American men, street kids—are apparent. So far we have seen that the deep divisions between vulnerable people are not necessarily an impediment, that people get past certain barriers because they have an already developed sense

---

60 Staughton Lynd, *Lucasville: The Untold Story of a Prison Uprising*, Philadelphia: Temple University Press, 2004.

of the perils and promise of movement, that the practice of circulating within regions underlies potential interpretations of possibility and alliance, and finally that multiply rooted people have a sense of the ways that "elsewhere" is simultaneously "here" (another way of saying that "I is an Other").

When organizers against industries of last resort take to the road, they constantly meet a reasonable question: If not this, then what? In fact, in left-ish discourse in the United States, an insistence that "winnable" solutions be proposed along with problems has become dominant. This dominance is in part an outgrowth of the professionalization of activism of all kinds and its formalization in not-for-profits, which are regularly required to generate "work products" to satisfy funders that the groups are doing what they say they will do. The "what-is-the-solution" imperative is also an outgrowth of the twentieth-century ascendance of the technocrat, especially skilled in breaking problems down into parts and solving them piecemeal. The trouble with technocracy, affecting engaged research and not-for-profit–based political experimentation, is that narrowness often stands in for specificity (and questions lose stretch and resonance along the way). Thus, the long struggle to shrink the US prison system through nonreformist reforms has sometimes been undermined by the technocratic imagination stifling work intended to advance the cause. For example, some advocacy research has narrowed the question "How do we shrink prisons?" to "How can we get some women out of prison?" and has ignored the facts—supported by experience—that the women released might wind up in jails or other lockups, or that the arguments advocated on behalf of decarcerating women might deepen and widen the net in which men and boys are captured and kept.

Yet since activist road-shows consistently encounter the question, they have to engage it as well as deconstruct it. Otherwise, the culture of human sacrifice kicks in, and what seems as reasonable as demanding a fully formed alternative is embracing the deferral of problems regardless of cost. For example, after I presented remarks on a plenary called "Militarization, the Economics of War, and Cultures of Violence" at the 2003 National Council for Research on Women's "Borders, Babies, and Bombs" conference, an Anglo retired career military woman scolded me that my antimilitarism was bad for young Black women, who develop leadership skills in the armed forces. She turned her back and strode off when I refused to agree that there was no better venue for such development outside the industrialized killing sector or that planning and carrying out the death of other people's children was an appropriate source of self-worth and livelihood for anybody.

Another error is double-edged: that vulnerable communities need mobile specialists who tell them what to do, yet at the same time have a completely thought-through revolutionary sensibility merely waiting to be set free by some visitors. This error recapitulates in two directions the bad thinking that posits structure and agency as opposites in ongoing struggles for self-determination. But if self-determination is a goal, and if *desakota* California, like anywhere else, is made by people but not under conditions of their own choosing, then a real engagement of people's creative thinking mixed with locally or externally available understandings of political and economic possibilities and constraints may be a way of getting at the question "If not this, then what?" In other words, the question becomes resilient and depends on people's immediate and longer range engagement—their own resilience—to realize any outcome.

In the winter of 2002, during a long-term decline in the number of women in California state prisons, the CDC closed one of its three new women's prisons, moving the eight hundred women kept there into bigger lockups. When the department originally sited the facility just east of Stockton in San Joaquin County in the mid-1980s, local boosters could and did "put conditions" to the CDC, which included that the prisoners be women and that the number locked up not exceed eight hundred. One way the county imposed restrictions was through the conditional-use permit—a standard instrument used to divide a territory into districts for different uses and to control the ways in which particular uses might change over time. This, in addition to mitigation funds, allowed the Anglo power elite to approve siting a prison in a former peach orchard.

Shortly after the prison closed, the CDC announced several possible reuses for the site: it could become a men's prison or a training facility for new guards, or it could be traded for some federal real estate and Immigration and Customs Enforcement (ICE) could redevelop the site as an immigrant detention center. Two Valley-based California Prison Moratorium Project organizers set themselves the task of creating a bottom-up movement against all these uses. They relied on research done by my former undergraduates at the University of California at Berkeley that the students decided to share, as well as research done as an academic studio course by graduate students in Berkeley's College of Natural Resources, to get a sense of what had happened in political jurisdictions and at the community level and where organizing might fit in.

The organizers learned that the chamber of commerce had opposed reopening the site as a prison, principally because in the nearly two decades since prison had seemed the only possible economic diversification scheme—to complement declining agriculture—the spread of residential hinterlands from the Bay Area and Sacramento put Stockton into a preferred development path of suburbanization (another in-between phenomenon, not dealt with in this essay). They also learned that some rising members of the city and county political class wished to use the fate of the site as a method to weaken the long-standing domination of the political elites. These newcomers were not necessarily opposed to prison, but they were opposed to decision making behind closed doors that excluded them. Finally, researchers saw that the demographic mix of Stockton was much like the rest of *desakota* California and that although agriculture was not the area's sole economic engine, it still figured prominently in the political economy of the place.

The Latino organizers, one an immigrant whose principal activity had centered on immigrant rights and the other a multigeneration Central Valley Chicana whose work had ranged widely, including to the margins of the Democratic Party, determined that the best way to get a sense of the lay of the land would be to hold a grassroots hearing about the site. They worked closely with several immigrants' rights organizers to reach out to farm and other low-wage workers. They also worked their connections in formal political associations to invite representatives of the rising political class to attend the session.

The meeting was announced for 6:00 p.m. At 5:55 the room was fairly empty except for Prison Moratorium Project members, elected officials' representatives, and leadership from a local of the Service Employees International Union (SEIU), some immigrants' rights organizations, and the Stockton League of Women Voters. It looked like a bust. But in the five minutes between the observation of failure and the time the proceedings were to begin, the room filled—mostly with Spanish-speaking workers. It was apparent that people had come to the neighborhood where the meeting was announced and had waited and scouted to see whether it was another of many ICE stings. ICE had been rounding up workers in an intense but random fashion throughout *desakota* California, and this meeting could have easily been such a trap. Once people came, they stayed, and although I was there, I cannot speak to how they would have secured themselves against an ICE invasion should one have occurred.

The organizers brilliantly invited the elected officials' representatives to sit in the front of the room, facing the audience, arguing that it would be useful for constituents to see them and that they need not speak but could just sit and listen. Good drama. The hearing was well orchestrated, involving a number of people who each spoke for three or four minutes condemning the reuse of the women's prison as a lockup for any purpose. Speakers of course directed their comments to the front of the room. At the end of the hearing, several representatives from Architects and Planners for Social Responsibility, who had been brought in by the Prison Moratorium Project to help set the stage to answer the expected question "If not this, then what?" invited the audience to attend a planning workshop in the same location the following month.

Since that time several community planning workshops, or *charrettes*, have been held in Stockton, in which people consider the prison buildings and site from every angle and propose their renovation for schools, museums, training centers, and other social investment uses. The *charrettes* have enabled people to think about the ways in which social investment works and the political levels at which the purse strings are held, by whom, and how tightly. Where are openings that ordinary people can enter to grasp and redirect a portion of the social wage?

As was seen in the previous section, not all resources that pour into a prison to build it come from a single source. The US state is a jumble of jurisdictions that have been newly federalized in the past twenty-five years. Some of the jurisdictions form a mosaic (as in the counties and states), some overlie others (counties and cities), and some are special-purpose regional governments (for example, for air quality or water). The unfunded devolution (or respatialization) of certain responsibilities, particularly in the area of social welfare programs, has caused many to think the state is no longer a crucial object of analysis. But if the object of the current analysis is at all correctly conceptualized, it seems more rather than less important to engage with the state at every turn. Certainly, devolution has produced belt tightening and boundary defending by many jurisdictions, and it underlies the widening bifurcation of all of California into richer and poorer.[61]

The *charrette* outcome can be turned to many uses, and planners have developed a volume to show what they are.[62] The resilience of planning, its reworking into the landscape of community action through both workshops and other kinds of political engagement, enables the creative imagination that self-determination requires. Around the United States, communities in other *desakota* regions have developed and implemented plans to revitalize shrunken economies in which revised values of place—as the repository and resolution of skills, talents, and preferences—enable concentrations of resources that, in the shadow of industries of last resort, seem scarce indeed. For example, in South Georgia a consortium of counties reorganized agriculture, food processing, and transportation to enable farmers to keep farming but not grow tobacco. They cobbled together sufficient collective capital from a wide array of public and other sources, finding in surprising corners of statutes and foundations resources that they could use to buy and build what they needed, transforming the landscape and therefore themselves. In the short run, everyone owns everything needed for processing and product movement, and everyone has also kept individual title to the small farms that they nearly wore out with tobacco. Similar counties that did not scale up or otherwise plan in developmentally imaginative ways have prisons and other industries of last resort. In Louisiana, families and friends of imprisoned young people fought to close down the murderous lockup and send the children home; they then continued fighting to have the site renovated and reopened as a community college. In these and other examples, the details of learning to make the future have animated rather than daunted

---

61   Gilmore and Gilmore, "Restating the Obvious."

62   Bill Lennertz and Aarin Lutzenhiser, *The Charrette Handbook: The Essential Guide for Accelerated, Collaborative Community Planning*, Chicago: APA/Planners Press, 2006.

the resilience of those who ask, "If not this, then what?" By deferring, if not defeating, the proliferation of industries of last resort, they have set a standard and created a context through which the material and ideological margins—*desakota* space—might be syncretically renovated to secure the future.

The purpose of this essay has been to think through both how to conceptualize a particular mix of socio-spatial relationships and how to operationalize engaged scholarship that matters. Forgotten places are historical geographies animated by real people. As fractured collectivities that are abandoned, yet intensely occupied by the anti-state state, these "between" or marginal places might be understandable as a singular region, spatially discontinuous, that is neither urban nor rural but in some way a version of *desakota*. How does the practice of engaged scholarship necessarily and ethically change the ideological and material field of struggle? If the fact of observation produces reality (not merely *afterwards*, as a representational artifact, but *during*, as a lived dimension of the field itself), then there are various kinds of work that a scholar might undertake in the mix.

Engaged scholarship and accountable activism share the central goal of constituting audiences both within and as an effect of observation, discovery, analysis, and presentation. Persuasion is crucial at every step. Neither engagement nor accountability has meaning without expanding recognition of how a project can best flourish in the mix. As a result, and to get results, scholar-activism always begins with the politics of recognition.[63] Whatever its ultimate purpose, the primary organizing necessary to take a project from concept to accomplishment (and tool) is constrained by people's practices of identification, fluidly laden with the differences and continuities of characteristics, interests, and purpose through which they contingently produce their individual and collective selves.[64]

---

63   Gilmore, "'You Have Dislodged a Boulder.'"
64   Stuart Hall, "Cultural Identity and Diaspora," in Jonathan

Such cultural (or ideological) work connects with, reflects, and shapes the material (or political-economic) relations enlivening a locality as a place that both links with and represents (as an example or outpost) other places at a variety of time-space resolutions—global, regional, postcolonial, and so on.[65] So here is another conundrum: it is *consistently* true that the engaged scholar of whatever political conviction works in the unavoidable context of dynamics that force her into self-conscious *inconsistency*; she must at times confirm and at times confront barriers, boundaries, and scales.[66] This is treacherous territory for all who wish to rewrite the world. Plenty of bad research (engaged or not) is produced for all kinds of reasons, and plenty of fruitless organizing is undertaken with the best intentions. Activist scholarship attempts to intervene in a particular historical-geographical moment by changing not only what people do but also how all of us think about ourselves and our time and place, by opening the world we make.

Rutherford, ed., *Identity: Community, Culture, Difference*, London: Lawrence and Wishart, 1994, 222–237; Gilmore, "'You Have Dislodged a Boulder.'"

65   Doreen Massey, *Spatial Divisions of Labor: Social Structures and the Geography of Production*, London: Macmillan, 1984.

66   Gilmore, *Golden Gulag*; Katz, *Growing up Global*; Jenna Morven Loyd, "Freedom's Body: Radical Health Activism in Los Angeles, 1963–1978," PhD diss., University of California at Berkeley, 2005.

18

The Worrying State of the Anti-Prison Movement

After declining for three consecutive years, the US prison and jail population increased in 2013. The widely declared victory over mass incarceration was premature at best. Below I raise four areas of particular concern about the state of the anti-prison movement.

1. A tendency to cozy up to the right wing, as though a superficial overlap in viewpoint meant a unified structural analysis for action.

Nearly forty years ago, Tony Platt and Paul Takagi identified as "new realists" the law-and-order intellectuals who purveyed across all media and disciplines the necessity of being hard on the (especially Black) working class.[1] Today's new "new realists"—the correct name for the "emerging bipartisan consensus"—exude the same stench. However differently calibrated, the mainstream merger depends on shoddy analysis and historical amnesia—most notably the fact that bipartisan consensus *built* the prison-industrial complex (PIC). The PIC isn't just the barred building, but the many ways in which unfreedom is enforced and continues to proliferate throughout urban and rural communities: injunction zones and intensive policing, felony jackets and outstanding warrants, as well as

[1] Tony Platt and Paul Takagi, "Intellectuals for Law and Order: A Critique of the New 'Realists,'" *Crime and Social Justice* 8 (1977): 1–16. Reprinted in *Social Justice* 40.1–2 (2013): 192–215.

school expulsions and job exclusions. Racial justice and economic democracy demand different paths from the one the new "new realists" blazed. Their top-down technocratic tinkering with the system renovates and aggrandizes it for the next generation.

The left-liberal side of the bipartisan consensus coopts vocabulary and rhetorical flourishes developed for different purposes by organizations engaged in bottom-up, anti-racist struggle. Slogans such as "education, not incarceration" willfully obscure the vital distinctions between the new "new realists" and the grassroots organizations whose work they distort. Unfortunately, many who point out the cynical appropriation of tactical principles or highlight underlying strategic differences find themselves accused of obstructionism or worse.

Even before the eponymous book appeared, grassroots organizations knew that "the revolution will not be funded."[2] That said, organizations rightly decided to take the available money and run in order to popularize constructively radical remedies for fundamental social problems. Not surprisingly, the very few sources that once funded innovative work have abandoned it, and they now wrap system-reinforcing work in phrases lifted from the thought and creativity of left and abolitionist grassroots struggle. Indeed, foundations cut loose the very organizations that came together in the 1998 Critical Resistance conference and consolidated the contemporary anti-prison movement. As a consequence, understanding and energy have taken a detour into reform for a few, while there is no change for the many.

Why the withdrawal of resources? From the perspective of the deep-pocket new "new realists," the organizations that built the movement over the past two decades are profoundly unrealistic: their politics are too radical, their grassroots constituents too unprofessional or too uneducated or too young

---

2 Incite, eds., *The Revolution Will Not Be Funded*, Cambridge, MA: South End Press, 2007.

or too formerly incarcerated, and their goals are too opposed to the status quo.

What is the status quo? Put simply, capitalism requires inequality and racism enshrines it. Thus, criminalization and mass incarceration are class war, as Platt and Takagi explained in 1977. Therefore, the struggle against group-differentiated vulnerability to premature death is waged in every milieu—environmental degradation, public-goods withdrawal, attacks on wages and unions, divide-and-conquer tactics among precarious workers, war, and so on. Police killings are the most dramatic events in a contemporary landscape thick with preventable, premature deaths.

Although it has become mildly mainstream to decry outrages against poor people of color, the new "new realists" achieve their dominance by defining the problem as narrowly as possible in order to produce solutions that on closer examination will change little.

2. A tendency to aim substantial rhetorical and organizational resources at the tiny role of private prison firms in the PIC, while minimizing the fact that the 92 percent constituting the vast money-sloshing public system is central to how capitalism's racial inequality works.

The long-standing campaign against private prisons is based on the fictitious claim that revenues raked in from outsourced contracts explain the origin and growth of mass incarceration. In any encounter about mass incarceration, live or on the Internet, in print or on video, sooner rather than later somebody will insist that to end racism in criminal justice, the first step is to challenge the use of private prisons.

Let us look at the numbers. Private prisons hold about 8 percent of the prison population and a barely measurable number (5 percent) of those in jails. Overall, about 5 percent of the people locked up are doing time in private prisons. What kind of future will prison divestment campaigns produce if they pay no attention to the money that flows through and is extracted from the public prisons and jails, where 95 percent of inmates are held? Jurisdiction by jurisdiction, we can see that contracts come and go, without a corresponding change in the number or the demographic identity of people in custody. In addition, many contracts are not even held by private firms, but rather by municipalities to whom custody has been delegated by state corrections departments.

3. A tendency to pretend that systematic criminalization will rust and crumble if some of those caught in its iron grip are extricated under the aegis of relative innocence.

One of the most troubling moves by the new "new realists" is to insist on foregrounding the relatively innocent: the third-striker in for stealing pizza or people in prison on drug possession convictions. The danger of this approach should be clear: by campaigning for the relatively innocent, advocates reinforce the assumption that others are relatively or absolutely guilty and do not deserve political or policy intervention. For example, most campaigns to decrease sentences for nonviolent convictions simultaneously decrease pressure to revise—indeed often explicitly promise never to change— sentences for serious, violent, or sexual felonies. Such advocacy adds to the legitimation of mass incarceration and ignores how police and district attorneys produce serious or violent felony charges, indictments, and convictions. It helps to obscure the fact that categories such as "serious" or "violent" felonies are not natural or self-evident, and more important, that their use is part of a racial apparatus for determining "dangerousness."

For example, campaigners for California's Proposition 47[3]

---

3 Passed by California voters in 2014, known for its ballot title "Criminal Sentences. Misdemeanor Penalties. Initiative Statute," and referred to by its supporters as the "Safe Neighborhoods and Schools

placed a widely touted "bipartisan" op-ed in the *Los Angeles Times*, coauthored by Newt Gingrich and B. Wayne Hughes Jr., in which the authors argued that "California has been overusing incarceration. Prisons are for people we are afraid of, but we have been filling them with many folks we are just mad at."

Note the use of the word "afraid." The new "new realists," with their top-down reforms, are trying to determine who constitutes "we"; worse, they also reinforce a criminal justice system, ideology, and image bank that justified Darren Wilson's grand jury testimony—just as it justified Bernhard Goetz's actions three decades ago. #BlackLivesMatter is an absolute statement, watered down to #sometimes by the opportunistic relativism of the new "new realists."

4. A tendency to virulently oppose critique from the left, as though the work of thinking hard about how and what we do interferes with the work of reform.

Opportunists beguile audiences and divert attention and resources away from people and organizations that have been fighting for decades to change the foundations on which mass incarceration has been built: structural racism, structural poverty, and capitalism devouring the planet. And they succeed in part because it has become unhip to subject the decisions, rhetoric, and goals of reform campaigns to any kind of thoughtful scrutiny. At stake is not only how we fight to win, but also how prepared we are for victories. *Prepare to win* means *be ready for the morning after.* If, for example, Proposition 47 actually releases savings that can be spent by school districts, who can ensure that the money goes to real educational programs, and not to school cops, school discipline, and school exclusion programs?

Fight to win.

Act"; it converted a number of nonviolent offenses from felonies to misdemeanors.

19

Race, Capitalist Crisis, and Abolitionist Organizing: An Interview with Jenna Loyd[1]

JENNA LOYD (JL): It's great to be talking with you, Ruthie. Can you tell us how you got involved in anti-prison work?

Ruth Wilson Gilmore [RWG]: I started working on anti-prison organizing about twenty years ago. It was never not on my agenda, but it became the focus of a good deal of my work when I realized that people who were trying to organize themselves around all different kinds of issues kept running up against the criminal justice system, which then seemed to become a focal point for people who were trying to achieve other goals, whether the goals were adequate education for children, health care, immigrant rights, you name it. People kept running up against the criminal justice system and what seemed to be a wholly new relationship with prisons and policing and jails.

I don't think once upon a time prisons and jails were used judiciously and then just got out of control recently. That is *not* what I think. But what I do know is that the use of prisons and jails as all-purpose solutions for all different kinds of social, political, and economic problems and challenges *is* different than what it was in the past. This is to say that the practices perfected in the past on the working class, people of color, and people without certain kinds of documentation have reached

---

1   This interview took place in February 2010.

a new level of industrialized efficiency, and we see all different kinds of people being sucked into that kind of machinery
at an incredibly fantastic rate. What has happened over the
last twenty years is that different kinds of people have found
themselves confronted with suddenly having to prove or assert
innocence or nonguilt in the face of criminalizing machinery,
including legislation and the ideologically produced representation of all different kinds of people as already criminals.

In recent years, one way that people have joined the struggle
against the all-purpose use of prisons to solve social problems
has been to try to assert that certain kinds of people are actually innocent. So they will say, for example, that long-distance
migrants who are not documented to work are not really criminals because they didn't do anything, they just showed up to
work. Or they will say, "Oh, look. People who are in prison
or who are in jail because they are addicted to certain kinds
of substances are not really guilty of any crimes. They're really
innocent and should be released."

In my view, while saving anyone is a good thing to do, to try
to assert innocence as a key anti-prison political activity is to
turn a blind eye to the system and how it works. The way the
system works is to move the line of what counts as criminal
to encompass and engulf more and more people into the territory of prison eligibility, if you will. So the problem, then, is
not to figure out how to determine or prove the innocence of
certain individuals or certain classes of people, but to attack
the general system through which criminalization proceeds.

JL: It seems like there's a gap between this analysis of criminalization as a political process and a widespread explanation
for prison expansion, which puts the blame on private prison
corporations as the major culprits. Could you talk about how
you think about the prison-industrial complex and how this
term can help us understand the dynamics of both criminalization and privatization?

RWG: The first thing I want to say is that over the last thirty years, the prison and jail capacity of the United States has swelled to such a point that one in a hundred adult residents in the United States is in a jail, in a cell, even as we speak. *Right now, one out of a hundred.* As this has happened, the percentage, or fraction, of cells that are operated or managed by private entities has stayed about the same. It's less than 10 percent of all capacity. Now, since absolute capacity has expanded, obviously the number of cages that are privately managed on behalf of public entities has expanded as well.

A lot of people imagine that it is private prison operators that lobby for the draconian laws that keep people locked up so they can make more money. While there is no doubt in my mind that there are places in which such private prison operators do lobby for certain kinds of laws, the fact of the matter is that they're parasites—and this is not to excuse them, they're totally nasty—coming in the wake of an entire criminalization project rather than being the people who make it happen. They're not the ones who make it happen.

What *do* they make happen? One of the things that has happened, especially in the area of immigrant detention, is that investment bankers—and this is separate from Corrections Corporation of America (CCA) or Wackenhut[2] or any other private prison entities—will persuade communities, especially communities in southern borderland areas and especially in South Texas, that if they agree to build or expand their jail in their county, that eventually the US Marshals Service or Immigration and Customs Enforcement (ICE) will put detained immigrants in them.

There are jails that have been developed that are "privately managed," but what makes them private is that they're not managed by the entity—the US Marshals or ICE—that is authorized by law to take people into custody. Some of these "private

---

2 In 2010, G4S Wackenhut changed its name to G4S Secure Solutions (USA).

prisons" are actually managed by private prison management companies, like Wackenhut and CCA. Others are managed by counties and cities; they're called private, but they're not actually private in the sense that you and I understand the term private. They are contracted with the entity that has jurisdiction to hold people against their will.

The second thing I want to say is that if we collectively could bring a halt to the private management of all cells tomorrow, including the management contracted with city and county officials, not a single person would get out of prison or jail. That would only end a certain kind of management activity. And the rooting out of CCA or Wackenhut or the city of Shafter [California] from managing these facilities would not at all change the laws and regulations under which the people who are in the cages are held in the cages. So it doesn't end the problem; it just shifts it back to the public sphere.

So that's a way of leading into a mini-rant on the prison-industrial complex. Rather famously, in 1995, Mike Davis published an article in the *Nation* magazine in which he more or less coined the phrase "prison-industrial complex";[3] it was modeled on the phrase used by Jim Austin, a criminologist, the "corrections-industrial complex." What both of these guys were trying to think through was whether the ways in which the courts and prisons and industry and the state operate in tandem, or complexly together, could be understood through the lens of the military-industrial complex. It wasn't, in my view, a cute phrase just to be cute. But what happened, in my view, is that people took up the phrase and they thought that all that Austin, Mike Davis, and by extension Critical Resistance —which picked up Mike Davis's phrase—meant was: "Are private corporations calling the shots?"

If we go back to Dwight Eisenhower (or his speechwriter), who coined the phrase "military-industrial complex," we can

---

3   Mike Davis, "Hell Factories in the Field: A Prison Industrial Complex," *The Nation* 260.7 (January 1995): 229–34.

think about what he meant. Who are included in that complex? What makes the "complex" complex? How is it not simply that weapons manufacturers were telling the United States Congress what to do and when to go to war? The latter is not exactly what Eisenhower was worried about when he warned against the military-industrial complex. Rather, Eisenhower—who revered war and who loved capitalism—was worried that this dyadic relationship between the Pentagon, on the one hand, which had become incredibly insulated and powerful by the end of the 1950s, and the military-industrial providers and beneficiaries, on the other hand, was going to set the stage and determine the path of *all* industrial development in the United States. That's what he was worried about. He wasn't worried about whether they were going to decide when the next war was, but rather that all of our industrial development would be shaped by the needs of perfecting the capacity to make war.

It's a slightly different emphasis, which is important for thinking about the prison-industrial complex because the complex evoked by the term "military-industrial complex" did not only include the elected and appointed officials in the Pentagon and in Washington, or the heads of corporations like McDonnell Douglas and General Electric, but also the places with military bases, all of the people who work for the military, the boosters who wanted more military installations in their communities in order to produce jobs, and the intellectuals in universities and think tanks who made plans about who should be appropriate targets for war, or the most efficient ways to kill the most people.

All of that is the military-industrial complex, which means to me that all of that is the prison-industrial complex. It's not only the private entrepreneurs or firms that make a profit, although they're important, but it's also the ways in which an entire path has been created around how to deal with certain problems. An entire development path has been created through the assumption that there is a perpetual enemy who must always be fought, but who can never be conquered. And that's where international militarization and domestic militarization meet— at this notion that there is the production of an enemy around which we organize everything, *everything*, not simply profit.

That said, when we think about the profit motive in prison expansion, in thinking in a detailed way through the notion of a *complex*, we are compelled to think about: What are all the ways in which people, firms, and entities—including law enforcement—are sweeping off from the top, as it were, the value that is circulating in the form of expenditures in policing, courts, and prisons? This means everyone who works in the courts. This means everyone who works in the prisons. This means every vendor who sells anything to the prisons. This means all those outrageous costs that are heaped on top of ordinary costs for telephones and so forth. But it also means what's happening in public education, not only the dollar trade-off, but the assumption that there is a place awaiting everyone who doesn't make it in the teach-to-the-test educational system in K–12, and for many the place is in some cage. *All of that*. It's an entire way of life that we're looking at when we think about the prison-industrial complex. And that is a lot to say to somebody who gets their interest fired up by the phrase "prison-industrial complex," who thinks that the problem is private prisons or slave labor. You can't say it fast!

JL: Who has been targeted by criminalization, and how does this fit with the recent history of class and capitalism?

RWG: When I describe who is in prison, the phrase that I always use is "modestly educated women and men in the prime of their lives." That phrase enables me—in fact, compels me— to think about: How do women and men *become* modestly educated? How is it that people in the prime of their lives who otherwise would be making, moving, growing, and caring for things instead are in cages? What has happened to the making, moving, growing, and caring for things that has changed through the participation of modestly educated women and men in those economic sectors? What did the activities and organizing of such folks become in capitalist terms? (And that's not always the same everywhere.) What is it about the regions that these folks come from that has changed, since once upon a time, without question, there was absorption into a certain labor market niche—often, but not always, a low-wage labor force—that is now unquestionably impossible?

Each of these questions enables a certain thinking about: How are these folks organized or not organized? What are potential, already-existing organizations or institutions through which organizing on behalf of, or in favor of, people sucked into prison might happen? What is working against them in an organized way? And, finally, are there new organizations that can come into being? I'm a firm believer in founding new organizations, not for the organizations to become the center of our attention such that what we do is tend the organization (which is where I think a lot of people in the voluntary sector have unwittingly arrived). Rather, new organizations make for new combinations and new possibilities. I totally agree with Paulo Freire and Myles Horton that organizations are the substance of social movements.

JL: How do you explain the paradox that so many modestly educated folks are being shoved out of the labor market, while other people, many of whom are migrating across national boundaries, are finding low-paid work? And on top of it, there's been an expansion of immigrant detention.

RWG: At least part of what's happened was that when the ideological and material conditions for the intense expansion of prisons took place, union busting was at the top of all agendas connected with how to revive capitalism in the Golden State after the difficult decade of the seventies. This was a period marked by a very long economic recession, by the United States being run out of Vietnam by the triumph of the Vietnamese People's Army, by the United States going off the gold standard, and by the beginning of the shift in who set prices for oil and what they called the "oil shock." All that economic ferment on a global scale was met not exclusively, but in a widespread way, in the United States by a very strong focus on getting rid of unions or at least weakening them.

So we see, starting in the late seventies and early eighties, outsourcing and multiple-tier contracts for union workers who entered a firm at different times. We see the busting of the unions, which was really profound. Firms wanted to employ people who were the least organized and most difficult to organize, so that having successfully clamped down on (and, in some cases, almost obliterated) the capacity of unions, the firms wouldn't have to go through that again.

Rather than imagining that workers line up outside a factory every day and that Brown workers without documents were hired before the Black workers with documents, this was actually much more structural and was much more systemically put into effect. For example, here in Los Angeles, janitors had organized from the 1930s forward. A lot of them organized during World War II under the Congress of Industrial Organizations and then continued to organize post–World War II. The janitorial services became eventually a niche dominated by Black men. (My grandfather was a Black man who was a janitor who organized on the East Coast, and my father was a machinist and janitor who did the same.) Black men fought and fought and fought to secure their jobs, wages, and benefits such that in 1980 janitors who were organized in Los Angeles County were making *good* money. They were making $10 an hour, which in 1980 was a lot of money. (I was making $5 at the time.) This meant a lot of things. It meant that they could pay for their houses, their little houses in South Central, they could let their children go to college. They didn't have to pay for it because it was free. They could allow their children to leave the household and not contribute to the household income because they had fought so hard.

It was right at the moment of success that failure kicked in systemically. Firms decided to lay off all their janitors and outsource janitorial services. They didn't hire new janitors who were undocumented people from Central America. They laid off all their janitors and then they hired Joe's Janitorial Contracting Firm to bring in new janitors. The contracting firms went and found people who were not already organized, who didn't have the local knowledge base, the local community networks, and so on, that those former janitors had developed in order to organize. And they hired those whom they imagined were the least organizable people—immigrants not documented to work, women rather than men (in many cases, although not exclusively)—and those are the people who succeeded the other janitors. And they succeeded them at less than half the hourly wages. What seems to be a conflict between group one and group two, and in some ways might actually play out to be a conflict, was actually a calculated decision made on the part of firms to reduce the cost of business. And, of course, the employers were wrong about the people they hired, as I'll discuss in a minute.

Now imagine that we're looking at a Los Angeles County graph of race and gender in relation to jobs and employment over time. You will see that as the best-waged jobs for Black men disappeared, the number of Black men going to prison shot up. Then we move across in time a little bit, and we see that as the well-waged jobs for Chicanos start to disappear, the number of Chicanos going to prison shoots up. And every time we see a certain labor market niche shrink, there's a sudden, secular rise—it's not just a spike; it goes up, and it keeps going up—in the number of people from that demographic category going to prison. When it comes to the question of long-distance migrants who are undocumented, we see again, as certain kinds of reorganizations in the economic landscape happen, that there's a rise in the percentage of people going to prison who are undocumented.

Thinking about these issues in this way gives us some insights into the various ways to connect the need to (re)organize low-wage workers as part of the struggle against the expansion of prisons as all-purpose solutions to social problems. One meeting I went to in the nineties, in which people who were organizing Justice for Janitors (the very immigrants whom firms thought were not organizable) presented what they had been doing, included representatives of the first Sandinista government in Nicaragua. When they finished their presentation, the Sandinista representative said, "That's really great, but what happened to the people who used to have these jobs? Are you organizing with them, too?" And that was exactly the right question. Not, "Should the long-distance migrants be organizing?" Of course they should. "And should they be organizing back along the migration trail so that people who might be coming from Central America or Mexico would understand that when you get there, you've got to join the union, so as not to be exploited?" But the question was, "What about the people who are right down the street? Why are you not organizing with them as well? Because if you're not, there's something wrong with this project."

JL: How do you understand the connections between slavery and prison?

RWG: I spend a lot of time trying to think about how to take the concept of slavery, which people respond to for good reasons, and open it up to a contemporary understanding of what is going on. Thinking through Orlando Patterson, and thinking through the constituent features of slavery as being secondarily or tertiarily about uncompensated labor, and more about the construction and consolidation of a certain kind of

enemy status is important.[4] What makes the enemy is what makes the enemy different from everybody else. So, while that difference might be conceived of or understood as race, which is to say "undifferentiated difference," Orlando Patterson's thinking can help us ask: What is it about people who have been criminalized that keeps them permanently, rather than temporarily (during an unfortunate period in their lives), in this enemy status?

The way that Patterson puts it in describing enemies, and the distinction between those who become enslaved who are from within the polity and those who become enslaved as a result of war with an external force, is: "The one fell because he was the enemy, the other became the enemy because he had fallen."[5] How can we think about this nexus between those who are "the enemy," that is, those who immigrate to the United States without authorization, and those who become the enemy because, although legally in the United States, they are criminalized?

Both groups being criminalized come to share certain features, and those constitutive elements of slavery have to do with alienation from their families and communities, and violent domination, which is to say, they are held against their will and made to do certain things that they otherwise wouldn't do. It's coercive, not consensual, force. And the third is general dishonor; who you are and what you are does not change because this singular category of criminal, which has been ascribed to you, becomes *the* category that defines everything about you in terms of the social order in which this coercion takes place. This doesn't mean that people who have been criminalized or enslaved themselves become this one thing to themselves; Du Bois's concept of double consciousness takes care of that analytical error for us.[6]

---

4 Orlando Patterson, *Slavery and Social Death: A Comparative Study*, Cambridge, MA: Harvard University Press, 1982.

5 Patterson, *Slavery and Social Death*, 44.

6 W. E. B. Du Bois, *The Souls of Black Folk*, New York: St. Martin's Press, 1997 [1903].

That said, if we start to think about all of the people who are caught up in this category as blending into a new category of person—a new category, thinking through the processes of racialization—then one of the things that we might be able to do is to echo what a former white supremacist, who is a prisoner, said in the wake of an uprising in which white supremacist prisoners organized with Black supremacist prisoners and Brown supremacist prisoners: "Well, maybe what we are is the prison race." This is endlessly interesting for me to think about and to try to get people to connect to.

JL: How do you think about organizing different groups of people together?

RWG: When I think about organizing, I ask myself: What would people actually do? Because organizing is constrained by recognition, and recognition is not only a matter of whether some people recognize other people who might become part of an organization as in some way similar to themselves, but also the recognition that this is something we *can* do. We *can* fight this, or we *can* protest that, or we *can* reorganize, whatever it is. As we all like to say, "You have to start where people are at." But as Stuart Hall reminds us, where people are at is more complicated than perhaps it might seem at first blush.

For example, people organize against three strikes.[7] What can happen that opens up that organizing focus to the multiple dimensions of the all-purpose use of prisons, even if the fight in the short term is to reform a law, which would still stand as a law? How can such organizing open people up to the consciousness of the *impossibility* for such a reform to be durable as long as that kind of law can also endure? How, in other

---

7 "Habitual offender" or "three-strikes" laws, present in numerous US States. In California, such a law was implemented after voters supported Proposition 184, "Three Strikes and You're Out," in 1994.

words, might organizing around a reform issue do significant work in building political consciousness?

I worked for many years with Families to Amend California's Three Strikes (FACTS), and I was around when it started. Another organization, Mothers Reclaiming Our Children (MROC), brought FACTS into being. The MROC constantly asked itself: "What can we do, what can we do, what can we do?" And the women from MROC decided to kick off FACTS because Three Strikes seemed the most blatant example of the whole set of laws and practices that was sweeping people into prison at a dizzying rate.

What we talked about at first was getting rid of that whole law because people completely understood what that law was really doing, which was taking modestly educated women and men in the prime of their lives, documented or not, and putting them into prisons for the rest of their lives. Everyone understood that, and having debated the perceived extent and purpose of the law, everyone understood that it was happening to all different kinds of people, but the high-profile way in which it was happening at the time to Black people made the struggle against the law understandable, acceptable, and justifiable to a whole political community, including Black people. The group developed a keen recognition of how anti-Black racism was doing the work of justifying mass incarceration and life terms and so on.

As FACTS transitioned from an idea for an organization into an organization for itself, people in the organization decided they would fight for an amendment, which would not completely blow up the law, but they were trying constantly to open up the law and make it vulnerable. What struck me was that there were people in that organization who were fighting for an amendment even though their loved ones in prison would not get out were the amendment to pass. That blew me away. These people were fighting just as hard as people whose loved ones would get out if the amendment were passed.

That's an example to me of people coming to the conscious-ness of how the complex works and therefore the complexity of arrangements that people would have to get themselves into to fight it out. People—and these are people who are them-selves modestly educated women and men in the prime of their lives, or elderly people—fighting for this amendment were fighting in a sense for a "non reformist reform," as André Gorz would have it, even though they knew that they ran the risk of just consolidating the rest of the law. They knew that but were willing to take that risk. That's an example of people who might not call themselves abolitionists having an abolitionist agenda.

Another example is the Central California Environmental Justice Network, which is composed mostly of environmental justice communities in the vast San Joaquin Valley struggling around issues of air quality and water quality. When we in the California Prison Moratorium Project (CPMP) went to the conference that led to the formation of the organization, we asked for some time to be on their agenda to explain why we thought that prisons fit the criteria by which the network was organizing itself, and therefore that CPMP would like to be part of any organizations that came out of the conference. They gave us twenty minutes to make our pitch, and at the end of twenty minutes everyone was convinced. They didn't have to think hard about it. People in urban areas of CPMP or Critical Resistance said, "They gotta be crazy!" We went out to rural California, and they said, "Oh, yeah. We see what you're saying." So we could talk about both the ways in which prisons are cities, and therefore their environmental footprint is huge, and we could talk about how part of the life-threatening condi-tions for people in rural California has to do with the ramping up of policing and criminalization there. Everyone saw that. It wasn't rocket science, just a little harder.

Therefore, the CPMP, which doesn't have the word "aboli-tion" in its mission statement, could join forces with grassroots environmental-justice organizations in the Central Valley in order to fight against prison expansion. And to fight against prison expansion, we would, by joining forces, also have to fight on behalf of clean water and adequate schools, and against pesticide drift, toxic incinerators, all of that stuff. This raised anti-prison organizing in that region to a true abolitionist agenda, which is fighting for the right of people who work in the Central Valley to have good health and secure working conditions and not be subject to toxicity, even though so many of the workers in the valley are not documented workers.

JL: This brings us to the specific connections that you see between abolitionist organizing and migrant-justice organizing.

RWG: Abolitionists should be thinking about what kinds of social practices and political and economic configurations make it possible for us to know that we finally ended the capacity for some of us to designate others as enemies in the way that Orlando Patterson so eloquently describes slavery as social death. In other words, if abolitionists are, first and foremost, committed to the possibility of full and rich lives for everybody, then that would mean that all kinds of distinctions and categorizations that divide us—innocent/guilty; documented/not; Black, white, Brown; citizen/not-citizen—would have to yield in favor of other things, like the right to water, the right to air, the right to the countryside, the right to the city, whatever these rights are. Of course, then, we have to ask ourselves: What is the substance of rights? What is a right anyway? Is it a thing, or is it a practice? If a right is a practice rather than a thing, then that requires that these little instances of social organization in which people work on behalf of themselves and others with a purpose in mind, rather than a short-term interest that can be met through a little bit of lawmaking or other haggling, changes the entire landscape of how we live.

To me, abolition is utopian in the sense that it's looking

forward to a world in which prisons are not necessary because not only are the political-economic motives behind mass incarceration gone, but also the instances in which people might harm each other are minimized because the causes for that harm (setting aside, for the moment, psychopaths) are minimized as well. In that sense, I think the greatest abolitionist organization that exists in the United States today, with all due respect to my beloved brothers and sisters in Critical Resistance, is the Harm Reduction Coalition. That's an abolitionist organization no matter what the people who do that work think of the word "abolition."

And that's where I'm at today. If we're not organizing between the very groups who imagine they have some "structural antagonism," we're never going to win. As a result, to go back to something I was saying earlier, the extent to which people try to differentiate between those who are convicted of crimes and sent to prison, those who are guilty, compared to people who aren't documented to work, but only showed up to work as non-criminals, is a *big* mistake. One, if the law has been set that crossing the border is a criminal act, you are a criminal. Two, that's not the issue. The issue is: Let's get everybody who's been criminalized together and figure out how we can undo this state of affairs.

JL: So, ending the possibility of defining other people as enemies comes back to not just an analogy with the military-industrial complex, but to the connections of the prison-industrial complex with the military-industrial complex.

RWG: Yes, exactly. Industrialized punishment and industrialized killing are following the same trajectories. The motives, the organizational strategies, in the United States the fiscal and bureaucratic capacities, are all modeled on each other. The great irony is that, as Greg Hooks so brilliantly showed, the whole structure, the fiscal and bureaucratic capacities and the organization of the Pentagon coming out of World War II, were modeled on the fiscal and bureaucratic structures that were designed, and never fully operationalized, for social and economic and cultural programs in response to the Great Depression.[8] They were formations organized for capitalism to save capitalism from capitalism and were sucked into the War Department and then emerged as the Pentagon and the warfare state. And then sucked into prisons and policing and emerged as the carceral state. Our job is to look at how capitalism saves capitalism from capitalism and figure out other directions— which does not mean helping save capitalism from capitalism, but to say, "Okay, there's something vulnerable here, obviously, because look at what changed. Let's get busy."

8   Gregory M. Hooks, *Forging the Military-Industrial Complex: World War II's Battle of the Potomac*, Champaign: University of Illinois Press, 1991.

20

Abolition Geography and the Problem of Innocence

> We were trying to find language to make sense of a time before whatever came after.
>
> —China Miéville, *Embassytown*

Money

Loot. Pay. Wage. Profit. Interest. Tax. Rent. Accumulation. Extraction. Colonialism. Imperialism.

The modern prison is a central but by no means singularly defining institution of carceral geographies in the United States and beyond, geographies that signify regional accumulation strategies and upheavals, immensities and fragmentations, that reconstitute in space-time (even if geometrically the coordinates are unchanged) to run another round of accumulation.

Prison rose in tandem with a world-historical transition in the role of money in everyday life. In retrospect the transformation looks just like a flip. From having been, as for most people it continues to be, a *means* to move stored energy between sellers and buyers of desired objects, money became the desirable *end*, not for hoarders' and misers' erotic caresses, but to touch differently and not for too long—to enliven through pressing into imperative motion irregular but perpetual cycles of transformation to make more money. Capitalism: never not racial, including in rural England, or anywhere in Europe for that matter, where, as Cedric Robinson teaches us, hierarchies among people whose descendants might all have become white depended for their structure on group-differentiated vulnerability to premature death, exploited by elites, as part of all equally exploitable nature-as-other, to justify inequality at the end of the day, and next morning as well.

Racial capitalism: a mode of production developed in agriculture, improved by enclosure in the Old World, and captive land and labor in the Americas, perfected in slavery's time-motion field-factory choreography, its chorographic imperative forged on the anvils of imperial war-making monarchs and the tributary peers who had to ante up taxes—in cash not kind—so the sovereign might arm increasingly centralized and regularized militaries who became less able to pay themselves, as they had in the past, by looting at each battle's end. Not that they stopped looting later or now.

Nor did the pay packet come all at once: in the United States many nineteenth-century citizen-soldiers went to their graves still waiting to be paid for having killed or agreed to kill Native Americans or French or their proxies. The compensation took the form of something that could be transformed into something else: title to looted land—an honor for the vast *herrenvolk* peerage of enfranchised white men—land, a good that can't be moved, though a deed can be pocketed or sold or borrowed against or seized for a lien, in other words, turned into money; and if not a title, a pension, an entitlement paid out regularly as money to ease one's golden years.

Indeed, modern prisons were born alongside, and grew up with, the United States of America. Penitentiaries established state-making at the margin of the early republic, whose every founding document recapitulated free as against other, imported as against immigrated, to clarify that sweeping ideals of defense and general welfare, long before the Thirteenth Amendment, had no universal remit but rather defined from the earliest pages who was in and who out.

Then, as now, competing concepts of freedom shaped the

planetary movement of people and relationships. Like lives, early sentences were short, absorbing one by one people who wouldn't toe their assigned or presumed line, play their part, hit their mark, in racial capitalism's dramatically scaled cycles of place-making—including all of chattel slavery, imperialism, settler colonialism, resource extraction, infrastructural coordination, urban industrialization, regional development, and the financialization of everything.

Racial capitalism's extensive and intensive animating force, its contradictory consciousness, its means to turn objects and desires into money, is people in the prime of life or younger, people who make, move, grow, and care for things and other people.

Who then was or is out of place? Unfree people who sold things they made or grew on the side, hiding the money in an emancipation pot. People who couldn't say where they worked, or prove that they were free, or show a ticket or a pass, a document to save their skin, or save themselves from the narrative that their skin, stretched in particular ways across muscles and bones, seemed or seems to suggest something about where they shouldn't be—caught.

Racial capitalism's imperative requires all kinds of scheming, including hard work by elites and their comprador cohorts in the overlapping and interlocking space-economies of the planet's surface. They build and dismantle and refigure states, moving capacity into and out of the public realm. And they think very hard about money on the move. In the contemporary world, when product and profit cycles turn faster and faster, with racial capitalism ever less patient with any friction on money-flow, sticking resources in prisons whence they might not emerge on time and in the quality required isn't all that attractive, even though the cages are full of millions of people in the prime of life.

We used to think that in the United States, contemporary mass un-freedom, racially organized, must be a recapitulation

473

of slavery's money-making scheme. But if these massive carceral institutions, weighted like cities, are not factories and service centers, then where's the profit, the surplus money at the end of the day? Today's prisons are extractive. What does that mean? It means prisons enable money to move because of the enforced *inactivity* of people locked in them. It means people extracted from communities, and people returned to communities but not entitled to be of them, enable the circulation of money on rapid cycles. What's extracted from the extracted is the resource of life—time.

If we think about this dynamic through the politics of scale, understanding bodies as places, then criminalization transforms individuals into tiny territories primed for extractive activity to unfold—extracting and extracting again *time* from the territories of selves. This process opens a hole in a life, furthering, perhaps to our surprise, the annihilation of space by time. A stolen and corrupted social wage flies through that time-hole to imprison employees' paychecks. To vendors. To utility companies. To contractors. To debt service. The cash takes many final forms: wages, interest, rent, and sometimes profit. But more to the point, the extractive process brings the mechanics of contemporary imperialism to mind: extraction, in money form, from direct producers whose communities are destabilized too. But money, too, gives us some insight into the enormity of the possible inhabitants and makers of abolition geographies—abolition geography, the antagonistic contradiction of carceral geographies, forms an interlocking pattern across the terrain of racial capitalism. We see it.

Abolition Geography

Abolition geography starts from the homely premise that freedom is a place. Place-making is normal human activity: we figure out how to combine people, and land, and other resources with our social capacity to organize ourselves in a variety of ways, whether to stay put or to go wandering. Each of these factors —people, land, other resources, social capacity—comes in a number of types, all of which determine but do not define what can or should be done. Working outward and down-ward from this basic premise, abolitionist critique concerns itself with the greatest and least detail of these arrangements of people and resources and land over time. It shows how rela-tionships of un-freedom consolidate and stretch, but not for the purpose of documenting misery. Rather, the point is not only to identify central contradictions—inherent vices—in regimes of dispossession, but also, urgently, to show how radical con-sciousness in action resolves into liberated life-ways, however provisional, present and past. Indeed, the radical tradition from which abolition geography draws meaning and method goes back in time-space not in order to abolish history, but rather to find alternatives to the despairing sense that so much change, in retrospect, seems only ever to have been displacement and redistribution of human sacrifice. If unfinished liberation is the still-to-be-achieved work of abolition, then at bottom what is to be abolished isn't the past or its present ghost, but rather the processes of hierarchy, dispossession, and exclusion that congeal in and as group-differentiated vulnerability to premature death.

Everyone was surprised in May 2011 when the notori-ously pro–states'-rights Supreme Court of the United States (SCOTUS) upheld a lower court order that the California Department of Corrections and Rehabilitation[1] reduce the number of people held in the stock of adult prisons and camps. SCOTUS affirmed a lower court's opinion that the Golden State could not "build its way out" of constitutional violations so severe they could be measured in premature, which is to say preventable, death: averaging one per week, every week, for decades, due to well-documented medical neglect.

---

1 The California Department of Corrections (CDC) was renamed Cal-ifornia Department of Corrections and Rehabilitation (CRCR) in 2004.

The decision, although a victory, did not mark a clear turn away from nearly forty years of life-shortening mass criminalization, even though five judges recognized the accumulated catastrophe of premature death happening to the people whom most Americans of all races, genders, and ages have learned to abhor and ignore. And yet, in the context of the global war on terror coupled with domestic wars on vulnerable people, we know that challenges to murderous outrage (torture, drone strikes, police killings, poisoned water) readily dissolve into frenzied analytical activity that produces fresh justification, cancelling out prohibitions by the combined force of applied violence, revised legal reasoning, and lengthy commission reports. In the wake of scandal and demand for prison reform, the ruthless principles and procedures of criminalization remain intact, noisily tweaked at the margin but ever hardening at the center where most people in prison languish: average sentences, average conditions, average cages, average charges, average misery. In other words, against the scandal of documented deliberate neglect, criminalization remains a complicated means and process to achieve a simple thing: to enclose people in situations where they are expected, and in many ways compelled, to sicken and so die.

The processes contributing to both the development and epochal ordinariness of mass criminalization have been the focus of research, action, advocacy, and other forms of study trying to make sense of experience. A general but not exhaustive summary goes like this: In the United States, the multidecade crisis-riven political economy threw off surpluses that became prison expansion's basic factors: land, people, money-capital, and state capacity. The elements of "the prison fix" neither automatically nor necessarily combined into extensive carceral geographies. Rather, an enormously complicated people-, income-, and asset-rich political economy made a relatively sudden turn and repurposed acres, redirected the social wage, used public debt, and serially removed thousands and thousands and thousands and thousands and thousands and thousands and thousands and thousands of modestly educated people from households and communities.

As we can see, something changed. Crucially, instead of imagining the persistent reiteration of static relations, it might be more powerful to analyze relationship dynamics that extend beyond obvious conceptual or spatial boundaries and then decide what a particular form, old or new, is made of, by trying to make it into something else. This—making something into something else—is what negation is. To do so is to wonder about a form's present, future-shaping design—something we can discern from the evidence of its constitutive patterns, without being beguiled or distracted by social ancestors we perceive, reasonably or emotionally, in the form's features. (I'll come back to ancestors in a few pages.) To think this way is to think deductively (there are forms) and inductively (interlocking patterns reveal generalities which might or might not be structural). I suppose I became a geographer because this kind of back and forth is what we do, trying to see and explain the formalities and improvisations of place-making, which are shaped by human/environmental relationships, always elaborated by dependency—the coupling or connection of power with difference—and sometimes but not inevitably interrupted by preventable fatalities. Deliberately propagated fatalities, and the forms and patterns that coalesce into premature death, reveal human sacrifice as an organizing principle, or perhaps more precisely as an unprincipled form of organizing, which returns us to racial capitalism and the role of criminalization in it.

The prolific advocacy shaping efforts to foster anti-prison awareness and action partially reveals, campaign by campaign, bits of mass incarceration's breath-taking structure. The selection and arrangement of categories inspiring sustained action ironically tend to legitimize the system as such by focusing on how it's specifically harmful to youth, women, parents, mothers, men, gender-nonconforming people, the aged, or the infirm, or that it's the outcome of the war on drugs, stop-and-frisk, racism, privatization, and so forth. And yet the extraction of time from each territory-body specifically and viscerally changes lives elsewhere—partners, children, communities, movements, the possibility of freedom. At the same time, the particular also implies entire historical geographies in constant churn. For some examples, think: Gentrification. Auto or steel manufacturing. Coal mining. Gold mining. Conflict minerals. Fracking. New shipping technologies. Robotics. Commodity chains. Finance capital. The challenge is to keep the entirety of carceral geographies—rather than only their prison or even law-enforcement aspects—connected, without collapsing or reducing various aspects into one another. Any category or system has many dimensions, analytically necessitating scalar stretch in order to perceive the material world in a variety of overlapping and interlocking totalities. This basic imperative requires more in the way of self-critical consciousness than additional data (we already have too much): although what's real matters absolutely, the experience of it will never automatically reveal how and why negation (the thorough reworking of materiality and experience) sometimes succeeds.

Worldwide today, wherever inequality is deepest, the use of prison as a catchall solution to social problems prevails—nowhere as extensively as in the United States, led by California. Ideologically, which is to say in thought and everyday culture, the expression and normalization of the twin processes of centralization and devolution—patterned as they are by the sensibility of permanent crisis—shape structures of feeling and therefore, to a great extent, socially determine the apparent range of available oppositional options. In other words, the doctrine of devolution results in a constantly fragmenting array of centers of struggle and objects of antagonism for people who seek equal protection, to say nothing of opportunity. In crisis, in resistance, in opposition: To whom, at whom, against whom does one carry one's petition or raise one's fist?

Devolution is partition, sometimes provisional, sometimes more secure. Its normalizing capacities are profound, patterning political imagination and thus contouring attacks on the carceral form. As a result, many such attacks exhibit trends which, not surprisingly, coalesce tightly around specific categories: policing, immigration, terrorism, budget activism, injunctions, sexuality, gender, age, premature death, parenthood, privatization, formerly and currently incarcerated people, public-sector unions, devalued labor, and (relative) innocence. Racism both connects and differentiates how these categories cohere in both radical and reformist policy prescriptions—in other words, how people (and here I cite Peter Linebaugh's exquisite phrase) "pierce the future for hope." Insofar as policies are a script for the future, they must be sharp, a quality often confused with excessive narrowness—narrowness being something that devolution's inherent patterning encourages to a fault. As A. Sivanandan teaches, while economics determine, the politics of race define techniques and understanding, even though racial categories and hierarchies—at any moment solid—are not set in concrete. If, as Stuart Hall argued back in the late 1970s, race is the modality through which class is lived, then mass incarceration is class war.

And yet, breadth carries analytical and organizational challenges as well. It's not news that we find the answers to the questions we ask. What then might the most adequate general term or terms be that usefully gather together for scrutiny and action such a disparate yet connected range of categories, relationships, and processes as those conjoined by mass criminalization and incarceration? Seventeen years ago, the abolitionist organization Critical Resistance came into being, taking as its surname "Beyond the Prison-Industrial Complex." The heuristic purpose of the term "prison-industrial complex" was to provoke as wide as possible a range of understandings of the socio-spatial relationships out of which mass incarceration is made by using as a flexible template the military-industrial complex—its whole historical geography, and political economy, and demography, and intellectual and technical practitioners, theorists, policy wonks, boosters, and profiteers, all who participated in, benefited from, or were passed over or disorganized by the Department of War's transformative restructuring into the Pentagon.

In other words, we meant "prison-industrial complex" to be as conceptually expansive as our object of analysis and struggle. But I think in too many cases its effect has been to shrivel —atrophy, really—rather than to spread out imaginative understanding of the system's apparently boundless boundary-making. As a result, researchers spend too much time either proving trivial things or beating back hostile critiques, and activists devote immense resources to fighting scandals rather than sources. And yet there *is* a prison-industrial complex. So it has occurred to me, as a remedial project, to provisionally call the prison-industrial complex by another name—one I gave to a course I developed in 1999 and taught for half a decade at Berkeley—the somewhat more generic "carceral geographies." The purpose here is to renovate and make critical what *abolition* is all about. Indeed, abolition geography is carceral geography's antagonistic contradiction.

I will return to this point at the end, but here—as you who know me will expect—I will remind us that, in the archival record of self-organization and world-making activity among the Black people of the South under Reconstruction, the great communist W. E. B. Du Bois saw places people made—abolition geographies—under the participatory political aegis of what he called "abolition democracy." (Thulani Davis has most recently and exquisitely elaborated this work through tracing its expansion and contraction across space-time.) People didn't make what they made from nothing—destitute though the millions were as a result of the great effort to strike, free themselves, and establish a new social order. They brought things with them—sensibilities, dependencies, talents, indeed a complement of consciousness and capacity Cedric Robinson termed an "ontological totality"—to make where they were into places they wished to be. And yet they left abundant evidence showing how freedom is not simply the absence of enslavement as a legal and property form. Rather, the undoing of bondage—abolition—is quite literally to change places: to destroy the geography of slavery by mixing their labor with the external world to change the world and thereby themselves— as it were, habitation as nature—even if geometrically speaking they hadn't moved far at all.

Such Reconstruction place-making negated the negation constituted as and by bondage, and while nobody fully inhabits its direct socio-spatial lineage because of the counterrevolution of property, the consciousness remains in political, expressive, and organizational culture if we look and listen. (Indeed, 2015 is the 100th anniversary of *The Birth of a Nation*—a tale that made the wages of whiteness not only desirable but in many senses obligatory.) What particularly concerns us here is a general point: to enhance their ability to extract value from labor and land, elites fashion political, economic, and cultural institutions using ideologies and methods acquired locally, nationally, and internationally. They build states. Tweak them. Aggrandize and devolve them. Promote and deflate explanatory and justificatory explanations of why things should either be otherwise or as they are. But even in the throes of periodic abandonment, elites rely on structures of order and significance that the anarchy of racial capitalism can never guarantee. Further, as the actual experience of the Negro during the Civil War and Reconstruction shows, non-elites are never passive pawns. Ordinary people, in changing diversity, figure out how to stretch or diminish social and spatial forms to create room for their lives. Signs and traces of abolition geographies abound, even in their fragility.

* * *

Gaza and the West Bank: During the First Intifada (1987–93) popular committees throughout the territories organized an astonishing array of institutions that would constitute the outline of an infrastructure for postcolonial Palestine. The projects included health clinics, schools, shops, food-growing and -processing capacities, and clothing factories. The people who organized and worked in these places discussed the work as partial although necessary to liberation and requiring persistent work on consciousness through imaginative education, training, and other programs. For example, some of the women who worked in food processing discussed how the revolution-in-progress could not be sustained unless patriarchy and paternalism became as unacceptable and unthinkable as occupation. The work in popular education depended on stretching awareness from the particular (an inoculation, an irrigation ditch, an electrically powered machine) to the general requirements for the ad hoc abolition geographies of that time-space to become and become again sustained through conscious action.

Domestic Violence: Carceral feminism has failed to end violence against women or domestic violence in general, although sometimes law enforcement intervention makes time and space for people to figure out alternatives. So, INCITE! Women of Color against Violence and many other people organized in a variety of ways around the world have tried to figure out how to make that time-space in the context of household or community building rather than criminalization. The idea here is, rather than punish violence better or faster, to end violence by changing the social relationships in which it occurs. As a result, and as the Story Telling Organizing Project demonstrates, people around the world have devised many approaches to stopping the central problem—violence—without using violence to achieve successful change, involving friends, neighbors, wider communities, and different strategies.

Decolonial Education: Sónia Vaz Borges's 2016 PhD thesis on the liberation schools established by the anti-colonial forces during the Guinea-Bissau thirteen-year liberation war shows the intricate interrelation of place-making, space-changing activities. Educated to be a member of the Portuguese state's overseas professional managerial class, Amílcar Cabral's role in the development of revolutionary consciousness drew in part from his training as an agronomist. Having walked the land of Guinea-Bissau and Cape Verde to evaluate problems and solutions for soil productivity, he also got to know the people who lived on and worked that land. The Party for the Independence of Guinea and Cape Verde (PAIGC) created a curriculum for alphabetical, practical, and political literacy, wrote textbooks, and trained soldiers to become teachers. The schools, built and staffed as soon as possible after expulsion of the colonial military in each region of the country, articulated possible futures for localities and beyond, with particular emphasis on Pan-African and Third World connection.

Oakland Anti-Gang Injunctions: The range of concrete control exercised by the criminal justice system doesn't stop at the system's border. Rather, local administrators can use civil law to extend prison's total-institution regime to households and communities, while employers can discriminate at will against the 65 million or more people in the United States who are documented not to work because of disqualifying arrest or conviction records. In Oakland, a coalition of formerly incarcerated people, several social and economic justice organizations, family members, and others launched a campaign to compel the city government to cancel an established injunction zone and not establish more planned zones. In a zone, people named in the injunction, and the places they live and frequent, have no barriers to police questioning and searches. Further, household members become involuntary deputies, expected to enforce injunction terms or get into trouble themselves.

Transforming the zone into an abolition geography required transforming consciousness, as officially and locally mocked and reviled individuals had to develop their persuasive power both at city hall and in the streets and empty lots where they built community and trust through extraordinary commitment to ordinary things: creating a garden and a mural. Being the first to respond in times of trouble. Leading by following. Curiously, people not afraid to die had to demonstrate their fearlessness anew in altogether novel contexts.

The Problem of Innocence

I noted earlier that many advocates for people in prison and the communities they come from have taken a perilous route by arguing why certain kinds of people or places suffer in special ways when it comes to criminalization or the cage. Thus, the argument goes, prisons are designed for men and are therefore bad for women. Prisons are designed for healthy young men and are therefore bad for the aged and the infirm. Prisons are designed for adults and are therefore bad for youth. Prisons separate people from their families and are therefore bad for mothers who have frontline responsibility for family cohesion and reproductive labor. Prisons are based on a rigid two-gender system and are therefore bad for people who are transgender and gender-nonconforming. Prisons are cages and people who didn't hurt anybody should not be in cages. Now this does not exhaust the litany of who shouldn't be in prison, but what it does do is two things. First, it establishes as a hard fact that some people should be in cages, and only against this desirability or inevitability might some change occur. And it does so by distinguishing degrees of innocence such that there are people, inevitably, who will become permanently not innocent, no matter what they do or say. The structure of feeling that shapes the innocence defense narrative is not hard to understand:

after all, if criminalization is all about identifying the guilty, within *its* prevailing logic it's reasonable to imagine the path to undoing it must be to discover the wrongly condemned.

The insistence on finding innocents among the convicted or killed both projects and derives energy from all the various "should not be in cages" categories such as those I listed above. But it also invokes, with stupefying historical imprecision, a cavalcade of other innocents to emphasize the wrongness of some aspect of mass incarceration. In particular, it is as if mass incarceration were the means through which we are presumed to have inherited duty for some set of the uncompensated tasks because of what our ancestors were violently compelled to do. It's a reasonable extension given the historical facts of convict leasing and chain gangs that once upon a time were widespread. However, since half of the people locked up are not, or not obviously, descendants of racial chattel slavery, the problem demands a different explanation and therefore different politics. This does not mean that the lineage of abolition extending through chattel slavery is not robust enough to form at least part of the platform for ending mass incarceration in general. However, as it stands, to achieve significance, the uncritical extension of a partial past to explain a different present demands a sentimental political assertion that depends on the figure of a laboring victim whose narrative arc—whose structure of feeling—is fixed, and therefore susceptible to rehabilitation—or expungement—into relative innocence. The turn to innocence frightens in its desperate effort to replenish the void left by various assaults, calculated and cynical, on universalism on the one hand and rights on the other. If there are no universal rights, then what differentiated category might provide some canopy for the vulnerable? In my view, the proponents of innocence are trying to make such a shelter, but its shadow line or curtilage—like that "legally" demarcating people drone-murdered or renditioned by the United States abroad—can and does move, expunging the very innocence earlier achieved through expungement. In other words, dialectics requires us to recognize that the negation of the negation is always abundantly possible *and* hasn't a fixed direction or secure end. It can change direction, and thereby not revive old history but calibrate power differentials anew.

Consider this: a contemporary development in the relative innocence patrol, highlighted by the Supreme Court decision but not born of it, is toward the phenomenal spread of both saturation policing (stop-and-frisk; broken windows; and various types of so-called "community policing") and its new formation (which echoes some Second Klan practices): carceral or police humanitarianism. One of the results of contemporary racial capitalism's relentlessly restructured state-institutional capacities, and the discourses and practices that combine to enliven them, is "the anti-state state"—governmental capacity dominated by mainstream parties and policies that achieve power on the platform that states are bad and should shrink. Mass incarceration might seem inconsistent with something named the anti-state state. I think, to the contrary, mass incarceration is its bedrock. In other words, the dominant trend that goes hand-in-hand with mass incarceration is devolution—the off loading to increasingly local state and non-state institutions responsibility for thinning social welfare provision. At the same time, increased centralization (the strong executive) belies one of democracy's contemporary delusions—the notion that more local is somehow more participatory.

Carceral/police humanitarianism is a domestic counterinsurgency program spreading rapidly throughout the United States and abroad. Like mass incarceration, this humanitarianism is a feature of what I've long called the anti-state state: a dynamic pattern among the patterns shifting and reconsolidating the anti-state state form, dispensing (to riff on Du Bois) the wages of relative innocence to achieve a new round of anti-state state building. It's not new, but now altogether notable in the general landscape of exclude and define, capture and reward. This too is part of devolution, and more aggrandizing of police organizations coupled with not-for-profit and parastatal partners to identify and attend to the (relatively) innocent victims of too much policing and prison—sometimes formerly incarcerated people, sometimes their families, sometimes their neighborhoods. Police humanitarianism targets vulnerable people with goods and services that in fact everybody needs—especially everybody who is poor. But the door opens only by way of collaboration with the very practices that sustain carceral geographies, thereby undermining and destroying so many lives across generations in the first place.

We have already seen that innocence is not secure, and it's a mystery why it ever seemed reliable. And while nothing in this life is secure, sitting down to make common cause with the intellectual authors and social agents who unleashed and manage the scourge of organized abandonment—highlighting for the present discussion the organized violence on which it depends—puts into starkest terms the peril of the innocence defense.

Let's think about this problem in another way: While all those who benefited from chattel slavery on both sides of the Atlantic, and from all the forms of slavery that preceded and intersected with and since have followed it, are responsible for vicious injustices against individuals and humanity, to prove the innocence of those who have been or are enslaved for any purpose ought to play no role in the redress of slavery. In his controversial but indispensable *Slavery and Social Death*, Orlando Patterson notes that the power to kill is a precondition for the power of "violent domination, natal alienation, and general dishonor." The power to put humans in cages also derives from the power to kill—not only by way of the ritualized punishment of the death penalty, but also by life sentences, as well as the ritual of serially excused police killings that transformed #BlackLivesMatter from a lament to a movement. Patterson gives us the elegant turn of phrase that helps us, sadly, wrap our minds around the continuum of killing to keeping: "The one fell because he was the enemy, the other became the enemy because he had fallen."[2] Human sacrifice rather than innocence is the central problem that organizes the carceral geographies of the prison-industrial complex. Indeed, for abolition, to insist on innocence is to surrender politically because "innocence" evades a problem abolition is compelled to confront: how to diminish and remedy harm as against finding better forms of punishment. To make what I'm discussing a bit more explicit, I turn to the words of the great armed thief and spy Harriet Tubman. She told this story:

> I knew of a man who was sent to the State Prison for twenty-five years. All these years he was always thinking of his home, and counting the time till he should be free. The years roll on, the time of imprisonment is over, the man is free. He leaves the prison gates, he makes his way to the old home, but his old home is not there. The house in which he had dwelt in his childhood had been torn down, and a new one had been put in its place; his family were gone, their very name was forgotten, there was no one to take him by the hand to welcome him back to life.
>
> So it was with me. I had crossed the line of which I had so long been dreaming. I was free, but there was no one to welcome me to the land of freedom, I was a stranger in a strange land, and my home after all was down in the old cabin quarter, with the old folks and my brothers and sisters. But to this solemn resolution I came; I was free, and they should be free also; I would make a home for them.[3]

---

2   Orlando Patterson, *Slavery and Social Death: A Comparative Study*, Cambridge, MA: Harvard University Press, 1982, 44.

3   "Harriet Tubman Narrative, 1849 (Based on an interview with Sarah Bradford after the war)," in *Broken Utterances: A Selected Anthology of 19th Century Black Women's Social Thought*, ed. Michelle Diane Wright, Baltimore: Three Sistahs Press, 2007, 89–90.

Infrastructure of Feeling

W. E. B. Du Bois interviewed Harriet Tubman late in her life. For a while in the mid-twentieth century, a small but rather raucous scholarly competition developed to "prove" how many (which is to say how *few*) people Tubman helped "keep moving" along the Underground Railroad. By contrast, Harvard- and Humboldt-trained historian and sociologist Du Bois, a numbers guy if ever there was one, said hundreds. Then thousands! Why? Did he just get sloppy? Or did he begin to see how abolition geographies are made, on the ground, everywhere along the route—the time-route as well as the space-route. Indeed, was he able to redo in *Black Reconstruction in America* his earlier research on the Freedmen's Bureau because of the insights—truly visionary—he gained from talking with the ancient Tubman? It's here that I think the concept "infrastructure of feeling" might help us think about how we think about the development and perpetuation of abolition geographies, and how such geographies tend toward, even if they don't wholly achieve, the negation of the negation of the overlapping and interlocking carceral geographies of which the prison-industrial complex is an exemplar—while absolutely nonexhaustive, as the examples of abolition geographies show.

Raymond Williams argued more than fifty years ago that each age has its own "structure of feeling," a narrative structure for understanding the dynamic material limits to the possibility of change. Paul Gilroy and many others have engaged Williams's thinking and shown that ages and places necessarily have multiple structures of feeling, which are dialectical rather than merely contemporaneous. Williams went on to explain how we might best understand tradition as an accumulation of structures of feeling—that gather not by chance, nor through a natural process that would seem like a drift or tide, but rather by way of what he calls the "selection and re-selection of ancestors."[4] In this, Williams disavows the fixity of either culture or biology, discovering in perpetuation how even the least coherent aspects of human consciousness—feelings—have dynamically substantive shape.

The Black Radical Tradition is a constantly evolving accumulation of structures of feeling whose individual and collective narrative arcs persistently tend toward freedom. It is a way of mindful action that is constantly renewed and refreshed over time but maintains strength, speed, stamina, agility, flexibility, balance. The great explosions and distortions of modernity put into motion—and constant interaction—already-existing as well as novel understandings of difference, possession, dependence, abundance. As a result, the selection and reselection of ancestors is itself part of the radical process of finding anywhere—if not everywhere—in political practice and analytical habit, lived expressions (including opacities) of unbounded participatory openness.

What underlies such accumulation? What is the productive capacity of visionary or crisis-driven or even exhaustion-provoked reselection? The best I can offer, until something better comes along, is what I've called for many years the "infrastructure of feeling." In the material world, infrastructure underlies productivity—it speeds some processes and slows down others, setting agendas, producing isolation, enabling cooperation. The infrastructure of feeling is material too, in the sense that ideology becomes material as do the actions that feelings enable or constrain. The infrastructure of feeling is then consciousness-foundation, sturdy but not static, that underlies our capacity to recognize viscerally (no less than prudently) immanent possibility as we select and reselect liberatory lineages—in a lifetime, as Du Bois and Tubman exemplify, as well as between and across generations. What matters—what materializes—are lively re-articulations and surprising syncretisms.

---

4 Raymond Williams, *The Long Revolution*, London: Penguin, 1965, 69.

If, then, the structures of feeling for the Black Radical Tradition are, age upon age, shaped by energetically expectant consciousness of and direction toward unboundedness, then the tradition is, inexactly, movement away from partition and exclusion—indeed, its inverse.

Unboundedness, Against Conclusion

Thus, abolition geography—how and to what end people make freedom provisionally, imperatively, as they imagine *home* against the disintegrating grind of partition and repartition through which racial capitalism perpetuates the means of its own valorization. Abolition geography and the methods adequate to it (for making, finding, and understanding) elaborate the spatial—which is to say the human-environment processes —of Du Bois and Davis's abolition democracy. Abolition geography is capacious (it isn't only by, for, or about Black people) and specific (it's a guide to action for both understanding and rethinking how we combine our labor with each other and the earth). Abolition geography takes feeling and agency to be constitutive of, no less than constrained by, structure. In other words, it's a way of studying, and of doing political organizing, and of being in the world, and of worlding ourselves.

Put another way, abolition geography requires challenging the normative presumption that territory and liberation are at once alienable and exclusive—that they should be partitionable by sales, documents, or walls. Rather, by seizing the particular capacities we have, and repeating ourselves—trying, as C.L.R. James wrote about the run-up to revolutions, trying every little thing, going and going again—we will, because we do, change ourselves and the external world. Even under extreme constraint.

A last story: in the 1970s, the California Department of Corrections decided to reorganize the social and spatial world of people in prison in response to both reformist and radical mobilization. Evidence shows that the Department of Corrections experimented with a variety of disruptive schemes to end the solidarity that had arisen among its diverse (although then mostly white) population in the prisons for men. Cooperation, forged in study groups and other consciousness-raising activities, had resulted in both significant victories in federal courts over conditions of confinement and deadly retaliation against guards who had been killing prisoners with impunity. In spite of twenty years of Washington, DC rule-making forbidding, among other things, segregation, failure to advise of rights, lack of due process, and extrajudicial punishment, the Department of Corrections decided to segregate prisoners into racial, ethnic, and regional groups labeled gangs, to remand some of them to indefinite solitary confinement, and to restrict the ending of punishment to three actions: snitch, parole, or die. To reify the system as the built environment, the Department of Corrections created two prisons for men and one for women with high-tech Security Housing Units (SHU—a prison within a prison). The history of SHUs has yet to be fully told; it is indisputable that they induce mental and physical illness, which can lead to suicide or other forms of premature, preventable death. Indeed, the United Nations defines solitary confinement in excess of fourteen days as torture.

The people locked up in the Pelican Bay State Prison SHU, some from the day it opened on December 10, 1989, might or might not have done what they were convicted of in court; their innocence doesn't matter. For many years lawyers and others have worked with people in the SHU trying to discover the way out, not picking and choosing whom to aid, but interviewing any willing subject about conditions of confinement and struggling to devise a general plan. Activists created handbooks and websites, lobbied the legislature, testified to administrative law judges, devised lawsuits, held workshops, organized with family members, and otherwise sought to bring the SHU scourge to light. (In 1998, at a hearing into the cover-up of seven SHU prisoners shot dead by guards, a producer for Mike Wallace's *60 Minutes* asked: "Tell me why to care about these guys." "Do you care about justice?" "Of course. But the audience needs to care about people. Why should they care?")

The Department absolves itself of breaking laws and violating court decrees by insisting that the gangs it fostered run the prisons and the streets. After almost forty years of people churning through the expanded Department of Corrections, it's impossible that there's no stretch or resonance across the prison walls. SHU placement mixes people from ascriptive (what the Department says) and assertive (what the prisoners themselves say) free-world social geographies in order to minimize the possibility of solidarity among people who, the circular logic goes, are enemies or they wouldn't be in the SHU. They can't see or touch one another, but across the din of television sets and the machine-noise of prisons they can talk, debate, discuss. And while race is not the SHU's only organizing factor, race is the summary term that ordinary people, inside and out, use to name the divisions. For many years some of the most active SHU residents debated racism versus racialism, first embracing and then challenging a variety of supremacies, while for years continuing to accept the structure of feeling that keeps race constant as naturally endowed or culturally preferable.

People make abolition geographies from what they have; changing awareness can radically revise understanding of what can be done with available materials. It's clear that the SHU, in calculated opposition to 1970s Soledad or San Quentin or Attica, thins social resources to the breaking point. But what breaks? In many cases the persons locked up. But consciousness can break into a different dimension, shedding common-sense understandings of being and solidarity, identity and change. A negation of violence through violence is possible, which returns us to the territory of selves invoked in the opening pages of this discussion. Even in a total institution, sovereignty is contradictory, as resistance to torture demonstrates. The regime—its intellectual authors and social agents, its buildings and rules—tortures captives one by one. They can turn on the regime through shifting the object of torture into the subject of history by way of hunger strikes. Participating individuals turn the violence of torture against itself, not by making it not-violent but rather by intentionally repurposing vulnerability to premature death as a totality to be reckoned with, held together by skin.

The first strike, whose organizers represented all of the alleged prison gangs, sent its demands upward to the Department of Corrections, asking for modest improvements for all SHU dwellers' experience and fate: better food, improved visitation, and some way to contest SHU sentences based in evidence rather than system aggrandizement. People in many non-SHU prisons joined the strike in solidarity, and one died. The Department offered to negotiate; the strike ended. Nothing changed.

A second strike erupted, well-covered both by the ever-active in-prison grapevine and the organizing collective's free-world support infrastructure. In the context of the Supreme Court decision concerning medical neglect and of uprisings in many parts of the planet—North Africa, West Asia, South Africa, the streets of the United States—the demands took a new direction, against the partitions that, especially in the contemporary era, normalize devolved imaginations and shrunken affinities when expansive ones seem absolutely necessary. The collective sent its demands out, horizontally as it were, to their constituent communities inside and out, calling for an end to the hostilities among the races. Although some people interpret the call as "Black-brown solidarity"—because race seems to mean people who are not white—the collective's documents are radical and all-encompassing. The call has a history as old as modernity, however anachronistic contemporary labels might be.

The racial in racial capitalism isn't epiphenomenal, nor did it originate in color or intercontinental conflict, but rather always group-differentiation to premature death. Capitalism requires inequality and racism enshrines it. The Pelican Bay State Prison collective, hidden from one another, experiencing at once the torture of isolation and the extraction of time, refigured their world, however tentatively, into an abolition geography by finding an infrastructure of feeling on which they could rework their experience and understanding of possibility by way of renovated consciousness. The fiction of race projects a peculiar animation of the human body, and people take to the streets in opposition to its real and deadly effects. And in the end, as the relations of racial capitalism take it out on people's hides, the contradiction of skin becomes clearer. Skin, our largest organ, vulnerable to all ambient toxins, at the end is all we have to hold us together, no matter how much it seems to keep us apart.

Acknowledgments

Our comradely thanks to Rosie Warren and the team at Verso for encouraging and welcoming this project, to Patrick DeDauw and Michael Carr for their editorial work on the manuscript, and to Geoff Mann for his comments on a draft of the introduction.

Below are the author's original acknowledgments for essays included in this collection.

Decorative Beasts
Thanks to many who helped this paper along with encouragement and critique: Cathay Che; Sid Lemelle; Salima Lemelle; Michael Cadden and Valerie Smith who arranged for an early version's presentation at the Modern Language Association Commission on the Status of Women in the Profession; Bay Area Women's Writing Collective; Pew Seminar on Black Feminist Theory; Women of Color of the Claremont Colleges; Selma James; Karen Barad; CS&RI; Craig Gilmore.

"You Have Dislodged a Boulder"
For criticism and encouragement at various stages of this project, thanks to: Barbara Balliet, Ann Blum, Sue Cobble, Mike Davis, Allen Feldman, Leela Fernandes, Ann Markusen, Neil Smith, Caridad Souza, and Brackette Williams; The Rutgers Center for the Critical Analysis of Contemporary Culture 1995–96 Seminar. Special thanks to Craig Gilmore. Gratitude, respect, and honor to Mothers Reclaiming our Children. All errors are my responsibility.

Race and Globalization

I thank Craig Gilmore, Lauren Berlant, Rachel Herzing, and the editors of *Geographies of Global Change* (Ron Johnston, Peter J. Taylor and Michael J. Watts) for their thoughtful criticism of earlier drafts.

The Other California

Thanks to all those in rural California and elsewhere who are fighting back; the battles can be long, rough, and lonely. This essay is only a sketch of their remarkable work. Our crew of "outside agitators" has included Jean Caiani, Eric Ettlinger, Michelle Foy, Sarah Jarmon, Sonja Sivesind, Peter Spannagle, Ashle Fauvre, and Abby Lowe, the *compañeras* of California Prison Moratorium Project. Thanks also to Joe Morales and the rest of Center on Race, Poverty, and the Environment; John & Rosenda Mataka and all the rest of the Central California Environmental Justice Network; Bradley Angel of GreenAction; Yedi Nuñez, Michael Murashige, Laura Pulido, Babak Naficy, Celeste Langille, Kassie Siegel, Brigette Sarabi, and the Western Prison Project and the Prison Activist Resource Center. Particular mention should be made of Tracy Huling, whose advocacy against rural prison siting has been crucial, and Rose Braz and the remarkable group of activists who work with Critical Resistance who have logged thousands of dusty miles with us.

Scholar-Activists in the Mix

I thank Alec Murphy for the opportunity to share these thoughts during a Presidential Plenary at the AAG Centenary Meetings (March 2004). Thanks also to Alec, the editors of this journal, Jack Danger, and Craig Gilmore for helpful criticism. The work emerged from a path-breaking Social Science Research Council–sponsored workshop—and forthcoming book—on scholar-activism conceived and convened in April 2003 by Charlie Hale and Ted Gordon. I presented an earlier and much longer version of these remarks at the University of Texas Center on Mexican American Studies (February 2004).

Forgotten Places and the Seeds of Grassroots Planning
I thank Charlie Hale, Ted Gordon, Gill Hart, Laura Pulido, Jack Danger, Yong-Sook Lee, Bae-Gyoon Park, James Siddaway, Denise Ferreira da Silva, and Fred Moten for helping me think through various stages of this project; Mica Smith for research assistance; the California Prison Moratorium Project, and especially Debbie Reyes and Leonel Flores for their astonishing work; the Open Society Institute, the Social Science Research Council, and the National University of Singapore for their generous support; and Craig Gilmore for everything.

Restating the Obvious
For continuing guidance, thanks to Dana Kaplan and Avery Gordon; and for translation and much more, thanks to Tiago Pires e família.

Abolition Geography and the Problem of Innocence
Versions of this lecture were delivered at the twenty-ninth annual Sojourner Truth Lecture for the Department of Africana Studies of the Claremont Colleges (September 2014); Confronting Racial Capitalism: A Conference in Honor of Cedric Robinson at the CUNY Graduate Center (November 2014); the Antipode Institute for Geographies of Justice, Women's Gaol, Johannesburg (July 2015); the American Studies Association (October 2015); and the biannual conference of the Center for American Studies and Research at the American University of Beirut (January 2016). I am grateful to the editors of *Futures of Black Radicalism*, Gaye Theresa Johnson and Alex Lubin, and to many interlocutors for encouraging criticism.

Index